8th International Congress on Mathematical Education. Selected Lectures

8º Congreso Internacional de Educación Matemática. Selección de Conferencias

Sevilla
14-21
July / *julio*
1996

Edited by / *Editado por:*

Claudi Alsina
José Mª Alvarez
Bernard Hodgson
Colette Laborde
Antonio Pérez

Prof. Alba Thompson
In memoriam / *En su memoria*

Cover Design / *Diseño de la Portada:*
José Ignacio García Severón

Cover Picture / *Fotografía de la Portada:*
Ismael Roldán Castro

Published by / *Publicado por:*
S.A.E.M. 'THALES'

Printed by / *Imprime:*
Doble Cero Sevilla, S.L.

ISBN:
84-923760-3-1

Depósito Legal: SE-2152-98

CONTENTS
ÍNDICE

PREFACE / *PREFACIO*

This book comprises selected lectures from the 8th International Congress on Mathematical Education (ICME-8), held in Sevilla, Spain, from July 14 to 21, 1996. There were some 56 "regular lectures" given during ICME-8 and 33 of them are included in the present volume, with authors coming from 19 different countries. (We do not take into account here the four "plenary lectures" presented at ICME-8, which are to be found in the book of Proceedings of ICME-8.)

As was the case with previous ICMEs, the Executive Committee of the International Commission on Mathematical Instruction (ICMI) appointed an International Programme Committee (IPC) for ICME-8, responsible for setting up the structure of the scientific programme and for inviting the main speakers and the organizers of various components of the programme. One of the first decisions of the IPC was to maintain the practice reintroduced at the previous ICME congress (ICME-7, Québec, 1992) of having an important number of lectures, in addition to the customary plenary lectures or the mini-lecture presentations to small groups. While adhering to the principle that an essential aspect of the quadrennial ICME congresses is the opportunity they provide for face-to-face debate and discussion among mathematics educators, either in the context of Working Groups, Topic Groups, Poster Presentations or informal gatherings, the IPC felt the "traditional lecture", in spite of all its well-recognized deficiencies, still provides an excellent medium for putting participants in contact with key issues in mathematics education.

The ICME-8 IPC therefore reserved six one-hour slots on the programme for the regular lectures, about 10 presentations being scheduled simultaneously each time. Invitations were issued to a selection of the best theoreticians, researchers and practitioners in the field around the world. Speakers were chosen according to their professional quality, theircommunication abilities, the selection of topics and the levels of education the IPC wished to cover. The written versions of thirty-three of these presentations make up this volume.

The reader should be aware that the set of lectures we offer here is in many ways biased. It is a proper subset of the lectures presented at ICME-8, which were themselves only one component in the scientific programme. We make pretence that it gives a complete picture neither of the field of mathematics education nor of the ICME-8 programme as a whole. The reader should consult the ICME-8 Proceedings to see how the lecture topics complement the topics treated in other programme strands: the plenary lectures, the Working Groups, the Topics Groups, the reports of ongoing work by the official Study Groups of ICMI, the reports of the ICMI Studies, etc. Here, however, the reader will find written versions of some fine talks well worth reading and reflecting upon.

As was the case with ICME-7, the Sevilla congress results in the production of two books, one being the Proceedings of ICME-8 themselves and the other, the present volume of selected lectures. A difficulty in the production of such a book is that for many authors, English (the "lingua franca" in mathematics education at the international level) is a second, if not a third, language. Although all efforts have been made to insure a high level of correction in the written language, it was the policy not to change authors' style, staying as close as possible to the original versions.

The editors wish to acknowledge the contribution of a number of people to the production of this volume. First, and above all, we extend our thanks and gratitude to the authors themselves: by investing the extra effort, in addition to the preparation of their oral presentation, necessary for their presentation to be brought in a written format, they have made this volume possible. We also wish to thank all the Local Institutions and sponsors, which made all their best to contribute to the success of ICME 8.

Bernard R. Hodgson
for the Editing Committee:
Claudi Alsina, José Mª Alvarez Falcón, Bernard R. Hodgson, Colette Laborde, Antonio Pérez Jiménez.

LAS CONCEPCIONES SOCIOEPISTEMOLÓGICAS DE FRÉCHET EN SUS INVESTIGACIONES SOBRE LA TEORÍA DE LOS ESPACIOS ABSTRACTOS Y LA TOPOLOGÍA GENERAL

Luis Carlos Arboleda A.

Luis Cornelio Recalde C.[1]

1. Introducción

La forma como el científico se representa su proyecto investigativo es algo que llama constantemente el interés en los estudios sociales sobre la ciencia. Uno de los aspectos importantes del análisis sobre las condiciones socioculturales de la producción de las teorías, es la explicación del sistema de valores y conceptos del matemático creador y, muy particularmente, de los procedimientos prácticos y conceptuales que pudieron haberlo conducido a ciertos resultados empleando determinadas estrategias.

Con el término de **representación** nos referimos, de manera aproximada, a las formas en las que se revisten los objetos de los mundos matemáticos en el ámbito de la conciencia, por efecto de la intermediación de *doble vía* de la práctica matemática de los individuos con un sistema de valores y creencias (sociales, culturales, religiosas, etc.). Que algunos matemáticos mantengan fervientemente que el único objetivo de la ciencia -como decía Jacobi refiriéndose a la teoría de números- es 'la búsqueda del honor del espíritu humano'[2], o que otros crean que incluso las nociones más simples como los números enteros no son intuiciones puras o juicios sintéticos a *priori,* sino 'conceptos primigenios que surgieron de complicadas nociones humanas'[3], unas y otras son representaciones

---

1 Profesores-investigadores del Grupo de Historia de las Matemáticas - Departamento de Matemáticas-, y del Grupo de Educación Matemática–Instituto de Educación y Pedagogía-, Universidad del Valle, Cali, Colombia.

2 Dieudonné, J., **Pour l'honneur de l'esprit humain. Les mathématiques aujourd'hui**. Hachette, Paris, 1987.

3 Fréchet, M., **Les mathématiques et le concret**. P.U.F., Paris, 1955; idea expresada en el capitulo sobre los *Orígenes de las nociones matemáticas,* al cual volveremos páginas más adelante.

orgánicamente relacionadas con estrategias cognitivas e investigativas contrapuestas. Uno y otro tipo de enfoques son construcciones articuladas estrechamente por configuraciones sociales, como puede comprobarse a través de una indagación cuidadosa de carácter histórico y cultural.

El propósito de la presente comunicación es aprovechar algunos materiales documentales de la investigación socio-histórica que adelantan los autores sobre la teoría de los Espacios Abstractos del matemático francés Maurice Fréchet (1878-1973)[4], con el fin de analizar algunas de las representaciones del científico sobre su obra. Especialmente nos interesa destacar aquellas apreciaciones y valoraciones filosóficas de Fréchet sobre la relevancia para la creación matemática, de los procesos de generalización fundamentados en lo concreto de las modelizaciones abstractas con soporte empírico.

Una adecuada comprensión sobre este problema puede contribuir a explicar a matemáticos, filósofos, historiadores, sociólogos y educadores matemáticos, la naturaleza y función de los factores del contexto social y cultural en la formación de pensamiento matemático. En particular en el campo de la educación matemática, es sabido que la **transposición didáctica** tiene como propósito explicar los mecanismos que permiten el paso de un objeto de saber a un objeto de enseñanza. En el estudio de caso de la noción de *distancia* de Fréchet,[5] se señala una vía fecunda para explorar estrategias didácticas viables sobre esta noción, las cuales tienen en cuenta aquellas representaciones del matemático que son asociadas con el pensamiento creador, y no solamente las ideas acabadas que se establecen por acuerdos consensuales entre la comunidad matemática. Tales acuerdos constituyen el llamado saber erudito (*savoir savant*) que es, por naturaleza, despersonalizado. Una de esas representaciones consisitió, según el mismo Fréchet, en generalizar en los espacios abstractos una idea muy *simple*: que una *cualidad* (la proximidad o vecindad en torno a un elemento) se puede expresar por un *número* (la noción de *distancia*).

---

4 Arboleda L.C, y L.C. Recalde. **Matemáticas y experiencia: La generalización de la noción de espacio abstracto en Maurice Fréchet.** Proyecto financiado por Colciencias y la Universidad del Valle. 1996-1998

5 Chevallard Y., y Joshua M.-A., Un exemple d'analyse de la transposition didactique: la notion de distance, **Recherches en didactique des mathématiques**, vol. 3, 2, 1982

2.Fréchet y la Matemática de las Formas.

En lo que sigue nos limitaremos a analizar las ideas de Fréchet sobre su producción matemática a partir de dos ejes fundamentales que, como veremos, se presentan íntimamente ligados al observador histórico:

i) En relación con el programa filosófico de orientación leibniziana que articula su obra, y

ii)En relación con sus concepciones sobre el origen fundamentalmente empírico de la producción matemática en general, y de la suya en particular.

Estas ideas de Fréchet se encuentran reunidas básicamente en dos publicaciones suyas: la **Noticia** sobre sus trabajos científicos [6], y **Las Matemáticas y lo Concreto** [7]. La primera es un ensayo sobre su contribución matemática durante el período 1904-1928. En este trabajo Fréchet explica lo específico y original de la misma a los evaluadores del concurso para ser admitido como miembro correspondiente de la **Academia de Ciencias de París.** La segunda es una recopilación de artículos divulgativos y pedagógicos elaborados a lo largo de su carrera como investigador y profesor. Entre ellos, hay dos particularmente útiles para los propósitos de la presente comunicación en cuanto abordan temas relacionados con sus concepciones empiristas: *Desaxiomatización de la ciencia* y *Orígenes de las nociones matemáticas.* Este último artículo contiene, como aspecto a destacar, una reseña del debate que mantuvo Fréchet con algunos colegas y filósofos contemporáneos suyos (Enriques, Gonseth, Bernays, Lukasiewisz, Wavre y Kérékjarto), en las **Entretiens de Zürich,** realizadas entre el 6 y el 9 de diciembre de 1938, alrededor del tema de los fundamentos y el método de las ciencias matemáticas.

En la **Noticia,** Fréchet escoge el siguiente epígrafe de Leibniz para explicarle a sus colegas de la Academia, la naturaleza del programa filosófico que articula y soporta su contribución en diversos campos (análisis funcional, análisis general, análisis clásico, geometría, probabilidad y matemáticas aplicadas):

> *Quienes prefieren avanzar en los detalles de las ciencias deprecian las investigaciones abstractas y generales, y quienes profundizan en los principios, entran raramente en particularidades. En cuanto a mí, le doy igual importancia a lo uno y a lo otro, porque he descubierto que el análisis de los principios permite el avance en las invenciones particulares.*

---

[6] Fréchet, Maurice. **Notice sur les travaux scientifiques.** Paris. Hermann, 1933.
[7] Fréchet, Maurice. **Les mathématiques et le concret.** Paris. PUF, 1955.

Fréchet explica enseguida las razones por las cuales encuentra que su obra se enmarca en el programa filosófico leibniziano sobre las matemáticas. En primer lugar, se destaca el interés de ambos en orientar las investigaciones dentro de estrategias de generalización específicas; Leibniz en el análisis infinitesimal de **R**, y Fréchet en el análisis general de espacios de naturaleza cualquiera. Los resultados obtenidos por Fréchet durante el período 1904-1928 al aplicar este enfoque de generalización a distintas teorías matemáticas (topología general, análisis funcional, teoría de funciones, etc.), fueron sistematizados en su célebre obra de 1928 sobre los Espacios Abstractos[8].

El análisis de los principios que se preservan en las generalizaciones hace parte de un programa filosófico con una cobertura que va más allá del campo matemático. La idea de Leibniz era elaborar una especie de alfabeto del pensamiento humano, de tal suerte que a partir de él se pudiera inferir y discutir sobre cualquier aspecto, en lo que denominó **charasteristica generalis** (característica universal). Buscaba crear una **Mathesis universalis** con el propósito de registrar en el pensamiento simbólico aquello que la percepción nos permite percibir, ya que "todo lo que la imaginación empírica abarca a partir de las figuras, lo deriva el cálculo de signos por una demostración inequívoca; e incluso conduce a otras consecuencias a las que la facultad de imaginar no puede llegar"[9].

Fréchet comparte el propósito central del programa leibniziano de desarrollar esa **matemáticas de las formas** que permitiera registrar en el pensamiento simbólico aquello que la percepción nos permite observar[10]. La idea de una matemática universal articula sus estrategias investigativas en cuanto a la construcción de un lenguaje matemático integrador de una red conceptual de teorías especializadas, y que en los años 1920 se centraban en el Análisis General de los Espacios Abstractos. Pero también se haya presente en actividades que Fréchet emprendió sistemáticamente como proyecto de vida, en tanto ciudadano y como intelectual.

Recordemos que Fréchet fue durante muchos años, promotor y organizador de la **Unión Universal de Esperanto**, lengua en la cual

---

[8] Fréchet, Maurice. **Les espaces abstraits et leur théorie considérée comme introduction à l'Analyse Générale.** París. Gauthier-Villars, 1928.

[9] Leibniz citado en Granger, Guilles-Gaston. **Formes, opérations, objets**. Paris. Mathesis, Vrin. 1994; capitulo
"Philosophie et Mathématique Leibniziennes", p.p. 216.

[10] Leibniz citado en Granger, **op. cit.**, p.216.

publicó interesantes resultados matemáticos. Si bien esto implicaba reducir el impacto científico esperado en la circulación de tales investigaciones, Fréchet quería así convencer a sus colegas de que era posible y deseable escoger una lengua "ordinaria" muy general y tal vez más apropiada que otras para comunicar enunciados matemáticos del nivel "universal" de los suyos.

Como sabemos,[11] la creación del cálculo leibniziano reposa sobre algunos principios lógico-filosóficos: la **combinatoria** (en la cual procedimientos como la diferenciación se establecen al margen de consideraciones infinitesimales y en relación con las propiedades del triángulo característico de Pascal); la ley de **continuidad** (principio metafísico que permite la extensión de propiedades de lo finito a lo infinito; permite entender, por ejemplo, cómo la tangente conserva en el límite las propiedades de la secante a través de la relación invariante entre la subtangente y la ordenada); y el conocimiento de los objetos matemático a través de su representación en el **universo simbólico**. En relación con este último principio, la solución más general posible de un problema, por el ejemplo el de la tangente, pasa por encontrar un algoritmo en el cual se expresen simbólicamente todos los pasos implicados en el proceso de generalización.

En el contexto de este programa filosófico se entiende mejor la manera en que Leibniz introdujo las conocidas técnicas y simbolismos del cálculo, como las notaciones "∫" y "**d**" para la integración y la diferenciación, entendidas éstas en tanto operaciones recíprocas. También sabemos que precisamente la fuerza notacional del cálculo de Leibniz jugó un papel determinante en la aceptación de su enfoque con relación al de Newton. Entre otras cosas porque siendo para Leibniz los símbolos "∫" y "**d**" muy próximos a nuestra idea actual de operadores, se llegaba fácilmente a resultados fecundos en el análisis. Por su parte, la engorrosa metodología newtoniana de las fluxiones y la notación de punto, complicaba inútilmente los procesos. En fin, mientras que el enfoque de Newton estaba referido a variaciones infinitesimales en el tiempo, el de Leibniz trataba variables más generales en las cuales, no sólo el tiempo podía ser tomado como un caso particular, sino que su manejo era independiente de consideraciones infinitesimales.

No deja de llamar la atención que en cierta medida algunos de estos principios lógico-filosóficos se encuentran subyacentes a la creación

---

[11] Ver, por ejemplo, Granger, **op cit**, y Belaval, Yvon. **Leibniz critique de Descartes**. París, Gallimard. 1960; capitulo "La géométrie algébrique et le calcul infinitésimal"

matemática más general y abstracta de Fréchet. Así como se los halla contribuyendo y validando al campo teórico del cálculo infinitesimal, también es posible reconocerles esta misma función dentro del proyecto de establecer el análisis general, entendido como el estudio de las correspondencias entre variables de naturaleza cualquiera. En la obra de Fréchet se realiza el propósito leibniziano de encontrar en el análisis más general y absoluto de los principios (la matemática de las formas), la explicación más fecunda de los objetos particulares a la cual se refiere el ya citado epígrafe de la **Noticia**.

3. La diferencial de Fréchet y la generalización de principios útiles y sencillos.

Una excelente ilustración de la filiación de sus investigaciones sobre el análisis en los espacios abstractos con el programa de Leibniz, es la llamada 'diferencial de Fréchet', o diferencial de una función definida sobre un espacio particular de funciones, con la bien conocida aplicación al caso de una transformación definida entre partes de dos espacios lineales normados. Refiriéndose a los procedimientos y criterios que utilizó en esta extensión de la diferencial a los espacios abstractos, Fréchet recalca que inicialmente su interés se orientó en la dirección de generalizar aquel principio 'útil y necesario' que originó la noción de diferencial en el cálculo infinitesimal; esto es, que la diferencial dF es la función más **simple** con respecto a la variación Δx de la variable, y más **aproximada** a la variación ΔF de la función. [12]

En su noticia necrológica de 1977 sobre Fréchet, Szolem Mandelbrojt escribió:[13]

---

[12] En su conferencia de 1925 en Berna sobre la *Désaxiomatisation de la science* (**IN: Mathématique et le Concret, op. cit.,** pp. 8-9), Fréchet afirma que con esta definición había querido retornar a la concepción de los inicios del cálculo diferencial, y darle a la diferencial un uso más intuitivo y riguroso.

[13] *Notice nécrologique sur M.F.. par Szolem Mandelbrojt,* le 19 novembre 1977. **IN:** Dossier Administratif, Fonds Fréchet, Académie des Sciences, Paris. En un trabajo posterior analizaremos con detenimiento los procedimientos de Volterra y Fréchet en relación con dos 'estilos' diferentes de generalizar la diferencial. Anotemos por el momento como hecho interesante, que Mandelbrojt encontró en su Noticia razones para establecer la conexión entre las generalizaciones de Fréchet y la búsqueda consecuente de un ideal leibniziano que habria caracterizado las distintas facetas intelectuales, matemáticas y humanas de su vida.

En el Análisis funcional concebido por Vito Volterra (actualmente se le da ese nombre a otra rama más general de las matemáticas), se estudian las funciones cuya variable es una línea o una función, llamadas 'funcionales' por Hadamard. Al explorar ese nuevo dominio Volterra empleó el método del paso de lo finito a lo infinito, el cual no es siempre riguroso en esta disciplina.

Y destacando entre otras contribuciones suyas al análisis funcional la introducción de la diferencial abstracta de Fréchet, Mandelbrojt agregó enseguida lo siguiente:

Fréchet comenzó sus investigaciones a este respecto utilizando un método directo, general y muy riguroso. Sustituyó la definición de la diferencial de una función de línea por una definición valedera en casos mucho más amplios.

En efecto, trabajando en un espacio de funciones de línea, Vito Volterra había introducido en 1887 las nociones de derivada y diferencial. Volterra empieza analizando la variación de $F(\ f\ (x))$, con pequeños cambios de la función f en la vecindad de un punto particular x. Volterra define la derivada de F en relación a f en el punto x, como la funcional $F'(f\ ,\ x)$, la cual es continua en cada variable bajo ciertas condiciones

---

[14] V. Volterra, *Sopra le funzioni che dipendono da altre funzioni,* **Rend. R. Accad. dei Lincei,** ser. 4, vol. 3 (1887); tres notas respectivamente en las pp. 97-105, 141-146, 153-158.

[15] La evolución de los principales resultados sobre la diferencial hasta alcanzar su estado canónico, se encuentra expuesta con todo detalle en: Taylor, A.E., *A Study of Maurice Fréchet III: Fréchet as Analyst, 1909-1930,* **Arch. for History of Exact Sciences,** vol. 37, 1987; pp. 25-76. El estudio de la cuestión desde la perspectiva italiana -particularmente interesante por la argumentación en contra de la polémica explicación dada por J. Dieudonné a la contribución de Volterra a los inicios del Análisis funcional-, se encuentra, entre otros, en Fichera, G., *Vito Volterra and the birth of functional analysis.* IN: Pier, J.-P. (ed.), **Development of Mathematics, 1900-1950,** Birkhäuser, Berlin, 1994; pp. 171-183. En una próxima publicación los autores del presente trabajo harán un balance sobre estas diversas interpretaciones, en el marco de su investigación sobre las ideas de Fréchet en relación con el problema de las generalizaciones matemáticas a partir de la experiencia.

restrictivas, obteniendo a partir de allí la expresión:

$$\underset{\varepsilon \to 0}{Lim} \frac{F(f + \varepsilon\, g) - F(f)}{\varepsilon} = \int_a^b F'(f,x)\, g(x)dx$$

donde f y g están definidas sobre $[a, b]$. La expresión $\varepsilon\, g(x)$ es llamada la variación de $f(x)$, y será denotada por δf. De lo anterior se sigue que:

$$F(f + \varepsilon\, g) - F(g) = \varepsilon \int_a^b F'(f,x)\, g(x)dx + \rho$$

donde ρ es tal que $\rho/\varepsilon \to 0$ cuando $\varepsilon \to 0$.

A la expresión $\delta F = \varepsilon \int_a^b F'(f,x)\, g(x)dx$

Volterra la llamará 'primera variación' de F.

En 1902, Hadamard muestra que la definición de Volterra es demasiado restrictiva, pues no puede extenderse a casos más generales de funcionales en los cuales él mismo estaba interesado. Propone someter la definición a hipótesis más generales, para ampliar su campo de incidencia y posibilitar así que a tales funcionales se les pudiesen aplicar los métodos del cálculo infinitesimal. En particular Hadamard recomienda que se tengan en cuenta las funcionales F cuya variación es una funcional lineal de la variación de f.

En 1912, Fréchet, retoma las ideas de Hadamard con respecto a la diferencial abstracta como parte de su programa de extender los principios fundamentales del cálculo diferencial al cálculo funcional. Es una comunicación enviada a Volterra el 30 de julio de 1913, Fréchet explica el método empleado por él para obtener tal generalización: [16]

---

16   Nurzia, L, *La Corrispondenza tra Vito Volterra e Maurice Fréchet sui Fondamenti dell'Analisis Funzionali.* **Revista di storia della scienza**, vol. 4, 3, 1987; pp. 391-416. En este trabajo se publican por primera vez apartes de la correspondencia de Fréchet a Volterra que aportan información histórica importante para valorar las contribuciones de estos autores a los comienzos del análisis funcional, así como para comprender las diferencias de 'estilos cognitivos', motivaciones y representaciones –particularmente de Fréchet- sobre la naturaleza de los conceptos y del razonamiento matemático

(...) La idea que constituye la sustancia de mi artículo y que me parece original, consiste en adoptar el punto de vista de Hadamard [recordemos que Hadamard había propuesto atender a la variación de f] pero aplicándolo no a la variación de f (x) sino a su crecimiento (...)

Más adelante, en 1914, Fréchet escribe:

Me incliné pues a tratar de retomar la antigua definición, generalmente olvidada hoy en día: la diferencial es la parte principal del crecimiento de la función cuando el crecimiento de la variable se considera infinitamente pequeño.

Un paso decisivo para llegar a la generalización del tipo que buscaba Fréchet, consistió en apoyarse en una definición previa de la diferencial total de una función de varias variables. En este aspecto, Fréchet incorpora un nuevo elemento teórico en la definición de la diferencial de una función $f(x, y)$, al hacer depender la diferencial de la existencia de una función homogénea y de primer grado con relación a los crecimientos Δx, Δy. Se dice que la función $f(x, y)$ tiene una diferencial en (x, y), si existe una función lineal homogénea
$A \Delta x + B \Delta y$, tal que:

$$\frac{1}{\Delta}\left(f(x + \Delta x, y + \Delta y) - f(x, y) - A\Delta x - B\Delta y\right) = \varepsilon$$

donde $\varepsilon \to 0$, cuando $\Delta \to 0$. La función lineal homogénea $[A \Delta x + B \Delta y]$ es la diferencial de f.

La definición para el caso de la funcional $F(f)$ que propone Fréchet, se 'vislumbra' ya en la expresión anterior:

$F(f)$ es diferenciable en f si existe ε y una funcional $\delta F(f; g)$, lineal en relación a g, tal que:

$$F(f + g) - F(f) - d(f; g) = \varepsilon M(g)$$

donde, $M(g) = max|g(x)|$ en $[a, b]$ y $\varepsilon \to 0$, cuando $M(g) \to 0$.

Pero Fréchet no se detiene en este nivel de generalización de la diferencial. En 1925 aplica su definición a una clase de espacios que él había introducido años atrás y que se habían revelado extremamente importantes en teorías de naturaleza diferente: los 'espacios distanciados vectoriales' o espacios normados lineales:

Sean E_1, E_2 espacios normados lineales. Si $M = f(m)$ es una transformación del punto m de E_1 en el punto M de E_2, y si m_0 es un punto interior del conjunto, donde está definido $F(m)$, se dice que la transformación es diferenciable en m_0 si existe una transformación lineal Ψ de E_1 en E_2 tal que:

$$F(m_0 + \Delta m) - F(m) - \Psi \Delta(m) = \varepsilon \ || \Delta m \ U, ||$$

donde U es un vector unitario variable en E_2 y $\varepsilon \to 0$, cuando $||\Delta m|| \to 0$.

Observemos la expresión simbólica simple del algoritmo; principio lógico que era característica común a los procesos de generalización y abstracción en el análisis matemático de los siglos XIX y XX. Así mismo se puede comprobar la intervención -en este proceso de definición de la diferencial abstracta de Fréchet-, de otros de principios filosóficos como, la ley de los homogéneos (simbolización y manipulación teórica distinta entre variables y cantidades respectivamente comparables), y la aceptación de que a nivel de lo general y abstracto –por simetría con lo que ocurre en el mundo de lo concreto-, también se pueden establecer relaciones y manipulaciones teóricas entre objetos con un cierto grado de vaguedad, aproximación e indeterminismo.

4. Las ideas de Fréchet sobre la relación de las Matemáticas con la Experiencia.

Además de los mencionados principios lógico-filosóficos de factura leibniziana, el campo de representación de la creación matemática de Fréchet nos parece que está articulado por sus concepciones sobre el origen empírico de las nociones más generales y abstractas. Resulta interesante estudiar la cuestión de si existe una cierta recurrencia entre estos dos órdenes de representación en el sistema de valores y conceptos matemáticos de Fréchet. Es decir, preguntarse hasta qué punto cabe hablar de las concepciones socioepistemológicas de Fréchet como factor movilizador de sus investigaciones sobre la teoría de los espacios abstractos y la topología general. Este es un asunto que los autores abordarán en otros trabajos. Por ahora limitémonos a considerar las concepciones de Fréchet sobre la naturaleza de los conceptos y el pensamiento matemático.

Las nociones fundamentales de todas las ramas matemáticas son construidas a partir de la experiencia.[17] La experiencia conduce a la abstracción, y la abstracción sustituye y enriquece la experiencia. El Análisis General se fundamenta en ideas que a través de la experiencia de matemáticos en diferentes campos teóricos particulares se revelaron **simples, útiles y fecundas,** pero que sin embargo antes de Fréchet nadie había examinado en forma tan sistemática ni en toda su generalidad. Fréchet reconoció tales ideas "candidatas a generalización", a través de su propia experiencia y la de su entorno intelectual. Escrutó en las distintas teorías cuáles eran las condiciones necesarias y suficientes en las que radicaba su éxito; separó los aspectos accesorios de los fundamentales, y les imprimió a los fundamentales su forma a la vez simple y fecundidad conceptual. Por último validó sus generalizaciones de nuevo a través de la experiencia, y comprobó que permitían desarrollar nuevos campos teóricos y experimentales, al mismo tiempo que perfeccionaban los ya existentes tanto en el nivel conceptual como técnico. Veamos las fases del procedimiento de doble vía entre abstracción y realidad concreta que explica -de acuerdo con Fréchet-, la dinámica del pensamiento matemático.

La primera etapa de generalización a partir de lo concreto se opera con la **síntesis inductiva.** Esta tiene que ver con ese a menudo largo proceso que consiste en articular en un mismo campo teórico las versiones particulares que tiene la teoría general en campos restringidos y hasta entonces inconexos. Muchas veces la generalización matemática se produce mediante procesos de iteración. Una teoría o modelo abstracto que es reconocido como válido en la experiencia dentro de espacios restringidos, se extiende entonces a campos generales, incluso a espacios de naturaleza cualquiera.

En sus investigaciones científicas Fréchet utilizó corrientemente este procedimiento de generación inductiva sobre nociones **simples y útiles.** Como tratamos de demostrarlo en nuestro proyecto, en ello habría podido influir, aparte de ciertos principios lógico-filosóficos, la experiencia de utilización **exitosa** de este método en los trabajos de análisis funcional que hacia comienzos del siglo XX ya había hecho célebres a matemáticos como Ascoli, Volterra, Arzelà e Hilbert, y a su propio maestro Hadamard. Fréchet tenía la convicción profunda de que las generalizaciones se hacen poco a poco, respondiendo a necesidades del campo teórico, en la

---

[17] Fréchet, M., *Entretiens de Zürich,* **IN: Les Mathématiques et le concret, op. cit.,** pp. 11-51.

medida que ellas son reconocidas como tales por los propios investigadores.

La segunda etapa corresponde a los procedimientos clásicos de la axiomatización de la teoría. A través de esta fase se busca la organización racional del campo teórico, la reconstrucción del objeto y la reproducción del mismo campo. Esta fase es la que permite reemplazar experiencias directas demasiado dispendiosas o simplemente alejadas del alcance de nuestras posibilidades empíricas, por experiencias indirectas que se apoyan en proposiciones de la teoría deductiva. En la tercera fase se trata de constatar que la teoría abstracta así generalizada y axiomatizada, preserva las propiedades fundamentales de la red de teorías particulares asociadas con la teoría abstracta.

En este punto es necesario hacer una acotación sobre las apreciaciones de Fréchet con respecto a los peligros del formalismo excesivo. En varios de sus trabajos se refiere a la situación de autonomización del pensamiento abstracto, en virtud de la cual, en la medida que se extienden los procesos de generalización, la comunidad matemática se encierra en ella misma, desarrollándose cada vez más los conceptos y métodos dentro de un mundo matemático hermético[18]. Las teorías progresivamente se vuelven más difíciles de relacionar y analizar de acuerdo con categorías familiares al mundo de la experiencia y de la vida cotidiana. Como dice Sal Restivo[19], el mundo matemático va dejando atrás los mundos de las representaciones y de los paisajes de cosas identificables, para reducirse a un mundo de símbolos y notaciones autoreferenciado.

Fréchet observa esta situación (el comienzo de la hegemonía de programa de Hilbert), y alerta sobre el hecho de que las matemáticas no se pueden reducir a su parte deductiva, so pena de convertirlas en un juego del entendimiento sin ningún alcance práctico. Llega incluso a afirmar que, no obstante todas las ventajas que se le reconocían al método axiomático, "sería interesante identificar igualmente una

---

[18] Por ejemplo, en su biografía del matemático alsaciano Louis Arbogast (1759-1803) (IN: **Revue du Mois**, 1920, pp. 337-362), Fréchet se apoya en las políticas educativas por las cuales Arbogast abogó en la Convención Nacional, para denunciar el dogmatismo del logicismo puro que estaba en boga entonces sobre todo entre los jóvenes investigadores. Decía que si bien tal dogmatismo podía ser cómodo, correspondía a un programa de trabajo estrecho. Había pues, necesidad de luchar por desterrar esas concepciones de las mentes de los candidatos a la agregación impara quienes la comodidad de la lógica de exposición era lo portante.

[19] Restivo, Sal. **The social construction of mathematics.** Zentralblatt der mathematik, 1988.

construcción científica basada sobre principios diferentes e incluso opuestos" (in [4]; **op.cit.**, pp. 3). Su propuesta parece aplicarse en todo caso a aquellas teorías "que hubieran ya alcanzado un alto grado de abstracción".

Dentro de la concepción de Fréchet sobre la relación matemática y experiencia, se pone en cuestión la creencia generalizada de la autonomía de las matemáticas con respecto a la realidad. Aún en el trabajo matemático más abstracto interviene inevitablemente -con un efecto epistémico determinado sobre la teoría- algún tipo de representación de la experiencia. Fréchet constata que la orientación de las ciencias matemáticas, el sentido hacia donde se producen sus progresos, no está condicionada solamente por necesidades internas (organización, sistematización, simplificación de resultados de tales transformaciones lógicas). También son motivadas por demandas externas, por problemas concretos planteados por la naturaleza y la técnica.

5. La estrategia comunicativa de Fréchet sobre sus ideas sobre las matemáticas.

Enfrentado como estaba en el período de entreguerras, a un contexto intelectual en el cual se comenzaban a valorar más los enfoques estructuralistas, formalistas y axiomáticos, Fréchet se vio conducido a poner en práctica una verdadera estrategia de divulgación de las concepciones socio-epistémicas, con orientación empírica, en las cuales reposaban sus propias investigaciones. Las ideas que hemos venido comentando en este trabajo, están articuladas en función de una *retórica persuasiva* que a todas luces utiliza Fréchet para hacer comprender a sus diferentes interlocutores (académicos, comunidad matemática en general, profesores, distintos usuarios científicos y no científicos), la construcción, naturaleza y función de sus teorías más abstractas y generales. El gusto que siempre manifestó por el uso de citaciones de autores consagrados en la literatura matemática y en la historia de las ciencias, se convierte en muchos casos en un instrumento privilegiado para reforzar la argumentación persuasiva sobre sus concepciones socioepistemológicas o pedagógicas.

Conviene traer a colación en esta parte final de la exposición uno de los tantos textos y citaciones en los cuales acostumbraba Fréchet sustentar la defensa de sus delicadas argumentaciones. En el escrito es el cual propendía claramente por la **Desaxiomatización de la ciencia**[20]

---

[20]   Fréchet, **op. cit.**, p. 10.

TEACHING AND LEARNING ELEMENTARY ANALYSIS

Michèle ARTIGUE, Equipe DIDIREM,
University Paris 7 and IUFM of Reims

I. INTRODUCTION

It is not easy for students to enter the conceptual field of analysis.Thanks to the educational research carried out in this area during the last years (Tall, 1991), today we better understand the real nature of students' difficulties and we are aware of the general failure of standard teaching strategies. As a consequence, all over the world, new curricula are developed, trying to find the way for a meaningful and accessible entrance into this conceptual field (Artigue & Ervynck, 1992). More intuitive and experimental approaches relying on the use of new technologies seem to be widely privileged now. What are their potential and their limits? What can we learn from the experience of countries where such approaches were established some years ago? In this text, I would like to address these important issues.

Firstly, I shall try to synthesize the main results obtained by didactical research in this area. I do not pretend to be exhaustive but just try to give a personal view of the present state of the art. Then, I shall analyse teaching practices and their evolution, by referring to one particular case : the case of French secondary curricula which, in my opinion, illustrates the general tendency, fairly well. Finally, I shall come to the potential and limits of the new approaches, as one can evaluate them from the French experience.

II. STUDENTS' DIFFICULTIES WITH THE CONCEPTUAL FIELD OF ANALYSIS

Didactical research in this area has evidenced the existence of strong and resistant difficulties. They have different origins but they tightly intervene and reinforce mutually, in a kind of complex network. Nevertheless, in order to facilitate the synthesis, I have chosen to group them according to three categories, which are the followings :

• Difficulties linked to the mathematical complexity of the basic objects of the field : real numbers, functions, sequences, objects which are still in a construction phase when the official teaching of analysis begins.

• Difficulties linked to the conceptualization of the notion of limit at the core of the field, and to its technical mastery.

• Difficulties linked to the necessary breach with algebraic thinking.

II.1. DIFFICULTIES LINKED TO THE BASIC OBJECTS OF THE FIELD:

We cannot consider that the basic objects of analysis are new notions for students when they enter the field. In France, for instance, irrational numbers, linear and affine functions are introduced at grades 8 and 9 and, at grade 10, the notion of function becomes a central notion. Nevertheless, we cannot say that these objects are yet stabilized; on the contrary, analysis will play an essential role in their conceptualization and maturation.

Real Numbers

Various pieces of research tend to show that conceptions developed by students about real numbers are not really adequate. The distinction between the different categories of numbers remains fuzzy and strongly dependent from their semiotic representations (Munyazikwiye, 1995). Moreover, the increasing and uncontrolled use of pocket calculators tends to reinforce the assimilation real number / decimal number.

At this level of schooling, real numbers are algebraic objects. Real order is recognized as a dense order but, depending from the context, students can conciliate this property with the existence of numbers just before or just after a given number : for instance, 0.999... is often said to be the number just before 1 ; more than 40% students entering French universities consider that, if two numbers A and B satisfy the condition : $\forall n > 0 \ |A-B| < \frac{1}{n}$, they are not necessarily equal, just very close, in some sense successors. The association between real numbers and the real line also lacks coherence. Even if a priori students accept the principle of a one to one correspondence between R and the line, they are not necessarily convinced that such or such precise number has a place on the line (Castela, 1996).

Functions

As far as functions are concerned, the situation is even more complex and it is difficult to summarize in a few words the huge amount of existing research results. I will only mention some main categories of difficulties, which, once more, do not act independently.

• *Difficulties in identifying what really a function is and in considering sequences as functions.*

It is well known that the criteria used by students in order to check functionality are at variance with the formal definition of the notion, even for students who are able to reproduce this formal definition (Vinner & Dreyfus, 1989). These criteria depend more from typical examples taken as prototypes and from associations such as the association : function - formula or the association function - curve. So, the same object may be considered as a function or not, depending from the form of its semiotic representation : for instance, the function f defined by f(x)=2 is not recognized as a function because the given algebraic expression does not depend from x, but is considered as a function if given through its graphic representation as it is represented by a straight line. Such phenomena led researchers to differentiate between what they call « concept definition » and what they call « concept image » (Tall &Vinner, 1981).

• *Difficulties in going beyond a process conception of functions and being able to link flexibly the process and the object dimension of this concept, and develop with respect to it a proceptual view (Tall & Thomas, 1991).*

Research clearly shows the qualitative gap existing between these two levels of conceptualization : process level and object level (Sfard, 1992) (Dubinsky & Harel, 1992). One can trace it, for instance, in the difficulties students often meet at considering as equal functions defined by two equivalent processes, or at working with functions defined by a general property. Mathematical work in analysis becomes very difficult if students can only rely on a process view of functions, as they have to engage them as objects, in more complex processes (such as integration, differentiation...) and as they also have to consider not only particular objects but classes of functions defined by specific properties : continuous, C1, Riemann integrable ...functions.

• *Difficulties in linking the different semiotic registers which allow us to represent and work out functions.*

These difficulties have been extensively analyzed (Romberg, Carpenter, Fennema, 1994), both those related to the translation from one semiotic register to another one, especially from the graphical register to the algebraic one, and those related to the use of information referring to different notions within a given register : function and its derivative, in the graphical register, for example. Research has also evidenced the poor sensitivity of usual teaching to these difficulties and nicely explained how these practices tend to reinforce difficulties by the way they treat graphical representations and the low status they give to graphical reasoning.

• *Difficulties in going beyond numerical and algebraic modes of thinking.*

This category of difficulties is less mentioned in the literature, perhaps because students are rarely given the responsibility of the kind of thinking they have to develop in problem solving. Nevertheless, it is an essential one as analysis is, since Euler at least and his famous book : «Introductio in analysin infinitorum», a mathematical field organized around the notion of function, around functional thinking. Current research in France (Pihoué, 1996) tends to prove that, when entering grade 11, students who have been exposed to functions during three years at least, do not really see the interest and economy of functional thinking. For a great majority, it remains a simple matter of didactic contract.

II.2. DIFFICULTIES LINKED TO THE CONCEPT OF LIMIT

Difficulties students must face are not reduced to this first category. Those associated to the conceptualization of the notion of limit are well documented in the research literature (Cornu, 1991). As regards this specific domain, it has to be noticed that several researchers refer to the notion of epistemological obstacle introduced by the philosopher Gaston Bachelard (Sierpinska, 1988), (Schneider, 1991). According to Bachelard, scientific knowledge is not built in a continuous process but results from the rejection of previous forms of knowledge, which constitute «epistemological obstacles ». So these authors make the hypothesis that some learning difficulties, especially the more resistant ones, result from forms of knowledge, which have been, for a time, coherent and efficient in social or scholar contexts met by students. In other words, they focus on difficulties which can be expressed as resulting from coherent and locally efficient forms of knowledge, appearing both in the historical development of the concept and in its current learning, even if they do not take exactly the same form, due to evident cultural differences.

As far as limits are concerned, the different authors seem to agree on the following epistemological obstacles at least :

• the common sense of the word « limit » which induces resistant conceptions of the limit as a barrier or as the last term of a process, or tends to restrict convergence to monotonous convergence,

• the over-generalization of properties of finite processes to infinite processes, according to the continuity principle stated by Leibniz,

• the strength of a geometry of forms which prevent from clearly identifying the objects involved in the limit process and their underlying topology. This makes difficult the subtle game between the numerical and geometrical settings at play in the limit process.

The strength of such an obstacle is attested by the difficulties encountered by students and even graduate students when they are asked the following unfamiliar question : why the same method : cutting a sphere into small slices and approximating it by the corresponding pile of small cylinders, then taking the limit, gives a correct value for the volume of the sphere and an incorrect value for its area ? As the pile of cylinders has the sphere as evident geometrical limit, most of them do not understand why the different magnitudes associated to the pile of cylinders do not necessarily converge towards the corresponding magnitudes for the sphere !

In the research literature about limits, the identification of epistemological obstacles plays an important role, but students' difficulties cannot be reduced to those relevant of this particular category. The concept of limit, as the concept of function, has two facets : a process facet and an object facet and the ability to cope efficiently with these two facets requires cognitive processes whose complexity and difficulty are well known, now. This fact contributes to explain why students, all over the world, have so strong difficulties in identifying 0.999... and 1. The first semiotic representation 0.999... is obviously of a process type and the second of an object type. Equaling the two imposes not to be trapped by these semiotic characteristics, it imposes to be able to see beyond the infinite process described by 0.999..., the number created by this process and detached from it.

Another important category of difficulties arises from the characteristics of the formal definition of the concept, at least in the standard analysis which is taught nowadays : its logical complexity and the fact that it requires to reverse the direction of the function process which goes from the variable x to the value of the function f(x). But, beyond these formal characteristics, there is one essential point : between an intuitive conception of limits and a formal conception, there is a major qualitative gap. The formal concept of limit is a concept which partially breaks with previous conceptions of the same notion. Its role as unifying concept, as foundational concept is as important, perhaps more important than its productive role in problem solving. We meet there an epistemological dimension of the concept whose didactic transposition is not evident. In fact, some re-searchers such as A.Robert (Robert & Robinet, 1996), have got the conviction that it needs specific mediations, at a meta-level. Some relation-ship could certainly be made with the ideas developed by Vigotsky about the formation of scientific concepts.

II.3. DIFFICULTIES LINKED TO THE NECESSARY BREACH WITH ALGEBRAIC THINKING.

Mathematical activity in analysis, strongly relies on algebraic skills and competencies but, at the same time, entrance in « analysis thinking » requires to take some distance from algebraic thinking (Legrand, 1993). The breach between algebraic thinking and analytic thinking has various different dimensions but I shall limit to some essential points.

Firstly, in order to enter analysis thinking and be efficient in it, one has to develop another vision of equality, to develop and master new techniques for proving equalities. Note that a similar change was evidenced by didactical research in the transition from numerical thinking to algebraic thinking. Briefly speaking, in algebra, in order to prove that two expressions $a(x)$ and $b(x)$ are equal, the standard strategy is the following: to transform one or the two of them by successive equivalencies, up to obtain two obviously equivalent expressions, or to transform their difference (resp. quotient) up to obtain 0 (resp. 1). In analysis, of course if one does not restrict analysis to its algebraic part, this strategy is often out of range or at least not the most economic one, as we do not know the objects of analysis as we know the algebraic ones and as we often work with local properties. We have to develop a vision of equality linked to local « infinite proximity », that is to say linked to the fact that if : $\forall \varepsilon > 0 \ d(A,B) < \varepsilon$, for an adequate distance d, $A=B$. As a consequence, inequalities are taking in analysis a predominant role over equalities and reasoning locally by sufficient conditions on algebraic expressions becomes a fundamental mode of reasoning.

For instance, if you have to prove that there exists a neighborhood of x_0 such that : $a(x) < b(x)$, you do not try to solve this inequality as you would certainly do in algebra. You transform it by introducing successive expressions : $a_1(x)$, $a_2(x)$... $a_n(x)$, and by reducing if necessary the initial neighborhood such as locally : $a(x) < a_1(x) < ... < a_n(x)$, up to get the evidence that for some neighborhood of x_0, you can assure : $a_n(x) < b(x)$. Each step of the process can require difficult choices : you have to accept to loose information on $a(x)$, but not too much as you want to stay locally under $b(x)$ and you have to combine these choices with a subtle game on neighborhoods.

Looking at these changes, at the underlying increase in technical difficulty, helps us to understand better the distance which separates the ability to articulate the formal definition of the limit, even to illustrate it by examples and counter-examples, by graphical representations, from the ability to technically master this definition, that is to say to be able to use it as an operational tool in problem solving and proofs.

In order to close this section, I would like to stress another dimension of this breach between ancient modes of thinking and analytical thinking. Entering the world of analysis requires also to reconstruct objects which were familiar, but in other worlds. The notion of tangent provides us with a typical example of such necessary reconstruction. As showh by (Castela, 1995), the educational system, in France at least, is not sensitive to this problem and this poor sensitivity has evident negative effects.

III. THE EVOLUTION OF FRENCH SECONDARY CURRICULA

III.1. THE 1902 REFORM :
A PRAGMATIC AND ALGEBRAIC APPROACH TO ANALYSIS

As in many other countries, analysis appeared in the classical secondary curriculum at the beginning of this century with the 1902 reform (Artigue, 1996). This was a successful introduction, supported by the most eminent mathematicians of the time : Poincaré, Borel, Hadamard... not to quote the others, as attested by the ICMI study devoted to these questions ten years after (Beke, 1914).

For the mathematicians involved in the reform process, taught analysis had to be rigorous, free from any kind of metaphysics (thus from any kind of infinitesimals), but, at the same time, it had to be accessible to students and useful, both for mathematics and physical sciences. The following quotations from a famous conference given by H.Poincaré on mathematical definitions (Poincaré, 1904) and from the report of the ICMI study illustrate these positions :

« No doubt, it is difficult for a teacher to teach something which does not satisfy him entirely, but the satisfaction of the teacher is not the unique goal of teaching : one has at first to take care of what is the mind of the student and what one wants it to become » (Poincaré)

« Our main duty is to introduce the notions of differential and integral calculus in an intuitive way, by starting from geometrical and mechanical considerations, and gradually rise to the necessary abstraction. All our affirmations have to be true, but we do not have to target the whole truth. » (Beke)

These mathematicians were convinced that it was possible to develop a curriculum in analysis coherent with these principles without major difficulties and, with regard to the notion of limit, one can read in the final report of the ICME study :

« The notion of limit is so present in secondary teaching and even at beginning levels (unlimited decimal fractions, area of the circle, logarithm, geometrical series...) that its general definition would not be likely to occasion any difficulty. »

What was taught in fact, at that time, was standard calculus, but we have to be aware that the increase in power and rigour offered by this algebraic analysis for solving classical problems at secondary level was so evident that the interest of this new calculus could not be denied.

III.2. THE SIXTIES' REFORMS AND THE NEW MATH REFORM: TOWARDS A FORMAL APPROACH OF ANALYSIS

The curriculum remained stable until the beginning of the sixties. At that time, structuralism was becoming dominant. Mathematicians had discovered the power of algebraic structures and foundation issues were taking a predominant role. In France, it was the golden age for the Bourbaki Group created in 1937, with the aim of renewing the universitary course of differential and integral calculus. Traditional teaching of analysis was then seen as an obsolete object, unable to cope with the central ideas of the field. Renovation entered the secondary curriculum in 1960, introducing a conception of analysis less empirical and pragmatic, with more emphasis on fundamental concepts and their structural dimension. At the same moment, quantifiers were officially introduced as well as elements of set theory and algebraic structures. The formal definition of the limit was explicitly mentioned in the syllabus. This was a real renovation, reinforced in 1965, but not a revolution. A careful look at textbooks shows that it was in fact a transition period, that newness introduced did not bowl over the ancient organization.

The new math reform definitively turned the page at the beginning of the seventies. Analysis was not its main part but teaching of analysis was deeply influenced by the spirit of the reform. It became essentially formal and theoretical, focusing more on definitions and foundation issues than on problem solving. It was rejected soon after within the wave of global rejection of the new math reform.

III.3. THE REJECTION OF THE NEW MATH REFORM AND THE INTRODUCTION OF INTUITIVE AND EXPERIMENTAL APPROACHES

The last important reform directly resulted from the rejection of the new math reform and took place in 1982. It was influenced by the reflection and experimental work undertaken in the IREMs. It was supported by the vision of mathematics as a science historically and culturally produced and, as such, dependent from historical and cultural contexts, which was becoming predominant. It tried to find a more adequate equilibrium between the mathematical coherence of the field and students' cognitive development. It tried also to find a better equilibrium between the « tool » and « object » dimensions of analysis, according to R.Douady (Douady, 1986), that is to say between the internal development and structuration of the fundamental concepts of the field and their use as tools for solving problems internal or external to mathematics. The proposals of the commission interIREM Analyse published in 1981 reflected these ambitions. They were the followings :

• to modify the relationships between theory and applications and organize the syllabus around the solving of problems rich enough and epistemologically representative of the field, a field being now considered, according to J.Dieudonné, as a field where « approximating, majoring, minoring » were core processes,

• to find better equilibrium between qualitative analysis and quantitative analysis, by giving more importance to quantitative problems, thanks to the use of calculators,

• to give particular importance to typical and simple examples which could then serve as a reference, and to avoid any early interest in pathological cases,

• to theorize only when necessary with reduced levels of formalization accessible to students,

• and last but not least, to develop a constructivist approach to teaching.

These proposals were directly reflected in the new curriculum, proposed in 1982 and the general strategy used in order to introduce the different key notions clearly illustrates these positions:

> • explore typical simple behaviors, both numerically and graphically, with the help of calculators for the numerical part,
> • use these explorations in order to produce quantitative definitions adapted to the most simple cases and work them out,
> • by introducing more complex cases, let students become aware of the limitations of the first approach and introduce general and qualitative definitions.

For instance, the notion of derivative was introduced through the notion of first order expansion by exploring numerically and graphically the local behavior (at 0) of typical functions allowing majorations of the form : $|f(x+h)-f(x)-f'(x)h| \leq Mh^2$. Later on, functions which did not allow such simple majorations were introduced and led to the general definition of a first order expansion.

Formalization was strongly reduced. Only one formal definition was introduced for the limit in 0 and teachers were explicitly asked not to use it extensively. This formal definition whose role was vanishing, disappeared in the curriculum adjustment which took place three years later and the paragraph of the syllabus devoted to limits was modestly renamed «language of limits ».

Mathematical activity was organized around problem solving : optimization problems, approximation of numbers and functions, modelisation of discrete and continuous variations... The notions of derivative, and above all of derivative function, essential tool for solving these problems, became the central notion. The logical order : limits - continuity - derivatives was thus broken : a minimal intuitive language of limits was introduced for supporting the introduction of the derivative, then the derivative function was the central piece of the edifice, the notion of continuity nearly disappeared, all the more as, with the definition chosen for the limit, every function having a limit at a point in its definition domain was necessarily continuous.

The influence of analysis was already evident at grade 10, one year before its official introduction, as attested by the following excerpt of the syllabus :

> « Themes for activities :
> 1. Majoration and minoration of a function on an interval
> 2. Research for extremum in optimization problems
> 3. Rate of variation - inequalities such as : $|f(x)-f(y)| < M|x-y|$. Geometrical interpretation
> 4. Use of variations of functions in order to solve equations $f(x)=b$ and inequalities. »

This was an ambitious curriculum. It tried to make alive the epistemological value of analysis as a field where approximation played a central role and to organize the progressive entrance of students in it, both at conceptual and technical levels. In this introduction, links between algebraic, numerical and graphical representations and techniques played an essential role, as explicitly stressed in the syllabus. Analysis taught was not a formal one, it was approached in an intuitive and experimental way, and there was a desire not to limit it to algebraic practices. This syllabus was then modified in 1985, 1990, 1993, in order to better fit the increasing democratization of high schools but the spirit remained the same, at least as expressed in the syllabus. So we can measure today the long term effects of nearly 15 years of such intuitive and experimental approaches.

IV. SOME POTENTIALS AND LIMITS OF THESE APPROACHES

Firstly, there are some evident positive outcomes. I would like to only mention three of them which, in my opinion, are specially important :
• Such an approach made the field accessible to any category of students, up to a certain point, and this positive outcome cannot be considered as unimportant, above all if one takes into account that the great majority (about 70%) of what we call each « age class » of the population enters high school and is taught analysis,
• Very soon, students are in contact with important problems at the core of the field, such as optimization and approximation problems ; analysis is not reduced to its algebraic part, and according to the syllabus, textbooks try to give importance to the numerical and graphical dimensions of both concepts and techniques,
• Calculators and even graphic calculators are regularly used by students. They help to make viable the numerical and graphical approaches encouraged in the syllabus.

In spite of these evident positive outcomes, I am far from thinking that we found some ideal way towards analysis. Some very important issues remained unsolved and new problems are emerging. Once more, I would like to focus on some of them.

• *The limits of the help provided by calculators and the issues linked to their integration*

Calculators and even graphic calculators are widely spread out in France, as mentioned above. In 1981, a decision of the Ministry of Education allowed them to be freely used in assessments at secondary level and this is still the case today. Students for instance can take the « Baccalauréat » with a graphic calculator or even a TI92. This decision was taken in order to foster the institutional integration of such technological means. But, even now, calculators are mostly considered as private students' tools. Recent research (Trouche, 1996) shows the negative effect of such an uncontrolled use on the conceptions developed by students, about concepts such as the concept of limit, about numerical approximations or graphical representations. An effective learning of analysis with graphic calculators requires the development of specific competencies, of specific knowledge. This fact is not easily recognized by the educational system which remains reluctant to devote time to such specific learning.

•*The difficulties of viability of the* « *approximation* » *dimension of analysis*

Recent evolution has also put to the fore the difficulties encountered by the educational system with the « approximation » dimension of analysis. As stressed above, developing this dimension requires to take some distance from usual modes of thinking and relies on difficult techniques whose learning is a long term process. Teachers encounter evident difficulties at organizing and preserving an « ecological niche » for such mathematical practices, all the more as they cannot avoid the competition between approximation techniques and algebraic techniques, which look easier (Artigue, 1993).

• *The difficulties of viability of teaching through rich and significant problems.*

New curriculum wanted to organize analysis approach around rich and significant problem solving activities. We note an increasing gap between these ambitions which are still explicit in the syllabus and the content of textbooks. What one can find in most recent textbooks tends more towards an unstructured accumulation of problems with a limited scope whose solving is so much decomposed in sub-questions that students can hardly understand their global coherence. Such an evolution clearly shows the strength of didactic transposition processes which shape and condition the real curriculum (Chevallard, 1985). In the educational world too, as far as assimilation remains possible, accommodation is not the rule.

• *The difficulties resulting from the increasing lack of structuration*

Once more, these difficulties are evidenced by recent textbooks. Status of objects, notions, assertions remains fuzzy. Formal definitions have been banished, replaced by descriptive sentences expressed in

« natural language », these being a priori thought more accessible and intuitive. In fact, these sentences only have the appearance of natural language : they have nothing to do with the vernacular language spoken by students. They do not support an operational control of practices. Moreover, as quantifiers are generally situated partly at the beginning of the sentence, partly at the end, they do not help students to become sensitive to the complex game quantifiers play in the corresponding definitions. Theorems are accepted on the base of a few explorations and not necessarily labeled as such. At reading textbooks, one has the uncomfortable feeling that the coherence induced by the logical constraints of knowledge has progressively fainted without being replaced by another evident coherence.

For many of our students, what we are developing, beyond the standard algebraic part of analysis, is perhaps more a world of « pottering about » than the mathematical world we wanted to begin to make alive.

V. SOME CONCLUDING REMARKS

Didactical research clearly attests that it is not easy for students to enter the conceptual field of analysis, if analysis is not reduced to its algebraic part, if entrance in this conceptual field aims at developing the modes of thinking and the techniques which are now considered as fundamental in it. Secondary education has been facing this problem for about one century. At the beginning of the century, analysis entered the general secondary curriculum, and this introduction, which provided teachers with very efficient tools for solving classical problems, both in mathematics and physical sciences, was highly appreciated. With the reform undertaken in the early sixties, new ambitions entered the secondary curriculum in analysis : roughly speaking, analysis taught took its autonomy from algebra and the object dimension emerged from the tool dimension. Soon after, the new math reform imposed a formal vision where foundation issues tended to become predominant. This formal vision was soon rejected and, in the early eighties, a new organization around problems and techniques at the core of the field emerged ; experimental and intuitive approaches were encouraged. These intuitive and experimental approaches to analysis progressively imposed themselves and today, they appear as the only reasonable entrance gate, all the more as analysis teaching is no longer limited to some mathematical or social elite. But, we have to confess that they did not succeed in making teaching and learning analysis miraculously easy and satisfactory. They helped to solve some problems but, in the long range, if they are not carefully controlled, they tend to generate some unavoidable problems. The necessity to better control these approaches is evidenced by the evolution of the didactic transposition process along the last fifteen years in France and the cognitive effects this evolution produces. Current didactical research in the field, in France, is addressing these crucial issues, both at high school level and at the transition form high school to university.

Analysis of this particular didactic transposition process also evidences the difficulties raised by the exploitation of didactical results or local successful experimentations, for undertaking substantial and global actions on the educational system. For this purpose, epistemological and cognitive approaches which have been predominant in the field and essentially used, up to now, are obviously insufficient. We have to integrate approaches to didactical research which allow us to better take into account the role played by institutional and cultural constraints in both learning and teaching processes.

References

Artigue, M. & Ervynck, G. (Eds) (1992) : *Proceedings of Working Group 3 on students' difficulties in calculus,* ICME-7, Université de Sherbrooke.

Artigue, M. (1993) : *Enseignement de l'analyse et fonctions de référence,* Repères IREM, vol. 11, 115-139.

Artigue, M. (1996) : *Réformes et contre-réformes dans l'enseignement de l'analyse au lycée (1902-1994),* in Les sciences au lycée - *Un siècle de réformes des mathématiques et de la physique en France et à l'étranger,* B. Belhoste, H. Gispert et N. Hulin (eds), 197-217, Ed. Vuibert, Paris.

Beke, E. (1914) : *Rapport général sur les résultats obtenus dans l'introduction du calcul différentiel et intégral dans les classes supérieures des établissements secondaires,* L'Enseignement Mathématique, vol. 16, 246-284.

Castela, C. (1995) : *Apprendre avec et contre ses connaissances antérieures - un exemple concret : celui de la tangente,* Recherches en Didactique des Mathématiques, vol.15.1., 7-47.

Castela, C. (1996) : *La droite des réels en seconde: point d'appui disponible ou enjeu clandestin ?,* IREM de Rouen.

Chevallard, Y. (1985) : *La transposition didactique,* La Pensée Sauvage, Grenoble.

Commission interIREM Analyse (ed) (1981) : *L'enseignement de l'analyse,* IREM de Lyon.

Cornu, B. (1991) : *Limits,* in Advanced Mathematical Thinking, 153-166 , Kluwer Academic Publishers.

Douady, R. (1986) : *Jeux de cadre et dialectique outil-objet*, Recherches en Didactique des Mathématiques, vol. 7.2, 5-32.

Dubinsky, Ed & Harel, G. (Eds) (1992) : *The concept of Function : Some aspects of Epistemology and Pedagogy*, MAA Notes, N°25.

Legrand, M. (1993) : *Débat scientifique en cours de mathématiques et spécificité de l'analyse*, Repères IREM, vol. 10, 123-159.

Munyazikwiye, A. (1995) : *Problèmes didactiques liés aux écritures de nombres*, Recherches en Didactique des Mathématiques, vol. 15/2, 31-62.

Pihoué, D. (1996) : *L'entrée dans la pensée fonctionnelle en classe de seconde*, DEA, Université Paris 7.

Poincaré, H. (1904) : *Les définitions en mathématiques*, L'Enseignement Mathématique, vol. 6, 255-283.

Robert, A. & Robinet, J. (1996) : *Prise en compte du meta en didactique des mathématiques*, Recherches en didactique des mathématiques, vol. 16/2, 145-176.

Romberg, T., Carpenter, T., & Fennema, E. (1994) : *Integrating research on the graphical representation of functions*, Hillsdale, N.J. Lawrence Erlbaum.

Schneider, M. (1991) : *Un obstacle épistémologique soulevé par des découpages infinis de surfaces et de solides*, Recherches en Didactique des Mathématiques, vol. 11 2/3, 241-294.

Sfard, A. (1992) : *On the dual nature of mathematical conceptions : reflections on processes and objects as different sides of the same coin,* Educational Studies in Mathematics, N°22, 1-36.

Sierpinska, A. (1988) : *Sur un programme de recherche lié à la notion d'obstacle épistémologique*, Actes du Colloque : Construction des savoirs : obstacles et conflits, Montréal, CIRADE.

Tall, D. (Ed) (1991) : *Advanced Mathematical Thinking*, Kluwer Academic Publishers.

Tall, D. & Thomas, M. (1991) : *Encouraging versatile thinking in algebra using the computer*, Educational Studies in Mathematics, vol. 22, 125-147.

Tall, D. & Vinner, S. (1981) : *Concept image and concept definition in mathematics with particular reference to limits and continuity*, Educational Studies in Mathematics, vol. 12/2, 151-169.

Trouche, L. (1996) : *A propos de l'apprentissage des limites de fonctions dans un « environnement calculatrice »: étude des rapports entre processus de conceptualisation et processus d'instrumentation*, Doctoral thesis, Université de Montpellier 2.

Vinner, S. & Dreyfus, T. (1989) : *Images and Definitions in the Concept of Function*, Journal for Research in Mathematics Education, vol. 20/4, 356-366.

INNOVACIÓN EDUCATIVA: UN RETO PROFESIONAL

Luis Balbuena

La innovación educativa puede ser definida, descrita e interpretada desde múltiples ópticas. Como en el proceso educativo intervienen investigadores, administraciones públicas, maestros, padres, alumnos, etc., cada uno puede tener, y de hecho lo tiene, un modo de entender y de hablar de la innovación en el área de la educación. Y por si esta complejidad fuese poca, en la literatura dedicada al tema existe un conjunto de palabras tales como reforma, cambio, renovación, investigación, mejora, innovación, etc., de significados parecidos y sin que exista aún un acuerdo generalizado sobre cuáles son o deben ser los límites de unas y de otras.

Por eso considero importante que trate de delimitar lo mejor que me sea posible cuál es el entorno educativo en el que centraré mis reflexiones.

Si se ha leído con atención el extenso programa de este 8º ICME, se habrá podido comprobar que esta preocupación que les intento transmitir es la parte central de varias actividades. Significa que estamos ante un problema que ocupa la atención de los que nos movemos en el mundo de la Educación Matemática, aunque quizás preocupe más a los que cada día hemos de practicar con grupos de alumnos más o menos extensos. Quizás seamos también los que tengamos más difuso nuestro rol en el área de la Educación Matemática.

El tema es abordado directa o indirectamente en varias conferencias regulares, es el eje específico de un grupo de trabajo y seguro que planeará en muchas más de las actividades que contiene el programa.

Pero empecemos a precisar los conceptos.

Parece que hay un cierto consenso en considerar la Reforma educativa como un cambio en el sistema a gran escala. Un cambio que afecta, no sólo al curriculum de las distintas disciplinas y a las formas de enseñar, de evaluar, etc., sino que puede introducir cambios estructurales sobre lo ya existente. Así, por ejemplo, en España, se acomete en estos momentos una reforma del sistema educativo que modifica la estructura existente hasta hoy de manera sustancial. Introduce dos segmentos absolutamente novedosos: Educación Infantil (de tres a cinco años), y la Enseñanza Secundaria Obligatoria (de 12 a 16 años), con lo que la obligatoriedad se amplía de los catorce años actuales a los dieciséis. Por otra parte, reduce la enseñanza primaria de los ocho años que tiene ahora a seis y también el actual Bachillerato (incluyendo el Curso de Orientación Universitaria) pasará de cuatro a dos años.

Es, por tanto, una reforma que como indica Sack (1981) "es una forma especial de cambio, que implica una estrategia planificada para la modificación de aspectos del sistema de educación de un país, con arreglo a un sistema de necesidades, de resultados específicos, de medios y de métodos adecuados".

La reforma educativa va generalmente ligada a políticas y programas gubernamentales con las que se intenta dar algún rumbo a todo el país. Los gobernantes son conscientes de que ningún cambio profundo puede realizarse en una sociedad si no se reforma y se orienta el sistema educativo hacia esos objetivos. Nuestros gobiernos, en España, orientan el sistema educativo hacia la nueva situación del país: hacia la democracia y hacia la plena integración con Europa.

Queda claro, por tanto, cuál es concepto de reforma aplicado a la educación.

La investigación en Educación Matemática es otro término que conviene clarificar, aunque parece que hay un cierto consenso en considerar a la investigación en esta área como aquella que se realiza siguiendo los métodos propios de un proceso investigador. Dice G. Vázquez (1987) "... deben formularse dos requisitos para dar validez a la investigación en esta área: primero, que sea científica y segundo, que sea pedagógica, esto es, adecuada a la naturaleza de nuestro objeto de estudio: la educación como resultado y como proceso ".

D.J. Fox en su "Modelo del proceso de investigación" habla de 17 etapas divididas en tres partes:

Primera parte: diseño del plan de investigación (trece etapas).

Etapa 1.- Idea o necesidad impulsora y área problemática.
Etapa 2.- Examen inicial de la bibliografía.
Etapa 3.- Definición del problema concreto de la investigación.
Etapa 4.- Estimación del éxito potencial de la investigación planteada.

Etapa 5.-   Segundo examen de la bibliografía.
Etapa 6.-   Selección del enfoque de la investigación.
Etapa 7.-   Formulación de las hipótesis de la investigación.
Etapa 8.-   Selección de los métodos y técnicas de recogida de datos.
Etapa 9. -   Selección y elaboración de los instrumentos de recogida de datos.
Etapa 10. -   Diseño del plan de análisis de datos.
Etapa 11. -   Diseño del plan de recogida de datos.
Etapa 12. -   Identificación de la población y de la muestra a utilizar.
Etapa 13.-   Estudios pilotos del enfoque, métodos e instrumentos de recogida de datos y del plan de análisis de recogida de datos.

Segunda parte: ejecución del plan de investigación (tres etapas).

Etapa 14. -   Ejecución del plan de recogida de datos.
Etapa 15. -   Ejecución del plan de análisis de datos.
Etapa 16. -   Preparación de los informes de la investigación.

Tercera parte: aplicación de resultados (una etapa).

Etapa 17. -   Difusión de los resultados y propuesta de medidas de actuacion.

Sobre la investigación en Educación Matemática creo que se ha estudiado y teorizado suficientemente. Los criterios de calidad están establecidos y más o menos aceptados por todos, pero creo que es la práctica, esa tercera parte que apunta Fox, la que, en la mayoría de los casos, determina la validez y la viabilidad de cualquier investigación por muy sesuda y rigurosa que sea.

Generalmente se piensa que la labor del investigador acaba con la elaboración de un informe y su presentación ante un tribunal cuando se trata de una tesis doctoral. Opino, sin embargo, que es responsabilidad del investigador, no sólo la difusión de su estudio, sino también procurar que sus deducciones y conclusiones lleguen a producir los cambios y mejoras que investigó, máxime, cuando la mayor parte de las veces, su investigación ha sido financiada con dinero público.

Por otra parte, nadie pone en duda la trascendencia y las aportaciones de la investigación en Educación Matemática para la mejora del aprendizaje y de la enseñanza de esta disciplina. Esto es un axioma.

No voy a incidir más en este aspecto que considero del máximo interés, porque quizás me desvíe demasiado de mi objetivo aunque pienso que es necesario que reflexionemos acerca del papel que juega o puede jugar la investigación en los cambios que se producen en el sistema educativo. Resulta cuando menos preocupante, la frecuencia con que los cambios que se proponen (desde las administraciones, sobre todo), no se basen en investigaciones contrastadas y no deja de causar cierta inquietud y perplejidad que, a los que enseñamos día a día en el aula, no nos lleguen tampoco ni ideas ni resultados producto de investigaciones que nos ayuden a enseñar mejor o a conseguir que nuestros alumnos aprendan con más intensidad y eficacia.

Y llego así al tercer concepto que quisiera intentar precisar y delimitar:

Innovación educativa.

No existe demasiada literatura sobre este concepto y ello, quizás, debido a lo complicado que resulta marcar con claridad sus límites y los criterios de calidad y eficacia que debe conllevar toda innovación educativa. Hay incluso quien piensa que se trata de una distinción (entre investigación e innovación), interesada y artificiosa. Pero también he escuchado a investigadores, como el Prof. Rico (Universidad de Granada), hablar de la necesidad de aceptar ambas concepciones como perfectamente diferenciadas, coexistentes y potenciables.

Empezaré exponiendo algunas opiniones sobre la innovación educativa que puedan orientar al profesor "de aula" a la hora de intentar clarificar su rol innovador.

Según T. González y J.M. Escudero (1987) "... suele emplearse el término innovación para referirse a cambios a menor escala o más concretos ". Desde hace años otros autores hablan de la innovación como cambios deliberados que pretenden dar al sistema educativo una mayor eficacia para el cumplimiento de sus objetivos.

Así pues, parece que se quiere reservar el término "reforma" para aquellos cambios cuantitativamente amplios; el término "investigación" (en nuestro caso, en Educación Matemática), para cambios cualitativamente más profundos y se reserva la "innovación" para cambios cualitativa y cuantitativamente menores. Esa ambigüedad nos sitúa ante una idea difícil de delimitar, para la que no existe una medida adecuada que permita precisar cuándo se rebasan los límites de la innovación para situarnos en otra cosa.

Debemos, no obstante, intentar establecer criterios y conceptualizaciones que acerquen la innovación a sus protagonistas que son (y en esto parece que no existe demasiada controversia), los profesores y profesoras que cada día desarrollan su labor profesional en centros educativos, ante grupos de estudiantes cuya correcta formación depende, en gran medida, de las actitudes y de las aptitudes de sus profesores.

Esa tendencia de reservar la innovación para lo que podríamos llamar "la práctica educativa" es la visión que, sobre el tema, sostienen J.M. Sancho y otros (1992) que hablan de "procesos deliberados y sistemáticos" que intentan producir cambios en la práctica educativa. También M.V. García (1995) indica que "... para algunas personas la innovación es algo cotidiano, algo propio del quehacer profesional, vinculado a su preocupación por la educación y por el aprendizaje de sus alumnos". Creo que esta visión del concepto nos sitúa sobre la pista de lo que muchos entendemos por innovación educativa, de qué es lo que cabe en él y qué tipo de trabajos y actividades se pueden considerar como innovadores.

Surge, pues, una pregunta clave: ¿pueden establecerse principios que permitan identificar procesos innovadores en Educación Matemática?

Intentaré aportar algunas señas de identidad sobre lo que considero como innovación educativa.

Como punto de arranque, considero la innovación aplicada a nuestro campo, como aquellas experiencias que suponen acciones prácticas y sistemáticas por medio de las cuales se intenta introducir y promover ciertos cambios tanto en la forma de aprender y de enseñar matemáticas, como para conseguir actitudes más positivas en torno a nuestra disciplina. Este último aspecto tiene, para mi, una gran importancia. Se trata de conseguir que los estudiantes se acerquen a las matemáticas de una forma distinta a como suele hacerse, que se superen ciertos tabúes e ideas preconcebidas, que la vean y la consideren como a una amiga. Es posible.

La innovación no siempre está motivada por algún grado de insatisfacción, bien ante el sistema educativo en su conjunto o bien ante la práctica cotidiana. El profesor debe considerar la innovación como algo propio de su quehacer y con la cual puede mejorar su práctica. Ahora bien, la alteración que supone pasar de una situación inicial a otra final diferente, no debe hacerse sin una programación que clarifique al detalle el por qué, el para qué, el cómo y el cuándo se hace. El objeto de nuestra innovación es tan delicado y preciso que nos debe obligar a meditar y reflexionar sobre el proceso de cambio que deseamos realizar.

Pero ahí no debe acabar la innovación. En ningún caso debe plantearse el cambio por el cambio. Es necesaria la evaluación de lo realizado. Él por qué, el para qué y el cómo, han de analizarse y comprobar si los objetivos propuestos con la innovación se han cubierto o no. Se debe verificar si el producto final es mejor que el del punto de partida. En resumen, en toda innovación educativa, ha de existir una programación y una evaluación. Sobre todo una evaluación, pues aunque pueda parecer paradójico, existe poca "cultura evaluativa" entre los profesores. En pocas ocasiones realizamos una evaluación de nuestro propio trabajo y esta es una de las condiciones básicas para garantizar la calidad de cualquier trabajo innovador. Debemos aplicarla a nuestra labor como algo habitual y como una especie de control de calidad de nuestro trabajo.

Otra característica que, a mi juicio, debe contener la innovación para que pueda concedérsele la categoría de eficaz, es que sea transferible. Que se pueda repetir. Que pueda ser aplicada por el mismo profesor o por otro en distintas circunstancias. Así, las innovaciones que un profesor decida realizar no quedarán restringidas sólo a los alumnos de su grupo, sino que deben ser conocidas, aplicadas y desarrolladas, si así se deseara, por otros también.

Por otra parte, la innovación debe ser proyectada y desarrollada tratando de ajustarse al máximo al método de trabajo que requiere una investigación. Es evidente que existen múltiples limitaciones para que una innovación, hecha desde el aula, pueda seguir estrictamente los pasos que requiere una investigación. El profesor en ejercicio está sometido a muchas restricciones: de medios, de tiempo, de formación, etc. , que, en general, le impiden realizar investigaciones siguiendo todas y cada una de las pautas que éstas requieren. El importante rastreo bibliográfico, que Fox señala en dos etapas, por ejemplo, es una seria limitación. Pero aún cuando todas las etapas no puedan realizarse en toda su extensión, el espíritu que anime al innovador, a aquel profesor que pretenda introducir algún cambio en su práctica docente, debe ser el mismo que anima al que quiere hacer una profunda investigación: ha de seguir un proceso totalmente deliberado y sistemático.

La innovación debe actuar directa e inmediatamente sobre el sistema educativo. Esta es una de las características que permite reconocer una innovación, pues ésta se plantea y diseña para producir efectos inmediatos. Es parte de su grandeza y también de su peligro. El profesor desea experimentar un nuevo material didáctico (manipulable o no), que le permita mejorar la introducción de un determinado contenido;

o bien quiere conseguir desarrollar mejor ciertas capacidades del alumno (abstracción, generalización,...) a través de contenidos nuevos o de contenidos del curriculum pero enfocados de otra manera o desea, en fin, cambiar la actitud de sus alumnos hacia las matemáticas proporcionándoles ideas y actividades más creativas y acordes con sus capacidades y con su formación. En cualquiera de los casos, el profesor innovador no se plantea obtener resultados a medio o a largo plazo, como suele ocurrir con la investigación, sino que desea obtener resultados (buenos, malos o neutros) de forma inmediata. Es que, además, esos resultados actúan como estímulo para proseguir mejorando e innovando. Creo conveniente clarificar que no es la innovación un factor discriminante entre el buen y el mal profesor. Un profesor con inquietudes innovadoras, realizadas con las condiciones de calidad, suele corresponder a un buen profesor. Sin embargo, el recíproco no siempre es cierto.

Tras estas caracterizaciones de la innovación, demos un simbólico paseo por la realidad.

Desgraciadamente el sistema educativo, casi nunca, procura las mejores condiciones para que el "profesor de aula" se sienta estimulado a realizar labores innovadoras. En general, lo hace o ha de hacerlo "a pesar del sistema", derrochando grandes dotes de profesionalidad y utilizando parte o gran parte de su tiempo libre, en el supuesto de que disponga de él, pues cada vez es más escaso...

El profesor innovador ha de superar, por tanto, diversas situaciones que le inducen a la desmoralización. Entre otras:

- La formación. Generalmente tenemos poco tiempo para la formación permanente, sobre todo en los aspectos docentes: leer revistas, libros, asistir a cursos, a congresos, etc. . Nada de esto suele ser fácil. Unas veces por falta de recursos económicos, otras porque la estructura del sistema (horas de clase, burocracia, permisos oficiales,...) lo impiden. Por otra parte, tampoco suele enseñarse el cómo innovar. Es algo que tenemos que aprender con nuestros medios y si tenemos interés por hacerlo. (Obsérvese que no he hecho referencia a la formación científica porque doy por supuesto que se tiene la suficiente e incluso más).

- El encorsetamiento de los sistemas educativos. Aunque en este aspecto hay una cierta superación, aún los sistemas educativos son demasiado rígidos. Se marcan no sólo los contenidos, sino que muchas veces se señalan las metodologías. Y si no lo hace la administración responsable, lo hacen las editoriales a través de sus libros de texto que, en general, marcan y obligan a seguir pautas.

- Falta de incentivación. Es una de las más graves deficiencias de los sistemas educativos. En casi todos los trabajos (sobre todo en los promovidos por la empresa privada), el trabajador tiene unos incentivos que le estimulan a procurar hacerlo cada vez mejor. En nuestra profesión esos estímulos sólo se encuentran en la profesionalidad de cada uno, pues las administraciones educativas no suelen ofrecer más que el sueldo, que no siempre está acorde con la labor que desarrolla el docente. Y cuando hablo de incentivos, no me refiero sólo a los de tipo económico. Existen formas de reconocer la labor y el esfuerzo del docente que no pasan necesariamente por elevar sus emolumentos.

Si bien para el profesor universitario la actividad investigadora forma parte de lo que podría ser su propia definición, en el profesor no universitario no sólo no toma parte de su definición, sino que ni siquiera es tenida en cuenta de forma adecuada entre sus méritos profesionales. En numerosas convocatorias de las que suele hacer la administración educativa para seleccionar profesores que han de desarrollar labores que requieren cierta especialización en temas didácticos, los trabajos realizados por un profesor aspirante relacionados con la innovación o con aportaciones al sistema educativo (publicaciones, artículos en revistas especializadas, comunicaciones o ponencias en congresos e incluso una tesis doctoral), son considerados méritos "no preferentes" y baremados con ínfimas puntuaciones. Es evidente que esta falta de reconocimiento conlleva una general inhibición del profesorado a la hora de plantearse proyectos de innovación y no digamos ya, de investigación.

Un reconocimiento formal de esta parcela de nuestro trabajo traería como consecuencia una transformación de nuestro perfil profesional. Posiblemente la subliminar y solapada "carrera docente" actual, basada en la consecución de la máxima titulación y de conseguir un máximo de certificados de cursos y más cursos, daría paso a otra basada más en las aportaciones que cada cual sea capaz de hacer al sistema educativo, con lo enriquecedor que eso podría ser para todos.

- Es evidente que no está cerrada la lista de limitaciones (soledad, incomunicación, dificultad para publicar resultados, burocratización cada vez mayor del sistema, y otras tal vez de tipo más particular de una zona, país o estrictamente personales). Sin embargo, creo que a pesar de todas esas limitaciones (que nos pueden afectar en mayor o menor medida), nuestra profesionalidad, es decir, el amor hacia nuestro trabajo y el convencimiento de que estamos desarrollando una labor de gran trascendencia para la sociedad, nos debe obligar a estar por encima de esas posibles trabas y hemos de convertir la innovación permanente en una de las características definitorias de nuestra profesión. Esa actitud de constante búsqueda de mejoras es buena para el sistema, es buena para nosotros, los profesores, porque nos obliga a reflexionar sobre nuestro quehacer, pero, sobre todo, es buena para nuestros alumnos porque entre otros efectos positivos, es un buen referente de profesionalidad que perdurará.

Existen infinitos campos en los que aquel que lo desee, puede innovar. En este sentido hemos de tratar de superar la falta de autoestima que suele tener el profesor de aula; el maestro que día a día se comunica con sus alumnos en el grandioso recinto de su aula. Ese hecho ya es en sí, sumamente importante. Pero es que, además, nuestros ensayos, nuestras innovaciones, por muy sencillas que nos parezcan, tienen el mérito de ser realizadas sin que nadie nos obligue a ello. Tendemos a pensar que nuestras experiencias no tienen valor y, en general, ni nos preocupamos de comunicarlas y mucho menos nos esforzamos en escribir acerca de ellas para transmitirlas, bien a través de congresos, bien por medio de revistas o por cualquier otro sistema. Sin embargo, tengo la convicción de que esa tendencia va a cambiar. Los profesores de aula hemos de ser conscientes de que nuestros problemas los tendremos que resolver nosotros mismos, ayudándonos y comunicándonos unos con otros. No podemos seguir esperando a que mi problema cotidiano sobre cómo estimular a un alumno para que comprenda y ame las matemáticas me sea resuelto ni se sabe cuándo, ni se sabe por quién, ni se sabe desde dónde. Nosotros también tenemos resultados que aportar en la Educación Matemática. Nosotros también debemos aportar resultados a la Educación Matemática. En ese sentido es esperanzador constatar la gran cantidad de comunicaciones presentadas por profesores de aula.

Por otra parte, los sistemas educativos se están reformando en muchos países. Es un deseo en todos, que el sistema que resulte sea bueno, el mejor posible y creo que una condición "sine qua non" para que un sistema educativo sea considerado bueno es que consiga que su profesorado se sienta con deseos de innovar, que se sienta apoyado y estimulado para ello y que se pongan a su disposición medios para poder hacerlo. Por eso hay un rayo de esperanza para que, si esto se comprende, podamos tener en el futuro mejores sistemas educativos y una mejora de nuestro rol profesional.

En definitiva, como se deduce de lo anterior, la innovación educativa necesita de la contribución de todos para conseguir una sistematización, una fundamentación teórica, la legitimación conceptual, clarificar su contenido, diseñar y consensuar unos criterios de calidad que garanticen la utilidad, la generalización y, sobre todo, que incida en la práctica escolar. Es necesaria la innovación permanente para afianzar y ampliar nuestro prestigio ante la sociedad. Nos queda, pues, tarea por hacer.

Como no quisiera que mi planteamiento fuera estrictamente teórico o que quedase en el terreno de los deseos, quisiera explicarles sucintamente una actividad que venimos desarrollando en mi centro de trabajo, que es un Instituto de Bachillerato (enseñanza Secundaria) con unos 850 alumnos y alumnas de edades comprendidas entre los 14 y los 18 años. Es, concretamente, el I.B. "Viera y Clavijo" de la ciudad de La Laguna - Isla de Tenerife - Canarias - España. Los ocho profesores que impartimos matemáticas en el centro formamos el Seminario de la asignatura y un equipo de trabajo compactado.

La actividad en cuestión la titulamos "Semana de Matemáticas" y la venimos desarrollando desde hace varios años. Cada edición nos permite ampliar y mejorar la anterior. El título de la actividad puede resultar engañoso porque el trabajo se desarrolla prácticamente durante todo el curso escolar. Moviliza en torno a las matemáticas a un buen número de alumnos del centro debido, principalmente, a que procuramos ofrecer un variado conjunto de actividades en las que poder participar. Esquemáticamente incluye:

- Concurso del cartel anunciador (se convoca un mes después de empezar el curso).
- Concurso de "Fotografía y Matemáticas" (también se convoca en noviembre).
- Liguilla matemática "¡Yo qué sé!" (Los alumnos se organizan en equipos para participar en las cuatro sesiones de que consta).
- Revista "¡Yo qué sé!" (Se edita paralela a la liguilla publicando trabajos diversos sobre matemáticas).
- Talleres impartidos por los alumnos.
- Show matemático.
- Conferencias Ilusiones ópticas, La medida del tiempo, Las matemáticas ¿para qué?, Las celosías, Los números y la numerología: lo serio y lo menos serio,...
- Visitas pedagógicas (museo de la Ciencia y el Cosmos; Centro provincial de meteorología; planetario; observatorio astronómico; ...).

-Concurso de trabajos científicos.

-Construir aparatos y sencillas máquinas.

-Exposición de trabajos realizados por equipos durante el curso (celosías, la medida del tiempo, los cuarenta principales, ilusiones ópticas, simetrías,...).

-Realización de alguna actividad mascota: icosaedro de doce metros de diámetro, superficies regladas con rectas directrices de diez metros, laberinto gigante de 222 nudos y 40 vértices cambiables.

-Exposición de material manipulable; incluye un amplio conjunto de actividades que se realizan con material manipulable, elaborado, en muchos casos, por los propios alumnos: puzzles planos y espaciales, demostraciones visuales, puentes de Köningberg, mundo de los espejos, grafos, aparatos de Galton, la cicloide, la torre de Hanoi, la mesa de las celosías y las teselaciones,...

Es una actividad que entre otros muchos efectos positivos, permite presentar otra cara de las matemáticas y ser un punto de atracción para muchos alumnos.

Además de la actividad brevemente relatada, solicitamos a la autoridad educativa poder implantar una asignatura optativa para los alumnos de 2º y 3º (15 - 16 años) que hemos titulado "Taller para re-crear matemáticas" y que nos fue concedida. Este taller, con dos horas semanales, nos permite dar "rienda suelta" a la creatividad matemática toda vez que la programación tiene ese aspecto como uno de sus objetivos. La innovación está presente de manera casi permanente ya que intentamos desarrollar actividades que complementen la formación algoritmizada que se les ofrece en las clases ordinarias. Así que se profundiza en procesos que contengan grandes dosis de abstracción, creatividad, intuición matemática, estrategias de resolución de problemas matemáticos y no matemáticos, procesos lógicos, acercamiento a la historia de las matemáticas y de las ciencias en general, etc. En síntesis, desarrollar capacidades más que conocimientos estrictamente matemáticos.

Como conclusión quisiera animar a todos a innovar. Esta actitud no debe ser una excepción sino la regla general. Necesitamos las aportaciones de todos para que los profesores de aula encontremos y definamos claramente nuestro rol en el área de la Educación Matemática.

Debemos ser reflexivos y creadores de nuestro propio trabajo. Creo que es una forma honrada y directa tanto de ejercer la profesión como de dignificar y prestigiar al profesor ante la sociedad.

No quiero terminar sin hacer una mención expresa a Gonzalo Sánchez Vázquez, al maestro y amigo que convalece. Él nos ha enseñado el camino cuando dice que la Educación Matemática la debemos construir entre todos. En ocasiones nos ha hablado de la necesidad de formar equipos de trabajo en los que participemos no sólo los profesores de aula (a los que gusta llamar "profesores de a pie"), sino también investigadores, psicólogos, pedagogos y todos cuantos puedan y tengan algo que decir en esta área a la que él ha dedicado parte de su vida y de su sabiduría.

Muchas gracias.

DRAWING INSTRUMENTS:
HISTORICAL AND DIDACTICAL ISSUES

Maria G. Bartolini Bussi
Dipartimento di Matematica Pura ed Applicata
Università degli Studi di Modena

Introduction

The aim of this paper is to present some cultural artefacts, originally developed as drawing instruments, and to analyse them from two different, yet related, perspectives, namely their status in the historical development of geometry and a possible use in didactics of mathematics at secondary and tertiary level. As for the first problem, we shall base our arguments on well known results in the history of mathematics, whom the interested reader is referred to. As for the second problem, we shall hint at some recent and ongoing research studies in didactics of mathematics and in the psychology of mathematics education.

The following discussion is mainly drawn from the results of a fifteen years long research project in didactics of mathematics in secondary school, i. e. the project *Mathematical Machines*, that has been developed in cooperation by an academic researcher (the author of this presentation) and a group of secondary school teachers. Among them the contribution of Annalisa Martinez, Marcello Pergola and Carla Zanoli has to be especially acknowledged: they did the historical research and built more than one hundred and fifty models of historical relevance and used them systematically in the classroom (grades 9-13). The whole collection is temporarily kept in the laboratory of mathematics of their school (Liceo Scientifico 'A. Tassoni' at Modena) and is waiting to be moved to a more suitable site.

The context of the teaching experiments on *mathematical machines* has two characteristic features (Bartolini Bussi & Pergola 1996):
(a) the presence of manifold teaching aids, among which physical large size models (either statical or dynamical), the so - called mathematical machines, that give the name to the whole project.;
(b) the recourse, under teacher's guidance, to selected historical sources,

1) to contextualise problems, 2) to describe the functioning of machines, 3) to approach the problem of the historical development of mathematics in a broad perspective.

This context, in spite of the presence of intrusive physical models is highly mathematised: it allows students to go through the history of some mathematical theories from the very starting of their existence as geometrical objects.

In the following section we shall present some historical sheets that contextualise some of the models available in the mathematical laboratory. They refer to two topics, i. e. conics and geometrical transformations. In the other section we shall discuss the didactical use of these models by presenting shortly a teaching experiment on pantographs.

Drawing Instruments: Historical Issues
Descartes' Curve Drawers

It is well known that the Greek approach to geometrical construction relied upon the use of straightedge and compasses. The theory of conic sections was three dimensional, whence the name of *solid problems* for the problems which required conics to be solved. Surely other mechanical instruments had been built, like curve drawers (e.g. Nicomedes' conchoid) or mean finders (e.g. Erathostenes' mesolabon). Mechanical ways of generating conics too, on the base of their 3d-definition were known for centuries, as the enclosed figure 1 shows: it is a parabolic compass, drawn by Leonardo da Vinci. But their use was not accepted in scholarly geometry.

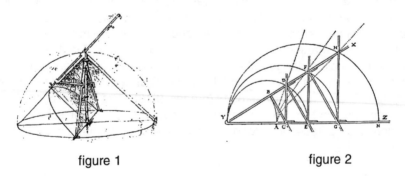

figure 1   figure 2

We can contrast this position with Descartes' one. In the Géométrie he started his program of refounding geometry, that would have produced modern algebraic geometry, by introducing, in a very interlaced way, the so-called Cartesian geometry, i.e. the method of describing curves by means of measuring numbers, with respect to two lines, and the recourse to mechanical generation of curves, by means of movements whose relation admits exact determination (figure 2).

Consider the lines AB, AD, AF and so forth, which we may suppose to be described by means of the instrument YZ. This instrument consists of several rulers hinged together in such a way that YZ being placed along the line AN the angle XYZ can be increased or decreased in size, and when its sides are together the points B,C,D,E,F,G,H, all coincide with A; but as the size of the angle is increased, the ruler BC, fastened at right angles to XY at the point B, pushes towards Z the ruler CD which slides along YZ always at right angles. In like manner, CD pushes DE which slides along YX always parallel to BC; DE pushes EF; EF pushes FG; FG pushes GH and so on. Thus we may imagine an infinity of rulers, each pushing another, half of them making equal angles with YX and the rest with YZ.

Now as the angle XYZ is increased the point B describes the curve AB, which is a circle; while the intersections of the other rulers, namely the points D,F,H describe other curves, AD, AF, AH, of which the latter are more complex than the first and this more complex than the circle. Nevertheless I see no reason why the description of the first cannot be conceived as clearly and distinctly as that of the circle, or at least as that of the conic sections; or why the second, third or any other that can be thus described, cannot be as clearly conceived of as that of the first: and therefore I see no reason why they should not be used in the same way in the solution of geometric problems.

(Descartes, *La Géométrie*, 1637)

This very short quotation shows that in Descartes' geometry the status of mechanical devices such as curve drawers is theoretical. The existence of a curve drawer that allows one to determine exactly movements is the criterion to accept the product curve inside geometry.

It is important to recall that Descartes poses the problem of algebraic curves but does not solve it. Actually the identification of the set of plane algebraic curves with the set of curves that can be drawn (at least locally) by a linkage is solved only two centuries later by Kempe, as we shall see in the following (see also Bos 1981).

In the laboratory several models of curve drawers are available, dating back to either the classical age or to the systematic studies of post-cartesian age. Most of them can be simulated by computer (e.g. Cabri-Géomètre software) in order to draw the curve as a locus of points.

Approach to Geometric Transformations in the Seventeenth Century

The figures 3 and 4 from Dürer, show drawing activity with the help of instruments.

In the first figure the painter uses the picture plane as a 'window' from which to look at the space of the room. In the second figure the painter uses an instrument to obtain, point by point, a correct perspective drawing of a lute. A thread, weighted to keep it taut, is stretched from a point (the position of the eye) to a point of the lute: it passes through a point of the window that is later marked by means of two adjustable threads (that function as coordinate lines in the window); then the thread is moved out of the way and the 'little door' carrying the drawing paper is swung round into the picture plane, so that the position of the point (the intersection of the two threads) can be marked in the drawing.

| figure 3 | figure 4 |

In the mathematical laboratory a large size model of the first Dürer's perspectograph is available together with several models of pairs of perspective planes, made out of wood and/or plexiglas, with corresponding points joined by weighted threads. Some pairs of planes are movable up to the complete superimposition of each other. During the movement the eye's point (if any) changes, but the projection is conserved, according to Stevin's statement:

If the picture plane rotates round the ground line and if the observer rotates in the same sense round his own foot so as to be parallel to the plane, the perspective will not be troubled and will be kept also when the picture plane is turned over on the horizontal plane.

(Stevin,, Oeuvres Mathematiques, augmentees par A. Girard, Leyde, 1634)

This set of models embodies the birth of the projective approach to geometrical transformations in the seventeenth century. This approach, even if grounded on the tradition of Greek geometry (e. g. Euclid and Apollonius) represents a change for several reasons, e. g.:

(1) while in Greek geometry the attention was focused on figures, conceived as isolated realities, in the seventeenth century the attention is shifted to the whole plane (or space);

(2) while in Greek mathematics infinite existed only potentially, in the seventeenth century infinite is conceived also in actuality;

(3) while in Greek culture the separation between geometry and practical knowledge was emphasised, in the seventeenth century geometry develops in a dialectical relationship with other fields of knowledge, not only offering but also adopting methods, e. g. algebra (from commercial arithmetic), drawing (from architecture, technology - e. g. sundials and astrolabes - and art - the theory of perspective).

Some of these reasons seem to be understandable inside mathematics, but actually they depend on inside as well as outside factors, as some historians point out (Raymond 1979, Kline 1972).

The introduction of ideal points in the plane is the mathematical counterpart of the introduction of vanishing points in the picture plane, as centres of the pencils of lines obtained by projecting pencil of parallel lines: the vanishing points on the horizon of the picture plane can be conceived as external representations of the ideal points, which are at infinite distance from the observer. Besides the introduction of ideal points allows the unified treatment of conics, according to the general need of finding general methods that apply to individual cases (i. e. combinatoric reasoning), that is typical of the whole development of science in the seventeenth century (Raymond 1979).

The work of mathematicians such as Desargues has to be contextualised in this complex cultural space. Desargues brings from the practical tradition to the scholarly tradition of geometry two crucial elements:

(1) the concern with problems as being three-dimensional, as the practical tradition deals with the real world and not with diagrams on paper;

(2) the concept of projection from object to image.

However Desargues' concept of projection is not the same as in earlier texts on perspective: in Renaissance usage, objects rendered in per-spective are usually said to be 'degraded': as the emphasis is upon what has been changed by the projection (dimensionality and shape), the essentially symmetrical relationship between object and image is lost. The important original contribution of Desargues seems to have been the concept of invariance (Field & Gray 1987).

The Pantograph of Scheiner

The instrument we are describing now is the so - called Scheiner's pantograph, used in the seventeenth century either to make a scale copy of a drawing (figure 5) or as an aid to drawing in perspective (figure 6).

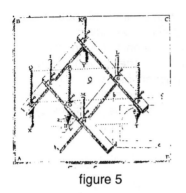

figure 5   figure 6

The second use is so described by Scheiner (1631) himself:

The object, to be seen, sends its own image or visible species - called intentional by philosophers - to the eye through air or other diaphanous body, in pyramid's shape, whose base is the very object and the vertex is in the centre of our eye. This pyramid, wherever it is mathematically cut, has always on the section surface the lively and right image or portrait of the object. When we draw distant bodies, we cannot physically touch them with the pointer and extract immediately from them the copy by pen; hence, if we portray their species represented on the section of the segment of the visual pyramid, that we can touch mathematically with the pointer, as it is close to us, we shall make in the same time a copy very similar to the very object; as in optics there is a proposition, credited by everybody as true, that if two things are similar to another, they are similar to each other. Hence, as both the object and the image formed by us with the instrument are similar to the visible species, they are similar to each other.[..] As the image to be touched by the pointer is not real, but is only the intentional species of the object on the surface of the segment of the visual cone, and the copy formed by the pen must be real and physical, the plane on which we work must be partly real and physical and partly rational and mathematical.

Two copies of the Scheiner's Pantographs are available in the Laboratory. The first is designed to make a scale copy of a drawing. The second is for perspective drawing. The rational part is on the left and the physical part (where a sheet of paper can be stuck) on the right.

From Scheiner's Pantographs to Linkages

The Scheiner's pantograph is one of the early documented linkages used for realising geometrical transformations. If we use the linkage to make a scale copy of a drawing, we allude to a plane similarity that transforms the drawing into a smaller, equal size, or larger drawing. The use of the Scheiner's pantograph in perspective drawing alludes in modern terms to a composition of application, the first from the object to its 'intentional' species and the second from the intentional species to the physical copy made on the paper.

The study of such linkages arises from practical purposes, such as perspective drawing, but the attitude towards mathematical activity of the mathematicians of the seventeenth century is deeply contrasting with the attitude of ancient mathematicians. The introduction of linkages for theoretical purposes is reconsidered also in the nineteenth century. We can quote from Kœnigs (1897) the historical reconstruction of this theory:

The theory of linkages dates back to 1864. There is no doubt that such articulated systems have been used also before: maybe some passionate and precise investigator can track them down in remote antiquity. [...] When in 1631 Scheiner published for the first time the description of his pantograph, he surely did not know the general concepts that his small instrument contained in embryo; we can actually state that he could not know them, because these concepts are linked to the abstract theory of transformations, a theory peculiar of our century, which gives a unitary imprint to all the fulfilled progresses.

The merit of Peaucellier, of Kempe, of Hart, of Lipkine was not so much to have been able to trace some special curves by means of linkages as to have seen there a technique to realise real geometrical transformations. This is the very generality of the theory of linkages

It is well known the device called the parallelogram of Watt: it is a device which aims at describing, in an approximate way a line segment by means of the pole of a piston. Peaucellier in 1864 found a rigorous solution by means of a simple linkage. [...] Sylvester was very interested in this discovery and engaged to disseminate and to extend it. His intervention made the linkages very popular in England, where they were extensively studied by Hart, Clifford, Roberts, Cayley and Kempe.

(Kœnigs 1897)

The studies of the quoted geometers concern mainly the mechanical description of individual algebraic curves and individual birational transformation. But later Kempe proves that every algebraic curve can be traced by means of an articulated system, and that every birational transformation can be realised by means of an articulated system (Lebesgue 1950).

Later the study of linkages stops being interesting for pure mathematicians, but becomes a fundamental part of the Theory of Machines and Mechanisms and Robotics (Bartolini Bussi & Pergola 1996).

In the laboratory there are more than a dozen elementary linkages that realise geometrical transformations together with dozens of composed linkages that combine elementary ones to give mechanical proofs of theorems on composition of transformations

Drawing Instruments: Didactical Issues.
The Small Group Study of the Pantograph of Sylvester

In the previous section we have presented some sets of instruments available in the laboratory, by means of their historical contextualisation. In this section we shall briefly describe how they are actually used in mathematics lessons. The small group study of these models, historically contextualised by the teacher, defines the activity in the mathematical laboratory.

Small group study of a model is realised by means of a task, given by the teacher: the students are not completely free to manipulate the model, but they are given a precise list of questions to be answered. For instance, the study of a pantograph of Sylvester is done by means of a list of questions to be answered in writing: in particular, we shall focus on two questions (further details in Bartolini Bussi 1993, Bartolini Bussi & Pergola 1996):

A specimen of the pantograph, see figure 7, is given to a small group of students (11th grade) together with a list of questions. We shall focus on only two of them.

QUESTIONS

1. Represent the mechanism with a schematic figure and describe it to somebody who has to build a similar one on the base of only your description.

4. Are there some geometrical properties which are related to all the configurations of the mechanism? Try to prove your statements.

The first question is a typical communication task. It is well studied in didactics of mathematics (Brousseau 1986). The mathematical task of describing the geometrical structure of the pantograph is inserted into the social task of communicating it to an interlocutor. The small group acts on the mechanism with the aim of producing a written message, including a figure: the decoder, in this case a fictitious one, is supposed to gain the information, by means of which he has to reconstruct the building action. As the students have not handled the pantograph before, they do not know anything about it: so, also the elementary features of the polygons which constitute the schematic figure (a parallelogram and two similar isosceles triangles) are to be discovered, by means of handling and even measuring, to be sure that some bars have the same length and some angles have the same width. Yet, even if the students are allowed to measure, they are given this physical object in a school setting, in a mathematics laboratory, where a typical situation of speech communication is given. This very setting inhibits the recourse to a practice-oriented message, such as the one that could have been used in some out-of-school setting. The students immediately realise that coding essential points with letters is crucial: in small group they can point at the mechanism ostensively and speak of 'this point', 'that angle', and so on, but, as a student says, if we write so, he (i. e. the fictitious interlocutor) will understand nothing. Hence, coding points by letter is given a new sense: it is no more a social rule of the contract between the teacher and students, based on the tradition of all the school books ; rather, it is a true need of communication.

The fourth question requires three different processes, described in (Bartolini Bussi 1993): (a) guessing and stating a conjecture; (b) looking for a proof; (c) writing down a proof.

The conjecture is produced with the help of the teacher. It is a difficult conjecture as it concerns objects that are not directly observable in the mechanism, namely the line segment OP and OP'

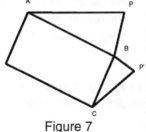

CONJECTURE
OP = OP'
POP' is constant

It means that, during the deformation of the mechanism, the point P' is always the image of P under a rotation around O. The rotation angle is PAB = BCP'.

Figure 7

The process of looking for a proof is quite interesting. It could be described as a continuous exploration of a metaphorical space that contains 'known' facts and statements to be proved. Among known facts there are not only results from geometrical theory that has been already studied by students but also empirical information from the configurations of the mechanism. The pieces of available knowledge are used without investigating whether they are empirical information or theoretical statements. So, for instance (see details and further examples in Bartolini Bussi 1993, but the same structure has been found in different experiments carried out with graduate students too), we can observe the following path in the process of proof search:

A: 'OP = OP' and the angles POP' are equal for all the configurations of the linkages' (it is the conjecture to be proved and it has been stated on the base of empirical observation);
B: 'OP = OP' because we have proved that the triangles OAP and OCP' are congruent';
C: 'As the angle POP' is constant and the triangle POP' is isosceles, all the triangles of the infinitely many configurations of the linkage are similar'.

In the step C two information of different nature are treated as if they had the same status: actually *'POP' is constant'* is based on empirical evidence, while *'POP' is isosceles'* is based on an already produced proof. Later, during small group work, the statement *'POP' is constant'* will be proved independently, i. e. connected to the available knowledge by means of theorems on the angles.

In the following process of writing down the proof, the time order of exploration has to be changed. According to the standard script of proofs, it is necessary to build a path from the geometrical properties of the model of the physical mechanism to the statement to be proved. The conjecture is the thesis and cannot be used any more as available information. An implicit or explicit separation between known facts (either axioms, or theorems or inference rules) and facts to be proved (thesis) will be introduced.

However the shift from looking for a proof to writing down a proof is not simple and some traces of the old time organisation are still evident in the final text produced by the students:

Thesis. The angle POP' is constant.
The angle POP' is constant as the triangles POP' obtained by means of the deformations of the mechanism are always similar, whatever the position of P and P'.

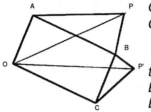

Figure 8

In fact OP=OP', because the triangles OCP' and OAP are congruent, as CP'=OA,CO=AP and OCP'=OAP (BCO=OAB and P'CB=BAP)

The above triangles are also similar to a third triangle PBP', because, as the triangles BCP' and BAP are similar, it follows:
BP' : BP = CP' : CO
and the angle P'BP = OCP' as (posing that CP'B = CBP' = α and CBA =β) we have
PBP' = 360 - (2α+β)

OCP' = 360 - (2a+β).

This is true because prolonging the line BC from the side of C the angle supplementary to BCP' is equal to 2α and the angle supplementary to BCD is equal to β as two contiguous angles of a parallelogram are always supplementary

Discussion

The introduction of mathematical machines in the classroom at secondary school level seems to answer to two related problems of didactics of mathematics
1) the socio-cultural construction of consciousness;
2) the construction of a pragmatic basis for proof.
The first issue is related to the first part of this paper. The small group work is historically contextualised by the teacher by means of wide historical introductions, like the ones that have been presented, and put in this way in a broader perspective. The importance of this historical perspective extends well beyond the students' discovery that similar problems existed a long time ago. In the course of a historical study, what is in the foreground is the process of constructing meaning and the idea that this process is not individual but collective (Otte & Seeger 1994).

The second issue is related to the second part of this paper. During small group work, the students are confronted with the global process of production of 'new' theorems: they are put in the situation of exploring, making and testing conjectures, and devising their own proofs. They are working on physical objects, to be transformed into geometrical objects; they are coping with the complex epistemological relationship between deductive reasoning on the one hand and its application on the other (Hanna & Jahnke 1993). The deep connections between the exploring phase, the conjecturing phase and the proving phase that have been only hinted at in this paper are the focus of some research studies that are now in progress on the early approach to mathematical proof in the field of experience of sunshadows (Boero, Garuti & Mariotti 1996, Boero, Garuti, Lemut & Mariotti 1996) or in the context of Cabri-geometry (Laborde, personal communication). In the studies, the standard habit of asking the students to understand and repeat proofs of statements supplied by the teacher is upset. In all the cases the standard paper-and-pencil context for geometrical proofs is substituted by a dynamic context (i. e., linkages, sunshadows and Cabri-geometry), that encourages exploration and the statement of conjectures. Further research studies seem to be necessary to ascertain whether this not episodic experience could provoke effects on proof construction in more traditional paper-and-pencil contexts and outside geometry as well.

References

Bartolini Bussi M. (1993), Geometrical Proofs and Mathematical Machines: An Exploratory Study, *Proceedings of the 17th PME Conference*, vol. II, 97-104, The Program Committee of the 17th PME Conference, Tsukuba (Japan).

Bartolini Bussi M. & Pergola M. (1996), History in the Mathematics Classroom: Linkages and Kinematic Geometry, in Jahnke H. N., Knoche N. & Otte M. (eds), *History of Mathematics and Education: Ideas and Experiences,* Goettingen: Vandenhoeck & Ruprecht, 39-67.

Boero P., Garuti R., Lemut E. & Mariotti M. A. (1996), Challenging the Traditional School Approach to Theorems: a Hypothesis about the Cognitive Unity of Theorems, *Proceedings of the 20th PME Conference,* The Program Committee of the 20th PME Conference, Valencia (Spain).

Boero P., Garuti R. & Mariotti M. A. (1996), Some Dynamic Mental Processes Underlying Producing and Proving Conjectures, *Proceedings of the 20th PME Conference*, The Program Committee of the 20th PME Conference, Valencia (Spain).

Bos H. J. M. (1981), On the Representation of curves in Descartes' *Géométrie, Archive for History of Exact Sciences*, 24, pp. 295-338.

Brousseau G. (1986) *Théorisation des Phénomènes d'Einseignement des Mathématiques.* Université de Bordeaux: Thèse d'état

Field J. V. & Gray J. (1987), *The Geometrical Work of Girard Desargues*, New York: Springer Verlag.

Hanna G. & Jahnke H. N. (1993), Proof and Application, *Educational Studies in Mathematics,* 24 (4) 421-438.

Kline M. (1972), *Mathematical Thought from Ancient to Modern Times,* New York: Oxford University Press.

Kœnigs G. (1897), *Leçons de Cinématique,* Paris: Hermann.

Laborde C., (personal communication), *The Hidden Role of Diagrams in Pupils' Construction of Meaning in Geometry.*

Lebesgue H. (1950), *Leçons sur les constructions géométriques.* Paris: Gauthier-Villars.

Otte M. & Seeger F. (1994), *The Human Subject in Mathematics Education and in the History of Mathematics,* in R. Biehler, R. W. Scholz, R. Straesser, B. Winkelmann, *Didactics of Mathematics as a Scientific Discipline,* 351-365, Dordrecht, Kluwer Academic Publishers.

Raymond P. (1979), *La storia e le scienze,* Roma: Editori Riuniti.

Acknowledgements: The Project Mathematical Machines is supported by the CNR and the University of Modena.

BASIC IMAGERY AND UNDERSTANDINGS FOR MATHEMATICAL CONCEPTS

Peter Bender
Universität-GH Paderborn Fb 17

Basic Imagery and Understandings for Mathematical Concepts

1. Despite immense progress in the field of mathematics didactics there are still a lot of mathematics educators as well as teachers who adhere to a rather narrow picture of their subject, namely consisting on the whole of abstract relations between abstract objects and some calculation. For them, intuitive, vivid, enactive or application oriented ways of doing mathematics do not belong to true mathematics, but are mere approaches. The advantage of this picture is that the contents can be identified exactly, and can easily be made accessible to presentations in textbooks, as well as to empirical research on how students handle them, or to (so-called) intelligent tutorial systems.

Yet, this picture is not a suitable foundation for teaching and learning mathematics (neither for doing or applying mathematics), as in it the category of **meaning** is ignored and hence the constitution of meaning is not a matter of education. — But in every thinking or learning process the individual assigns some meaning to some notion, situation or circumstances, and teachers, in particular mathematics teachers, have to take into account these processes of assignment.

Closely connected to the difficulties in recognizing and controlling the students' learning processes is the problem of matching concepts in the realms of mathematics, epistemology and psychology (which I will call 'mathematical', 'epistemological' and 'psychological concepts' respectively). — The conception of basic imagery and understandings (BIU) offers a didactical frame for this matching problem. In German mathematics education this conception has a long tradition. Rudolf vom Hofe (1995) investigated its history and found a lot of variants in the last 200 years, most of them tackling the matching problem by designing ideal normative mathematical concepts in the epistemological mode (vom Hofe names them "basic ideas") serving as models for the students' formation of concepts in the cognitive mode (which he names "individual images").

It seemed to be natural to all those educators to found their conceptions on an analysis of subject matter and to include their rich teaching experience as an empirical background. Thus they were much closer to their students than many mathematics professors at the universities or teachers at the Gymnasiums (in former times with the top 10 % of each age-group) who taught (and often still do teach) mathematics — maybe in an elementarized, but still — in a rarely modified manner as a pure discipline. On the other hand, those educators, too, did often not care for what really happens in the students' brains, and, furthermore, in spite of their good ideas, their efforts had only little success.

But one must admit that only since the 1970s has there been reasonable technology for thoroughly studying classroom actions, namely video recordings. Of course, even with this technology one does still not know how cognition 'really' works. Neither the mathematical formalization of thinking processes, nor the definition of man as an information processing being similar to a computer (Simon 1969) brought about much new insight in to **human** cognition. But based on the talents of video technology we learned a lot about communicative and social interaction in the classroom, in particular, how mathematical meaning is implicitly and explicitly negotiated between the participants (cf. Bishop 1985).

Due to the constructivist and connectionist roots of their theories, some cognitive scientists underestimate, ignore or deny a dominant influence of the teacher and, consequently, of the subject matter on the students' learning processes. — In fact, during painstaking examinations of videotaped and transcribed micro situations, middle and long term effects can easily get out of sight. If one concentrates on social and communicational characteristics of a situation, the subject matter tends to play only a minor role. And comparing students' deviating verbal and non-verbal manifestations with teachers' obvious original intentions may support severe doubts in the efficacy (or even possibility) of extraneously deter-mined learning processes. — These tendencies are supported by the researchers' aim to overcome the old theories because of their meager success.

On the other hand, careful re-analyses of classroom situations under **subject matter aspects** often lead to plausible recasts or improvements (as well as to verifications) of former interpretations based on interaction-theoretical grounds. So to me it sounds unreasonable to exclude these aspects when exploring such a situation. As I pointed out before, in German mathematics didactics, for a lot of mathematical concepts there are well known elaborated teaching routines. Whether a teacher relies on such a routine or not: From the words, diagrams etc. that she or he uses, from her or his rejection or acceptance of students' answers etc., the observer frequently can disclose the teacher's own imagery and understandings about the mathematical concept in question. (Throughout this talk, the notion of mathematical concept includes theorems, mathematical structures, procedures etc.) — Surprisingly often, the teacher's own imagery and understandings seem to be inadequate, or at least the teacher evokes inadequate imagery and understandings among the students. — These problems can be tackled didactically with the help of the conception of BIU, which is meant to be a theoretical and practical frame for a normative, descriptive and constructive treatment of concept formation processes.

A radical constructivist would argue that there is no adequacy or in adequacy of imagery and understandings. Here we have reached a point of discourse where there might be no agreement. For me, **adequacy** of concepts or adequacy of imagery and understandings is a useful and important didactical category. Of course, adequacy cannot be proved like a mathematical theorem. Whether a student's concept is adequate even cannot be stated uniquely, neither in the prescriptive, nor in the descriptive mode. But there are strong hints in either mode: If a student's statements about, and actions with a mathematical concept sound plausible and seem to be successful to her or his own common sense as well as to experts, we would concede some adequacy (for more details cf. E.J. Davis 1978).

From a didactical point of view, it is not crucial whether teachers actually 'teach' their students or whether they only **stimulate** their students' concept formation processes. Good 'teaching' always contains stimulating the students' own activities.

2. By the adjective 'basic' there are expressed several essential characteristics of the conception of BIU:
    — It includes a tendency of **epistemological homogenity and obligation** how mathematical concepts should be understood.
    — **Psychologically** speaking, it indicates that students' individual concepts normally are, and in the teaching processes the epistemological concepts should be, **anchored in** the students' **worlds of experience.**
    — With respect to **subject matter** it stresses the importance of **fundamental ideas** (in the sense of Halmos' elements, 1981, or Schreiber's universal ideas, 1983) guiding the study of any mathematical discipline.

Epistemological homogeneity: This tendency seems to be in contradiction with modern pedagogical and didactical paradigms like "the students should create their own mathematics", or "the students have to find their individual ways in solving mathematical problems" etc. In fact, teaching does not mean telling (Campbell & Dawson 1995), but it means stimulating students' cognitive activities, negotiating mathematical meaning in the classroom etc.

But this way of conceiving the teaching-learning process does not entail any obligation for the teacher to tolerate or even to support inadequate individual concepts; on the contrary: it makes the teacher's task much more difficult. She or he must be provided with a good theoretical and practical competency in mathematics, mathematics applications, epistemology, pedagogy, psychology, social sciences etc., in order to

— develop her or his own view of the epistemological kernel (which must not be identified with a mathematical definition) of some mathematical concept which the students shall acquire,
— perceive the students' actual individual concepts as truly as possible and to judge their adequacy,
— help the students, if necessary, to improve or to correct their individual concepts into adequate ones near the epistemological kernel,
— possibly learn by the students and improve her or his own individual concepts.

This task imparts a predominant role in the teaching-learning process to the teacher's own imagery and understandings and to their transposition into didactical action. For example, if for the calculation of π a circle is approximated by a sequence of polygons and the teacher uses a phrase like "in this sequence the polygons have more and more vertices, and finally they turn into the circle", the students' formation of an adequate concept of limit is obstructed.

The epistemological kernel of a concept corresponds to a commonly shared socio-psychological kernel. Such a socially constituted kernel is an important prerequisite for the construction of individual argumentation and its introduction again into classroom interaction (cf. Krummheuer 1989). — It is obvious that this commonly shared kernel should be as extensive as possible, which, again, gives the teacher a central position in the teaching-learning process.

Anchoring mathematical concepts in the students' worlds of experience: Even working mathematicians need some real world frame for doing mathematics ("we consider ...", "if x runs through the real line ..." etc.; cf. Kaput, 1979, and many others). All the more do students need such frames so that they can constitute meaning with the subject matter they are about to learn (Davis & McKnight, 1980, Johnson, 1987, Fischbein, 1987, 1989, Dörfler 1996 etc.). As such frames do not belong to the epistemological concepts, the teacher is rather free when constructing real world situations where basic imagery and understandings can be unfolded.

These situations need not be absolutely realistic; on the contrary, by alienating them with the help of fairy-tale traits and concentrating on the essence they can be turned into metaphors with their explanatory power. One can take human beings, animals, things, which are more or less anthropomorphized and more or less mathematized. These participants in the situation have to act somehow, following some arbitrary rules, pursuing some arbitrary plans, obeying arbitrarily physical and other natural laws, or not.

For a lesson about the integral as area function for a given function I designed the following situation: The x-axis is a hard-surface road; to the north of this road (in the coordinate system) there is a uniformly wet swamp which is bounded by the road and the graph of the function in question. A vehicle drives on the road in the positive (eastern) direction, with an arm perpendicular to the road which is sufficiently long to reach all parts of the swamp during the trip. With the help of this arm the water is **absorbed** uniformly from the swamp (on the basis of some uninteresting technology) and collected in a cylindrical jar. Thus, at any moment the level of the water in the jar is a linear measure of that part of the area which has already been passed by the vehicle.

If the vehicle reaches a position where the function is negative, the metaphor has to be extended: To the south of the road there is a desert which is bounded by the road and the negative parts of the graph and which has to be **watered** uniformly by the vehicle. For this purpose the vehicle has a second arm perpendicular to the road which is sufficiently long to reach all parts of the desert during the trip. Again, the exact mechanism is not interesting; the only important thing is that the level of the water in the jar drops proportionally with the desert area passed.

Of course, this metaphor contains a lot of technical and didactical problems which have to be considered thoroughly: — What happens if the jar is full (empty) and there is still swamp (desert) area to be drained (watered)? — Draining the swamp and watering the desert have to be accomplished with the same velocity of flow (whatever this physical notion means). — In principle, one needs a new coordinate system for the function of the water level (the integral function). — When the vehicle makes a half turn and then drives in the negative (western) direction, the two arms change their positions, and now the desert has to be to the north and the swamp has to be to the south of the road (in accordance with the mathematical changing of positive and negative area). — But if the starting point of the vehicle is finally made a variable, the efficiency of the metaphor comes to an end.

Every metaphor has its limitations (cf. Presmeg 1994), but this is no drawback. The one which I just described should make plausible
— continuous measurement,
— the transfer from area measurement into linear measurement and
— the concept of negative area.
It thus appeals to common sense, and if the teacher wants the students to maintain their common sense, it is a must to emphasize the limitations of any metaphor.

Situations which are appropriate for mathematics teaching rarely come along by themselves. Genuine mathematics applications are often not suited for supporting concept formation, as they are frequently over-loaded with alien problems. At the same time the teacher should not evoke the impression that some artificial situation, designed for the use in mathematics teaching, would be an example for genuine mathematics applications. Sometimes, this coincidence can happen, but usually it does not; and students with common sense realize the artificial character of such a situation.

Fundamental ideas for mathematical disciplines (in an epistemological and psychological sense): Basic imagery and understandings are not only meant as a peg on which to hang some mathematical content, but they shall lay the foundations for further meaningful interpretations of concepts within a mathematical discipline.

3. The notions of imagery and understanding stand for two fundamental psychological constructs. There exists an extensive literature about them. Different authors have different definitions, most of them not very concise. A lot of contemporary cognitive scientists disregard these two constructs anyway, as they escape hard empirical research and do not fit a computer related view of intelligence. — But it is just these — seen behaviouristically — shortcomings, their vagueness and flexibility, which turn these constructs into suitable means for analyzing (and promoting) such complex didactical objects as human teaching-learning processes.

Imagery can be grasped as: mental, often visual (but also auditory, olfactory, tactile, gustatory and kinesthetic; cf. Sheehan 1972) representations of some object, situation, action etc. having their sensory foundations in the long term memory and being activated in **conscious** processes. A person activating some imagery has already some meaning, some intentions in mind and organizes these processes according to these intentions (Bosshardt 1981). — Imagery is closely related to intuitions, but its objects are more concrete, and meaning plays a more important role.

The objects of imagery (and understandings) can be given in different modes, namely analogous or propositional. I don't want to resume the cognitive scientists' quarrel in the 1970s about the interrelations between these two modes or about their separate existence as ways of thinking. In my opinion both are valuable means for analyzing imagery and understandings in teaching-learning processes.

Apparently, imagery is more closely connected to the analogous mode, and understandings are more closely connected to the propositional mode of thinking. But it is difficult for a person to activate some imagery without propositional elements, in particular in didactical situations, as in these situations verbalization is **the** fundamental means for a participant to communicate either with others or with her- or himself (this communication with oneself being a transposition of a social situation to one's mind which is typical for teaching-learning processes). On the other hand, there can be no process of understanding without recurring to any plausible imagery and to analogous elements.

Obviously, thinking in the analogous mode can be stimulated by analogous means like pictures, diagrams etc. (with a lot of limitations; cf. Presmeg 1994), and the propositional mode can rather be stimulated by propositional means like verbal communication. In the age of paper and pencil and of books, analogously given objects frequently are of a visual, static nature, and the learners have to undertake some effort to make these 'objects' plausible, meaningful, vivid imagery matching their worlds of experience. In the nearest future the use of multi-media in schools (in the western world) possibly will relieve the students from these efforts.

Whether multi-media will be conducive to the students' learning processes, is not yet settled: The students' inclinations and abilities to undertake efforts to generate mathematical concepts could be undermined. — This problem is complementary to the following classical one, related to the use of visualizations (diagrams, icons etc.): Among educators there is a naive belief that visualizations do facilitate the students' learning processes. But as, for example, Schipper (1982) showed with primary graders, many visualizations are not self-explanatory at all, but they are subject matter which has to be acquired for its own sake, on the one hand, and in relation to the visualized contents, on the other hand. — As a matter of course, visualizations can be successful didactical means, but not because they would reduce necessary effort, but because they demand more effort and give hints how to direct and structure this surplus effort and thus make it effective.

There are didactical situations, as well as mathematical concepts, as well as students, for which respectivily one of the modes is more suitable. For teaching and learning mathematics it is important that there has to be a permanent transformation between the two modes. Maybe geometry can be treated predominantly in the analogous mode, and algebra in the propositional mode; maybe the teacher is even able to take into consideration the preferences of single students. But in principle, both modes must be present.

Taking into account the widespread propositional appearance of mathematics teaching, in particular on the secondary level, there is need of an increased use of the analogous mode all over the world. — By stressing the students' anchoring of their individual concepts in their worlds of experience, the conception of BIU lays some accent on the analogous mode, as a prophylactic counterweight to the preponderance of the propositional mode in the upper mathematical curriculum.

The psychological construct of understanding is still more complicated and non-uniform. For didactical reasons the following aspects are relevant:

> (1) One can understand people, their actions, situations, the motives or the aims of the participants (practical knowledge of human nature, **common sense**).

> (2) One can understand utterances **medially** and **formally** (e.g., if they are made loud enough and in a language one knows).

> (3) One can understand the **content** of a **message** made by someone (understand what this someone **means** by a certain communication, text, phrase, word, symbol, drawing etc.).

> (4) One can understand technical matters, working principles of gadgets, mathematical structures, procedures etc. **(expertise).**

At first glance, aspect (4) seems to be most suitable for the conception of BIU. But it becomes immediately clear that each of these aspects is important for the learning of mathematics and has to play an essential role in the conception, in particular (3). This aspect is a classical psychological paradigm, but the general opinion about it has changed: Today, one does not believe anymore that it consists just of finding some objective meaning of given signs, but that the receiver of a message tends to and has to embed the message in some context and, in doing so, tries to reconstruct its meaning (cf. Engelkamp 1984), thus getting near aspect (1).

It goes without saying that there is no understanding (3) without (2): the sender and the receiver of a message have to have a common language, not only in a direct, but also in a figurative sense: As Clark & Carlson (1981) put it, there has to be a "common ground", which, again, refers to aspect (1). — In school teaching, and in particular in mathematics teaching, the common ground of teachers and students is often rather thin, if existing at all. — But, extending the common ground does not only mean that the students have to be better instructed so that they make the teachers ground their own. Rather the teacher must engage in the students, attach importance to them (and not only to the subject matter), understand them as human beings (again, aspect (1)), and try to reconstruct or to anticipate their ways of thinking.

By following the conception of BIU, to some extent the teacher is forced to do so, and furthermore, her or his expertise can be promoted. But this way of teaching and learning demands much more effort for both parts, in comparison with the ususal way, where teachers, in good harmony with the students, are satisfied with students' instrumental understanding (in the sense of the late Richard Skemp 1976).

In the following example, the teacher (resp. the researcher) did not quite understand the student's ways of thinking. It was originally described by Malle (1988) and re-analyzed by vom Hofe (1998): In order to develop the concept of negative numbers, Ingo, the student, was given the following situation: "In the evening the temperature is 5 degrees (Celsius) below zero. During the night a warm wind moves inland, and the temperature rises **by** 12 degrees. — What is the temperature next morning?" Ingo answers correctly: "7 degrees", but in the dialogue with the interviewer, he shows inadequate imagery. When he sketches the situation, he asks whether he must draw three thermometers, and later he explains that at midnight the temperature went up to +12 degrees, and in the morning it dropped to +7 degrees.

Malle gives well known and, of course, correct explanations for Ingo's obvious inadequate dealing with the situation: Ingo is not able to identify the elements which are important for solving the problem, but invents additional information and tells fairy tales, and he does not distinguish between the starting and the final state (i.e. the starting and final temperature, represented on the thermometer), on the one hand, and the change between the states (the rise of the temperature), on the other hand.

In his careful re-analysis, vom Hofe shows that the problem lies in Ingo's imagery about the physical situation, which is no suitable basis for the formation of the mathematical concept. Whereas the interviewer expects Ingo to focus on the changes of the mercury column (as a direct model of the number line), Ingo imagines two masses of air, a cold and a warm one, which mix and result in a third mass with average temperature. Therefore he needs **three** thermometers, and in the night the temperature does not rise **by** 12 degrees, but **up to** 12 degrees, and goes down again in the morning. The idea of mixing air masses is, physically speaking, not at all inept, but it merely does not fit the mathematics that the interviewer has in his mind. For Ingo, there are two states of temperature which result in a third one, the weighed arithmetical mean, and not one state which changes into another.

Granted that every human being tends continually to conceive, or to make and to keep her or his environment meaningful and sensible, one must admit that usual mathematics teaching in large parts has a contra-productive effect. — The striving for "constancy of meaning" (Hörmann, 1976) is in my opinion a characteristic trait of humans which, for example, is largely ignored in Piaget's biologistic theory of equilibration.

Mathematics teaching, too, is such an environment which humans who are in touch with it try to make meaningful and sensible. As an **extreme** example, (in a famous French movie from 1984) in a physics lesson in Paris the absent-minded student from Algeria understands "le thé au harem d'Archimède", when he hears "le théorème d'Archimède" (which means: "tea time in Archimedes's harem" instead of "the theorem of Archimedes"). Even if we omit such extreme cases, it still seems to be rather normal all over the world that students tend to develop their own non-conforming imagery and understandings, which, however, often remain implicit.

Fischbein (1989) calls them "tacit models" and characterizes them as simple, concrete, practical, behavioural, robust, autonomous and narrowing. Their robustness results from their simplicity, their anchoring in the students' worlds of experience, and their short term success with convenient applications (see the example of Ingo and the temperature). Inadequate tacit models come into being because of lack of adequate basic imagery and understandings, which in their turn would also be concrete, practical, etc., successful and therefore robust, and not narrowing, but capable of expansion.

So the conception of BIU includes the strategy of occupying the students' frames with adequate basic imagery and understandings from the beginning, i.e. to give them the possibility and to enable them to develop such imagery and understandings by themselves.

Nevertheless, students will still generate a lot of inadequate tacit models, and teachers must be able to recognize them and to help the students to settle them. In this, again, the teachers can be supported by the theoretical and practical frame of the conception of BIU, thus using the constructive aspect of the conception (as vom Hofe, 1995, puts it).

Fischbein (1989), like many other educators and cognitive scientists, recommends that the students should undertake meta-cognitive analyses in order to discover and eliminate the defects in their frames. — I couldn't find evidence in the literature that students would be able to successfully analyze their own (wrong) thinking without massive interventions by the teacher or by some interviewer. According to my own experience with young people in all grades, they are overstrained if they reflect reflexively about their own reflections.

Indeed, in many classroom situations there can be found actions of understanding on a meta-level; for example, if students recall how they solved a certain problem, or if they try to find out the teacher's intentions, instead of trying to understand the contents of her or his statements. But, in general, this kind of understanding (aspect (1)) is not explicitly reflected by the students.

One essential trait of every didactical situation is (or should be) that the participants strive for understanding the contents of some message given, verbally or non-verbally, by the teacher, students, the textbook etc. (aspect (3)), with the underlying aim that the students shall acquire expertise (aspect (4)). Whereas aspect (3) stresses the **processes** of under-standing, aspect (4) stands for the **products** of these processes. The products are not only results, but at the same time they are starting points for new processes, and each understanding process starts on the ground of some already existing understanding.

In mathematics teaching, both aspects of understanding ((3) and (4)) deal with the same objects: the messages, seen ideally, deal with mathematical concepts, about which the students shall acquire expertise. — In the humanities and in the social sciences, as well as (in an indirect way) in mathematics, this expertise again often refers to social situations (in a wide sense) and thus is in parts identical with aspect (1). — So, finally, in normal teaching-learning processes all the aspects of understanding discussed here belong together and are essential for success.

In my view, there is no understanding without imagery, and no imagery without understanding. With the notion of imagery there are stressed the analogous mode, roots in everyday lives, intuitions etc., — whereas with the notion of understanding there is laid some accent on the propositional mode, on subject matter, on predicates etc., — but not only do both notions appear together, they have a large domain of essence in common.

4. There can be identified roughly four types of BIU for use in mathematics teaching in the primary and secondary grades:

A. More or less **global** BIU, especially for the formation of the concept of number and for elementary arithmetic: multiplication as repeated addition; division as partitioning (splitting up; 'Aufteilen') or distributing (sharing out; 'Verteilen'); fractions as quantities or as operators, negative numbers as states or as operators, the machine model for operators, the little-people metaphor for running through an algorithm. Basic imagery and understandings are not bound to primitive, non-quantifiable actions (in the sense of intuitive understanding according to Herscovics & Bergeron, 1983), and their formation is not a kind of mathematical propedeutics or pre-mathematics, but — in my opinion — genuine mathematics (just without calculus with symbols). They would be useful in the upper secondary grades as well, for example, with the concept of limit and infinitesimal thinking as a whole.

B. More or less **local** BIU, e.g. the arithmetical mean, the internal rate of return of an investment, the circumcircle of a regular polygon.

C. BIU for **extra-mathematical** concepts, situations, procedures (from physics, economics, everyday lives etc.), which are to be used in mathematics teaching (example: Ingo and the temperature).

D. BIU for **conventions,** e.g. the meaning of symbols, or of diagrams. Example: The teacher tries to explain subtraction with the help of the following situation: "Mother baked six cakes for her daughter's birthday; the dog Schnucki ate four of them. How many are there left?" She draws 6 circles on the blackboard and crosses out four of them (each with one line), hoping to support visually the understanding of the problem 6–4=2: But Ralph, a learning disabled child, wonders why the teacher halves the marbles (Mann 1991).

It goes without saying that the prototypes, metaphors, metonymies (Presmeg 1994) used for BIU should not obscure the concepts they refer to, as in the following example:

Euclidean geometry: As a preparation for proving the existence and uniqueness of the incircle of a triangle, the teacher asks the students: "Imagine a cone with several balls of ice cream intersecting each other physically, and a plane section through the cone containing its axis of rotation. Do so three times, by identifying the tip of the cone with the three vertices of the triangle one after another." — A more suitable imagery would be to stick a small circle near one vertex between its adjacent edges. When the circle is blown up like a two-dimensional balloon, it moves away from that vertex, still touching the two edges, until it meets the third edge and thus reaches its final position as incircle. In dissociation from the pure Euclidean way of doing geometry, this metaphor makes use of kinematic and continuous physical phenomena from the students' worlds of experience.

Of course, mathematical concepts should not be falsified, as is the case with the concept of circle in Papert's (1980) original idea of **turtle geometry.** The children shall draw a circle by programming the turtle to do a straight motion of length 1, then to do a right turn of the amount 1, and to repeat these two actions 360 times, i.e. by drawing a fuzzy regular polygon with 360 vertices. In fact, the result looks like a circle, but the way in which it was produced belongs to a concept which is essentially different from the Euclidean circle. It's true that every line on the computer screen is a sequence of squares; but this is not the point, as students with some experience with paper and pencil as well as with computer screens will recognize the shortcomings of any realization of geometric forms and will be able to idealize these forms, if at least the underlying activities are appropriate. — But the procedure for making a Logo circle is not appropriate for Euclidean geometry. — Furthermore, I doubt that the Logo geometry is a good preparation for differential geometry, — eventually it is a helpful model for someone who already has the concept of mathematical limit at her or his disposal, whereas it is likely to be a mental obstacle for someone who is still on her or his way of acquiring this concept, let alone for primary graders.

Transformation geometry: When in the late 1960s and early 1970s transformation geometry was pushed into the mathematics curriculum, it was assumed that real motions of real objects could serve as BIU. In fact, the students accepted these BIU willingly and transferred them easily into continuous motions of point sets in the plane. But the crucial point was the abstraction of the motions, which the students in general did not manage to perform. Their BIU of transformations grounded on motions were so robust that the good advice to focus their attention to the starting and final positions of the geometric forms or to the plane as a whole remained useless, because, for example, the notions of starting and final position, again, evoked imagery about motions (cf. Bender 1982).

Thus, mathematicians and mathematics educators failed to establish in the curriculum the full algebraization of geometry by transformation groups, and up to today geometric transformations are not treated as objects on their own, but only as means to investigate geometric forms. The idea of embodying Piaget's groupings of thinking schemes in geometric transformation groups proved to be too naive.

By the way, there are reasonable didactical applications of continuous motions, e.g. in good old **congruence geometry** by Euclid and Hilbert: Two geometric forms are conguent if they can be moved to each other in a way that both exactly cover one another. In German there is a synonym for the word 'kongruent' which is due to this reciprocal covering (='decken'), namely 'deckungsgleich' ('gleich'= 'equal'). In congruence geometry, different from transformation geometry, the specific form of these motions is not essential at all. So the students need not, cannot and, in fact, do not memorize them, and motions are not likely to turn into mental obstacles against viewing congruence as an interrelation between two stationary geometrical forms.

For **functional reasoning** in geometry and other mathematical disciplines, like calculus, there is needed a different, and slightly more abstract, concept of motion: What happens in the range of a function, if one 'walks' around in its domain? Example: The area function assigns to each triangle of the Euclidean plane its area. Starting with one triangle, one changes one of its vertices, and one observes, how the area changes. — The metaphorical character of this situation is obvious: There is a space (the domain, i.e. the set of all triangles) and someone or something (the variables) who 'walks' around; and the motions of this someone or some thing are transferred by some mechanism, like an abstract pantograph, into another space (the range, i.e. the positive real numbers).

One more example, where 'dynamic' imagery and understandings seem to be not helpful for basic concept formation, is the **concept of sequence and limit:** Many students have the wrong idea that a mathematical sequence would possess a last element or that one could at least reach such an element (whatever the notion of reaching should mean). — The ground for this misconception is often laid in mathematics teaching itself, e.g. when determining the number π by an approximation:

The students consider a sequence of polygons which have more and more vertices until they finally turn into a circle. Even if the teacher carefully avoids such wrong diction, the students still can easily get the impression that the circle would be the last element of that sequence: Firstly, because of optical reasons, and secondly, because the aim of the lesson is to determine a limit by a sequence of elements, and all the activities evoke this impression, whether or not the teacher expresses verbally that the limit cannot be reached. Even if the students accept that it is impossible to reach it, they tend to ground the impossibility on limited time and limited arithmetic of human or electronic calculators.

Another example, which is dealt with in the curriculum even earlier, is the decimal fractions of **rational numbers**. The students prove, e.g., that $^1/_3 = 0,333...$, The teacher states that the equality holds if there are infinitely many digits '3', and finally, in Germany, there is written $^1/_3 = 0,\hat{3}$ as abbreviation. By this notion the double nature of the concept of limit is expressed. The symbol 'lim...' stands for a request to run through a process and, at the same time, for the result of this process.

For an **algebraic** term, like a+b , this double nature (to be a request for some activity and to be the result of this activity) is well known and useful, but it fails when the activity includes some infinite process. So the students are right when they refuse to accept the correctness of the equality $0,\hat{3} = {}^1/_3$ and all the more $0,\hat{9} = 1$. They take the dynamic part of the double nature of limit seriously (because this part, grounded on the didactical principle of supporting 'dynamical' thinking, is always stressed), and they correctly deny that running through that infinite process, for which an expression like $0,\widehat{9}$ stands, will result in the limit. Fischbein (1989) observed that students even deny the symmetry of the equality sign, as they accept $^1/_3 = 0,\widehat{3}$, because this expression can be read from left to right, and the digits on the right can be written down one after the other, whereas they refuse $0,\widehat{3} = {}^1/_3$, because one can never have on the left side all the needed ingredients to produce the result, one never comes to an end and one is not able to say " $= {}^1/_3$ ".

5. In all times, all over the world, mathematics educators reflected and still do reflect on basic imagery and understandings for mathematical concepts, though they usually do not name them like that and possibly have different or no conceptual frames. There is still missing a theory unifying the relevant disciplines 'mathematics', 'epistemology' and 'psychology'. The work of vom Hofe and my work is one attempt. But the realization in didactical and teaching practice is at least as important as the theory. Which basic imagery and understandings do we think to be adequate? How can we support the students generating adequate basic imagery and understandings? Which inadequate basic imagery and understandings can occur? How are they caused? How can they be improved or corrected? — In my opinion, these are fundamental questions of mathematics education.

6. In the discussion after the talk I was asked, what the conception of BIU had to do with learning. — This question was a harsh criticism, as in my opinion I hadn't talked about anything but what the conception of BIU has to do with learning.

References

Bender, Peter (1982): Abbildungsgeometrie in der didaktischen Diskussion. In: *Zentralblatt für Didaktik der Mathematik 14*, 9–24

Bishop, Alan J. (1985): The Social Construction of Meaning — a Significant Development for Mathematics Education. In: *For the Learning of Mathematics 5*, no.1, 24–28

Bosshardt, Hans–Georg (1981): Vorstellungen — Grenzgänger zwischen Wissenschaft und Alltagsverstand. In: *Zeitschrift für Semiotik 3*, 363–370

Campbell, Stephen & A.J. Dawson (1995): Learning as Embodied Action. In: Rosamund Sutherland & John Mason (eds.): *Exploiting Mental Imagery with Computers in Mathematics Education*. Berlin etc.: Springer, 233–250

Clark, Herbert H. & Thomas B. Carlson (1981): Content for Comprehension. In: J. Long & A.D. Baddeley (eds.): *Proceedings of the International Symposium on Attention and Performance IX*. Hillsdale, N.J., & London: Lawrence Erlbaum, 313–330

Davis, Edward J. (1978): A Model for Understanding Understanding in Mathematics. In: *Arithmetic Teacher 26*, September, 13–17

Davis, Robert B. & Curtis McKnight (1980): The Influence of Semantic Content on Algorithmic Behavior. In: *Journal of Mathematical Behavior 3*, no. 1, 39–87

Dörfler, Willibald (1996): Means for Meaning. In this book

Engelkamp, Johannes (ed.) (1984): *Psychologische Aspekte des Verstehens*. Berlin etc.: Springer

Fischbein, Efraim (1987): *Intuition in Science and Mathematics*. Dordrecht etc.: Reidel

Fischbein, Efraim (1989): Tacit Models and Mathematical Reasoning. In: *For the Learning of Mathematics 9*, no. 2, 9–14

Halmos, Paul R. (1981): Does Mathematics Have Elements? In: *The Mathematical Intelligencer 3*, 147–153

Herscovics, Nicolas & Jacques C. Bergeron (1983): Models of Understanding. In: *Zentralblatt für Didaktik der Mathematik 15*, 75–83

Hörmann, Hans (1976): *Meinen und Verstehen*. Frankfurt: Suhrkamp

Hofe, Rudolf vom (1995): *Grundvorstellungen mathematischer Inhalte*. Heidelberg etc.: Spektrum

Hofe, Rudolf vom (1998): On Concepts of the Generation of Adequate Images and Basic Ideas — Normative, Descriptive and Constructive Aspects. In: Anna Sierpinska and Jeremy Kilpatrick, eds., *Mathematics Education as a Research Domain*. Dordrecht: Kluwer

Johnson, M. (1987): *The Body in the Mind: The Bodily Basis of Meaning, Imagination and Reason*. Chicago: University of Chicago Press

Kaput, James J. (1979): Mathematics and Learning: Roots of Epistemological Status. In: Jack Lochhead & John Clement (eds.): *Cognitive Process Instruction. Research on Teaching Thinking Skills*. Philadelphia: The Franklin Institute Press, 289–303

Krummheuer, Götz (1989): Die Veranschaulichung als "formatierte" Argumentation im Mathematikunterricht. In: *Mathematica Didactica 12*, 225–243

Malle, Günter (1988): Die Entstehung neuer Denkgegenstände — untersucht am Beispiel der negativen Zahlen. In: Willibald Dörfler (ed.): *Kognitive Aspekte mathematischer Begriffsentwicklung*. Wien: Hölder–Pichler–Tempsky, 259–319

Mann, Iris (1991): *Ich war behindert an Hand der Lehrer und Ärzte*. Weinheim: Beltz

Papert, Seymour (1980): *Mindstorms. Children, Computers, and Powerful Ideas*. New York: Basic Books

Presmeg, Norma C. (1994): The Role of Visually Mediated Processes in Classroom Mathematics. In: *Zentralblatt für Didaktik der Mathematik 26*, 114–117

Schipper, Wilhelm (1982): Stoffauswahl und Stoffanordnung im mathematischen Anfangsunterricht. In: *Journal für Mathematik-Didaktik 3*, 91–120

Schreiber, Alfred (1983): Bemerkungen zur Rolle universeller Ideen im mathematischen Denken. In: *Mathematica Didactica 6*, 65–76

Sheehan, Peter W. (ed.) (1972): *The Function and Nature of Imagery*. New York & London: Academic Press

Simon, Herbert A. (1969): *The Sciences of the Artificial*. Cambridge, Mass.: MIT Press

Skemp, Richard R. (1976): Relational Understanding and Instrumental Understanding. In: *Mathematics Teaching 77*, 20–26

TRANSFORMING MATHEMATICS INSTRUCTION IN EVERY ELEMENTARY CLASSROOM: USING RESEARCH AS A BASIS FOR EFFECTIVE SCHOOL PRACTICE

Patricia F. Campbell
Center for Mathematics Education
Department of Curriculum and Instruction
University of Maryland at College Park

Project IMPACT (Increasing the Mathematical Power of All Children and Teachers) is a National Science Foundation-funded collaborative venture that joins university researchers at the University of Maryland at College Park with school district coordinators and teachers in Montgomery County Public Schools, Maryland, USA. The purpose of the project was to design, implement, and evaluate a teacher enhancement model that sought to enhance student understanding and to support teacher change in predominantly minority urban schools in the United States. The emphasis was on teaching mathematics for understanding, focusing on problem solving and concept development. The model intended for instruction was consistent with a constructivist perspective on mathematical learning, emphasizing interaction and collaboration. The project accessed intact mathematics faculties within schools. Evaluation addressed both student achievement and teacher change. This research was conducted in demographically diverse elementary schools, enrolling children of ages 5 through 10 or 11, in low socio-economic communities in Maryland, just outside Washington, D.C. The area served by the schools was urban, but not what is termed "inner-city" in the United States. This longitudinal project began in December, 1989, and concludes in February, 1997.

Two Perspectives to be Merged

Two perspectives influenced this project. First, the school district wanted to address student mathematics achievement in racially diverse, low socio-economic schools. The district was attempting to implement a new kindergarten through eighth-grade mathematics curriculum based on the NCTM *Curriculum and Evaluation Standards for School Mathematics.* They recognized the need for a more focused and supportive teacher enhancement model, because prior professional development efforts had led to only limited student achievement. Further, student achievement data indicated persistent and continuing differential performance by student racial ethnicity. As a university researcher, I was interested in investigating the use of research as the basis for transforming school practice in elementary mathematics. A study was designed that would implement and evaluate a teacher enhancement model based on constructivist principles and existing research on the teaching and learning of elementary mathematics. This project was to involve *all* elementary mathematics teachers in the participating schools and to be evaluated in terms of student achievement, not just in terms of teacher beliefs.

This project presumed a constructivist theory of knowledge, and this provided the theoretical basis for Project IMPACT. In particular, two basic principles were: (a) learners actively construct knowledge through interaction with their surroundings and experiences, and (b) learners interpret these occurrences based on prior knowledge and their rendering of their observations and actions (Noddings, 1990).

Assumptions for Project IMPACT

In 1989-90, when this Project was initiated, there was "no 'constructivist teaching model' out there waiting to be implemented" (Pirie & Kieren, 1992, p. 506). But there were researchers who had hypothesized characteristics of instructional approaches that would be compatible with a constructivist perspective. Further, research studies on addition, subtraction and place value offered evidence that when teachers had knowledge of children's thinking and focused on fostering understanding through problem solving, increased student achievement and teacher change resulted (Carpenter, Fennema, Peterson, Chiang, & Loef, 1989; Cobb, Wood, & Yackel, 1991; Cobb, Yackel, Wood, Wheatley, & Merkel, 1988).

There were two important assumptions in Project IMPACT. One assumption addressed application of constructivist theory to all children. The other assumption addressed school-based reform.

First, it was assumed that all children can understand and construct mathematical meaning. This meant that the Project had to implement a policy of expecting and fostering the mathematical understanding of each child, not a policy of remediation. Therefore, the Project had to address teachers' pedagogical and mathematical content knowledge, encouraging instructional change and decision making to support children's construction of knowledge. Further, the intention of the Project was to move beyond equal opportunity for students to educational justice in terms of treatment and outcomes.

Second, this Project assumed that the critical unit for change in mathematics instruction is the school. Therefore, the study's design did not rely on teachers to volunteer for enhancement nor did it scatter the enhancement across partial faculties in many schools. The Project accessed intact mathematics faculties in the participating schools. This was done because it was believed that programmatic and instructional reform could not depend on isolated, heroic teachers who were left to work independently. Generally, when given sufficient notice, teachers viewed the expected summer in-service program with either acceptance or eagerness.

School Selection

The 21 predominantly minority elementary schools in the district were ranked on the following criteria: percentage of minority students enrolled; percentage of families receiving free or reduced-fee breakfast, lunch, or both; percentage of low scores on the Grade 3 statewide assessment; and percentage of students categorized as below grade level on the school system's mathematics curriculum assessment upon leaving Grade 3. Third-grade achievement was used as a measure of academic tradition because the project was initially funded only for kindergarten through third-grade implementation.

The principals of the six highest ranking schools in these categories were invited to join the Project. Of the six schools initially identified, two schools decided against participation and the next two schools on the listing agreed to participate. These six cooperating schools were matched in demographic pairs and identified as either a treatment site, participating in the teacher enhancement, or a comparable site, receiving no enhancement from the Project. Schools had to commit to Project IMPACT prior to identification of treatment or comparable-site status. The assignment of project status was determined by three coin tosses, conducted in the presence of the school principals or their designees. Designation of treatment or comparable-site status was the choice of the winning schools. Both treatment and comparable-site schools had to permit classroom observations in the fall and the spring and student assessment in the winter and spring. Following the coin toss, two of the principals requested treatment status; one principal requested that his school be a comparable site. These schools participated in a longitudinal study from June, 1990, through June, 1993. There were two years of implementation support at each grade beginning with the kindergarten and first grade in 1990, adding the next grade in each successive year.

Three of the six cooperating schools were primary schools, enrolling children through Grade 3. The other three schools were elementary schools, enrolling children through Grade 5. In 1993, the school district funded the Project's summer in-service program for the primary grade teachers in the comparable-site schools. At the same time, the teacher enhancement model was implemented in Grades 4 and 5 across all Project schools. At that time, two more schools became involved in the Project. These were the fourth- through sixth-grade schools that enrolled the children who had come from one of the three original primary schools participating in the Project. There were no comparable-site schools for the fourth and fifth grade. The Project was implemented at the fourth and fifth grade from June, 1993, through June, 1995.

The Project schools enrolled a diverse student population. The 9% Asian population were primarily children from Cambodia and Vietnam with other children from the nations of Southwest Asia and the Middle East. Another 26% of the children were coded White; these were children from the United States, with some children from Eastern Europe. This category included children who were not coded as Black, Asian or Hispanic by a caregiver. The Hispanic children constituted 30% of the student population. They were primarily from Central America, with some children from the northern countries of South America. The remaining 35% of the children were coded Black. These included African-American children from the United States and children from Africa, Haiti, and islands in the Caribbean. In each of the five implementation years, approximately 500 children formed a grade-level cohort across the schools. Of these, 60% of the children received free or reduced-fee breakfast, lunch, or both meals at schools, and 25% of the children were enrolled in English classes for speakers of other languages.

The Teacher Enhancement Model

The Project IMPACT teacher enhancement model involved (a) a summer in-service program for all teachers of mathematics, (b) an on-site mathematics specialist in each school, (c) manipulative materials for each classroom, and (d) teacher planning and instructional problem solving during a common grade-level planning time each week. This report only addresses the summer in-service program.

The summer program was grade related, involving all of the kindergarten and first grade teachers in the participating schools during the first summer and teachers of subsequent grade levels participating by grade in the following summers. Each summer in-service addressed:

(a) adult-level mathematics content; (b) teaching mathematics for understanding, including questioning, use of manipulative materials, and integration of mathematical topics; (c) research on children's learning of those mathematics topics that were deemed critical to the grade-level focus as well as research addressing a constructivist theory of learning; and (d) teaching mathe-matics in culturally diverse classrooms. The summer in-service program accessed a summer school program for children, providing teachers with an opportunity to begin instructional change with a small group of children without all the demands associated with academic year instruction. The in-service program also included time to plan for the coming academic year.

Consider one approach that was used to address research on children's learning. Videotapes of teaching and videotapes of children solving mathematics problems were used. These two kinds of tapes served different purposes. The teaching tapes were to illustrate and provoke discussion about how "constructivist teaching" might look. In particular, the sessions addressed the teacher's role as a facilitator of learning, the crucial nature of teacher questioning, and the meaning of student responses. The children's problem-solving tapes provided a context for discussing re-search. After watching one of these tapes, teachers struggled to characterize how the understanding of a particular child might be interpreted. Further, the teachers would discuss what approaches they might use or what issues they might want to address if that child was in their class. The reason for using videotapes was to focus the teachers' attention on children's learning, whether thinking about examining mathematical meaning, considering instructional approaches, or defining curricular emphases. Thus, in this Project, the intention was to make a research perspective a critical basis for making decisions.

Evaluation and Results

Project IMPACT sought to evaluate the effectiveness of its efforts by examining student achievement and by collecting data regarding teacher change. Surveys of teacher beliefs and confidence were administered in order to characterize the rationale that might be guiding teachers' actions. Classroom observations provided information regarding the teachers' actual conduct. Student achievement was evaluated by assessments administered twice each year, using both student interviews and written tests.

Teacher Change

Two surveys were constructed to examine the teachers' rationale and perspectives. One survey characterized teachers' beliefs about mathematics, mathematical pedagogy, and equity; the second survey estimated teachers' confidence for implementing instructional reform.

The primary teachers assumed a more constructivist perspective regarding how children learn mathematics and how mathematics should be taught than did the upper grade teachers. Further, the primary teachers' perspectives of equity in mathematics education favored supporting every child's access to challenging mathematics whereas the upper grade teachers were more likely to base instructional decisions on an evaluation of children's existing skills and assessed needs. There was no difference between upper and lower grade teachers' change in beliefs regarding (a) the relationship between skill and understanding or problem-solving instruction, (b) the way mathematics instruction should be sequenced, or (c) the nature of mathematics. Within each of these, the primary and upper grade teachers made comparable shifts toward a more reform-based perspective.

Although the confidence level of each group of teachers changed in a direction indicating more willingness to interact with mathematics and to implement instructional approaches supporting reform, this change was more pronounced among the primary teachers. Both sets of teachers made a strong shift evidencing more confidence for interacting with mathematics over the course of the academic year. As the reality of classroom practice became evident, primary teachers became slightly more confident about their ability to implement a reform perspective whereas the upper grade teachers became slightly less confident, but this difference was not statistically significant.

Classroom instruction was observed in order to characterize the growth and changes evidenced within the teachers. If a teacher was still in the classroom of an IMPACT school after two years of implementation, the status of instruction at the end of those two years is characterized. If a teacher left an IMPACT school prior to two years of implementation, the evaluation of her instructional change was fixed at the level evidenced when she was last observed at an IMPACT site. Therefore, the characterizations that follow present a distribution skewed towards less change for the upper grade teachers as none of the fifth grade teachers had had two years of supported implementation. Finally, each of the following frequency estimates are truly only educated predictions, subject to further analysis and interpretation of the classroom observation data.

About 10% of the primary teachers (5 out of 52) and 17% of the upper grade teachers (7 out of 41) made no real change in their instruction. Another 17% of the primary teachers (9 out of 52) and 24% of the upper grade teachers (10 out of 41) moved considerably beyond routinized practice and direct instruction. These teachers used manipulatives and small-group activities. They asked how problems were solved and accepted different strategies, but they did not pursue the meaning of student explanations. They generally did not use know how to use an incorrect answer as an instructional probe, typically ignoring incorrect answers or telling the errant child the correct response. About 19% of the primary teachers (10 out of 52) and 37% of the upper-grade teachers (15 out of 41) evidenced instructional changes consistent with a constructivist perspective. These teachers sought the input of their colleagues and asked questions when manipulative materials were in use to keep a mathematical focus. In these classrooms, it was not uncommon to hear a teacher probing the reasoning behind a child's response, but these teachers generally did not relate strategies as a way to highlight mathematical meaning. In about 54% of the primary classrooms (28 out of 52) and 22% of the upper grade classrooms (9 out of 41), instruction was supportive of children's construction of knowledge and attentive to mathematics. These teachers made links between mathematical topics and frequently asked questions to focus the children's attention towards mathematical generalizations or abstractions. These teachers often used questioning to address the similarities or differences between offered strategies. When students responded incorrectly, these teachers tried to ask questions that might cause the children to reexamine their procedure or reasoning.

Student Achievement

The data for grades 4 and 5 are still being analyzed, so this report is limited to the kindergarten through third-grade data. The students were assessed at the middle of the school year and at the end of the school year each year, using both a scripted problem-solving interview and, in Grades 2 through 5, a written test. The assessments were administered in one of six languages. The assessment addressed numerical and computational skill, whole number and place-value concepts, problem solving and reasoning, geometric properties and relationships, and rational number.

Student data indicated that there was no significant difference in total mean achievement through first grade. However, there was a significant difference in mean achievement favoring the children in the treatment classrooms in second and third grade. Other significant effects were attributable to race and English language proficiency. To better understand the source of the effects, the items in the assessment were subsequently categorized by mathematical topic and were re-analyzed.

This analysis revealed no significant difference in numerical and computational skill over the four-year data set. A significant difference in geometry achievement was noted in the first grade favoring the treatment group; this persisted in each successive grade. Similarly, there was no difference in problem solving and reasoning through the middle of first grade, however, a significant difference became evident favoring the treatment group at the end of first grade. This difference was due to increased performance on graphing and word problem items, and it persisted through third grade. The significant difference in achievement on whole number and place-value concepts became evident at the middle of second grade and continued in the next year's data. Finally, the rational number achievement data showed a significant difference favoring the treatment children at the middle of second grade and again throughout third grade.

Conclusion

Project IMPACT's influence on student achievement was not immediate. It seemed to become evident first in the least abstract mathematics represented in the curriculum and then increase in breadth over time. The beneficial effect of focusing on conceptual understanding and problem solving became more evident and persistent as the level of the mathematical abstraction became more pronounced.

Instructional change is not easy. It is demanding, threatening, and risky. The evidence of Project IMPACT is that change in urban centers can happen when individual teachers are not left alone to accomplish it in isolation. It is easier to attempt change in an atmosphere of support. It is easier to succeed when people work together for a common goal relevant to their needs.

Finally, IMPACT addressed both the mathematical and pedagogical knowledge of teachers in order to support decision making. Both components are critical. Research on children's learning provides an important lens for teacher enhancement, but so does mathematical content.

Project IMPACT demonstrates the potential of applying research to instructional decision making across whole schools. It has done so in the reality of public schools that do not have a tradition of strong mathematics achievement. If the potential and problems associated with reform are to be understood, if the implications of reform are to be recognized, and if the vision of mathematical power for all is to be realized, then reform cannot just be carried out in idealized settings.

We, as mathematics educators, must accept the challenge to expand and to maintain our commitment, not to just selected classrooms, but to educational change across schools.

References

Carpenter, T. P., Fennema, E., Peterson, P. L., Chiang, C. P., & Loef, M. (1989). *Using knowledge of children's mathematics thinking in classroom teaching: An experimental study.* American Educational Research Journal, 26, 499-531.

Cobb, P., Wood, T., & Yackel, E. (1991). *A constructivist approach to second grade mathematics.* In E. von Glasersfeld (Ed.), Radical constructivism in mathematics education (pp. 157-176). Dordrecht: Kluwer Academic Publishers.

Cobb, P., Yackel, E., Wood, T., Wheatley, G., & Merkel, G. (1988). *Creating a problem-solving atmosphere.* Arithmetic Teacher, 36(1), 46-47.

Noddings, N. (1990). *Construction in mathematics education.* In R. B. Davis, C. A Maher & N. Noddings (Eds.), Constructivist views on the teaching and learning of mathematics (Journal for Research in Mathematics Education Monograph No. 4, pp. 7-18). Reston, VA: National Council of Teachers of Mathematics.

Pirie, S., & Kieren, T. (1992). *Creating constructivist environments and constructing creative mathematics.* Educational Studies in Mathematics, 23, 505-528.

ACCOUNTING FOR MATHEMATICAL LEARNING IN THE SOCIAL CONTEXT OF THE CLASSROOM

Paul Cobb
Vanderbilt University

This paper focuses on the issue of accounting for students' mathematical learning as it occurs in the social context of the classroom. In the opening section of the paper, I first clarify why this is a significant issue for myself and my colleagues and develop criteria for classroom analyses that are relevant to our purposes. In the second part of the paper, I outline the interpretive framework that we currently use by presenting a sample analysis. In the final section, I reflect on this analysis to address four more general issues. These concern the contributions of the type illustrated by the sample analysis, the relationship between instructional design and classroom-based research, the role of symbols and other tools in mathematical learning, and the relation between individual students' mathematical activity and communal classroom processes.

Social Context and Developmental Research

In recent years, there has been a shift away from theoretical perspectives that focus on individual, isolated learners and towards those that bring to the fore the socially- and culturally-situated nature of mathematical activity (e.g., Bishop, 1988; Nickson, 1992; Nunes, 1992). Analyses conducted from this latter viewpoint continue to be vitally concerned with the process of mathematical development. However, in contrast to purely psychological perspectives, individual students' mathematical interpretations, solutions, explanations, and justifications are seen not only as individual acts, but simultaneously as acts of participating in collective or communal classroom processes. Viewed in this way, mathematical learning is seen to be necessarily situated in social context. It should be acknowledged that this paradigm encompasses a range of theoretical positions that include various versions of constructivism, sociocultural theory, and sociolinguistic theory. Comparing and

The general theoretical analysis reported in this paper was supported by the Office of Educational Research and Improvement under grant number R305A60007. The analysis of the sample instructional sequence was supported by the National Science Foundation under grant No. RED-9353587. The opinions expressed do not necessarily reflect the views of either OERI or the Foundation.

contrasting these alternatives is beyond the scope of this paper, and I will instead focus directly on the version of social constructivism to which I and my colleagues subscribe.

From the social constructivist perspective, the challenge of accounting for learning in social context involves analyzing both 1) the evolution of the communal practices in which students participate, and 2) the development of individual students' mathematical understandings as they participate in and contribute to the evolution of these classroom practices. Consequently, from this point of view, a first criterion when accounting for learning in social context is that such analyses should *focus on the mathematical development of both individual students and of the classroom communities in which they participate.*

Stated in this way, the rationale for this first criterion is primarily theoretical and reflects a particular view of the relation between individual activity and communal practices. In considering other criteria, I attempt to ground the issue of accounting for mathematical learning in social context in my own and my colleague's classroom-based activity of collaborating with teachers to design learning environments for students. In this work, we draw on the theory of Realistic Mathematics Education developed at the Freudenthal Institute when developing sequences of instructional activities for students. In following this approach, we initially conduct an anticipatory thought experiment in which we envision how students' mathematical learning might proceed as an instructional sequence is enacted in the classroom (Gravemeijer, 1994). These thought experiments involve conjectures about both 1) students' possible learning trajectories, and 2) the means of supporting, organizing, and guiding that development. These conjectures are then continually tested and modified as we engage in classroom-based research and attempt to make sense of what is actually happening as the instructional activities are realized in interaction between a teacher and his or her students in the classroom. It is here that the issue of accounting for students' mathematical learning in social context gains pragmatic force in that the ways in which we look at communal classroom practices and at individual students' activity profoundly influences the instructional decisions that we make when we experiment in classrooms. Given our agenda as mathematics educators who conduct classroom-based developmental research, a second criterion is therefore that analyses of mathematical learning in social context should *feed back to inform the ongoing process of instructional development.*

In addition to conducting ongoing analyses of classroom events on a daily basis, we also video-record all classroom lessons so that we can conduct retrospective analyses of teaching experiments that typically last several months. The time frame of these analyses gives rise to further challenges in that analyses that locate students' mathematical activity in social context often deal with only a few lessons, or perhaps focus on just a few minutes within one lesson. The issue that I and my colleagues have been struggling with is therefore that of stepping back from and coming to grips with what transpires in a classroom not during a ten-minute episode but over, say, a three-month time period. A third criterion that arises when conducting developmental research is therefore that analyses should document the mathematical learning of both the classroom community and of individual students over extended periods of time.

Interpretive Framework

The interpretive framework that has emerged from our attempts to analyze classroom events while engaging in developmental research involves the coordination of social and psychological perspectives (see Figure 1). The social perspective is an interactionist perspective on collective or communal classroom processes (Bauersfeld, Krummheuer, & Voigt, 1988) and the psychological perspective is a constructivist perspective on individual students' and the teacher's interpretations and actions as they participate in and contribute to the development of these communal practices (cf. Cobb & Yackel, 1996). The entries in the column headed "social perspective" - social norms,

Social Perspective	Psychological Perspective
Classroom social norms	Beliefs about own role, others' roles, and the general nature of mathematica activity in school
Sociomathematical norms	Mathematical beliefs and values
Classroom mathematical practices	Mathematical conceptions

Figure 1. An Interpretive Framework for Analyzing Mathematical Activity in Social Context.

sociomathematical norms, and classroom mathematical practices - refer to aspects of the classroom microculture that we have found it useful to differentiate given our research agenda. The corresponding entries in the column headed "psychological perspective" refer to what, for want of better terminology, might be called their psychological correlates.

I will give an extended example taken from a year-long teaching experiment to illustrate how analyses can be organized in terms of the framework. This experiment was conducted in a first-grade classroom with six- and seven-year-old students and focused on the development of core quantitative concepts. A series of three individual interviews conducted with all 18 students at the beginning, middle, and end of the school year indicated that the experiment was reasonably successful in that the students made significant progress (Cobb, Gravemeijer, Yackel, McClain, & Whitenack, in press). The data collected in the course of the teaching experiment therefore constitute an appropriate setting in which to explore ways of accounting for students' mathematical development as it occurs in the social context of the classroom. In the following paragraphs, I summarize this analysis by briefly outlining the social and sociomathematical norms established by the classroom community and then considering the classroom mathematical practices in more detail.

Social norms. The first step in the analysis of the first-grade teaching experiment involved documenting the social norms to delineate the classroom participation structure. This participation structure proved to be relatively stable by the midpoint of the school year and can be summarized as follows:

1) Students were obliged to explain and justify their reasoning.
2) Students were obliged to listen to and to attempt to understand others' explanations.
3) Students were obliged to indicate non-understanding and, if possible, to ask the explainer clarifying questions.
4) Students were obliged to indicate when they considered solutions invalid, and to explain the reasons for their judgment.
5) The teacher was obliged to comment on or redescribe students' contributions, sometimes by notating their reasoning.

As shown in Figure 1, we take the psychological correlates of the social norms to be students' beliefs about their own roles, others' roles, and the general nature of mathematical activity in school. We therefore conjecture that in guiding the renegotiation of social norms, teachers are simultaneously supporting students' reorganization of these beliefs. This conjecture, it should be noted, is open to empirical investigation.

Sociomathematical norms. It is apparent from the list of social norms given above that such norms are not specific to mathematics, but apply to any subject matter area including science or social studies classes as well as to mathematics classes. The second aspect of the classroom microculture that we differentiate focuses on normative features of students' mathematical activity (Yackel & Cobb, 1996). With regard to the analysis of the first-grade classroom, one sociomathematical norm that emerged was that of what counted as an acceptable mathematical explanation. In the most general terms, acceptable explanations in this classroom had to be interpretable by other members of the classroom community as descriptions of actions on numerical entities (cf. Sfard, 1994). A second sociomathematical norm that emerged concerned what counted as a different mathematical explanation in this classroom. It appeared that solutions to additive tasks were judged as different if they involved either 1) different quantitative interpretations (e.g., the task "14 cookies are in the cookie jar and I take 6 out. How many cookies are in the jar now?" interpreted as $6+\_=14$ rather than $14-6$), or 2) difference in calculational processes such that numerical entities were decomposed and recomposed in different ways (e.g., a solution in which a student reasoned $14-4=10$, $10-2=8$ would be judged as different to that of another student who reasoned, $7+7=14$, $14-7=7$, $7-1=6$). Significantly, by the midpoint of the school year, various counting methods that would be judged as different by researchers (e.g., counting all versus counting on) were not judged as different in this classroom, but were all simply described as counting. This observation highlights the claim that what counts as a different explanation can differ markedly from one classroom to another, and that these differences can profoundly influence the mathematical understandings that students develop.

A third sociomathematical norm that emerged concerns what counted as an *insightful mathematical solution*. It is important to clarify that, by the midpoint of the school year, the teacher responded differentially to students' contributions, and that in doing so, she indicated that she particularly valued what she and the students called grouping solutions. This appeared to be an important facet of her effectiveness in supporting her students' learning in that it enabled them to become aware of more sophisticated forms of mathematical reasoning. This, in turn, made it possi-ble for their problem solving efforts to have a sense of directionality (cf. Voigt, 1995). In accomplishing this, however, the teacher continued to accept and actively solicited counting solutions from students who she judged were not yet able to develop grouping solutions. In doing so, she actively managed the tension between proactively supporting the evolution of classroom mathematical practices and ensuring that all students had a way to participate in those practices.

As is shown in Figure 1, we take students' specifically mathematical beliefs and values to be the psychological correlates of the sociomathematical norms. We therefore conjecture that in guiding the renegotiation of these norms, teachers are simultaneously supporting students' reorganization of the beliefs and values that constitute what might be called their mathematical dispositions. Once again, this conjecture is open to empirical investigation.

Classroom mathematical practices. The third aspect of the interpretive framework concerns the mathematical practices established by the classroom community and their psychological correlates, individual students' specifically mathematical interpretations and actions. The objective when analyzing the evolution of classroom mathematical practices is to trace the mathematical development of the classroom community against the backdrop of the social and sociomathematical norms. For illustrative purposes, I will focus on one short instructional sequence called the Candy Shop that was enacted during 12 lessons midway through the school year. The instructional intent of this sequence was to support students' initial construction and coordination of units of ten and of one. The teacher first introduced the anchoring scenario by developing a narrative with her students about a character called Mrs. Wright who owned a candy shop. In the course of these initial discussions, the teacher and students established the convention of packing candies into rolls of ten.

The first mathematical practice identified was that of counting by tens and ones to evaluate collections of candies. For example, in one of the first instructional activities, the teacher gave the students bags of lose unifix cubes and asked them to act as packers in the candy shop. Before they began, however, the students estimated how many rolls of ten they thought they would make. This served to orient them to enumerate the candies/unifix cubes as they packed them. In a subsequent instructional activity, the teacher used an overhead projector to show the students a pictured collection of rolls and individual candies and asked them to figure out how many candies there were in all. In both of these instructional activities and in others, solutions in which students first counted rolls by ten and then individual candies by one became routine and beyond need of justification. As this first mathematical practice illustrates, a practice does not necessarily correspond to a particular type of instructional activity but can instead cut across several activities. It is also important to clarify that the emergence of a practice typically involves a process of negotiation. For example, several students participated in the first instructional activity described above by counting rolls by ten, 10, 20, 30, ..., 80, but then said that they had made 80 rolls. Other students challenged them, arguing that they had made eight rolls that contained 80 candies. The actual process by which the practice of counting by tens and ones emerged can be documented by conducting detailed microanalyses of this and other specific episodes.

A second mathematical practice emerged as the teacher and students continued to discuss solutions to tasks involving pictured collections of rolls and candies. The graphic the teacher used when presenting one task is shown below. The reasoning of the first student who gave an explanation, Chris, proved difficult for the teacher and other students to follow. However, he appeared to mentally group ten individual candies together.

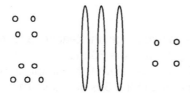

T: How did you figure it out, Chris?
Chris: Well, I knew there was 13 pieces not counting the rolls, all those pieces that are loose,
T: OK.
Chris: and then those three rolls make 30 and if you go up and I got past ten, and I got to 13, so I got past 30, and then I knew if you added ten and three, and I used up two of those, I mean three of those (points towards the screen from his position sitting on the floor). You have 30, and you add the ten, you used up the ten on the 30 and then you had three left and that made 43.

Chris' subsequent clarifications indicate that when he spoke of "using up a ten on the 30," he probably meant that if he counted ten more from 30 he would complete the 30s decade and have 40, and that three more would be 43.

The teacher asked Chris to repeat his explanation and then began to redescribe his solution, possibly to verify her interpretation with him.

T: Chris, you said this was 30 (writes 30 beneath the rolls). Then you have five here (circles a group of five candies).
Chris: Yes.
T: Then you had (circles a group of four candies).
Chris: Four, and then that one over there made five. (T circles the candy he points to.) So that's ten. I used up that 30 right there, I used up that 30 with ten, you see 30 is a whole entire ten almost, it's not

really a whole entire ten—after 39 comes 40 and that used up the ten.

T: So there's the 30 that he used (points). Now does everybody see the ten that he used? He had five there, and then you saw he had four and one more made another five. So did you add the five and five to make ten?

Chris: Yes.

T: So then you had 30 plus ten and that got you up to 40.

Chris: Yes.

T: And then you still had these three more (circles the group of three candies) made 43.

Chris: Yes.

In the course of this exchange, the teacher accommodated to Chris' way of speaking, saying "there's the 30 that he used." However, in doing so, she assumed that Chris was referring to the three picture rolls when he in fact seemed to be referring to the 30s decade. Thus, there was a subtle difference in their individual interpretations. Nonetheless, they appeared to communicate effectively as the exchange continued. To take account of such differences, I and my colleagues speak of interpretations being taken-as-shared rather than shared.

As the discussion continued, several other students indicated that they did not understand Chris' reasoning and he gave a series of increasingly articulate explanations. In the remainder of this lesson and in subsequent lessons, the act of mentally grouping ten pictured candies gradually emerged as an established classroom mathematical practice. The teacher for her part indicated that such solutions were particularly valued. For example, after several students had explained how they had figured out how many candies there were in a picture showing eight rolls together with groups of six, four, and three individual candies, she asked, "Is there another way that you could group to figure out 93?"

Ben: (Walks to the screen.) I think it's 93 because I took this six (points to the group of six individual candies) and I broke it up and I took one away and I put it with the four (points to the group of four individual candies) to make five and five, to make ten, and I knew that was 80, so it would be 90, and then 93.

As Ben described his solution, the teacher indicated that she particularly valued it by writing arithmetical sentences to record his reasoning. In addition, the protracted discussion of Chris' solution had also implicitly served to legitimize solutions of this type.

The third mathematical practice identified during the Candy Shop sequence emerged when the teacher introduced a new type of instructional activity in which the students generated different partitionings of a given collection of candies. The teacher explained that Mrs. Wright was interrupted as she packed candies into rolls.

Teacher:What if Mrs. Wright had 43 pieces of candy, and she is working on packing them into rolls. What are different ways that she might have 43 pieces of candy, how many rolls and how many pieces might she have? Sarah, what's one way she might find it?

The students, as a group, were able to generate the various possibilities with little apparent difficulty.

Sarah: Four rolls and three pieces.
Elizabeth: 43 pieces.
Kendra: She might have two rolls and 23 pieces.
Darren: She could have three rolls, 12 pieces, I mean 13 pieces.
Linda: One roll and 33 pieces.

The teacher for her part recorded each of their suggestions on the whiteboard as shown in Figure 2. Previously, the students had evaluated pictured collections of candies. In contrast, the teacher now drew pictured collections to record the results of their reasoning as they generated alternative partitionings.

At this point in the exchange, one of the students, Karen, volunteered, "Well see, we've done all the ways." She then went on to explain how the configurations the teacher had drawn could be arranged in order. Most of the students seemed to take Karen's purpose for ordering the configurations as self-evident, and a second student proposed an alternative scheme for numbering the pictures. The discussion during the remainder of the session then focused on the merits of different ways of organizing and labeling the configurations.

Summary. This necessarily brief account of the mathematical practices that emerged during the Candy Shop sequence can be summarized as follows:
1. Counting by tens and ones to evaluate collections of candies.
2. Grouping ten candies mentally when evaluating collections.
3. Generating alternative partitionings of a given collection of candies.

We, as observers, can see in this sequence of mathematical practices the initial emergence of the invariance of quantity under certain transformations. In this regard, it can reasonably be argued that the learning of the classroom community was mathematically significant. As a further point, it is important to stress that an analysis of mathematical practices

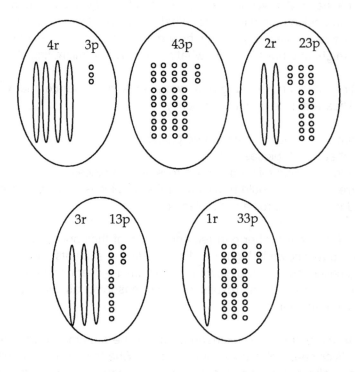

Figure 2. The Teacher's Record of the Students' Responses to the Task Involving 43 Candies.

does not merely involve listing a sequence of activities, methods, or strategies. The analysis also has to sketch the collective developmental route the classroom community has taken by indicating how one practice might have emerged from previously established practices. For example, consider again Ben's reasoning when he evaluated a collection of eight rolls and 13 candies.

I think it's 93 because I took this six (points) and I broke it up and I took one away and. I put it with the four (points) to make five and five, to make ten, and I knew that was 80, so it would be 90, and then 93.

Here, in reasoning "80, so it would be 90, and then 93," Ben in effect established nine units of ten and three units of one as an alternative to 93 organized as eight tens and 13 ones. This, of course, is not to say that he consciously related these alternative partitionings. Instead, the relationship was implicit in his activity as he participated in the second mathematical practice. As the third mathematical practice emerged, what was previously implicit in students' activity became an explicit topic of conversation. This example is paradigmatic in that it illustrates that an analysis of classroom mathematical practices should account of the process of the classroom community's learning.

Reflections

My purpose in the final section of this paper is to step back from the analysis of the candy shop sequence to address several more general issues. The first of these concerns the contribution of analyses that delineate sequences mathematical practices. To this end, imagine that, at the end of the school year, we had interviewed not only the students in the teaching experiment classroom but also those from another first-grade classroom in the same school. I am sure that if we shuffled the video-recordings of these interviews, most viewers could almost unerringly identify the classroom from which each student came. It is precisely this contrast between the mathematical reasoning of the two groups of students that is accounted for in terms of participation in the differing mathematical practices established in the two classrooms.

To continue the thought experiment, suppose that we now focus only on the students in the teaching experiment classroom. The contrast is now between the activity of individual students in the same classroom community and it is here that qualitative differences in their reasoning come to the fore even as they participate in the same practices. In my view, psychological analyses of the individual students' diverse ways of participating in these practices are needed in order to account for these qualitative differences. An analysis of this type, when coordinated with an analysis of communal practices, documents the process of individual students' mathematical development as they participate in and contribute to the evolution of the classroom mathematical practices.

The second more general point is to note that, in documenting the evolving mathematical practices, we have in effect documented the Candy Shop sequence as it was realized in interaction in the classroom. However, participating in these practices also constituted the immediate social situation in which the students' mathematical learning occurred. As a consequence, the analysis also documents the evolving social situation of their mathematical development. These interrelations between 1) an analysis of classroom mathematical practices, 2) the instructional sequences as realized in interaction, and 3) the evolving social situation of the students' mathematical development is encouraging in that it brings together the two general aspects of developmental research -- instructional development and classroom-based research. Analyses of classroom mathematical practices might therefore make it possible to develop a common language in which to talk both about instructional design and about individual and collective mathematical development in the classroom.

The third more general point concerns the role of symbols and other tools in mathematical learning. It should be apparent from the sample analysis that ways of symbolizing do not stand apart from classroom mathematical practices but are instead integral aspects of both these practices and the activity of the students who participate in them. For example, participation in the second. mathematical practice involved reasoning with pictured collections of candies. This observation in turn implies that the ways of symbolizing established in the teaching-experiment classroom profoundly influenced both the mathematical understandings the students developed and the process by which they developed them. It is in fact possible to trace the evolution of the ways of symbolizing:

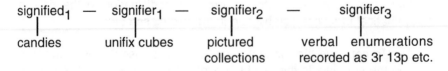

$$\text{signified}_1 \ — \ \text{signifier}_1 \ — \ \text{signifier}_2 \ — \ \text{signifier}_3$$

| candies | unifix cubes | pictured collections | verbal enumerations recorded as 3r 13p etc. |

In Walkerdine's (1988) terms, one can speak of a chain of signification emerging as the mathematical practices evolved. Walkerdine notes that succeeding signifiers may initially be established as substitutes for preceding terms, with the assumption that the sense of those terms is preserved through the links of the chain. For example, pictured collections were initially introduced as substitutes for collections of candies/unifix cubes. However, Walkerdine goes on to argue that the original sign combination (i.e., candies/unifix cubes) is not merely concealed behind succeeding signifiers. Instead, the meaning of this sign combination evolves as the chain is constituted. Walkerdine's fundamental contention is that a sign combination that originates in a particular practice slides under succee-ding signifiers that originate in other practices motivated by different concerns and interests. In the case of the Candy Shop sequence, for example, the meaning of the candies/unifix cubes sign combination was initially constituted within a narrative about Mrs. Wright's candy shop. The concerns and interests in this instance were those of a simulated buying and selling activity. Later, the concerns and interests were primarily mathe-matical and involved structuring collections of candies in different ways. When the students participated in the third mathematical practice, rolls of ten candies instantiated units of ten of some type, and the activity of packing candies by making bars of ten unifix cubes had been displaced by that of mentally creating and decomposing such units. In a very real sense, they were no longer the same candies that the students had acted with as when they participated in the first mathematical practice. An analysis of the chain of signification that was constituted as the classroom mathe-matical practices evolved accounts for this change of meaning and thus for the underlying process of mathematization in sociolinguistic terms. It should be stressed that, in such an account, the symbols themselves do not have any particular magic. Instead, the focus is on ways of symbolizing -- on symbols as integral aspects of individual and collective activity rather than as separate entities that stand apart from thought and reasoning.

The final more general point concerns the relationship between individual students' mathematical activity and communal classroom practices implicit in the sample analysis. To put the matter as succinctly as possible, we take this relationship to be reflexive. This is an extremely strong relationship and does not merely mean that individual activity and communal practices are interdependent. Instead, it implies that one literally does not exist without the other (cf. Mehan & Wood, 1975). I would therefore question an account that spoke of classroom mathematical practices first being established, and then somehow causing students to reorganize their mathematical understandings. Similarly, I would question an account that spoke of students first reorganizing their understandings and then contributing to the establishment of new practices. The theoretical position inherent in the interpretive framework and in the sample analysis is one that focuses on both individual students' activity and on the social worlds in which they participate without attempting to derive one from the other. From this point of view, individual students are seen to contribute to the evolution of classroom mathematical practices as they reorganize their mathematical understandings. Conversely, their participation in those practices is seen to both enable and constrain the ways in which they reorganize their understandings.

In this analytical approach, the process of coordinating psychological and social analyses is not merely a matter of somehow pasting a conventional psychological analysis on to a separate social analysis. Instead, when conducting a psychological analysis, one analyzes individual students' activity as they participate in the practices of the classroom community. Further, when conducting a social analysis, one focuses on communal practices that are continually generated by and do not exist apart from the activities of the participating individuals. The coordination at the heart of the interpretive framework is therefore not that between individuals and a community viewed as separate, sharply defined entities. Instead, the coordination is between different ways of looking at and making sense of what is going on in classrooms. What, from one perspective, is seen as a single classroom community is, from another, seen as a number of interacting individuals actively interpreting each others' actions. Thus, the central coordination is between our own ways of interpreting classroom events. Whitson (in press) clarifies this point when he suggests that we think of ourselves as viewing human processes in the classroom, with the realization that these processes can be described in either social or psychological terms. Throughout this paper, I have attempted to illustrate that both of these perspectives are relevant to the concerns and interests of mathematics educators who engage in developmental research. The interpretive framework I have outlined represents one way of coordinating these perspectives that is rooted in classroom-based research of this type.

References

Bauersfeld, H., Krummheuer, G., & Voigt, J. (1988). Interactional theory of learning and teaching mathematics and related microethnographical studies. In H-G Steiner & A. Vermandel (Eds.), *Foundations and methodology of the discipline of mathematics education* (pp. 174-188). Antwerp: Proceedings of the TME Conference.

Bishop, A. J. (1988). *Mathematical enculturation: A cultural perspective on mathematics education.* Dordrecht, The Netherlands: Kluwer.

Cobb, P., Gravemeijer, K., Yackel, E., McClain, K., Whitenack, J. (in press). Mathematizing and symbolizing: The emergence of chains of signification in one first-grade classroom. In D. Kirshner & J. A. Whitson (Eds.), *Situated cognition theory: Social, semiotic, and neurological perspectives.* Hillsdale, NJ: Lawrence Erlbaum Associates.

Cobb, P., & Yackel, E. (1996). Constructivist, emergent, and sociocultural perspectives in the context of developmental research. *Educational Psychologist, 31*, 175-190.

Gravemeijer, K. E. P. (1994). *Developing realistic mathematics education.* Utrecht, The Netherlands: CD-b Press.

Mehan, H., & Wood, H. (1975). *The reality of ethnomethodology.* New York: John Wiley.

Nickson, M. (1992). The culture of mathematics: An unknown quantity? In D. A. Grouws (Ed.), Handbook of research on mathematics teaching and learning (pp. 101-115). New York: Macmillan.

Nunes, T. (1992). Ethnomathematics and everyday cognition. In D. A. Grouws (Ed.), *Handbook of research on mathematics teaching and learning* (pp. 557–574). New York: Macmillan.

Sfard, A. (1994). Reification as a birth of a metaphor. *For the Learning of Mathematics,* 14(1), 44-55.

Voigt, J. (1995). Thematic patterns of interaction and sociomathematical norms. In P. Cobb & H. Bauersfeld (Eds.), *Emergence of mathematical meaning: Interaction in classroom cultures* (pp.163-201). Hillsdale, NJ: Lawrence Erlbaum Associates.

Walkerdine, V. (1988). *The mastery of reason.* London: Routledge.

Whitson, J. A. (in press). Cognition as a semiotic process: Grounding, mediation, and critical reflective transcendence. In D. Kirshner & J. A. Whitson (Eds.), *Situated cognition theory: Social, semiotic, and neurological perspectives.* Hillsdale, NJ: Lawrence Erlbaum Associates.

Yackel, E., & Cobb, P. (1996). Sociomath norms, argumentation, and autonomy in mathematics. *Journal for Research in Mathematics Education,* 27, 458-477.

CONCEPTUALIZING THE PROFESSIONAL DEVELOPMENT OF TEACHERS

Thomas J. Cooney
University of Georgia
USA

Introduction

Most mathematics educators are involved with teacher education in some way. The teachers may be at the preservice or inservice level and they may be oriented toward elementary, middle, or secondary schools. Regardless of their status or level of teaching most teachers participate in some form of teacher education designed to promote "better teaching" however we define that term. As such, teachers are learners. Brown and Borko's (1992) review of research on how teachers learn to teach mathematics emphasizes that teachers are rational and cognizing agents with all of the implications that entails. As with any learner, we can consider the conceptual development of the teacher as that development pertains to the different domains of knowledge acquired. The nature of those domains is complex as suggested by Lappan and Theule-Lubienski (1994) and Bromme (1994). Even a casual consideration of Shulman's (1986) notion of pedagogical content knowledge reveals the complexity of teachers' knowing as various elements of epistemology, psychology, mathematics, philosophy, and pedagogy are woven together by the teacher, implicit as that weaving process may be.

The notion of professionalism is likewise complex. Romberg (1988) identified four aspects he considered central to the concept of professionalism: (a) an accumulation of knowledge that sets the "professional" apart from others, (b) use of that knowledge when making occupational decisions, (c) membership in an organization that performs an indispensable public service and which has elements of self-regulation and autonomy, and (d) the presence of indicators that allow for change within the profession. Romberg (1988) and Noddings (1992) have argued that the presence of these conditions are frequently lacking in the professional lives of teachers. Noddings (1992) concludes that teachers generally fall short of professional status given the lack of prestige associated with teaching, the fact that teachers labor in isolation, and that they lack collegiality necessary for a rich professional life. An underlying factor in this lack of professional status is the question of legitimacy of the knowledge perceived necessary to become an accomplished teacher.

Simply put, is that knowledge commonsensical or the product of disciplined inquiry? I submit that it is both based on the following argument.

The professional development of teachers can be thought of in many ways. One could, for example, think of professional development in terms of the teacher's acquisition of knowledge and skills that lead to a particular model of teaching perhaps developed through disciplined inquiry. Good, Grouws, and Ebmeier's (1983) model of active mathematics teaching comes immediately to mind. Alternately, we can conceptualize professional development as moving toward some idealized notion of teaching as defined by recognized expert teachers. While we can debate the relative merits of different models of teaching, it is undeniable that some are grounded in knowledge derived from research. Most definitions of reform-oriented teaching assume teachers have acquired the kinds of knowledge suggested by Shulman (1986), Lappan and Theule-Lubienski (1994), and Bromme (1994). The commonsensical part is the artistic translation of this knowledge into action, an artistry that is dependent on the teacher's propensity to monitor his/her own actions and to generate alternatives for dealing with conceived constraints. These alternatives can be enhanced by the knowledge gained from studying teachers and classrooms.

Teaching ought to be about adapting to and taking advantage of students' cognitive structures while maintaining high expectations regarding what the student should eventually achieve. The adaptation to which I refer is a function of the teacher's ability to be a reflective being, to attend to various circumstances, and to sort out what constraints exist (and don't exist), and to envision ways of dealing with those constraints. Consequently, I think of professional development along a continuum in which a teacher acquires the ability to monitor his/her actions in accordance with the circumstances in which he or she is teaching or learning. The development involves the teacher's flexibility of thinking and adaptability when reacting to various constraints. Attention to context is an integral part of this conceptualization of development because it leads to questions of why an activity was effective in one situation and not in another or why some students seem to develop intellectually and others do not. The question then arises of how we can conceptualize such development among teachers.

Reflective Teaching and Mathematics

Presently the notion of reflective teaching and the value derived from the act of reflection has considerable currency. There are many factors that have contributed to this. Schön's (1983, 1987) seminal work on the reflective practitioner is foremost among them. His notions of reflecting-in-action and reflecting-on-action not only honor a practitioner's tacit knowledge but highlight the practitioner's ingenuity in translating knowledge into action via reflection. To watch a world class athlete or artist perform is to remind ourselves of the apparent ease with which the individual performs. "He/she makes it look so easy." is often the conclusion reached by observers. It is that kind of ease that marks the accomplished teacher as well--an ease punctuated by reflecting-in-action and adapting to a given context. I maintain that reflection and the recognition of constraints should be a central component to any teacher education program that desires to educate teachers to become adaptive agents in the classroom.

It is worth noting that a conception of teaching rooted in adaptation is consistent with recent developments in the philosophy of mathematics. Lakatos' (1976) classic work *Proofs and Refutations* emphasizes the proposition that mathematics, at least in part, consists of a dialogue among individuals in a societal context. His emphasis on dialogue embodies a characteristic of master teaching, namely, taking a student's intellectual hand and guiding his/her intellectual development. Davis and Hersh's (1981) descriptions of mathematical experiences reinforce the notion that mathematics is a function of human experience and is a far more problematic subject than often considered by the general populace. Nearly 20 years ago Tymoczko (1979) suggested the presence of a Kuhnian paradigm shift in mathematics in which the traditional notions of intuition and logic were being supplemented by the aid of computer explorations created by humankind. Witness the proof of the four-color map theorem. In his Quebec address Tymoczko (1994) drew the following conclusion.

> Educators ignore humanistic mathematics to their peril. Without it, educators may teach students to compute and to solve, just as they can teach students to read and to write. But without it, educators can't teach students to love, to appreciate, or even to understand mathematics. (p. 339)

This apparent shift in the notion of what constitutes mathematics has not gone unnoticed in the field of mathematics education. Ernest (1991) has taken arguments about what constitutes mathematics posited by various philosophers of mathematics and discussed the relevance of these arguments for mathematics education. While we can question whether these shifts in mathematical foundations have fueled reform in the teaching of mathematics or, as Tymoczko (1986) suggests, the relationship is the other way around, what seems clear is the consistency between thinking of mathematics as a human endeavor and the notion that teaching is an exercise in adaptation.

The question arises, then, as to what theoretical constructs can guide our thinking about teaching so conceived?

The Theoretical Challenge

As a profession we have come to accept that what a teacher believes about mathematics and the teaching of mathematics is integrally related to the quality of mathematics being taught in the classroom. (See Thompson, 1992.) We know less about how those beliefs are structured and the extent to which they are permeable in the face of tensions rooted in potentially conflicting evidence. Much of this permeability requires attention to context.

We have always honored context as an important contributor to understanding mathematics. For example, it is one thing to know the Pythagorean Theorem in the sense of finding the length of the missing side of a right triangle given the lengths of the two remaining sides. It is another matter to understand the Pythagorean Theorem as a special case of Pappus' Theorem or to understand the consequences of considering the existence of the Pythagorean Theorem in the hyperbolic plane. Similarly, our students learn that the graphs of the equations $y = (1/2)x + 3$ and $y = -2 x - 1$ are perpendicular but often fail to realize that the significance of this finding is rooted in the properties of the rectangular coordinate plane. Should the corresponding x and y axes intersect at a 60° angle, what then would we observe about the interesting graphs?

I use these examples to emphasize the importance of mathematical context in teaching mathematics. We all come to believe certain things about mathematics and about teaching mathematics. To what extent are our beliefs dependent on the contexts in which we have come to hold those beliefs? Why is it that we believe the Pythagorean Theorem or any other mathematical proposition? Because someone told us it is so? Because we formally deduced it? How do we come to believe anything? These questions are relevant as we examine the influence of the contexts on what we believe and on how those beliefs are held and, concomitantly, how they might be modified.

If we honor mathematics as a human endeavor then we must see the teaching and learning of mathematics as context bound, recognizing and dealing with constraints in the classroom, and generating alternatives for addressing those constraints. The challenge theoretically speaking is to identify and apply theoretical precepts that enable us to conceptualize a teacher's ability to be adaptive and attend to contexts. I will posit several perspectives that I think have particular merit in conceptualizing teachers' professional development so conceived.

Relevant Theoretical Constructs

I give considerable credence to the notion of self autonomy for I would claim that a person's autonomy is critical to being a reflective and adaptive individual. I do not mean autonomous in a boorish sort of way but rather autonomous in that the individual is capable of integrating a variety of perspectives into a cohesive set of beliefs to which the individual is committed. Bauersfeld (1988) speaks of the importance of the social dimension as an influencing factor on how we organize ourselves. To him, patterns of interaction are a product of social interactions, forever shaping our behavior in light of the implicit obligations we encounter as social beings. No less is true of teachers and students in classrooms. The issue arises whether the individual is capable of monitoring those interactions thereby having the ability to shape them. Von Glasersfeld's (1991) notion of reflection as the ability of an individual to "step out of the stream of direct experience, to re-present a chunk of it, and to look at it as though it were direct experience, while remaining aware of the fact that it is not" (p. 47) is particularly relevant to this discussion. For von Glasersfeld, reflection is a critical ingredient for an individual's ability to re-present the schemes that guide his/her thinking and actions. Dewey (1933) suggests that reflection involves a state of doubt and the act of searching for resolution. For Dewey, reflection is an explicit act, similar in many ways to Schön's (1983) notion of reflecting-in-action which necessitates an awareness of the action taken. This awareness is quite important for it emphasizes the individual's attention to context.

Green (1971) differentiates teaching and indoctrination, the former being a matter of creating contexts in which an individual comes to know in a personal and rational way, the latter being a matter of accumulating information verified solely by an external being. We see this difference being played out daily in classrooms around the world. On the one hand, we see teachers who invite students to explore, to reason, and to conclude that propositions are true by virtue of reasoning. On the other hand, we encounter teachers who emphasize students learning proclamations whose verification rests with them or the textbooks. This latter case is anti-thetical to reform in the teaching of mathematics. The distinction that Green makes involves how one positions himself or herself relative to an external authority. If mathematics is seen as a subject that is handed down, first from professors of mathematics to teachers of mathematics and then from teachers of mathematics to the students in our schools, then mathematics is cast as a subject devoid of human invention. It relies on some external authority to verify truth, that authority being external to the student. In contrast, a teacher who encourages students to learn and own their mathematics fosters a humanistic view of mathematics as it is the individual who builds mathematical knowledge, not an external being who transmits it. Much of this contrast has been couched in the language of constructivism and appropriately so. My interest here is to focus on the way that an individual comes to know and believe. Rokeach's (1960) analysis of the open and closed mind is another means of characterizing an externally (or not) oriented person. The closed minded person denies context as a mitigating factor as their judgments are absolute. To remind ourselves of the existence of this absoluteness, we have only to recall the number of times our preservice teachers have implored us to tell them the right way to teach mathematics. In contrast the open-minded person sees shades of gray depending on the contexts in which judgments are made. For example, a beginning teacher shared with me her experience in using cooperative learning groups, a technique she initially abandoned. She saw value in using learning groups and was analytical regarding the difficulties she encountered in her failed attempt. She was planning to use them again.

Attention to context differentiates teaching from indoctrination, the notion of open minded from close minded, and, to a great extent whether constructs are permeable (Kelly, 1955) or not. The basis for schemes developed by Perry (1970) and Belenky, Clinchy, Goldberger, and Tarule (1986) are rooted in the extent to which individuals come to know based on their own reasoning processes versus relying on external sources for their knowledge. Perry's (1970) analysis of the intellectual development of male Harvard students resulted in a scheme consisting of nine positions which can be clustered into four basic categories: dualism, multiplism, relativism, and commitment. Briefly, dualism involves seeing the world in absolute terms, truth being defined by an external being. The stage of multiplism consists of recognizing that various opinions exist but truth is still defined by an external authority which has yet to reveal which of the various positions have legitimacy. Brown, Cooney, and Jones (1990) noted various studies that revealed teachers often communicate a dualistic or multiplistic orientation toward the teaching of mathematics. Relativism is the ability to assess the merits of various perspectives which are recognized as not necessarily being of equal merit. Attention to context is an integral part of this analysis. Finally, Perry's stage of commitment involves not only analyzing the merits of various perspectives but making a personal commitment to one of the positions. A teacher who asks students to consider and analyze various ways of representing data, to analyze the value of each representation, and to make a case for the most appropriate representation would be encouraging this more sophisticated way of knowing.

Belenky, et al., (1986) use the metaphor of voice to describe different ways women come to know. Oversimplified, these positions are described briefly below.

    a. Silence--one who perceives herself as having no voice
    b. Received knower--one who listens to others often at the expen se of suppressing her own voice
    c. Subjective knower--one who listens to the voice of inner self and seeks self-identify
    d. Procedural knower--one who applies the voice of reason in separate or connected ways,
    e. Constructed knower--one who integrates many voices including her own voice

The Belenky, et al. (1986) scheme is not stage like as is the Perry scheme but it does characterize different ways that women and, I submit, others as well, come to know.

A critical aspect of both the Perry and Belenky et al. schemes is a transition from relying on external authority as the primary determiner of truth to valuing one's own voice and critically incorporating voices of others into one's belief systems. This transition point, no doubt evolutionary in nature, is a critical aspect of the professional growth of teachers as it marks the point at which a teacher values his/her own voice while integrating the voices of others. In Perry's scheme, this transition occurs in the movement from the position of true Multiplism Coordinate to the more evaluative stages of Relativism and Commitment Foreseen. Perry (1970) describes this transition as a "radical reperception of all knowledge as contextual and relativistic" (p. 109) rather than "assimilate the new, in one way or another, to the fundamental dualistic structure with which they began" (p. 109). For Belenky, et al., (1986) this shift occurs in the subjective knowledge position in which "an externally oriented perspective on knowledge and truth eventuates in a new conception of truth as personal, private, and subjectively known or intuited" (p. 54). These transitions are important for they signal the emergence of the teacher's ability to be analytical and attentive to context--both prerequisites for reflection as defined by Dewey (1933) and others.

Creating a Theoretical Perspective

Over the past five years we have studied preservice secondary teachers as they progress through their program at the University of Georgia and into their first year of teaching. More recently, this research has been conducted within a National Science Foundation supported project entitled Research and Development Initiatives Applied to Teacher Education (RADIATE) directed by Patricia Wilson and myself. We have found considerable merit in using the theoretical constructs previously described to characterize teachers' professional development. Some preservice teachers' orientations reflect Perry's (1970) dualistic or early multiplistic stages in that they seem unable or unwilling to reflect on the possible interpretations of teacher education activities. Henry's orientation (Cooney, Shealy, & Arvold, in press) seems to fit this category. Henry was convinced that he knew the right way to teach when he began his formal studies in mathematics education. He opposed the use of technology, a position that he maintained throughout his teacher education program. He was steadfast in his belief that good teaching consisted of effective methods of telling students what they needed to know. Throughout his teacher education program he felt uneasy with the methods of teaching being used and suggested. He was discouraged, almost to the point of withdrawing from the program. But Henry's student teaching assignment was with a traditional teacher who conducted a very teacher-centered classroom. This affirmed Henry's belief about teaching. He was critical of his teacher education program and felt that the University instructors were off the mark and failed to appreciate what teaching was really like in the schools. His first year of teaching consisted of teaching lower level classes. Observations of his classes revealed a very teacher-centered classroom. Henry wanted to teach higher level students so that he could *really* teach mathematics. (See Cooney, et al., in press.)

Harriet (Cooney & Wilson, 1995) was another student who seemed to gain little from her teacher education program. Her mathematics education courses placed considerable emphasis on reflecting and analyzing both mathematical and pedagogical situations. Harriet, too, had definite ideas about teaching, gained mostly from her mother, a highly respected middle school mathematics teacher. Over the 15 month period in which she took most of her courses in mathematics education, Harriet was resistant to activities that called for reflection or problem posing. Her orientation toward mathematics was decidedly arithmetical and computational. She cared deeply about helping students, an attitude that translated into helping students acquire basic skills. Harriet was not unhappy about her teacher education program as much as she just seemed oblivious to it. Observational data collected during her first year of teaching were consistent with interview data gathered during her preservice program in that she conveyed a caring attitude toward the students. But the mathematics she taught in her first year of teaching was limited and computational and was taught in a teacher-centered classroom which also characterized her student teaching. (See Cooney & Wilson, 1995.)

Although Henry was critical of his teacher education program, Harriet, in general, was not. She was pleased with her the field experiences and enjoyed exposure to topics such as alternative assessment (although she used none of the ideas in her teaching) and of the opportunity to share ideas with her peers (although she seemed not to incorporate the thinking of others into her own belief structures). Like Henry, her beliefs reflected Perry's notions of dualism or early stages of multiplism.

Nancy (Shealy, 1994/1995; Cooney, et al., in press), like Harriet, was influenced by family members to become a teacher. Nancy was oriented toward doing what others expected of her. Consensuality was very important to her. She saw creativity in others but not in herself. For the most part, Nancy's knowledge about teaching stemmed from the voices of others--her peers and her professors. She accepted diversity of views but saw herself as a spectator rather than a contributor to that diversity. Differences among her peers and professors were seen as misinterpretations rather than profound disagreements. She wanted students to like and respect her. In many ways, her way of knowing reflects what Belenky, et al., (1986) call a "received knower." We have only limited information about Nancy's first year of teaching, but we do know that she experienced considerable difficulty during her first few months of teaching and that she was quite discouraged. She did not seem to command the respect or love that she had hoped would come from the students. Although Nancy was sensitive to what others said and in that sense was reflective, it was not the kind of reflection defined by Dewey (1933), Schön (1983), or von Glasersfeld (1991). Although Nancy's orientation was not dualistic, neither was it relativistic. (See, Cooney, et al., in press.)

Despite their differences, Henry, Harriet, and Nancy have much in common. Shealy (1994/1995) used the term _naive idealist_ to characterize Nancy. He saw in Nancy a certain naiveté borne out her penchant for consensuality. Nancy was not resistant to new ideas. Indeed, she willingly received ideas from others suggesting an "idealist" nature to her orientation toward teaching mathematics. In contrast, Henry and Harriet were resistant to new ideas, Henry more openly so. They were absolute in their beliefs about teaching and generally failed to take context into consideration with respect to their beliefs. In this sense they were *isolationists.* (See Cooney, Shealy, & Arvold, in press.) It is difficult to see how an isolationist could become a reflective individual. On the other hand, it is possible that the naive idealist could move into a reflective mode. For example, there is reason to believe that a naive idealist like Nancy could eventually become a reflective practitioner when she realizes that her own voice is part of the choir of voices contributing to her beliefs about teaching.

Some preservice teachers were quite reflective. Greg (Shealy, 1994/1995), for example, held the core belief that his role of teacher was to help students prepare for life. This was a permeable belief. Initially, Greg saw technology as counterproductive to students developing their reasoning skills. As he progressed through his teacher education program, which involved extensive use of technology, he modified this belief and eventually became committed to the use of technology as a means of teaching mathematics. Greg's cohesive set of beliefs were based on the core belief that he would help prepare students for life. Greg had a relativistic orientation toward various situations as evidenced by his attention to the context in which he was teaching or learning mathematics. Other preservice teachers e.g., Sally (Cooney, et al., in press) and Kyle (Cooney & Wilson, 1995) were also reflective and generally analytical. They made connections but fell short of resolving conflicts involving beliefs about mathe-matics or the teaching of mathematics. For example, Kyle felt it quite important to demonstrate to students the importance of how mathematics could be applied to real world situations yet he felt that he missed some of the basics in calculus because his calculus professor spent a considerable amount of time solving application problems. Sally, who initially seemed to be a received knower, later developed a more sophisticated conception of teaching as she reflected on her experiences as a student and as she encountered new ideas about teaching. Yet there were contradictions that Sally never resolved perhaps because she was not committed to becoming a teacher as evidenced by the fact that she decided not to teach following her graduation in mathematics education. Kyle, too, was reflective and attended to context as evidenced by statements such as, "I would use cooperative learning, but not all the time. Don't make all your examples from the book. You can tell a lot about what they know about a problem by the mathematical terminology they're using." Kyle generally connected his experiences to his core belief that mathematics should be made interesting for students by enabling them to see connections between mathematics and the real world. Yet, Kyle felt tension between the importance he placed on basic skills and his orientation toward real world connections, a tension never fully resolved during his teacher education program. He seemed to relish and prosper from reflective activities in a way Harriet did not. Yet, neither did he develop a set of beliefs into a coherent whole as Greg had done. (See Cooney & Wilson, 1995.)

Cooney, et al. (in press) suggest that there are two kinds of connectedness that characterize preservice teachers. First, there is connectedness as demonstrated by Sally and Kyle in which connections are made through reflective activity and attention to context but tensions are not resolved. We describe this as *naive connectionism*. On the other hand, a student such as Greg not only made connections but was able to take various positions and weave them into a coherent set of beliefs. This permeability of beliefs represents a more sophisticated notion of connectedness which we call *reflective connectionism*. These various positions are also reflected in our research with other preservice teachers who have participated in project RADIATE.

Although we have less information about inservice teachers, they, too, reflect these different positions. Some are resolute that they are not interested in trying various methods of teaching mathematics such as cooperative groups, technology or alternative assessment. The reasons are varied and some with reasonable justification. But often they are rooted in their unwillingness to leave the security of traditional teaching. Ellen, for example, restrained from trying different ways of teaching for fear of loosing control of what the students would learn. Observations of her teaching revealed a very teacher-centered classroom, a position from which she was very reluctant to deviate. Ellen was an isolationist of sorts. Yet other inservice teachers dismiss reasons such as time constraints and lack of support and willingly venture into the unknown, confident that good things will happen. Usually these adventurous teachers are analytical and attentive to the context in which a particular teaching technique is more likely to be effective. David, for example, continually tried different ways of assessing students' understanding, monitoring his own assessment practices in the process. David fits the mold of a reflective connectionist.

Implications for Practice

During the instructional phase of project RADIATE we placed considerable emphasis on encouraging preservice teachers to reflect on various pedagogical and mathematical situations. Much of this material is based on the notion of integrating content and pedagogy as developed by

Cooney, Brown, Dossey, Schrage, and Wittmann (1996). In one scenario, Ms. Lopez presents "the biggest box problem" to her high school algebra students.

THE BIGGEST BOX PROBLEM
What size square cut from the corners of the original square maximizes the volume of the figure formed by folding the figure into a box without a top?

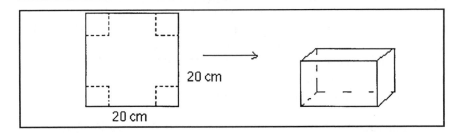

20 cm

20 cm

The students are asked to solve the problem using graphing calculators and spreadsheets. But when one student wants to know the "exact" answer, Ms. Lopez is not sure how to find that answer without using calculus which the students have not studied. As she fumbles mathematically, students become impatient and problems arise. The question then becomes one of having the preservice teachers not only solve the mathematical problem in various ways and extend it to related problems, e.g., what size cut would maximize the volume if no material was wasted, but consider the various options for handling the troublesome classroom situation.

In another situation teachers are asked to classify various representations of functions in much the way that Kelly (1955) advocates in his use of the imp grid technique. The activity below is but a sample of the materials presented in Cooney, Brown, Dossey, Schrage, and Wittmann (1996). The purpose of the activity is to consider various contexts in which functions appear and to focus on ways that functions are classified. This and other card sort activities are designed to promote recognition of the importance of classification in mathematics in general, functions in particular, and to consider how the activity can be adapted for use with other content areas in school mathematics.

THE CARD SORT PROBLEM

Consider the following six representations of functions. Group them into two or three piles using whatever criteria you wish.

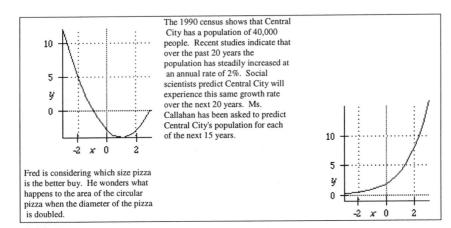

The 1990 census shows that Central City has a population of 40,000 people. Recent studies indicate that over the past 20 years the population has steadily increased at an annual rate of 2%. Social scientists predict Central City will experience this same growth rate over the next 20 years. Ms. Callahan has been asked to predict Central City's population for each of the next 15 years.

Fred is considering which size pizza is the better buy. He wonders what happens to the area of the circular pizza when the diameter of the pizza is doubled.

How many different groupings did you identify and what criteria did you use?

The following open-ended question was developed and used by the RADIATE project.

THE PENTAGON PROBLEM

Consider the pentagon drawn on a sheet of regular typing paper. What is the largest pentagon having the same shape that can be drawn on the paper?

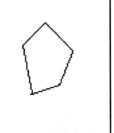

There are a variety of ways of solving the pentagon problem ranging from using dilations to using an overhead projector or even a copy machine to enlarge the figure. We ask our teachers to solve the problem and then create and analyze contexts in which the problem could be used with students. In short, they are asked to consider both the mathematical and pedagogical contexts of the problem. In all cases, convincing arguments must be given as to why the solution figure is similar to the original pentagon and why it is believed that the solution figure is the largest possible figure.

In project RADIATE preservice teachers use e-mail to communicate their reflections and analyses with the instructor and with each other. They are asked what influenced them to become mathematics teachers and what factors contributed to what they believe about mathematics. For example, they are asked whether they plan to become a mathematics teacher because of the mathematics or because of the desire to work with students. In another context, the teachers are asked to consider which of the following types of people would best fit their notion of being a mathematics teacher.

newscaster   orchestra conductor   physician   missionary   gardener

engineer   social worker   entertainer   coach

The issue is not what they pick but the rationale for their selection. The task, which serves both an instructional goal and as a source of data for research, is designed to encourage teachers to reflect on their beliefs about mathematics and teaching and to consider the implications of their biographies of becoming a mathematics teacher for the way that they might eventually teach mathematics.

A Concluding Thought

Properly conceived, teacher education ought not to be a random activity. It should take advantage of what the teacher brings to the enterprise just as we hope teachers consider what their students bring to the classroom. In part, this necessitates listening to what teachers tell us and basing teacher education on their perceived needs. Still, this cannot be the whole of teacher education as some teachers experience motivated blindness just as we do as teacher educators. That is, we sometimes lack the perception of what the real problems are because we are caught up in the particulars of a situation and fail to see the big picture.

I would claim that teacher education ought to be about providing visions of what teaching mathematics can be like in the idealized sense, of providing contexts in which teachers can define their vision and acquire the knowledge and skills to move toward that vision, and of enhancing their ability to be reflective and adaptive agents in the classroom so that they can monitor their own progress. With respect to this last point, I have argued that it is important for us to understand the struggles and tensions teachers experience as they strive to be adaptive agents and to understand what constitutes progress during that process. Such knowledge provides us a basis for conceptualizing both research and development activities in teacher education. More importantly, it provides a basis for allowing teachers to realize their potential and for them moving toward the type of professionalism of which Romberg (1988) and Noddings (1992) speak. Our tensions and struggles as teacher educators ought to focus on ways we can enable teachers to accomplish this end. For then, we will have moved teacher education beyond being activity bound and toward being a field of disciplined inquiry. What better way to spend our professional lives than finding means of enriching the professional lives of others and concomitantly enhancing our own as well?

References

Bauersfeld, H. (1988). Interaction, construction, and knowledge: Alternative perspectives for mathematics education. In D. Grouws, T. Cooney, & D. Jones (Eds.), *Perspectives on research on effective mathematics teaching* (pp. 27-46). Reston, VA: National Council of Teachers of Mathematics.

Belenky, M. F., Clinchy, B. M., Goldberger, N. R., & Tarule, J. M. (1986). *Women's ways of knowing: The development of self, voice, and mind.* New York: Basic Books.

Bromme, R. (1994). Beyond subject matter: A psychological topology of teachers' professional knowledge. In R. Biehler, R. Scholz, R. Strasser, & B. Winkelmann (Eds.) *Didactics of mathematics as a scientific discipline* (pp. 73-88). Dordrecht, The Netherlands: Kluwer Academic.

Brown, H. & Borko, C. (1992). Becoming a mathematics teacher. In D. A. Grouws (Ed.), *Handbook of research on mathematics teaching and learning* (pp. 209-242). New York: Macmillan.

Brown, S., Cooney, T., & Jones, D. (1990). Mathematics teacher education. In W.R. Houston, M. Haberman, & J. Sikula (Eds.), *Handbook of research on teacher education* (pp. 639-656). New York: Macmillan.

Cooney, T., Brown, S., Dossey, J., Schrage, G., & Wittmann, E. (1996). *Mathematics, pedagogy, and secondary teacher education: Reweaving the frayed braid.* Boston: Heinemann.

Cooney, T., Shealy, B., & Arvold, B. (in press) Conceptualizing Belief Structures of Preservice Secondary Mathematics Teachers. *Journal for Research in Mathematics Education.*

Cooney, T. & Wilson, P. (1995) On the notion of secondary preservice teachers' ways of knowing mathematics. In D. Owens, M. Reed, & G. Millsaps (Eds.)*Proceedings of the Seventeenth Annual Meeting of the North American Chapter of the International Group for the Psychology of Mathematics Education.*(pp. 2.91-2.96) ERIC, Columbus, Ohio

Davis, P. J., & Hersh, R. (1981). *The mathematical experience.* Boston: Birkhauser.

Dewey, J. (1933). *How we think: A restatement of the relation of reflective thinking to the educative process.* Boston: D. C. Heath.

Ernest, P. (1991) *The philosophy of mathematics education.* London: Falmer Press.

Good, T., Grouws, D., & Ebmeier, J. (1983). *Active mathematics teaching.* New York: Longman.

Green, T. (1971). *The activities of teaching.* New York: McGraw-Hill.

Kelly, G. A. (1955). *The psychology of personal constructs* (Vol. 1). New York: Norton.

Lappan G., & Theule-Lubienski, S. (1994). Training teachers or educating professionals? What are the issues and how are they being resolved? In D. F. Robitaille, D. H. Wheeler, & C. Kieran (Eds.), Selected lectures from the 7th International Congress on Mathematical Education (249-261). Sainte-Foy: Les Presses de L'Université Laval.

Lakatos, I. (1976). *Proofs and refutations.* New York: Cambridge University Press.

Noddings, N. (1992). Professionalization and mathematics teaching. In D. A. Grouws (Ed.), *Handbook of research on mathematics teaching and learning* (pp. 197-208). New York: Macmillan.

Perry, W. G. (1970). *Forms of intellectual and ethical development in the college years.* New York: Holt, Rinehart, & Winston.

Rokeach, M. (1960). *The open and closed mind.* New York: Basic Books.

Romberg, T. (1988). Can teachers be professional? In D. Grouws, T. Cooney, & D. Jones (Eds.), *Perspectives on research on effective mathematics teaching* (pp. 224-244). Reston, VA: National Council of Teachers of Mathematics.

Schön, D. (1983). *The reflective practitioner: How professionals think in action.* New York: Basic Books.

Schön, D. (1987). *Educating the reflective practicioner.* San Francisco: Jossey-Bass.

Shealy, B. E. (1995). *Conceptualizing the development of two first-year secondary mathematics teachers' beliefs.* (Doctoral dissertation, University of Georgia, 1994). Dissertation Abstracts International, 56-3A, 856.

Shulman, L. (1986). *Those who understand: Knowledge growth in teaching.* Educational Researcher, 15, 4-14.

Thompson, A. G. (1992). *Teachers' beliefs and conceptions: A synthesis of the research.* In D. A. Grouws (Ed.), Handbook of research on mathematics teaching and learning (pp. 127-146). New York: Macmillan.

Tymoczko, T. (1979). *The four color problem and its philosophical significance.* The Journal of Philosophy, 76(2), 57-83.

Tymoczko, T. (1986) *Making room for mathematicians in the philosophy of mathematics.* The Mathematical Intelligencer, 8(3), 44-50.

Tymoczko, T. (1994) *Humanistic and utilitarian aspects of mathematics.* In D. F. Robitaille, D. H. Wheeler, & C. Kieran (Eds.), Selected lectures from the 7th International Congress on Mathematical Education (327-340). Sainte-Foy: Les Presses de L'Université Laval.

Von Glasersfeld, E. (1991). *Abstraction, re-presentation, and reflection: An interpretation of experience and Piaget's approach.* In L. Steffe (Ed.), Epistemological foundations of mathematical experience (pp.45-67). New York: Springer-Verlag.

ETHNOMATHEMATICS: WHERE DOES IT COME FROM? AND WHERE DOES IT GO?

Ubiratan D'Ambrosio

My early thoughts on Ethnomathematics.

Mathematics, as a form of knowledge, is subordinated to the general behavior of the human being. Hence Mathematics results from the cummulative responses of the individuals and the communities to the drives towards *survival* and *transcendence.* These cummulative responses build into *culture.* In this process, individual actions are the result of different behaviors: *sensorial, intuitive* (and *instinctive), emotional* and *rational.* And individuals interact through *communication,* understood in the broad sense. Thus a body of knowledge is *generated,* which is *intellectualy* and *socially organized,* and is *diffused.* I try to understand knowledge, hence Mathematics, as the result of all these categories.

Particularly important are the relations between Mathematics and Society. I have been concerned with this issue for a long time. Five ICMEs ago, in the Third International Congress of Mathematical Education, in Karlsruhe in 1976, I was invited to prepare a paper reflecting the state of the art and to organize a discussion on the objectives and goals of Mathematics Education. In those years I had accumulated experience of work in Brazil and most Latin American countries, in the USA, in Europe and in a number of African countries. In this process, a broader conception of mathematics started to take shape in my mind. The paper, entitled "Why Teach Mathematics?", although published in several languages by UNESCO[1], did not draw attention. There I presented the basic ideas that led to the Program Ethnomathematics, mainly focusing on a socio-cultural critique of Western Mathematics. The name Ethnomathematics had not yet occurred to me.

Soon after I started to use the word Ethnomathematics. It looked adequate to me after learning about important works on Ethnomusicology,

---

[1] Ubiratan D'Ambrosio: "Overall Goals and Objectives for Mathematics Education Why Teach Mathematics?", *New Trends in Mathematics Teaching IV*, UNESCO- ICMI, Paris, 1979; pp. 180-196.

on Ethnobotanics, on Ethnohistory, on Ethnopsychiatry and on Ethnomethodology. These "ethnodisciplines" have much to do with work done by anthropologists and undeniably in my early work on Ethnomathematics I was very close to Anthropology and Ethnography. The name was explicitly used, in the broader sense I attribute to it nowadays, in the plenary talk I gave in the Fifth International Congress of Mathematics Education, ICME 5, in Adelaide, Australia, in 1984[2]. This broader sense challenges the usual way of understanding knowledge linearly, focusing on each of these categories which built into knowledge isolatedly, thus creating areas of study known as cognitive science [generation], epistemology [intellectual organization], history [social organization] and education [diffusion]. Also the drives which move materially and spiritually our species [survival and transcendence] and the dimensions of the responses to these drives [sensorial, intuitive/instinctive, emotional, rational] are usually studied as isolated categories. I see all of these categories of study as interdependent and interrelated. Thus my adoption of a holistic approach for understanding the human species. [3]

Ethnomathematics has only more recently been considered an area of Mathematics and Mathematics Education.[4] But since antiquity we recognize concerns similar to those that we label nowadays Ethnomathematics. Herodotus says: "If the river carried away any portion of a man's lot, he appeared before the king [Sesostris], and related what had happened; upon which the king sent persons to examine, and determine by measurement the exact extent of the loss; and thenceforth only such a rent was demanded of him as was proportionate to the reduced size of his land. From this practice, I think, geometry first came to be known in Egypt, whence it passed into Greece. The sun-dial, however, and the gnomon with the division of the day into twelve parts, were received by the Greeks from the Babylonian." [5] Most probably those persons whom

---

2 A short summary of the paper was published in the *Proceedings of the Fifth International Congress of Mathematical Education,* ed. Marjorie Carss, Birhäuser, Boston, 1986; pp. 1-6. The full paper was published as Socio-cultural bases for Mathematics education, UNICAMP, Campinas, 1985.

3 For a very brief and introductory discussion of the holistic approach see Ubiratan D'Ambrosio: "Uniting Reality and Action: A holistic approach to Mathematics Education" in *Teaching Teachers. Teaching Students,* eds. Lynn A. Steen and Donald J. Albers, Birkhäuser, Boston, 1981; pp. 33-42.

4 It appears Zentralblatt/Mathematics Reviews Subject Classification of 1991 as History: 01A07.

5 *The History of Herodotus,* translated by George Rawlinson, Book II, 109, Great Books of the Western World, 1994; p.70.

the king sent to examine the lands and determine the measurements were the "mathematicians" of ancient Egypt. We find similar considerations in Maya accounts.[6]

In every culture we recognize practices of measurement, of quantification, of observation, of classification, of inference. These practices were applied by distinguished members of the society for a variety of purposes, such as to record events and facts [scribes], to administer society [public officers], to change the face of the land through buildings and works [architects], to predict events and possibly to interfere with their course [diviners, magicians, astrologers, healers]. The corpora of knowledge that those distinguished members of society knew have many of the characteristics of what we call nowadays Mathematics. But they would never call themselves mathematicians nor Mathematics what they practiced. Much the less Ethnomathematics!

Throughout the history of mankind every culture has recorded, in different ways, reports of travellers who have seen or heard about ways of coping with reality and explainig facts and phenomena which are different from their own. The encounters of cultures are, evidently, responsible for the dynamics of cultural changes.

Ethnomathematics as a corpus of knowledge incorporate [Western] Mathematics.

Although I was led to use Ethnomathematics by similarity with other "ethnodisciplines", I soon recognized that it should be viewed as the recognition of different styles, forms and modes of thought [*tics*] aiming at explaining and dealing with reality [*mathema*], which were developed in different natural and cultural environments [*ethno*].[7] These developments

---

6   See Michael Closs (ed.): *Native American Mathematics,* University of Texas Press, Austin, 1986.

7   The search of a name to express all these ideas led me to commit *un abus d'étymologie* and use the Greek roots *ethno, mathema* and *tics* (a modification of *techné*). See my article "Ethnomathematics: A Research Program on the History and Philosophy of Mathematics with Pedagogical Implications." *Notices of the American Mathematical Society,* December 1992, vol. 39, n°10; pp. 1183-1185. Ethnomathematics is a reseach program, delineated in the name itself. Of course, it is supported by a broader view of History. Hence the discussions (Letters to the Editor) which appeared in subsequent issues of the Notices. Of course, it is of fundamental importance for this program to look for mathematical ideas in different cultures.

are not immune to cultural dynamics and reveal inumerous contributions from other cultures and run throughout history.

A corpus of knowledge results from a complex of needs and interests, of experiences and memories, of symbols and representations. The intangible process of imaginative thought which underlies the acquisition of knowledge distinguishes the human species from all other living creatures. The quest of men and women about themselves and the other, about nature and the cosmos, gives them their special dignity and the feeling of truth. The efforts to present images of truth in forms that will delight the mind and senses of the beholder gives meaning to humanity. Distortions in presenting these images lead to preposterousness, to arrogance and arrogation and to hegemony.

Western Mathematics does not escape from these considerations. Besides looking into the mathema of different cultures, my research program would naturally include an analysis of how these issues are seen in the development of Western Mathematics. Thus Ethnomathematics is also a research program in the History and Philosophy of Western Mathematics.

Western Mathematics developed out of the Mediterranean environment, hence they belong to the ensemble of behaviors of the Mediterranean cultures. This assertion is generally accepted. Even Herodotus comes in support of these remarks. But, for obvious reasons, those in power are zealous on reaffirming the intellectual hegemony of the West[8] . The strongest argument using to support this intellectual hegemony is Science. Hence the seemingly unchallengeable position of Mathematics.

The non-recognition of the process of cultural dynamics has lead to distorted views of history. The turning point was, undobtedly, the expansion of the West beginning in the last quarter of the XV century, which opened up the colonial enterprise.

---

8 There is a widely spread refusal to recognize this obviousness. I invite those reluctant in accepting my claim that the reasons are obvious to look into the qualitative changes in the state of the world in this century.

The colonial statute and a vision of history.

The colonial statute strongly relied on the strategies of conversion, which had been the main characteristic of both Christian and Islamic expansion, instead of allowing the flow of the process of cultural dynamics. This was particularly important in the evolution of mathematical ideas and in defining a style of mathematics education which was grounded in the ideals of the Enlightment, and acquired a firm standing in the XIX and XX centuries, clearly as a response to the major objectives of the colonial empires.

In the process of conquest it was decisive to remove historical and intellectual knowledge of the conquered, with the consequent elimination of their intellectual thrust and pride. To attain these goals, the strategy of religious conversion was efficacious. New religions brought to the new lands new conceptions of space [permanence] and of time [fluidity], which are the most relevant categories in the foundations of mathematical knowledge.

The era of political colonialism came to an end after the World War II. Since then there was the expectation of the emergence of a new protocol in economic and cultural relations. The Third World was a proposal for a new order.[9] Although the expectations are not yet realized, the process is irreversible and as a consequence there is evidence of the emergence, in just about every field of human activity, of new forms and styles of explanations, of understanding and of practices. Regretably, the former colonial mind are as yet reluctant in recognizing different styles of knowing, freed from the colonial biases.

A new historicity.

A new historicity, hitherto ignored and even repressed, now emerges and is increasingly accepted and adopted as a guide for action. It challenges truisms and social and cultural behaviors, taken as normal in modern civilization.

These studies combine the skills of the archaeologist, anthropologist, ethnographer, the conventional historian, the specialist in the disciplines,

---

9 The phrase "Third World" was coined by the Algerian writer Frantz Fanon in his book *Les damnés de la Terre,* Maspero, Paris, 1961, in writing about the newly-emergent nations after WW II. There was then an optimistic mood of hope that the era of damned peoples and cultures was approching its end.

and all this make up for a typical interdisciplinarian approach. The focuses include combining collection of data from tangible materials and from oral traditions, analysis of behavior, comparative studies and cultural dynamics. History thus gains a new breadth, for the concept of sources has to be largely amplified and the chronology entirely revised in order to include developments which followed different, in many cases unrelated, strands.

How could Mathematics stay unaffected by the opening of these new directions of critical inquiry? Thus the inevitability of Ethnomathematics. An excellent account of the trajectory of Ethnomathematics is given by Paulus Gerdes as Chapter 24 of the *International Handbook of Mathematics Education.*[10]

Ethnomathematics may be, and indeed it is, tolerated, even taught, admired and practiced in some academic environments. It is sometimes looked upon as a fashion. And regarded as politically correct. Indeed it is. But there is a cultural arrogance intrinsic to these views. There is a general acceptance and praise of the fact that some cultures show achievements that match -- even if minimally -- results of Western Mathematics, which continues to be the paragon of rationality.

No one would dare to challenge the fact that Western Mathematics is the paragon of rationality. Much of the research in Ethnomathematics today has been directed to identify results and practices that resembles Western Mathematics in non-Western cultures, and to analyze these results and practices by Western instruments. I entirely accept the need of this research. They are absolutely necessary and constitute the most accepted, attractive and indeed the most developed strand of Ethnomathematics research.

Different styles of knowing.

We now have the elements for going deeper into understanding other styles of cognition. The key issue, which sometimes is not explicit in most developments of Ethnomathematics, is the recognition that the Mathematical development of other cultures follow different tracks of intellectual inquiry, different concepts of truth, different sets of values,

---

[10] *International Handbook of Mathematics Education* , 2 volumes, eds. Alan J. Bishop et al., Kluwer Academic Publishers, Dordrecht, 1996.

different visions of the self, of the other, of mankind, of nature and the planet, and of the cosmos. These visions come all together and can not be considered isolated from each other. These visions build into the behavior of each human being and of societies and are inseparable from the history of each human being and of each society.[11] Civilization, as a category of historical analysis, is the result of this. This was the proposal implicit in Spengler's historiography and more explicit in the historiography of the Annales.

The frameworks of modern society, its science and technology, its religion and the arts, its political organization and philosophical schemes, all sprang out of the Mediterranean. From some elements an entire corpus of knowledge results.

Every culture reveals mythological attributes to facts of reality. The formalisms which derive from the mythological attributes generate distinct corpora of knowledge. Nowadays, all the discourse about indigeneous development refer to these broad aspects of knowledge.

There is a general acceptance that cultures are relative in the sense that something that is true or good in one cultural context may be false or bad in another. But this carries with it the adoption of standards of the outsider. Cultural relativism is indeed ethnocentric. And uses Mathematics as a standard, hence a demonstrative tool.

Much of the arguments are based on the claim of the universality of Mathematics, unique among all cultural manifestations. Of course, Mathematical knowledge is the same in Rome or Lapland or Amazonia, the same as myths, music and hot-dogs. But how about "producing" and "consuming" mathematics, myths, music and hot-dogs? All these cultural manifestations have to do with people.

What do the Lapps and Yanomami have to say about hot-dogs, music and myths? This is a good and respectable question. But if one puts similar questions about Mathematics, the answer is simply "this does not make sense". The claim is that Lapps and Yanomami do not have the intellectual tools to discuss Mathematics. To them we just say: learn Mathematics (of course, Western Mathematics).

---

[11] For a presentation of these issues, with special emphasis in the Navajo culture, see James F. Hamill: *Ethno-Logic. The Anthropology of Human Reasoning*, University of Illinois Press, Urbana, 1990.

These were key points in the conquest and the colonial process. Chroniclers have reported and identified all the contradictions resulting from the way the encounter was handled. To exhibit a "succesful" colonized has always been an important evidence of the magnanimity of the colonizers and the adequacy of their pedagogy. No one denies that some Lapp and Yanomami may even receive a Fields Medal! The undeniable possibilities of these results leave unresolved, indeed it masquerades, the real issue.

A theoretical approach and recent developments.

Current historiography is inadequate to deal with Ethnomathematics. The chroniclers of the conquest and colonization are not recognized sources in the History of Mathematics. Hence Ethnomathematics has been, and to a large extent continues to be, treated as curiosity, the same as ethnoreligions are seen as obscurantism and ethnomedicines as superstitions.

A theory of knowledge can be built on five main strands:

1. Description of *ad hoc* knowledge and recognition of methods.

2. How do methods give rise to theories?

3. How do theories lay the ground for invention?

4. What are the socio-political frameworks of knowledge?

5. How do we think? or How is knowledge generated?

A theory of Ethnomathematics should also focus in these five strands. These are not isolated strands. They twine and weave as in a fabric. The metaphor is specially appropriate for Ethnomathematics. How these strands come together in such an indissoluble way in Ethnomathematics is well illustrated in chapters 24 [by Paulus Gerdes], 26 [by Bill Barton] and 35 [by Ole Skovsmose and Lene Nielsen] of the *International Handbook of Mathematics Education* (see Note 9).

Much of the current research in Ethnomathematics has been directed to strand 1. This has also been the main objective of ethnography, psychology, and cultural and social anthropology. There is an increasing literature on these fields supported by the way peoples perform mathematically in different cultural environments in all the parts of the world. We have today a good amount of published research in these directions, which support Ethnomathematics, sometimes not explicitly. And a good amount of research on Ethnomathemastics following this strand.[12]

Of course, the pedagogical implications of these researchers is evident. From mere awareness of Ethnomathematics in different cultural environments to a deeper knowledge of these Ethnomathematics, it is undeniable that the classroom benefits benefits in several ways from it. We may think of a a practical and instrumental objective of Mathematics in Schools. Ethnomathematics relates to everyday uses in the more immediate cultural environment.[13] Political awareness and steps towards full citizenship, avoiding inequities, is more easily achieved, since Ethnomathematics is intrinsically critical, as a result of its dynamics. It has not the characteristics of frozen knowledge which prevails in most of academic mathematics.[14] But probably the most important is to restore cultural awareness and esteem of groups that have been subjected to iequities and discriminations which characterizes the colonial times, but still persits nowadays. This comes in the direction of strand 4.[15]

The arrogance of the dominator finds in Mathematics [academic, as practiced in the traditional school] a perfect ally. The interview with Paulo Freire, presented in this same congress, is very explicit on this. Freire reports that in his school days he never looked on Mathematics as accessible to him. This was regarded as something for individuals who were more like gods!

My early motivation for these thoughts came initially from artisan-ship (basketry in the Amazon), craftsmanship (boat builders in the Amazon basin), buildings (mosques in West Africa) and other cultural manifestations. This invited a reflexion on how these manifestations have, implicit in them, mathematical ideas and contents, which normally are not recognized,

---

[12] See Chapter 24, #4 [An Overview of Ethnomathematics Literatures] by Paulus Gerdes; op.cit. in Note 10.

[13] See the important book by Marilyn Frankenstein: *Relearning Mathematics. A different Third R: Radical Mathematics,* Free Association Books, London, 1989.

[14] The book of Marilyn Frankenstein, cited in note 13, is particularly concerned with this. See also the activities of the group "Political Dimensions of Mathematics Education", which was established and met for the first time in London, 1990.

[15] See my chapter in the NCTM Yearbook 1997.

while equivalente cultural manifestations of Western civilization support the relations between mathematics and society. We always talk about cathedrals, paintings and the medieval conceptions of God as decisive in the elaboration of what would be later called non-euclidean geometries. These facts are as common in other cultures and determine their developments of modes of explanation and of the more immediate needs of dealing with their environment [*mathema*]. Of course, this follows different paths in different cultural and natural environments. The same can be said about the techniques of registering space [cartography, maps], one of the most influential factors in the development of Western Mathematics. Corresponding techniques, with the same objectives, are present in every culture. Hence, they have determined specific developments of their "mathematical" ideas.[16] This is the typical approach to strand 1.

Strands 2. and 3. are as yet very incipient. Recent work by Samuel Lopez Bello with the Guarany Kayowáa, in Mato Grosso, of Chateubriand Amancio Nunes, with the Kaingang, in Southern Brazil, of Pedro Paulo Scandiuzzi, among the Kamaiurá nation in the Xingú region, aims at identifying the epistemological foundations of their Ethnomathematics.[17]

It is sure that a better knowledge about the generation and organization of knowledge in different cultural environments will shed light into the difficult strand 5. There is no point in attempting to understand the human mind by looking into the behavior of the dominant culture. Indeed this is preposterous. The theoretical understanding of Ethnomathematics and its history are essential elements for understanding both the human mind and the dynamics of cultural encounters.

The pedagogical benefits of the Ethnomathematics approach are easily recognized. There is considerable research supporting situated cognition and building-up on self-esteem. Both are intrinsic to the Ethnomathematics pedagogy. There has been much writing and several different proposals about this. Again, a good source of current developments is Chapter 24, by Paulus Gerdes, in the *International Handbook of Mathematics Education* (see note 12).

I see Ethnomathematics as a thriving field of research and of pedagogical practice.

---

16 The recent paper of Marcia Ascher touches this aspect of Ethnomathematics: "Models and Maps from the Marshall Islands: A Case in Ethnomathematics", *Historia Mathematica* 22, 1995; pp. 347-370. .

17 Some of these researches have been reported in the NEWSLETTER of the ISGEm. This periodical publication is, to my knowledge, the best source of new developments in Ethnomathematics.

SOME ASPECTS OF THE UNVERSITY MATHEMATICS CURRICULUM FOR ENGINEERS

Nguyen Dinh Tri
Hanoi university of technology

1. Introduction

The main objective of Hanoi University of technology is to train engineers for the country. The undergraduate education in our university is for 5 academic years, one year being composed of 2 semesters. The period of the first 2 academic years is for general education, the remaining period is for speciality education in engineering. There are 28 specialities in the university, including the speciality of applied mathematics.

Traditionally the Core Curriculum in mathematics for engineers includes :
- Calculus
- Linear algebra
- Probability and statistics
- Numerical methods

These courses are given as compulsory courses in the period of general education. In the remaining period, the departments offer specialized mathematics courses which are closely connected to the specific fields as Fourier analysis, special functions, equations of mathematical physics, differential geometry, approximation theory (splines, wavelets, ...), combinatorial optimization.

Over the years mathematics curriculum in our university have gone through a lot of changes. Due to various reasons, less probability and statistics, less numerical methods were being taught. Since 1988 the reform of curriculum in mathematics in the primary and secondary schools was carried out. Therefore we have to change our mathematics curriculum for providing a smooth transition from schools, to review the aims of mathematics education, the principles of implementation of mathematics curriculum in order to meet the requirement of our society in the coming century.

In this talk, I would like to expose what has been proposed for the core curriculum in mathematics for engineers at my university and for the mathematics curriculum of the Department of Applied Mathematics.

2. Role of mathematics in engineering education.

Throughout history it is well known that mathematics play the role of the key to engineering development and engineering development stimulates the development of mathematics .

> In the engineering curriculum, the role of mathematics is :
> - to provide a training in logical thinking
> - to develop a good level of knowledge (basic concept, basic ideas, basic techniques) and skills, of mathematics literacy
> - to provide a tool for the derivation of quantitative information about natural systems, a tool for learning across the disciplines, a modeling tool for other sciences.

We notice in the last decades the strong development of abstract activities of engineers : modeling, design of numerical models, using computers. However engineers are not mathematicians. Therefore mathematics education for engineering students is aimed not to train mathematical rigour but train the following abilities :

> - to develop mathematical thinking, to train mathematical reasoning
> - to understand elementary mathematical models of engineering and to solve them by computers
> - to formulate mathematically problems arising in engineering and to solve them by using mathematical ideas and techniques.

As the rate of technological change accelerates in the recent time, some engineering knowledges become outdated very quick. So the engineers must be able to learn independently for adapting successfully to the changes in demands upon them, to change their subjest of work. During the years of their professional lives, the engineers have to pass a number periods of technological updating for understanding new concepts and mastering new techniques. For this reason, our curriculum should be aimed to provide a training for change and not an education for life. We have to recognise and promote the role of mathematics in the continuing education of engineers in collaboration with industry.

As the specialisation in engineering increases due to the sophistication of technology, the engineers must be able to work with others, to work in team, in which engineers can collaborate, communicate easily with specialists of various domains.

3. Core Curriculum in Mathematics for engineers.
3.1 Incorporation of discrete mathematics in the Core Curriculum.

As I mentioned in the introduction, traditionally the Core Curriculum in mathematics for engineers in our university includes calculus, linear algebra, probability and statistics, numerical methods. It's clear that differential and integral calculus occupies a very important place in the mathematics curriculum in the last year of secondary school and the first year of university. Calculus provides methodology and techniques ne-cessary for the study of functions and e abstract tools which are fundamental for the further study of higher mathematics. Moreover, calculus provides the foundations for many applications of mathematics in other sciences and engineering. All these applications are based on continuous mathematical models.

With the widespread use of computers and the strong development of informatics in the last decades, the interest of discrete mathe-matics increases rapidly. Computers are discrete machines. Discrete mathe-matics play to the role of mathematical foundation of informatics. Moreover, the application of computers has stimulated the use and development of discrete mathematical models in many disciplines. So far the course of discrete mathematics is offered to the students of the third year of the department of informatics. Because computers are very efficient computing tools for all branches of sciences and technology, the students of all other departments have to learn some subjects of informatics, but they have no opportunity to learn discrete mathematics. For this reason, we would like to incorporate discrete mathematics in the core curriculum in mathematics for engineers. We prefer to develop a new mathematical course which includes algebraic structures, discrete mathematics and linear algebra. This course is given to all students of engineering of our university in the period of general education. So the new core curriculum in mathematics for engineers in our university now includes :

- calculus
- algebra (including discrete mathematics)
- probability and statistics
- numerical methods

3.2 Teaching of calculus.

We observe that engineers graduated from our university are not competent in mathematical modeling. When they investigate real problems arising in engineering, they are confused to identify the quantities which participate to the problem, to establish various relations between them, to find necessary and sufficient conditions so that the problem is well posed. The main reason of this fact is that the courses of calculus offered in our university are too abstract. In the lectures the mathematics teachers try to define precisely basic concepts of calculus, to expose main ideas, main methods, main results relative to these notions. Due to the pressure of time and the lack of knowledges of applications of calculus in various domains of applied sciences of professors, these applications are considered as auxiliary in the lectures of calculus. Our students are able to find the derivative or the integral of a wide class of functions, to integrate some classes of differential equation, but only very few students understand deeply the practical origin of derivative or integral and can apply these notions in the investigation of real problems in physics, mechanics, engineering. In the courses of calculus in our university, the demand of mathematical rigour in some fundamental aspect like in the construction of real number should be decreased, but the importance of calculus in various areas of applied sciences and and technology should be increased. To train engineers for the future, it is necessary to provide them the knowledges on the interpenetration between mathematics and other branches of sciences and technology, on the industrial dimension of mathematics, on the development of mathematical tools and the application of these tools in the resolution of mathematical models. The control of students knowleges should include some miniprojects which integrate the following aspects : modeling, numerical resolution of mathematical models by computers, discussion on received results. The project work should be included as a component of the mathematics curriculum. The project work contributes :

- to develop autonomy, initiative and personal work of students.
- to enhance the work in team
- to extend cultural perspectives of mathematics, of mathematics application, to promote the relevance of mathematics to industrial needs.

3.3 Core Curriculum in Calculus.

Calculus I. *Simple variable calculus*

* Sequences
* Functions : concept of mapping, function, graphical representation
* Differential calculus : definition and rules of differentiation, derivative of inverse function, higher derivatives, Taylor and Mac Laurin expansion, approximation and asymptotic behaviour of functions
* Integral calculus : indefinite integral and definite integral, fundamental theorems and standard techniques of integration. Engineering applications. Improper integrals

Calculus II. *Multivariable calculus*

* Function of n ($\geq$ 2) variables : representation, partial derivative, total differential, change of variables, implicit function theorem, Taylor expansion, extrema, Lagrange multipliers.
* Multiple integral : double integral, triple integral, change of variables
* Line integral, Green's theorem, surface integral, Stoke's theorem and Gauss theorem, with physical signifiance

Calculus III. *Infinite series. Ordinary differential equations (ODE)*

* Infinite series : convergence tests, absolute convergence, uniform convergence of series of functions, power series
* Fourier series
* ODE : first order differential equation, second order linear diferential equations with constant coeffcients, systems of differential equations.

3.4 Core Curriculum in Algebra

Set and mappings.
* Mathematical logic : propositions, connectives, truth-tables, rules, of inference, quantifiers, introduction to Boolean algebra, reasoning by recurrence
* Set : operations on sets, relation to Boolean algebra.
* Binary relations : equivalence, order

* Mapping : injection, surjection, bijection.
Combinatorics and graph.

* Counting techniques, the product rule, inclusion-exclusion
* Arrangenent, permutation, combination
* Graphs, directed, undirected, trees

Algebraic structure

* Group
* Ring
* Field

Linear space and transformations

* Space,linear independence, bases, subspaces, scalar product, Euclidean norm
* Linear transformation, matrix representation, change of basis, ortho-gonal transformation

Matrix algebra and system of linear equations

* Matrix representation of system of linear equations, solution of system of linear equations, by elimination method.
* Matrix algebra, inversion, rank
* Determinants
* Decomposition methods. Consistency, uniqueness of solution

The eigenvalue problem

* Algebraic methods for determining eigenvalues and eigenvectors
* Reduction a matrix to diagonal and Jordan form
* Quadratic form

3.5 Core Curriculum in Probability and Statistics.

Probability and basic laws

* Random events
* Definition of probability. Frequentist and combinatorial approaches
* Conditional probability

Random variable and probability distribution

* One-dimensional random variables. Basic distributions (binomial, Poisson, exponential, normal, ...)
* Multidimentional random variables. Conditional distributions, inpendences, linear combinations of random variables
The law of large numbers and the central limit theorem

Statistical treatment.

* Classical treatment : point estimation of parameters, unbiased estimator, consistent estimator, the maximum likelihood method, umbiased estimation of expectation and variance, estimating parameters of specific distributions, the confidence intervals for the mean and variance, for the parameters of the above distributions
* Bayesian treament

Estimation

* Point estimation
* Interval of confidence

Hypothesis testing

Linear regression

3.6 Core Curriculum in Numerical Methods

* Errors
* Numerical solution of algebraic and transcendantal equation : iteration, chord, bissection, Newton method, order of convergence
* Numerical solution of system of linear equations, method of iteration
*Polynomial interpolation
*Numerical solution of ordinary differential equation : Euler method, Runge-Kutta method.

4.Structure of the courses of Mathematics of the Department of Applied Mathematics

Applied mathematics is concerned with the development of mathematics models and techniques with applications to the resolution of problems arising in other sciences as physics, mechanics, computer sciences, in engineering. Computational techniques are of great interest to Applied Mathematics

The objective of the Department of Applied Mathematics is to train mathematics engineers. They have to master :
- mathematical aspects of modeling : differential and stochastic models
- scientific, economic computing and informatics
- some disciplines in applied areas : physics, mechanics, ...

The mathematics courses offered in the period of speciality education for Applied Mathematics are aimed to provide knowledges of higher level of abstraction, of deeper level of significance in mathematical modeling, in solving these models by mathematical tools, by computer. The courses comprises four areas of study : basic concepts, mathematical methods, computing and some domains of applied sciences.

The list of courses offered in the third and fourth years is as follows :

- Advanced discrete mathematics
- Data structure and algorithm
- Optimization
- Combinatorial algorithms
- Theory of programmation
- Functional analysis
- Equations of mathematical physics
- Advanced numerical analysis
- Finite difference and finite element methods
- Mathematical statistics and data analysis
- Time series
- System and control
- Economical models
- Signal processing
- Fluid dynamics
- Mechanics of deformable media

In the first semester of the fifth year, a reasonable flexibility in content is allowed. The last semester is for the memoir writing.

References

1. K.D. Graf, R. Frazer, ... : The effect of computers on the school mathematics curriculum. In: B. Cornu and A. Ralston, (edi), *The Influence of computers and informatics on mathematics and its teaching.*UNESCO, Document series No 44, 57-79

2. S.B. Seidman, M.D. Rice : *A fundamental course in Higher Mathematics incorporating discrete and continuous themes.* In: B. Cornu and A. Ralston, (edi), *The Influence of computers and informatics on mathematics and its teaching.* UNESCO, Document series 44, 80-86

3. John Mack. *Mathematics and Education for Mathematicians.* Proceedings of SEACME 6, Surabaya, 28-39

4. Hiroshi Fujita. *Principles in organizing the university mathematics curriculum for scientists and engineers.* SEACME 6, Surabaya, 1-11

GEOMETRY IN PARAMETER SPACES
A standard geometrization process

A. Douady

1. Introduction

Since the beginning of the 20th century – I could say following Hilbert– geometry has proved to be an extremely efficient way to tackle many problems in mathematics or other sciences. In many cases, it is not in Euclidean geometry in dimension 2 or 3 that one ends up, but in geometry in some space adapted to the problem –sometimes a space of parameters constructed ad hoc.

In very general terms, the strategy in this geometrization process, i.e. in the transfer from the initial framework to a geometrical framework, can be described as follows:

The initial problem is formulated as to find a configuration (in the given situation) satisfying certain requirements. One looks at the set of all configurations of that nature. One then identifies this set with some subset E of a space in which one is used to work geometrically (typically $\mathbf{R^n}$); the set E is then a *parameter space* for the configurations considered. The problem then becomes to construct a point in E with certain geometrical properties.

In this talk, we give three examples of implementation of this strategy:
1) A property of circle intersections
2) Possibility of reversing a line without letting it be tangent to a given curve;
3) Existence polynomials of degree 4 with prescribed critical values.

In the first two examples, the initial framework is already geometrical, but transfer to another geometrical framework is necessary (or at least useful) to solve the problem. In other words, we have to provide an already geometrical problem with a new geometrization.

In the third example, the initial problem is algebraic. It could be easily formulated in geometrical terms, but the geometric representation we use is different from the obvious one.

In each of these examples, the parameter space E is a part of $\mathbf{R}^3$ or $\mathbf{R}^2$, but it is easy to imagine that it is not always so. For instance, the set of possible orbits of a planet has dimension 5; in robotics, one has to deal with the set of all possible positions of a solid. This is a 6 dimensional manifold, which can be imbedded in $\mathbf{R}^9$.

We shall first give the statement of the problems in their initial framework, to allow the reader to investigate various ways to tackle them before looking at the one we propose.

2. The Problems
2.1 Circle intersections.

Let C_1, C_2, C_3, C_4 be 4 circles in the plane. We suppose that:
C_1 and C_2 intersect in a_1, a_2 ;
C_3 and C_4 intersect in a_3, a_4 ;
C_1 and C_3 intersect in b_1, b_2 ;
C_2 and C_4 intersect in b_3, b_4 (Fig. 1).

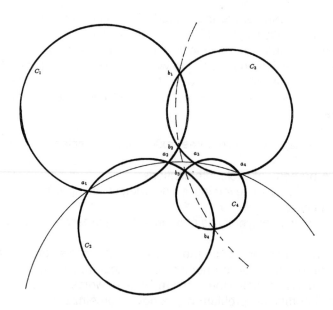

[Fig. 1]
Prove that, if a_1, a_2, a_3, a_4 are on a circle or a line, then b_1, b_2, b_3, b_4 are on a circle or a line.

2.2 Reversing a line (*a problem suggested by David Epstein*)

This problem has 3 versions. Consider in the plane an arc of curve Γ which is one of Γ_1, Γ_2, Γ_3 drawn in Fig. 2, and a straight line D not intersecting Γ. Is it possible to move D continuously and to take it back to its initial position with orientation reversed, without letting it to be tangent to Γ at any time during the movement ?

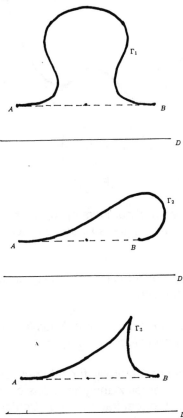

[Fig. 2]

Hint. The answer is not the same for the 3 curves: there are 2 yes and 1 no, or the other was around. Before you look at section 4, try to make guesses.

2.3 Polynomial with prescribed critical values.

Let f be a monic polynomial of degree 4 with coefficients in **R**:

$$f(x) = x^4 + a_3 x^3 + a_2 x^2 + a_1 x + a_0.$$

("monic" means $a_4 = 1$). We suppose that the derivative f' has 3 real roots $c_1 < c_2 < c_3$ (critical points). Then the critical value $v_i = f(c_i)$ satisfy $v_2 > v_1$ and $v_2 > v_3$ (Fig. 3).

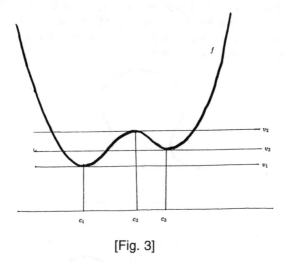

[Fig. 3]

Question 1: *Given real numbers v_1, v_2, v_3 such that $v_2 > v_1$ and $v_2 > v_3$, can one chose a_0, a_1, a_2, a_3, so that the critical values of f are v_1, v_2, v_3 ?*

If we translate f horizontally, i.e. replace it by $x \to f(x - b)$, the critical values are unchanged.

Question 2: *Is a monic degree 4 polynomial uniquely determined up to translation by its critical values v_1, v_2, v_3 ?*

This problem arises naturally for arbitrary degree d. There is a classical proof involving complex analysis. It was proposed as a challenge to get a proof staying in the real framework. P. Sentenac and I proposed a way to do so, I present here the case of degree 4, the simplest non trivial one.

3. Travel to the country of circles
3.0. Preliminary considerations

We are considering the first problem, that on circle intersections. This is a problem on circles: supposing that a_1, a_2, a_3, a_4 are on a circle, we are looking for a circle passing through b_1, b_2, b_3, b_4 (or at least trying to prove the existence of such a circle).

According to our general strategy, we have to look at the set C of all circles in the plane.

3.1. First attempt

A circle is determined by its center and its radius. Let us denote by $C_{a,b,r}$ the circle of radius r whose center has coordinates (a,b). Representing the circle $C_{a,b,r}$ by the point (a,b,r) of $\mathbf{R}3$, we identify the set C with the half space $\mathbf{R}^2 \times \mathbf{R}_+$ (the points on the frontier plane represent point circles).

This is very natural, but it leads to some trouble. Remember we are looking for a circle passing through 4 points. Given a point $P = (x,y)$ in the plane $\mathbf{R}^2$, the set $C(P)$ of circles passing through P is represented by the cone

$$\{(a,b,r) \mid r = d((x,y),(a,b))\}$$

The set $C(P,Q)$ of circles passing through two points P and Q is a branch of hyperbola. For 4 points, we are looking at the intersection of two hyperbolas in $\mathbf{R}^3$, this is very complicated, and we soon get drowned.

So we have to look for a more clever representation of the set C.

3.2. More algebraically

The equation of the circle $C_{a,b,r}$ is $(x - a)^2 + (y - b)^2 = r^2$, i. e.

$$(*) \qquad x^2 + y^2 - 2ax - 2by + c = 0$$

where $c = a^2 + b^2 - r^2$. Any equation of the form (*) describes a circle, provided $c \leq a^2+b^2$ (accepting point circles). Representing $C_{a,b,r}$ by the point (a,b,c) in $\mathbf{R}^3$, we identify C with the region exterior to the paraboloid Σ of equation $c=a^2+b^2$. Points on the paraboloid represent point circles; points in the region inside represent imaginary circles with no real points.

What are the goods and the odds of this new representation?

Disadvantages: This seems less natural. Moreover we get a region in $\mathbf{R}^3$ which is harder to describe.

Advantage: The set $C(P)$ is now a plane, namely that of equation (*) where a,b and c are the variables, x and y being considered as constant.

This plane touches the paraboloid Σ at the point representing the point circle $\{P\}$, otherwise it lies in region exterior to Σ. Given two points P and Q, the set $C(P,Q)$ becomes the intersection of two planes, i.e. a straight line (lying entirely in the region exterior to Σ).

3.3. Solving the problem

We use the second representation and identify C with the region E in $\mathbf{R}^3$ exterior to Σ. A circle C in $\mathbf{R}^2$ is represented by a point in E that we denote also by C. Given two points C and C' in $\mathbf{R}^3$, we denote by $D_{c,c'}$ the line passing through C and C'.

To say that a_1, a_2, a_3, a_4 are on a circle G means that there is a point $\Gamma \in$ E which lies both on the line D_{c_1,c_2} and on D_{c_3,c_4}, i.e. that these two lines meet. It implies that the points c_1, c_2, c_3, c_4 are in a plane, and therefore that the lines D_{c_1,c_3} and D_{c_2,c_4} meet or are parallel. If they meet in a point Γ', this point represent a circle passing through b_1, b_2, b_3, b_4.

Remains to see that, if the lines mentioned are parallel, the points b_i are on a line. There are several ways to show that, we will propose a limit argument.

3.4. Limit argument

Suppose that the lines $D_{c_1 c_3}$ and $D_{c_2 c_4}$ are parallel in a plane H. Move slightly the point C_4 in the plane H to a point $C_4(\varepsilon)$ so that the two lines intersect. Then we get 4 points b_1, b_2, $b_3(\varepsilon)$, $b_4(\varepsilon)$ on a circle. When e tends to 0, the points $b_3(\varepsilon)$ and $b_4(\varepsilon)$ respectively, while b_1 and b_2 remain fixed. Therefore b_1, b_2, b_3, b_4 are on a circle or on a line.

In the same way we can prove the converse. Applying it to $a1,...,a4$, we get that if these points are on a line, the lines D_{c_1,c_2} and D_{c_3,c_4} are parallel, thus the points $C_1,...,C_4$ are in a plane. We have seen that this implies that $b_1,...,b_4$ are on a circle or on a line.

This finishes the proof of the result.

4. Movement of a line
4.1. An unexpected Moebius strip

The problem suggested by D. Epstein is a problem about lines in the plane $\mathbf{R}^2$, so we have to look at the space D of lines in the plane.

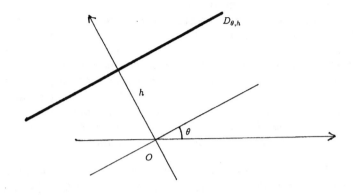

[Fig. 4]

Given θ and h in $\mathbf{R}$, let $D_{\theta,h}$ denote the line making an angle θ with the first axis Ox, and such that the projection H of O on it has abscissa h on the axis making angle $\theta + \pi/2$ with Ox (Fig. 4). Any line in the plane can be written as $D_{\theta,h}$, and this in several ways: given (θ,h) in $\mathbf{R}^2$, the pairs (θ',h') such that $D_{\theta',h'} = D_{\theta,h}$ are the $(\theta+2k\pi,h)$ and the $(\theta + (2k+1)\pi, -h)$. So D can be viewed as the quotient of $\mathbf{R}^2$ by the equivalence relation defined this way, or if you prefer as the strip $[0, \pi] \times \mathbf{R}$ with $(0, h)$ and $(\pi, -h)$ identified.

Note that $\mathbf{R}$ is homeomorphic to the open interval $]-1, 1[$ (and we can choose a homeomorphism ϕ so that $\phi(-h) = -\phi(h)$), so the strip $[0, \pi] \times \mathbf{R}$ is homeomorphic to $[0, \pi] \times]-1, 1[$, and finally D can be identified to $[0, \pi] \times [-1,1[$ with $(0,y)$ and $(\pi, -y)$ identified, i.e. to a Moebius strip with its boundary curve removed. (Fig. 5)

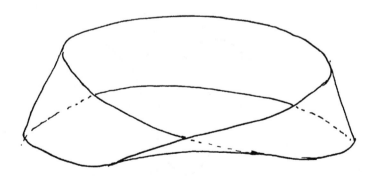

[Fig. 5]

Here I have a scruple, I feel I am cheating a little bit: D has been defined only as a set. But the statement of the problem implicitely involves a topology on D, since it mentions a continuous movement of a line, i.e. of a point in D. To be rigourous, we should define the natural topology on D, and show that the identification above is a homeomorphism. I don't want to develop on this theme here. We shall admit that saying that we have a continuous movement t $\rightarrow$ D_t parametrized by [0,1] means that $D_t = D_{\theta(t),h(t)}$ with $\theta(t)$ and $h(t)$ depending continuously on t, and that the requirement that D_t comes back to its initial position with orientation reversed means that $\theta(1) = \theta(0) + (2k + 1)\pi$ for some k, and $h(1) = -h(0)$.

So the question is whether it is possible to have such a movement avoiding the forbidden set: the set of lines tangent to Γ. What we have to do now is to describe this forbidden set in the 3 cases $\Gamma = \Gamma_1, \Gamma_2, \Gamma_3$.

4.2. Description of the forbidden set

Say we take as origin the midpoint O between the extremities A and B of Γ, and the axis Ox to be the line AB.

Let $M(s)$ be a point which ranges over Γ when s ranges from 0 to 1. Write the tangent to Γ as $D_{\theta^*(s),h^*(s)}$ with θ^* and h^* continuous. Then $(\theta^*(s),h^*(s))$ describes in $\mathbf{R}^2$ an arc Γ^*, and the forbidden set in $\mathbf{R}^2$ is the union Γ^{**} of copies of Γ^* translated by $(\theta,h) \rightarrow (\theta + k\pi, (-1)^k h)$ for $k \in \mathbf{Z}$. The sets Γ^*_ι and Γ^{**}_ι have the aspect drawned in Fig. 6.

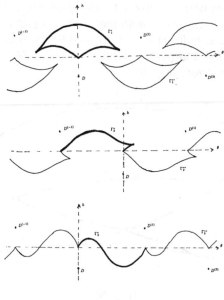

[Fig. 6]

The question is then whether it is possible to join the point D_0 to some $DO^{(k)}$ with k odd without meeting $\Gamma\iota^{**}$. It is clear on the picture that this is possible for $\iota = 1$ and impossible for $\iota = 2$ and $\iota = 3$.

4.3. Proofs

Let us try to transform this visual evidence into a proof. We start by Γ_3, for which it is the easiest. In this case θ^* is monotonous and ranges from 0 to π, so it is a homeomorphism $[0,1] \to [0,\pi]$. Therefore Γ_3^* is the graph of a continuous function $h : [0,\pi] \to \mathbf{R}$ with $\eta(0) = \eta(\pi) = 0$, and Γ^{**}_3 is the graph of the same function extended to $\mathbf{R}$ by $\eta(\theta+\kappa\pi) = (-1)\kappa\eta(\theta)$. Now, supposing we have q and h continuous $[0,1] \to \mathbf{R}$ with $\theta(1) = \theta(0) + (2\kappa+1)\pi$ and $h(1) = -h(0)$, then $h(f) - \eta(\theta(t))$ is continuous and takes opposite values at 0 and 1, so it must vanish somewhere. This means that there is a $t \in [0,1]$ so that $(\theta(t), h(t)) \in \Gamma^*_3$.   q.e.d.

Let us come to $\Gamma 2$. The important feature is that $\theta^*(s)$ varies continuously from 0 to $-\pi$ (it would work also with any $k\pi$, $k \neq 0$ in $\mathbf{Z}$). We shall use only this fact; maybe we could get a slightly simpler proof using other particularities of the situation, I think it is not worth trying.

We extend θ^* and h^* to $\mathbf{R}$ by $\theta^*(s+k)=\theta^*(s)-k\pi$ and $h*(s+k)=(-1)^k h*(s)$. The set Γ^{**} is then the image of $\mathbf{R}$ by $s \to (\theta^*(s),h^*(s))$. The functions $s \to \theta^*(s) + \pi s$ and h^* are continuous and periodic, thus bounded.

By hypothesis $D = D_{\theta(0),h(0)}$ does not intersect Γ, and we can suppose that $D_{\theta(0),h}$ does not intersect Γ for $h \leq 0$. We extend $t \to (\theta(t),h(t))$ by

$(\theta(t),h(t))$ $=$ $(\theta(0),h(0) + t)$ for $t \leq 0$;
                    $=$ $(\theta(1),h(1) + t - 1)$ for $t \geq 1$.

The result then follows from the following lemma (applied to $(-\theta^*,h^*,-\theta,h)$:

Crossing lemma.- Let $s \to (x1(s),y1(s))$ and $t \to (x_2(s),y_2(s))$ be two continuous maps $\mathbf{R} \to \mathbf{R}^2$. Suppose that the functions y_1 and x_2 are bounded, and that x_1 and y_2 range from $-\infty$ to $+\infty$. Then the two path cross, i.e. there is a pair (s,t) such that $(x_1(s),y_1(s)) = (x_2(t),y_2(t))$.

This lemma is classical in topology. The usual proof involves the notion of index of a loop around a point (number of turns).

4.4. The case of Γ_1

For the Ω-shaped curve Γ_1, the movement is possible. We can just exhibit it in the initial framework:

As the picture is drawned, the line AB and the two inflexion tangent limit a triangle below AB. Move D parallel to itself so that it passes through some point in this triangle, and then just rotate it by half a turn.

Remark: If we would take a curve Γ'_1 looking like Γ_1 but with the inflexion tangent intersecting Γ again, the result would be different: then there would be a double tangent L, and we could extract from $\Gamma'_1 \cup L$ a curve Γ'_3 looking like Γ_3 (but containing a line segment), and the answer would be NO as for Γ_3. (Fig. 7)

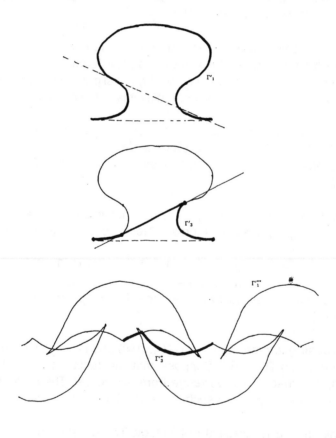

[Fig. 7]

5. The problem on degree 4 polynomials
5.1. Natural tackling of the problem

The set of monic polynomials of degree 4 is naturally identified to $\mathbf{R}^4$ via $f \to (a_0,...,a_3)$. In this set, polynomials having 3 distinct real critical points form an open set defined by a complicated inequation.

But we are interested only by polynomials up to horizontal translation: we could restrict to *centered* polynomials, i.e. those with $a_3 = 0$. Indeed each class modulo horizontal translation contains a unique centered polynomial. The centered monic polynomials of degree 4 form a space $\mathbf{R}^3$, in which those with 3 distinct critical points form the open set Ω defined by $a^3_2 - 27a^2_1 > 0$.

We want to show that the map $f \to (v_1,v_2,v_3)$ from Ω to $\{(v_1,v_2,v_3)|v_2>v_1,v_2,v_3\}$ is bijective. This is the natural way of tackling the problem, but we shall proceed in a slightly different way.

5.2. First transformation

We first draw our attention on the invariance of the problem by vertical translation. Indeed, if we have a polynomial f such that v_2-v_1 and v_2-v_3 have the prescribed values, then it is not difficult to adjust f by adding a constant so that v_1, v_2, v_3 have the prescribed values.

So we look at f up to vertical translation, i.e. we look at

$$f' = 4x^3 + 3a_3x^2 + 2a_2x + a_1$$

The critical points are the zeroes of f', we require that there are 3 distinct real ones $c_1 < c_2 < c_3$. Then v_2-v_1 and v_2-v_3 can be interpreted as areas:

$$v_2 - v_1 = A_1 = \int_{c_2 c_1} f'$$

$$v_2 - v_3 = A_2 = \int_{c_3 c_2} |f'|$$

So we can formulate the problem in the equivalent form:

Question: *Given A_1 and A_2 both positive, does there exist a polynomial $g = 4x^3 + b_2x^2 + b_1x + b_0$ with 3 real roots $c_1 < c_2 < c_3$ such that $\int_{c_2 c_1} g = A_1$, $\int_{c_3 c_2} = -A_2$? Is such a polynomial unique up to horizontal translation?*

5.3. Second transformation

We now take into account the invariance by horizontal translation. Note that $g = f'$ is given by

$$g(x) = 4(x - c_1)(x - c_2)(x - c_3)$$

Take as unknown
$l_1 = c_2 - c_1 > 0$
$l_2 = c_3 - c_2 > 0.$

These numbers determine f' up to horizontal translation. So they allow to compute A_1 and A_2, and we can look at the map

$$\Phi : (l_1, l_2) \rightarrow (A_1, A_2)$$

from $\mathbf{R}^2_+$ too itself. The question is now:
Question: *Is Φ a bijection? a homeomorphism?*

5.4. Study of the map Φ

Lemma 1 (homogeneity) .- If Δ is a half line from O, so is $\Phi(\Delta)$.
Proof: If $\sim l_1 = \lambda l_1$ and $\sim l_2 = \lambda l_2$, the graph of $\sim g$ is obtained from that of g by $x \rightarrow \lambda x$, $y \rightarrow \lambda^3 y$. So $\sim A_1 = \lambda^4 A_1$, $\sim A_2 = \lambda^4 A_2$.

Lemma 2.- If you increase l_1 and decrease l_2 so that $l_1 + l_2$ is unchanged, then A_1 increases and A_2 decreases.

Proof: Take $\sim c_1 = c_1$, $\sim c_3 = c_3$ and $\sim c_2 = c_2$, and define $\sim g$ from $\sim c_2$, $\sim c_2$, $\sim c_3$. Then $\sim g - g$ is a polynomial of degree 2 vanishing at c_1 and c_2, so it has a constant sign on $]c_1, c_3[$. This sign is it is > 0, because it is at $\sim c_2$.
Then $\sim A_1 = \int \sim c_2 c_1 \sim g > \int c_2 c_1 \sim g > A_1$
and $\sim A_2 = \int c_3 \sim c_2 |\sim g| < \int c_3 c_2 |\sim g| < A_2.$

5.5. What for d > 4 ?

For $d > 4$, the problem can be treated along the same lines, but we must make use of more sophisticated notions.

We define in the same way a map Φ from $\mathbf{R}^{d-2}_+$ to itself. Starting from a point inside $\mathbf{R}^{d-2}_{+}$, we can look at the linear map tangent to Φ at this point. By an argument similar to that of Lemma 2, we can see that this linear map is an isomorphism. Therefore Φ is a local homeomorphism.

Using homogeneity and extension to the boundary, we see that Φ is a proper map (i.e. the inverse image of a compact set is compact). Therefore it is a finite covering map, and since $\mathbf{R}^{d-2}_+$ is simply connected, Φ is a homeomorphism.

Conclusion

In the 3 examples treated here, we consider the set of objects (circles, lines, polynomials) of interest for the problem. This is an abstract set; in order to be able to work in it, we have to make a chart, i.e. to define a correspondance with a set of points in a space with already a geommetrical structure, or with a numerical set (typically a part of $\mathbf{R}^n$).

The choice of the chart is the crucial point. It is where one can show one's skill. It is not always the most natural choice which is the most efficient, as we have seen in examples 1 and 3. Sometimes, the correspondance is not bijective, as in example 2: the set of lines can be identified with a quotient of $\mathbf{R}^2$ homeomorphic to a Moebius strip, but the work actually takes place in its covering space $\mathbf{R}^2$.

In these examples, the work is rather easy after a proper geometrization has taken place. Certainly it is not always so, but such a process is often a very good first step.

SOCIAL CONSTRUCTIVISM AS A PHILOSOPHY OF MATHEMATICS

Paul Ernest
University of Exeter, UK

Introduction

My aim in this paper is two-fold. First to give a written report of my conference lecture at the International Congress on Mathematical Education in Seville. Second, to fill in a little the sketch of my current work in developing a social constructivist philosophy of mathematics which I presented there, briefly pointing to some the implications for mathematics education. But initially I need to spell out the problematic present position in the philosophy of mathematics and the need for a new approach.

Much of modern epistemology has understood knowledge to be made up of knowledge claims with ironclad warrants and justifications (Kant 1950, Moore 1959, Klein 1981). Thus, Ayer (1946), for example, claims that empirical knowledge of the world can attain certainty, and that the truths of mathematics and logic are both certain and necessary. However there is a sceptical tradition in epistemology stretching back to the presocratic philosophers and strongly present in contemporary philosophy which regards all knowledge as fallible and based on revisable foundations (Bernstein 1983, Everitt and Fisher 1995, Wittgenstein 1953, Rorty 1979, Rosen 1989). In the philosophy of science there has similarly been a shift in the leading views of knowledge away from infallibility and certainty (Feyerabend 1975, Kuhn 1970, Popper 1959). Likewise, in the sociology of knowledge and social studies of science there is a consensus that far from being necessary, scientific and mathematical knowledge, and indeed all forms of knowledge, are contingent social constructions (Bloor 1991, Fuller 1988, Latour 1993, Lyotard 1984).

Traditionally, mathematical knowledge has been understood as universal and absolute knowledge, whose epistemological status sets it above all other forms of knowledge. The traditional foundationalist schools of formalism, logicism and intuitionism sought to establish the absolute validity of mathematical knowledge. Although modern philosophy of mathematics has in part moved away from this dogma, it is still very influential, and needs to be critiqued. So I wish to begin by summarising some of the arguments against absolutism, as this position has been termed (Ernest 1991).

My argument is that the claim of the absolute validity for mathematical knowledge cannot be sustained. The primary basis for this claim is that mathematical knowledge rests on certain and necessary proofs. But proof in mathematics assumes the truth, correctness, or consistency of an underlying axiom set, and of logical rules and axioms or postulates. The truth of this basis cannot be established on pain of creating a vicious circle (Lakatos 1962). Overall the correctness or consistency of mathematical theories and truths cannot be established in non-trivial cases (Gödel 1931).

Thus mathematical proof can be taken as absolutely correct only if certain unjustified assumptions made. First, it must be assumed that absolute standards of rigour are attained. But there are no grounds for assuming this (Tymoczko 1986). Second, it must be assumed that any proof can be made perfectly rigorous. But virtually all accepted mathematical proofs are informal proofs, and there are no grounds for assuming that such a transformation can be made (Lakatos 1978). Third, it must be assumed that the checking of rigorous proofs for correctness is possible. But checking is already deeply problematic, and the further formalising of informal proofs will lengthen them and make checking practically impossible (MacKenzie 1993)

A final but inescapably telling argument will suffice to show that absolute rigour is an unattainable ideal. The argument is well-known. Mathematical proof as an epistemological warrant depends on the assumed safety of axiomatic systems and proof in mathematics. But Gödel's (1931) second incompleteness theorem means that consistency and hence establishing the correctness and safety of mathematical systems is indemonstrable. We can never be sure mathematics theories are safe, and hence we cannot claim their correctness, let alone their necessity or certainty. These arguments are necessarily compressed here, but are treated fully elsewhere (e.g., Ernest 1991, 1997). So the claim of absolute validity for mathematical knowledge is unjustified.

The past two decades has seen a growing acceptance of the weakness of absolutist accounts of mathematical knowledge and of the impossibility in establishing knowledge claims absolutely. In particular the 'maverick' tradition, to use Kitcher and Aspray's (1988) phrase, in the philosophy of mathematics questions the absolute status of mathematical knowledge and suggest that a reconceptualisation of philosophy of mathematics is needed (Davis and Hersh 1980, Lakatos 1976, Tymoczko 1986, Kitcher 1984, Ernest 1997). The main claim of the 'maverick' tradition is that mathe-matical knowledge is fallible. In addition, the narrow academic focus of the philosophy of mathematics on foundationist epistemology or on platonistic ontology to the exclusion of the history and practice of mathematics, is viewed by many as misguided. However there is still a heated controversy over whether the acceptance of mathematical knowledge is at root a social process, or whether proofs and hence the justification of mathematical knowledge are based on reason and logic alone, no matter how imperfectly these ideals are realised in actuality.

WHAT IS FALLIBILISM?

The term 'fallibilism' is ambiguous, and leads to some confusion, so it is useful to distinguish three versions. First of all, there is what might be termed fallibilism1 which asserts that mistakes occur in mathematics because humans make mistakes. Fallibilism1 is trivial because clearly human beings are fallible, i.e., make mistakes, and all philosophies of mathematics would accept this. So this version is discarded with no further ado.

Secondly, there is fallibilism2 which claims that mathematical knowledge is or may be, of itself, false. Two possible versions of this might be distinguished. The first subcase is the claim that all mathematical knowledge is or may turn out to be false. This is easily rejected because it is absurd to say that 2+2=4 is or may be absolutely false. The second weaker subcase is the claim that some mathematical knowledge is or may turn out to be false. To support this claim it is enough to find one falsehood in mathematics, or stronger, one contradiction. Gödel's Theorem means we cannot eliminate this possibility. However the implication of this version of fallibilism2 is that absolute true/false judgements can be made about ma-thematical knowledge, i.e. there is absolute truth, but mathematics fails or may fail to attain it. This version of fallibilism is thus absolutist.

Third, there is fallibilism3 which claims that mathematics is a relative, contingent, historical construct. This version denies the assumed absolutism of fallibilism2. According to fallibilism3 absolute judgements with regard to truth or falsity, correctness or incorrectness cannot be made. This is because the criteria and definitions of these concepts themselves vary with time, context, and never attain a final state. There are no absolutes concerning truth, correctness, certainty, necessity, and hence however good and well founded mathematical knowledge is or becomes it can never attain perfection, and no absolute or perfect criteria exist either.

Fallibilism3 is the position of social constructivism, which claims that the concepts, definitions, and rules of mathematics were invented and evolved over millennia, including rules of truth and proof. Thus mathe-matical knowledge is based on contingency, due to its historical development and the inevitable impact of external forces on the resourcing and direction of mathematics. But is also based on the deliberate choices and en deavours of mathematicians, elaborated through extensive reasoning. Both contingencies and choices are at work in mathematics, so it cannot be claimed that the overall development is either necessary or arbitrary. Much of mathematics follows by logical necessity from its assumptions and adopted rules of reasoning, just as moves do in the game of chess. Once a set of axioms and rules has been chosen (e.g., Peano's axioms or those of group theory), many unexpected results await the research mathe-matician. This does not contradict fallibilism3 for none of the rules of reasoning and logic in mathematics are themselves absolute. Mathematics consists of language games with deeply entrenched rules and patterns that are very stable and enduring, but which always remain open to the possibility of change, and in the long term, do change. And as they change, so does the range of possible discovered within a mathematical system.

Social constructivism and fallibilism3 reject absolutism, which involves the following three sub-theses (Harré and Krausz 1996). First of all, there is the thesis of universalism, which asserts that all knowing beings at all times and in all cultures would agree on truth and on mathematical knowledge. It may immediately be noted that this is false if 'do' is put for 'would', for groups such as intuitionists and classical mathematicians already disagree fundamentally on what is legitimate mathematical knowledge. But a more general problem for the thesis of universalism is the question of how would we know if it were true. Since people's knowledge and beliefs must be transformed to validate it, and this cannot be done universally, it must remain an indemonstrable article of faith. As such the thesis is rejected by social constructivism.

Second, there is the thesis of objectivism, which asserts that truth depends on objective reality, not views of persons or groups. This raises the problem of privileged access to 'objective mathematical reality', i.e., the 'god's-eye view' of mathematicians into the universe of mathematics. This thesis is unsatisfactory because it is not what mathematicians intuit which is taken as objective truth, but rather what they prove that is regarded as true. Thus how mathematical truth 'depends' on a mathematical reality that plays no part in its justification is unclear.

Third, there is the thesis of foundationalism, which asserts that there is a unique permanent foundation for knowledge. This foundation has not been identified historically. Foundationalist philosophies of mathematics (Logicism, Formalism, Intuitionism) have all failed, as I argue above. Furthermore, the idea that a basic foundation for mathematical knowledge exists leads to a vicious cycle, because no basic set of assumptions can ever ultimately be dispensed with (Lakatos 1962).

Lakatos' contribution

The philosopher of mathematics who has contributed most to the maverick tradition is Imre Lakatos. He is responsible for both the negative thesis (the rejection of absolutism by fallibilism3) and the positive thesis (philosophy of mathematics needs to be reconceptualised to include the history and methodology of mathematics) of the maverick tradition. He argued, as above, for a fallibilist epistemology of mathematics on the ground that any attempt to find a perfectly secure basis leads to infinite regress, and mathematical knowledge cannot be given a final, fully rigorous form. As he put it "Why not honestly admit mathematical fallibility, and try to defend the dignity of fallible knowledge from cynical scepticism" (Lakatos 1962: 184)

It should be mentioned that my interpretation of Lakatos is controversial. The editors of Lakatos (1976) claim that he had or would relinquish fallibilism3. He undoubtedly did change his position over time, and my account is of early Lakatos, where he unequivocally states that although formalisation of theories and logic increases rigour "one had to pay for each step which increased rigour in deduction by the introduction of a new and fallible translation." (Lakatos 1978: 90). Lakatos would not support social constructivism as I describe it here. He believed mathematics is fallible3 but wholly rational and not at root based on social agreement or conversation.

Lakatos's (1976) best known contribution is his logic of mathematical discovery (LMD) or the method of proofs and refutations, which is a methodology of mathematics with three functions. First there is the epistemological function: to account for the genesis and justification of mathematical knowledge naturalistically, as part of his fallibilism3 (concerning mathematical knowledge in the timeless present). Second, there is the historical function: to provide a theory of the historical development of mathematics (concerning mathematical knowledge in the past). Third, there is the methodological function: to account for the methodology of practising mathematicians (concerning mathematical knowledge in the future).

Lakatos's LMD is a cyclic theory of knowledge creation in mathematics with a dialectical form, which may be represented as follows.

Given a mathematical problem (or set of problems) and an informal mathematical theory, an initial step in the genesis of new knowledge is the proposal of a conjecture. The method of proofs and refutations is applied to this conjecture, and an informal proof of the conjecture is constructed, and then subjected to criticism, leading to an informal refutation. In response to this refutation, the conjecture and possibly also the informal theory and the original problem(s) are modified or changed (new problems may very well be raised), in a new synthesis, completing the cycle. This is illustrated schematically in Table 1, which shows one complete step, and the beginning of the next step in the cycle.

Table 1: Cyclic Form of Lakatos' Logic of Mathematical Discovery

STAGE	CONTEXT	COMPONENTS OF CYCLE
Some Stage in Process	Problem Set	Conjecture
	Informal Theory	Informal proof of conjecture
		Informal refutation of conjecture
Next Stage	New Problem Set	New Conjecture
	New Informal Theory	

Although Lakatos (1976) is explicit about the role of the conjectures, proofs and refutations in this cycle, the part played by problems and informal theory are often implicit in his account. He does stress the role of problems in the development of mathematics in some places, such as at the end of his dialogue where the teacher states that "a scientific inquiry 'begins and ends with problems'" (Lakatos 1963-4: 336, quoting Popper).

Wittgenstein's contribution

In looking for guidance on how to develop a broader, more inclusive social philosophy of mathematics, a unique source and inspiration is Wittgenstein (1953, 1956), who proposed a revolutionary naturalistic and fallibilist social philosophy of mathematics, which to this day remains under-appreciated under-developed. (My interpretation of Wittgenstein is also personal, and likely to be controversial).

Wittgenstein's philosophy is based on his key concepts of 'language games': how we use language co-ordinated with our actions and embedded in and inseparably a part of 'forms of life': which are our historico-cultural practices. "The term 'language-game' is meant to bring into prominence the fact that speaking of language is part of an activity, or of a form of life" (Wittgenstein 1953: 11). "Mathematics teaches you, not just the answer to a question, but a whole language-game with questions and answers." (Wittgenstein 1956: 381)

His naturalism gives priority to existing mathematical practice, as Maddy (1990) concurs. "You don't make a decision: you simply do a certain thing. It is a question of a certain practice." (Wittgenstein 1976: 237). His philosophy is fallibilist, because he grounds certainty in the accepted (but always revisable) rules of language games (Rorty 1979). "The ma-thematician is not a discoverer: he is an inventor." (Wittgenstein 1956: 111). "To accept a proposition as ... certain means to use it as a grammatical rule: this removes uncertainty from it." (Wittgenstein 1956: 170) He argues that proof serves to justify mathematical knowledge through persuasion, not by its inherent logical necessity. "In a demonstration we get agreement with someone." (Wittgenstein 1965: 62). Thus Wittgenstein puts forward what can legitimately be termed a social constructivist philosophy of ma-thematics. He challenges foundationalism, rejects the universally adopted prescriptive approach of his day, and demands the reconceptualization of the philosophy of mathematics so as to be descriptive of practice.

RECONCEPTUALIZING THE PHILOSOPHY OF MATHEMATICS

As I have indicated, traditional philosophy of mathematics seeks to reconstruct mathematics in a vain foundationalist quest for certainty. But this goal is inappropriate, as a number of philosophers of mathematics agree: "To confuse description and programme - to confuse 'is' with 'ought to be' or 'should be' - is just as harmful in the philosophy of mathematics as elsewhere." (Körner 1960: 12), and "the job of the philosopher of ma-thematics is to describe and explain mathematics, not to reform it." (Maddy 1990: 28). Lakatos, in a characteristically witty and forceful way which paraphrases Kant indicates the direction that a reconceptualised philosophy of mathematics should follow. "The history of mathematics, lacking the guidance of philosophy has become blind, while the philosophy of ma-thematics turning its back on the...history of mathematics, has become empty" (1976: 2).

Building on these and other suggestions it might be expected that an adequate philosophy of mathematics should account for a number of aspects of mathematics including the following:

1. **Epistemology**: Mathematical knowledge; its character, genesis and justification, with special attention to the role of proof

2. **Theories**: Mathematical theories, both constructive and structural: their character and development, and issues of appraisal and evaluation

3. **Ontology**: The objects of mathematics: their character, origins and relationship with the language of mathematics, the issue of Platonism

4. **Methodology and History**: Mathematical practice: its character, and the mathematical activities of mathematicians, in the present and past

5. **Applications and Values**: Applications of mathematics; its relationship with science, technology, other areas of knowledge and values

6. **Individual Knowledge and Learning**: The learning of mathematics: its character and role in the onward transmission of mathematical knowledge, and in the creativity of individual mathe-maticians (Ernest 1997)

Items 1 and 3 include the traditional epistemological and ontological focuses of the philosophy of mathematics, broadened to add a concern with the genesis of mathematical knowledge and objects of mathematics, as well as with language. Item 2 adds a concern with the form that mathematical knowledge usually takes: mathematical theories. Items 4 and 5 go beyond the traditional boundaries by admitting the applications of mathematics and human mathematical practice as legitimate philosophical concerns, as well as its relations with other areas of human knowledge and values. Item 6 adds a concern with how mathematics is transmitted onwards from one generation to the next, and in particular, how it is learnt by individuals, and the dialectical relation between individuals and existing knowledge in creativity.

The legitimacy of these extended concerns arises from the need to consider the relationship between mathematics and its corporeal agents, i.e., human beings. They are required to accommodate what on the face of it is the simple and clear task of the philosophy of mathematics, namely to give an account of mathematics.

SOCIAL CONSTRUCTIVISM

Social constructivism is proposed as a philosophy of mathematics building on the ideas elaborated above with the aim of potentially or possibly addressing these six aspects or dimensions of an enlarged philosophy of mathematics. Social constructivism is based first of all on Lakatos' Logic of Mathematical Discovery for negotiation and acceptance of mathematical knowledge, concepts and proofs.

The second source of social constructivism is Wittgenstein's notions of 'language game' and 'forms of life'. Thus mathematical knowledge is taken to rest on socially situated linguistic practices, including shared rules, meanings and conventions, i.e. on both tacit and explicit knowledge and symbolic practices.

A central element of social constructivism is the reinterpretation of objectivity as social and intersubjective. Following Bloor (1984), Fuller (1988), Harding (1986) and others objective knowledge is understood as social, cultural, public and collective knowledge, and not as personal, private or individual belief, nor as external, absolute or otherwise extra-human.

A novel central feature of social constructivism is that it adopts conversation as the basic underpinning representational form for its epistemology. Thus this position views mathematics as basically linguistic, textual and semiotic, but embedded in the social world of human interaction.

Conversation

Beyond the metaphor of the 'great conversation' for philosophy and the history of ideas used by Michael Oakshott, conversation is taken as a basic epistemological form by Rorty (1979), Harré (1983), Shotter (1993), Gergen (1985), and many others.

> If, however, we think of "rational certainty" as a matter of victory in argument rather than of relation to an object known, we shall look toward our interlocutors rather than to our faculties for the explanation of the phenomenon. If we think of our certainty about the Pythagorean Theorem as our confidence, based on experience with arguments on such matters, that nobody will find an objection to the premises from which we infer it, then we shall not seek to explain it by the relation of reason to triangularity. Our certainty will be a matter of conversation between persons, rather than an interaction with nonhuman reality. (Rorty 1979)

So what is conversation? The original form is naturally interpersonal conversation, which consists of persons exchanging of speech, based on shared experiences, understandings, values, respect, etc. That is, it is language-games situated in human forms of life. Two secondary forms of conversation are derived from this. First, there is intrapersonal conversation, i.e., thought as constituted and formed by conversation. According to this view (verbal) thinking is originally internalised conversation with an imagined other (Vygotsky 1978, Mead 1934, see Figure 2 below). Second, there is cultural conversation, which is an extended version, consisting of the creation and exchange of texts in permanent (i.e., enduringly embodied) form. Indeed, it can be said that the reading of any text is dialogical, with the reader interrogating it and creating answers from it.

These three forms of conversation are social in manifestation (interpersonal and cultural), or in origin (intrapersonal). Conversation has an underlying dialogical form of ebb and flow, comprising the alternation of voices in assertion and counter assertion. Conversation is the source of feedback, in the form of acceptance, elaboration, reaction, criticism and correction essential for all human knowledge and learning. Thus the different conversational roles include the following two forms, which occur in each of the three forms, but originate in the interpersonal:

1. The role of proponent or friendly listener following a line of thinking or a thought experiment sympathetically, for understanding (Peirce, Rotman)

2. The role of critic, in which an argument is examined for weaknesses and flaws.

Taking conversation as epistemologically basic re-grounds mathematical knowledge in physically-embodied, socially-situated acts of human knowing and communication. It rejects the cartesian dualism of mind versus body, and knowledge versus the world. It acknowledges that there are multiple valid voices and perspectives on knowledge, which has significant ethical implications (cf. Habermas 1981)

The conversational nature of mathematics

My claim is that mathematical text is conversational, for the following reasons. Mathematics is primarily a symbolic activity, using written inscription and language to create, record and justify its knowledge (Rotman 1988, 1993). Viewed semiotically as comprising texts, mathematics is conversational for it addresses a reader. "In all cases the word is orientated towards an addressee" (Volosinov 1973: 85)

Analysis of mathematical texts, proofs, etc., reveals the verb forms to be in indicative and imperative moods. The indicative mood is used to make statements, claims and assertions describing the future outcomes of thought experiments which the reader can perform or accept. (Peirce, cited in Rotman 1993: 76) The imperatives are shared injunctions, orders or instructions issued by the writer to the reader. (Rotman 1988, 1993). Thus mathematical texts comprise specific assertions and imperatives directed by the writer to the reader. The reader of mathematical text is therefore either the agent of the mathematician-author's will, whose response is an imagined or actual action, or a critic seeking to make a critical response. In all cases the mathematical text is conversational.

The conversational structure of mathematical concepts

Dialogical / conversational processes also underpin a substantial class of modern mathematical concepts as the underlying meanings or possible interpretations.

Table 2: Dialogical concepts in Mathematics

TOPIC	DIALECTICAL CONCEPT
Analysis	ε-δ definitions of the limit: for each value...there is...
Constructivist Logic	Interpretation of quantifiers: $\forall x \exists y$... "You choose x, and I show how to construct y"
Recursion theory	Arithmetical Hierarchy - $\forall \exists \forall \exists \forall \exists$...
Set theory	Diagonal argument:for any enumeration, omitted element
Set theory	Game-theoretic version of Axiom of Choice
Game Theory	Alternation of moves by opponents
Number theory	J. Conway's game theoretic foundations of number
Statistics	Hypothesis testing (H_0 versus H_A)
Probability	Analysis of wagers, betting games

Table 2 illustrates the wide occurrence of dialogical or conversational concepts in mathematics, through which the formal interplay between persons, or a back and forth movement of choices is structured into the concepts themselves. (For more details see Ernest 1994).

Origins and basis of proof

In Ancient Greece proof developed from of cultural practice of disputation, i.e. conversation (Struik 1967). The term 'dialectic' derived from verb 'to discuss'. (Cornford 1935). So the origins of proof may be said to be conversational. In modern Proof Theory many developments also treat proofs as if part of a dialogue. For example, according to Heyting (1956), in intuitionistic mathematics every assertion is a promise to provide a proof. Such claims are valid only if the opponent convinced. Natural Deduction techniques likewise build proofs based on sets of assumptions or hypotheses agreed by both a proposer and an opposer. In the method of semantic tableaux, the version or proof constructed is an explicit attempt to refute the claim or story as put forward by another in dialogue. Lorenzen's conversational proof method is likewise based on two disputants(Roberts 1992). One tries to maintain a thesis over other's objections, and the connectives used have explicit conversational meanings. Overall, it can be said that both the beginnings of logic and proof and modern developments confirm that mathematical proof is at root dialectical, based in human conversation and persuasion.

Acceptance of mathematical knowledge is conversational

A widespread but controversial view is that the acceptance of mathematical knowledge and proof is social act, a conversational act, as illustrated in the quote from Rorty, given above. Thus "A proof becomes a proof after the social act of 'accepting it as a proof'. This is as true of mathematics as it is of physics, linguistics and biology." (Manin). The structure of a proof is a means to this epistemological end of persuading others, and ultimately the mathematical community, to accept it as a warrant for a theorem. Furthermore, the acceptance of a proof depends on largely tacit criteria and informed professional judgement, just as a teacher's decision to accept mathematical answers from a student depends on professional judgement. In both cases such judgements are based on criteria including the rhetorical style of the proposed item of mathematical knowledge, not just on rigid and explicit logical rules of correctness.

The acceptance of mathematical knowledge depends on dual roles developed and internalised through conversation. These are, first of all, the role of proposer of would-be new knowledge, or analogously, of a sympathetic reader or listener. The second role is that of a critical reader or listener, a reviewer, assessor, or gatekeeper. These roles are deployed in the generalised logic of mathematical discovery, which is the proposed conversational mechanism for acceptance or modification of mathematical knowledge. This is illustrated in Table 3.

Table 3: The Generalised Logic of Mathematical Discovery

SCIENTIFIC CONTEXT for *Stage n* Background scientific and epistemological context: problems, concepts, methods, informal theories, proof criteria and paradigms, and meta-mathematical views.

THESIS *Stage n (i)* Proposal of new/revised conjecture, proof, solution or theory.
ANTITHESIS *Stage n (ii)* Dialectical and evaluative response to the proposal:

Critical Response	**Acceptance Response**
Counterexample, counter-argument, refutation,criticism of proposal	Acceptance of proposal. Suggested extension of proposal.

SYNTHESIS *Stage n (iii)* Re-evaluation and modification of the proposal:

Local Restructuring Modified proposals: new conjecture, proof, problem-solution, problems or theory.	**Globlal Restructuring of Context:** changed problems, concepts methods, informal theories. Changed proof paradigms, criteria, meta-mathematical views.

OUTCOME *Stage n+1 (i)* Accepted or rejected proposal, or revised scientific and epistemological context.

The generalised logic of mathematical discovery is so-termed because it is a generalisation of Lakatos's logic of mathematical discovery (Table 1) to overcome the criticism that it does not describe the full generality of mathematical knowledge developments, including 'mathematical revolutions' (Gillies 1992).

It is clear that conversation and dialectical processes play a key role in the generalised logic of mathematical discovery shown in Table 3. The underlying logic is dialectical, and that this underpins the genesis and warranting of mathematical knowledge. In this process mathematical proofs and other proposals are offered to the appropriate mathematical community as part of a continuing dialogue. They are addressed to an audience, and are tendered in the expectation of a response, drawing upon tacit and professional knowledge. Critical scrutiny of a proof by the mathematical community leads to either (a) criticism, requiring development and improvement (concerning the context of discovery), or (b) acceptance as a knowledge warrant (concerning the context of justification). The same conversational logic of mathematical discovery is at work in both cases. There can be no proofs in mathematics which are above critical scrutiny and this logic, no matter how rigorous. Thus mathematical proof has not only evolved from dialogical form, but its very function in the mathematical community as an epistemological warrant for items of mathematical knowledge requires the deployment of that form.

However, a word of caution is needed. Although mathematics is claimed to be at root conversational, it is also the discipline par excellence which hides its dialogical nature under its monological appearance, and which has expunged the traces of multiple voices and of human authorship behind a rhetoric of objectivity and impersonality. This is why the claimed conversational nature of mathematics might seem surprising: it is the exact opposite of the traditional absolutist view of mathematics as disembodied and superhuman, critiqued above.

See figure next page

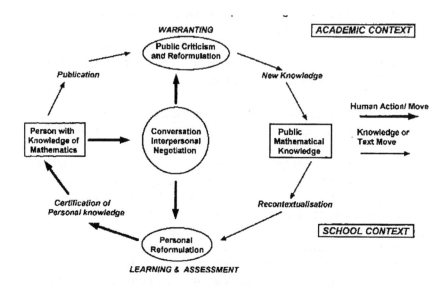

Figure 1: *The Cyclic Mechanism for the Social Construction of Mathematical Knowledge*

Figure 1 summarises the social construction of mathematical knowledge in the contexts of research and schooling, and shows how they are interrelated in an overall cyclic mechanism, and the role of conversation and negotiation in each. In the context of research mathematics, individuals use their personal knowledge both to construct mathematical knowledge claims (possibly jointly with others), and participate in the dialogical process of criticism and warranting of others' mathematical knowledge claims. In the context of mathematics education individuals use their personal knowledge to direct and control mathematics learning conversations both to present mathematical knowledge to learners directly or indirectly (i.e. teaching), and participate in the process of warranting and criticism of others' mathematical knowledge claims or performances (i.e. the assessment of learning). Ultimately, individuals emerge from this process with their personal knowledge warranted or certified, and may therefore be able to participate in these conversations as teachers or mathematicians, after further professional preparation.

As figure 1 illustrates, the mechanism for the social construction of mathematical knowledge has the form of a cycle. What travels for part of the cycle is embodied mathematical knowledge. This is represented publicly by mathematicians as a text, and after possible modification is then approved, if it passes muster, and then becomes part of the pool of accepted knowledge representations. Selections from this pool are recontextualised into the school context where they are offered to learners. Learners appropriate and internalise this knowledge, with a greater or lesser degree of personal reformulation (see Figure 2 below). Mathematical knowledge is now embodied in the skills and dispositions of individuals, i.e., as personal knowledge, and when these individuals are certified as knowledgeable, the cycle is completed. For potentially they can now participate in the construction of new mathematical knowledge, as research mathematicians, or can help the development of the personal knowledge of others, as teachers of mathematics.

The cyclic pattern of the social construction of mathematical knowledge finds a parallel in Harré's (1983) social model of mind (also referred to as Vygotskian space, in Shotter 1991). This also sees thought or knowledge cycling as it alternates between public and private manifestations, and between individual and collective social locations. This is illustrated in Figure 2.

Figure 2: Vygotskian space - Harré's social model of mind

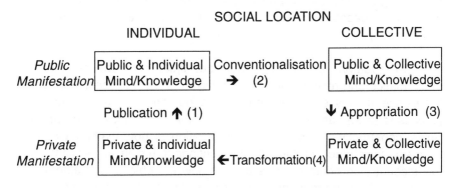

The cycle in Figure 2 is orientated differently from Figure 1, so the analogy is clarified by stating that the process of publication (marked 1) corresponds to the assessment and warranting of individual knowledge and learning, whereas the process of conventionalisation publication (marked 2) corresponds to the assessment of a new contribution to public knowledge. The process of appropriation (marked 3) corresponds to the recontextualisation of accepted mathematical knowledge into the context of schooling, and its offering to learners. The process of transformation (marked 4) corresponds to learner appropriating and assuming ownership of the knowledge as individual and personal knowledge.

Clearly this model has strong parallels and potentially strong implications for the teaching and learning of mathematics. There are many more aspects of the social constructivist theory which there is not space to report her, but which were indicated in the talk. These include an extended model of mathematical knowledge based on Kitcher (1984) and Kuhn (1970) incorporating both tacit and explicit knowledge elements. There is the important role of rhetoric in both research mathematics and school mathematics. There is the parallel with socially situated views of learning which are becoming more widely accepted in psychology and mathematics education. These are all treated in Ernest (1997), the source from which this article is a condensed selection.

Conclusion

In conclusion, it might be claimed that the novelty of social constructivism is to realise both that mathematical knowledge is necessary, stable and autonomous, but that this co-exists with its contingent, fallibilist3, and historically shifting character. As Vico said, with regard to geometry: the only things we can know completely are those we have made (because there is nowhere else to look than within our own construction).

In addition, social constructivism links both the learning of mathematics and research in mathematics in an overall scheme in which knowledge travels either embodied in a person or in a text, and the processes of formation and warranting in the two contexts are parallel. Social constructivism provides an explanation of how mathematics and logic seem irrefutably certain, yet are contingent, historical creations. The full account also offers explanations for how the objects of mathematics are cultural fictions emerging from the use of mathematical language and symbolism, yet seem so solid; and how mathematics is so unreasonably effective in providing the conceptual foundations of our scientific theories about the world. The central explanatory concept is emergence: the evolutionary history of culture and the individual, and the shaping role of conversation. However adequate arguments and explanations go beyond what I can offer here. This talk is based on my current book Ernest (1997), but other relevant publications are Ernest (1991, 1992, 1994).

References

Ayer, A. J. (1946) *Language, Truth and Logic,* London: Gollancz.

Bernstein, R. (1983) *Beyond Objectivism and Relativism,* Philadelphia, Pennsylvania: University of Philadelphia Press.

Bloor, D. (1984) A Sociological Theory of Objectivity, in Brown (1984), 229-245. Brown, S. C. Ed. (1984) *Objectivity and Cultural Divergence* (Royal Institute of Philosophy lecture series, 17), Cambridge: Cambridge University Press, 229-245.

Bloor, D. (1991) *Knowledge and Social Imagery* (Second Revised Edition), Chicago: University of Chicago Press.

Cornford, F. M. (1935) *Plato's Theory of Knowledge,* London: Routledge & Kegan Paul (Paperback edition, 1960).

Davis, P. J. and Hersh, R. (1980) *The Mathematical Experience,* Boston: Birkhauser.

Ernest, P. (1991) *The Philosophy of Mathematics Education,* London, Falmer Press.

Ernest, P. (1992).'The Nature of Mathematics: Towards a Social Constructivist Account', *Science and Education,* 1(1), 89-100.

Ernest, P. (1994).'The dialogical nature of mathematics' in Ernest, P. Ed. *Mathematics, Education and Philosophy: An International Perspective,* London, The Falmer Press, 1994, 33-48.

Ernest, P. (1997) *Social Constructivism as a Philosophy of Mathematics,* Albany, New York: SUNY Press.

Ernest, P. (1997) *Social Constructivism as a Philosophy of Mathematics,* Albany, New York: SUNY Press. In Science Technology and Society Series, Ed. Prof. S. Restivo, and Reform in Mathematics Series, Ed. Prof. J. Sowder.

Everitt, N. and Fisher, A. (1995) *Modern Epistemology,* London: McGraw-Hill.

Feyerabend, P. (1975) *Against Method,* London: New Left Books.

Fuller, S. (1988) *Social Epistemology,* Bloomington, Indiana: Indiana University Press.

Gergen, K. (1985) The social constructionist movement in modern psychology, *American Psychologist,* 40, 266-275.

Gillies, D. A. Ed. (1992) *Revolutions in Mathematics,* Oxford: Clarendon Press.

Gödel, K. (1931) translation in Heijenoort, J. van Ed. (1967) *From Frege to Gödel: A Source Book in Mathematical Logic,* Cambridge, Massachusetts: Harvard University Press, 592-617.

Habermas, J. (1981) *The Theory of Communicative Action,* 2 volumes, Frankfurt am Main: Suhrkamp Verlag (Trans. T. McCarthy, Cambridge: Polity Press, 1987 and 1991).

Harding, S. (1986) *The Science Question in Feminism*, Milton Keynes: Open University Press.

Harré, R. and Krausz, M. (1996) *Varieties of Relativism,* Oxford: Basil Blackwell.

Harré, R. (1983) *Personal Being,* Oxford: Blackwell.

Heyting, A. (1956) *Intuitionism: An Introduction,* Amsterdam: North-Holland.

Kant, I. (1950) *Prolegomena to Any Future Metaphysics,* Ed. L. W. Beck, Indianapolis: Bobbs Merrill Library of Liberal Arts. (First published in German in 1783)

Kilpatrick, J. (1992) A History of Research in Mathematics Education, in Grouws, D. A. Ed. (1992) *Handbook of Research on Mathematics Teaching and Learning,* New York: Macmillan, 3-38.

Kitcher, P. and Aspray, W. (1988) An opinionated introduction, in Aspray, W. and Kitcher, P. Eds. (1988) *History and Philosophy of Modern Mathematics,* Minneapolis: University of Minnesota Press, 3-57.

Kitcher, P. (1984) *The Nature of Mathematical Knowledge,* Oxford: Oxford University Press.

Klein, P. (1981) *Certainty: A Refutation of Scepticism,* Minneapolis: University of Minnesota Press.

Körner, S. (1960) *The Philosophy of Mathematics,* London: Hutchinson.

Kuhn, T. S. (1970) *The Structure of Scientific Revolutions,* (2nd edition), Chicago: Chicago University Press.

Lakatos, I. (1962) Infinite Regress and the Foundations of Mathematics, *Aristotelian Society Proceedings,* Supplementary Volume No. 36, 155-184 (revised version in Lakatos, 1978).

Lakatos, I. (1963-4) Proofs and Refutations, *British Journal for the Philosophy of Science,* Vol. 14, 1-25, 120-139, 221-243, 296-342.

Lakatos, I. (1976) *Proofs and Refutations,* Cambridge: Cambridge University Press.

Lakatos, I. (1978) *The Methodology of Scientific Research Programmes* (Philosophical Papers Volume 1), Cambridge: Cambridge University Press.

Latour, B. (1993) *We Have Never Been Modern,* Cambridge, Massachusetts: Harvard University Press.

Lyotard, J. F. (1984) *The Postmodern Condition: A Report on Knowledge,* Manchester: Manchester University Press.

MacKenzie, D. (1993) Negotiating Arithmetic, Constructing Proof: The Sociology of Mathematics and Information Technology, *Social Studies of Science,* Vol. 23, 37-65.

Maddy, P. (1990) *Realism in Mathematics,* Oxford: Clarendon Press.

Manin, Y. I. (1977) *A Course in Mathematical Logic,* New York: Springer, 48.

Mead, G. H. (1934) *Mind, Self and Society,* Chicago: University of Chicago Press.

Moore, G. E. (1959) *Philosophical Papers,* New York: Macmillan.

Popper, K. (1959) *The Logic of Scientific Discovery,* Hutchinson, London.

Roberts, J. (1992) *The Logic of Reflection,* New Haven and London: Yale University Press.

Rorty, R. (1979) *Philosophy and the Mirror of Nature,* Princeton, New Jersey: Princeton University Press.

Rosen, S. (1989) *The Ancients and the Moderns: Rethinking Modernity,* New Haven and London: Yale University Press.

Rotman, B. (1988) Towards a semiotics of mathematics, *Semiotica,* Vol. 72, No. 1/2, 1-35.

Rotman, B. (1993) *Ad Infinitum The Ghost in Turing's Machine: Taking God Out of Mathematics and Putting the Body Back in,* Stanford California: Stanford University Press.

Shotter, J. (1991) Rom Harré: Realism and the Turn to Social Constructionism, in Bhaskar, R. Ed. (1991) *Harré & his Critics,* Oxford: Basil Blackwell, 206-223.

Shotter, J. (1993) *Conversational Realities: Constructing Life through Language,* London: Sage.

Struik, D. J. (1967) A Concise History of Mathematics (Third revised edition), New York: Dover.

Tymoczko, T. Ed. (1986) *New Directions in the Philosophy of Mathematics,* Boston: Birkhauser.

Volosinov, V. N. (1973) *Marxism and the Philosophy of Language,* New York and London: Seminar Press.

Vygotsky, L. (1978) *Mind in Society,* Cambridge, Massachusetts: Harvard University Press.

Wittgenstein, L. (1953) *Philosophical Investigations* (Translated by G. E. M. Anscombe), Oxford: Basil Blackwell.

Wittgenstein, L. (1956) Remarks on the Foundations of Mathematics, revised edition, Cambridge: MIT Press, 1978.

Wittgenstein, L. (1976) *Wittgenstein's Lectures on the Foundations of Mathematics* (Ed.: C. Diamond), Ithaca, New York: Cornell University Press.

THE RUSSIAN STANDARDS: PROBLEMS AND DECISIONS

Victor Firsov

Alongside with space rockets and Bolschoy ballet, School Mathematics could be referred to the category of "sacred cows" of modern post-soviet Russia: it is accepted to be proud of them and not to criticize them. It is obviously no more than national myth that had its basis in achievements of the Past and that does not require today's confirmations. Typical for periods of social crisis the nostalgia on the Past promotes the creation of similar myths. At the same time mythological consciousness is dangerous for corresponding areas of human activity because it idealizes the Past and does not promote their development with taking into account the realities and the needs of modern Russia.

The critical analysis allows to see that some of past advantages of Russian School Mathematics are disappeared. Other ones have lost their significance in new system of school coordinates. Third ones have turned to the denying. In result the brilliant picture at one time has grown dull. The superiority myth becomes similar to an old mirror showing the image appreciably more attractive in comparison with the reality.

Large volume and high theoretical level of Mathematics courses were considered always as traditional advantages of Russian School. The question if it is necessary to each student, sounds increasingly stronger in modern conditions of greater freedom and greater openness of school to social demands. The opponents put forward the requirement of resolute humanitarization of school. They challenge the necessity of exceedingly ambitious goals of school mathematical education. They also ascertain significant break between the advanced requirements of the Mathematics Curriculum and the real achievements of the majority of the schoolchildren.

The officious soviet propaganda ignored break mentioned by the practice of overestimating minimum positive marks (writing "3" and keeping in mind "2"). Actually the data of researches of the Institute into Content and Methods of Education, USSR Academy of Pedagogical Sciences on check of mathematical preparation of the schoolchildren [1]* shows that from 30 up to 50 % of the pupils did not take possession of

---

*The numbers in parenthesis refer to the list of references at the end of the text.

basic Mathematics skills that are minimal necessary for continuing of education. There is no basis to hope that the today's situation is appreciably improved: the Curriculum and the textbooks have not practically changed, and, say, the indicators of health of the children fall down even in comparison with unsatisfactory ones of the last Soviet years [2].

Critics of Russian School Mathematics condemn excessive, by their opinion, enthusiasm for the formal goals of education to the detriment of real ones. Moreover in a part of achievement of the real goals of Mathematics Education the priority is given back to development of the technical apparatus instead of direct application of Mathematics to the solution of real practical problems.

The results of international comparative research like IAEP and TIMSS are indicative in this relation despite all their ambiguity. So, the Soviet Union looked not bad by results of IAEP [3]. The more detailed analysis [4] of test groups' results has compelled to change such evaluation. There was found out that Soviet students did not surpass practically the pupils from other countries in fulfilment of the tests requiring the understanding of Mathematics concepts and its practical application. Significant advantage was formed because of higher results on development of the technical part of Mathematics. Thus, by the price of serious expenditures of educational time and overloading of the children by mathematical technics it becomes possible to reach comparable results on those components of Mathematics that are most important from positions of General Education. We shall agree that even the opportunity of discussion of similar conclusion puts a question on efficiency of Soviet model of School Mathematics Education.

This model was developed for specific historic conditions of the period of Soviet industrialization in 30-ties. The model oriented to preparation of the future engineers at the system of high technical institutions. Till now each pupil in Russia is trained the Mathematics as if her (his) hot desire to receive the engineering diploma (and Soviet diploma of 30-ties namely) is known beforehand.

It effects the selection of School Mathematics content and style. It explains the orientation of Soviet School Mathematics to development of refined technical apparatus of transformations of algebraic and transcendent expressions and of algorithms for precise solution of the equations and inequalities appearing archaic today. It leads to the orientation of a subject to development of continuous Mathematics and to suppression of discrete Mathematics. Just mention the absence of such topics as combinatorics, data analysis and probability, elements of mathematical logic in modern Mathematics Curriculum for Russian School [5].

It is possible to continue the critical analysis of School Mathematics content. However, even if to take into account disputability and ambiguity of questions discussed above, we are nevertheless compelled to ascertain the necessity of Curriculum reform and it's reduction to greater conformity with the needs of our times.

The analysis of usual practice of teaching and learning Mathematics leads to similar conclusions [6]. It's orientation to needs of strong highly motivated learner (future student of university or technical institute) and neglect of interests of low-learners are the serious lacks. The aspects of School Mathematics as communications development and cooperative learning that are necessary for low-learners are developing unsatisfactorily. Assessment system imposes the penalties for non-achievement by the student of a level of the advanced requirements. Assessment system works under the circuit of "subtraction" that is opposite to cumulative assessment.

Unfortunately, the Russian Mathematics community does not welcome to discuss these questions. Powerful lobby of higher schools' professors and of Math educators works under the slogans "to increase the number of academic hours to study Mathematics at school" (one of the greatest in the world), "to raise the level of mathematical preparation of students" (meaning the future students and completely ignoring a consequence for other following to corresponding actions), "to keep high traditions of National Mathematics Education" (understanding it as the necessity of preservation of Soviet model). Honestly, there is hidden disrespect to the children (their rights not to love Mathematics are rejected resolutely) and to the Mathematics (educational and cultural values of School Mathematics for each pupil of school are declared on words whereas the course is designed actually according to the needs of the best pupils only).

Obviously it becomes impossible to carry out the contradictory social order within the framework of unique model of School Mathematics Education. The decisions conducting to a greater variety of Mathematics Education were found in conditions of Soviet school yet.

The development at schools since mid-30-ties of the system of voluntary mathematical circles and olympiads for students has become the most efficient of them. The names of such outstanding mathematicians and popularizators of Mathematics as I.Gelfand, I.Perelman and I.Yaglom are connected with the movement. Just this system has caused a large part of our mathematical elite. Just to it our country is obliged by outstanding results shown by the Soviet participants at International Mathematical Olympiads.

The schools with advanced studies of Mathematics at the high secondary stage are more known in the world. The names of A.Kolmogorov, A.Lyapunov and S.Shwarzburd are connected to its origin. Arising since 1959 as more systematized variant of mathematical circles, passing through period of official disallowance and fight for the existence, they have received "the rights of citizenship" to the end of Soviet epoch. Such schools become today the most popular model for "streaming" at high secondary school not only in a direction of Mathematics already.

Unfortunately significant overloading of pupils and teachers alongside with unreasoned state policy in the field of teacher's salaries have resulted to practical liquidation of mathematical circles as of a mass movement today. It is not enough completely to have the opportunities of diversity connected with streaming at high secondary school only.

The slogan of diversity as bases of organic development of school has an exclusive importance for modern Russia. Construction of a democratic civil society and market economical relations require freedom and pluralism and exclude the presence of "only right decisions". On the other hand, the positive achievement of Russian school that are answering to the realities of today's life should be protected from unreasonable innovations. Thus, new school appropriate to principles of unity and diversity [7] should come on change of extremely unified Soviet school that brought up the "small screws" of big state machine (according to metaphor of J.Stalin). These complementary and cooperating principles are called to ensure the evolutionary character of school's development just as heredity and variability provide biological evolution.

The development of new Russian School requires the creation of new generation of normative documents ensuring the goals. New Law of Russian Federation on Education named these documents as Educational Standards. The law provides that Educational Standards should determine "the compulsory minimum of the contents of Education", "the requirements to the levels of preparation of students graduated the stages of school" and "maximal allowable volume of study load of children" [8].

We shall notice at once that pedagogical public of Russia has apprehended extremely sensitively the term "standards" borrowed from American experience. For people in our country the word "standard" associates with compulsory uniformity of the Soviet times.

Really the goals of the standards' implementation in USA and in Russia look opposite diametrically. It seems that the authors of the project of National Standards [9] aspired to come to common understanding of the goals and objectives of School Mathematics Education in conditions of a superfluous variety of American schools. The similar problem does not arise at all in Russian school. Opposite, we here need more de-standardization of Education.

The collision of various interests and positions accompanies with the whole short history of creation of Russian Educational Standards. We shall designate basic conceptual "bifurcation points" where the positions of the parties differ essentially.

First and probably main distinction consists in understanding of the basic purpose of the Standards. The supporters of one position see it in maintenance of unity of Russian school [10]. Their opponents consider the maintenance of unity of school as one of a list of necessary conditions only. They specify priority purpose of the Standards as being the instrument of school's development [11].

The marked divergence has no scholastic character. It is directly connected with opposition of conservative guarding tendencies to the movement for reforming of Russian School that was described above. It is relevant to notice that this conflict has obvious political colour in today's Russia. If to finish up the first considered position to its logical end, the best decision will appear as return to the unified typical Curriculum of Soviet School, and complete refusal from a variety of the educational programs as a consequence.

Searches of ways of realization of a contrary position result to a new point of opposition. The conceptual divergences concern here to the ways, with the help of which future Standards would determine the directions of school's development.

Traditional approach (perceived often as only possible) supposes the setting of educational goals through the system of Educational Standards. In this case the standards are called to determine directly the major elements of Educational System, imposing them to school.

The opponents of the traditional approach remark that anybody cannot apply for knowledge what school should be. The achievement of public consensus in a question on the goals of Education looks perfect Utopia. In this context in Russia they always recollect the words from the song of outstanding poet and dissident A.Galich:

Do not fear of plague, do not fear of prison,
Do not fear of stench and of hell.
But fear of person only that could tell:
"I know as it should be!"

Within the framework of the alternative approach standards take a role similar to the role of the legislative restrictions in a lawful state: the standards specify what is forbidden to do. Thus, there are the conditions for realization of a democratic principle "it is allowed everything that it is not forbidden."

This principle means real freedom for schools, and apparent paradox only consists that freedom is provided by means of the interdictions. The standards become the expression of the similar interdictions concerning the content of Education at School. With their help the principle of "allowance" receives non-declarative mechanism of its realization.

Thus, in the alternative approach the standards set "a field of freedom" in a choice of the content of Education; freedom results in occurrence of various educational programs; the variety of the programs provides an opportunity of their choice by the parents and children. Through this choice the society would influence schools showing them people's educational needs and preferences. These needs and preferences will find reflection in the contents of the next variants of the standards, and so on... The democratic interaction of society and school will come true through the standards by such way.

Certainly, the serious discussions arise in the relation of the content and of the forms of standards presentation. These discussions go often around of some basic questions.

Whether It is necessary to adjust the content of Education that should be taught or which should be acquired by each student? Here the authors of the alternative projects took the same position: it should be both standards of "teaching" and standards of "learning". However, the different circuits of the forms of standards representation are selected with own advantages and lacks.

Should the standards be oriented on today or on prospect? In the first case the standards will easily enter School, but will fix those minuses which we aspire to take away from School. In the second case the standards will allow to specify urgent directions of development of School (for example, so necessary unload of compulsory educational content). At the same time such standards appear poorly connected to the textbooks available of schools. It is necessary to admit that this question did not find its satisfactory solution yet.

How to co-ordinate correctly federal and regional interests? How to distribute the responsibility for standards execution in appropriate way? How to alter the corresponding systems of assessment and control?

The search of the answers on these and similar questions continues. It is necessary to notice that in the field of Mathematics Education the alternative projects of the standards appear rather alike. Obviously it is connected to circumstance that in the field of School Mathematics the whole necessary way was passed much earlier in comparison with other subjects. The standards of School Mathematical Education in understanding as above entered into Soviet School already in 1982. Now the specification of the earlier entered standards comes true unless. Thus, our final conclusion is that existing projects of Standards could not ensure the required reform of Russian School Mathematics. The genuine reform is still ahead yet.

References

1. *On Results of the Theoretical and Experimental Study "Planning the Compulsory Outcomes of Education as the Base for Level Differentiation".* (Research Report).- Moscow, Institute into Content and Methods of Education, USSR Academy of Pedagogical Sciences, 1986. (in Russian).
2. *Normalization of Study Load of Students: Experimental Physiological and Hygienic Research.* - Moscow, "Prosvetschenie", 1988. (in Russian).
3. *Learning Mathematics.* IAEP Report. - New Jersey, ETS, 1992.
4. V.Firsov, G.Kovalyova, O.Loginova. *Transition to a Market Economy: Applications for Curriculum and Teaching in Post-Communist Society.* Report for World Bank. - Moscow.1994.

5. *Mathematics Curriculum for General Secondary School.* - Moscow, "Prosvetschenie", 1994. (in Russian).
6. V.Firsov. *The Basic Trends in the Improvement of Mathematics Teaching in the Present Day Soviet School.* The Report of Second Anglo-Soviet Seminar on Mathematics Education. - London, British Council, 1982.
7. V.Firsov. *United and Diverse.* - Moscow. "Soviet Pedagogy", Nr. 2, 1989. (in Russian).
8. *The Law of Russian Federation on Education.* - Moscow. "Novaya Shkola", 1992. (in Russian).
9. *Curriculum and Evaluation Standards for School Mathematics.* NCTM (USA). 1990.
10. *The Concept of Federal Educational Standards.* Project. - Moscow, Institute of General School, Russian Academy of Education, 1995 (In Russian).
11. V.Firsov. *To the Concept of Educational Standards.* Moscow Educational Standards. - Moccow, "Obrazovanie dlya vsekh", 1995 (In Russian).

HIGHLIGHTS AND SHADOWS OF CURRENT JAPANESE NATIONAL CURRICULUM OF MATHEMATICS FOR SECONDARY SCHOOLS

Hiroshi FUJITA
Meiji University; Japan

§1. Introduction

Firstly, focusing on SHS (Senior High School) mathematics curriculum, we describe the underlying philosophy, basic strategy, courses and their contents of the current Japanese national curriculum, which is called the Course of Study (CS). Actually, the author was involved in organizing this CS as a member of Council for Educational Curricula. Reports on initial experiences of implementation are mentioned.

Secondly, as a newly arising difficulty in mathematics education in Japan, we analyze recent tendency of Japanese youths' disinclination for mathematics as well as for science and technology, which has become a matter of national concern. It is our belief that the underlying idea and methods of the current CS will be effective also to overcome this crisis of Japanese mathematics education.

While some points of our discussion are specific to Japan, we think that the other points are of international interests and concern, at least, in some countries.

The paper is composed of 7 sections. In §2, we sketch the Japanese educational system, the process of text book authorization and the process of revision of CS. The second half of §2 is devoted to a description of the necessity of reform and the chronic issues of Japanese mathematics education which the current CS is intended to meet, particularly, the polarization of students, and backwardness in school use of computers.

In §3, we state our philosophy that the purpose of mathematics education (at the secondary level) is to cultivate students' mathematical intelligence with the two foci targets; fostering ML (Mathematical Literacy) and enhancing (MT (Mathematical Thinking Power). In order to be compatible with Japanese social tendency that dislikes apparent differentiations and, at the same time, in order to increase flexibility of curriculum, we have adopted an original structure, the so-called Core and Options curriculum (COM) structure as explained also in §3.

§4 gives a brief description of courses and topics of the current CS to be taught as the core or as optional modules. In fact, the program as a whole is a restricted realization of COM.

Reports on initial experiences of implementation of the current CS are mentioned in §5.

§6 is a brief analysis of Japanese crisis of mathematics education mentioned above. Serious symptoms are students' (even élite students') lowering of scholarship and running away from deep thought in mathematics. Possible causes of this crisis and related sociological backgrounds are mentioned, including the demographic factor that the number of Japanese youths is constantly decreasing.

In §7, this paper is concluded by a description of directions of our future efforts to improve mathematics education, including suggestions for the coming revisions of CS.

§2. Educational System in Japan

The Japanese school system is similar to the American one. Namely, its main body is of the 6-3-3-4 structure, while it is preceded by Kindergarten and is followed by the graduate school. Statistics for 1995 are:

school	years of study	type	enrollment ratio
Kindergarten (K)	1 – 3	volunteer	63.2 %
Elementary school (ES)	6	compulsory	99.99 %
Junior high school (JHS)	3	compulsory	99.99 %
Senior high school (SHS)	3	volunteer	96.7 %
University (Colleges) (UG)	4 (2)	volunteer	32.1 % (13.1 %)
Graduate school (GS)	2 + 3	volunteer	9.0 %

Remark

In Japan, Jyuku, (informal learning institute) is flourishing. Approximately, 20 % of pupils of elementary schools and 50% of students of junior high schools take evening and / or weekend courses in Jyukus for extra learning.

2.1. Course of Study

The contents of teaching in Japanese schools from Kindergarten to SHS are strongly controlled by the Course of Study (CS) issued by Monbusho (Ministry of Education, Science and Culture). In recent years, CS has been totally reorganized approximately every ten years. Actually, the current CS was announced in 1989, while previous revisions of CS had been made in 1978 (post-modernization), 1970 (modernization), 1969, 1955, · · · . Textbooks for school use must be written according to the CS and have to undergo authorization by Monbusho.

Usually, the formal process of revision of the CS starts with forming the Council of Education Curricula (CEC) and with an inquiry from the minister of Monbusho to the Council, which are often preceded by the minister's receipt of recommendations from a superior council, the Central Council of Education. After the answer of CEC is submitted, working committees for each school subject are formed and work out the new CS, which is then announced and put in force by Monbusho. Then publishers create textbooks in accordance with the new CS and submit them for authorization by Monbusho.

Thus, it takes several years to begin school teaching according to the new CS after its announcement. Actually, the current CS was announced in 1989, and firstly implemented 1992 with ES, 1993 in with JHS and in 1994 with SHS.

2.2. Recognized issues

The following issues were recognized as basic problems to be met by the new CS, when we started our informal and then formal preparation for organization of the current CS in 1980's.

1) *The nearly saturated high advancement rate to SHS,* which reaches 95% or over. This implies lowering and diversity of scholarships among the majority of students.

2) Practically and concretely, the mathematics part of the new CS has to meet *the polarization of students* into the following two groups;
• Students of better aptitude who are bound for university education, professional career and who need strength in mathematics.
• Majority of students who need mathematical literacy to live and work as intellectual citizens.

3) *Retarded state of use of computers* in mathematics teaching and learning has to be recovered. In spite of popularity of computers in Japanese society (workplace as well as home), introduction of computers in school education had been difficult without formal approval for it by CS.

Remarks

1) Generally speaking, the Japanese mathematics teachers are good in regard to the academic background. All of them are graduates of 4 years universities or higher.

2) The entrance examination to prestigious universities, good SHS, and excellent private JHS is very competitive. It exerts a strong driving force for students to work hard as well as distortion of sound learning of mathematics.

§3. Guiding Principles and Strategies

Our basic philosophy and strategies in organizing the current CS are as follows. Incidentally, in addition to publication of papers in references, these principles and strategies were orally presented by the author to the international community of mathematics education on occasions like ICME–5, Adelaide (1984), UCSMP & NCTM Conferences, Chicago (1988), ICME–6, Budapest (1988), ICMI Sessions in ICM'90, Kyoto (1990).

3.1. A historical view point

We claim that the current progress of mathematical sciences, where the new applied mathematics plays the core role, should be recognized as the fourth peak in the history of mathematics to follow the preceding three, namely, the birth of Euclidian geometry, the discovery of infinitesimal calculus and formation of abstract mathematics. Furthermore, the coming fourth peak of mathematics shares basic features with the second peak in the sense that they are both characterized by a vivid expansion of concepts and methods and by rich applications. Mathematics education must reflect these trends of mathematics.

3.2. The purpose of mathematics education

We have reviewed the purpose of mathematics education at SHS level and reached the assertion as follows. Particularly, as for SHS, the purpose of mathematics education is to cultivate mathematical intelligence of the students through the two-foci targets: namely, by fostering their

ML = mathematical literacy and *MT = mathematical thinking power.*

These two targets should be pursued in an appropriate balance depending on individual schools, classes or individual students and in view of the students' intended career and aptitudes.

To be a little more specific, we claim that

ML = mathematical competence of intellectual citizens
= mathematics for intelligent users,
MT = mathematical potentiality for future career.

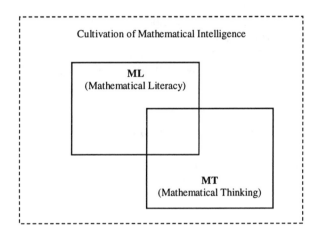

3.3. Flexibility curriculum

As a fundamental strategy, we have adopted the curriculum structure of *Core and optional modules (COM),* which was originally proposed by Prof. F. Terada.
Original structure of COM

Conceptually, the mathematics curriculum of the core-options structure is designed as follows.
• Math curriculum = { core } ∪ { option modules }
• Core = standard math-competence of intellectual citizens
• Option = { Remedial options } ∪ { advanced options }
– Core-Options diagram –

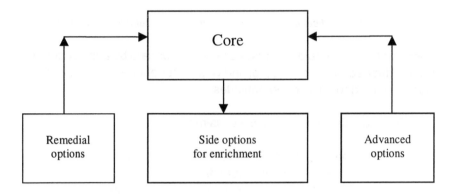

Intended merits of COM

1. Flexibility of curriculum to meet diversity of students without apparent differentiation.
2. More chances of self-adjustment.
3. Compatible with the two foci goals, ML and MT.
4. Compatible with introduction of computers and calculators into school mathematics.

§4. Current Courses of SHS Mathematics

The current SHS in accordance with 1989-CS is a restricted realization of COM, and is actually composed of courses as described below.

4.1. Courses

Course	Requirement	Standard Units	Structure	Year
Math I	compulsory	4	Omnibus	1st
Math II	selective	3	Omnibus	2nd
Math III	selective	3	Omnibus	3rd
Math A	selective	2	Option modules	1st
Math B	selective	2	Option modules	2nd
Match C	selective	2	Option modules	3rd

Remarks

As mentioned above, this program of the current CS can be viewed as a restricted realization of COM curriculum. Such restriction was necessary to avoid the impact of drastic change, to be feasible in the customary way of closed class teaching, to be practically compatible with the entrance examination to universities and finally to be subject to control by Monbusho through CS.

According to the current CS, we regard that the core for general students is

$$\{MathI\} \cup \{MathII\},$$

while the core for science and technology bound students is

$$\{MathI\} \cup \{MathII\} \cup \{MathIII\}.$$

The option modules are contained in Math A, Math B, Math C. If a student takes one of these courses, he/she is normally required to learn two of the modules of his / her choice among four modules belonging to each course. On the other hand, Math I, Math II and Math III are of integrated omnibus structure: If a student takes one of these courses, he/she must learn all topics in it.

It is emphasized that Math C should be learned with due use of computers and from the view point of applied mathematics.

The arrangement of topics through the whole program is not very systematic. Some of necessary knowledge to learn a topic or module may have to be prepared "on the spot" when needs come up.

4.2. Contents of courses

Math I	Math A
1) quadratic functions	1) numbers and expressions
2) figures and measurements, simple trigonometry included	2) plane geometry
3) number of elements and cases combinatorics	3) numerical sequence
4) probability	4) computation and computers

Math II	Math B
1) various functions e^x, $\log x$, trigonometric functions	1) vectors
2) figures and equations straight lines and circles	2) complex numbers and complex plane
3) change of values of functions simple differentiation and integration	3) probability distributions
	4) algorithm and computers

Math III	Math C
1) functions and their limit	1) matrices and linear computation
2) differential calculus	2) various curves including
	conics and polar coordinates
3) integral calculus	3) numerical computation
	4) statistical processing

§5. Report on Initial Implementation

Students to graduate from SHS in 1997 March are the first runners who have studied according to the current CS. Hence, reports only on the initial experiences of implementation of CS are available now.

5.1. Statistics of selective courses and modules

1) Selective courses are shown below by percentages of students who take them. For instance, since Math I is compulsory, its percentage is 100 %, while Math C is taken only by 19.8 % of students who are mostly bound for science and technology.

Math I	Math II	Math III	Math A	Math B	Math C
100 %	86.1 %	21.4 %	71.6 %	43.9 %	19.8 %

2) *Selective modules* taught are shown by percentages of schools which offer teaching of them. Statistics for Math C is not available yet in 1996.

Math A

Number and expression	Plane geometry
91.4 %	25.6 %

Numerical sequence	Computation and computer
81.9 %	6.4 %

Math B

Vector	Complex number and computer plane
76 %	70 %

Probability distribution	Algorithm and computer
25.0 %	3.2 %

5.2. Reports and comments

The following is a part of various reports and comments with appreciation or criticism from initial experiences of the CS.

1) *Text books:* Reliable but somewhat conservative text books have been created to match the new CS.

2) *Response of students:* In many schools, Math I matches the majority of students.

3) *Appreciation by teachers:* The flexible structure of the new CS is stimulating for enthusiastic or active teachers, while the non-systematic arrangement of topics is not liked by some conservative teachers who are mostly senior.

4) *Entrance examinations:* Notwithstanding the difficulty caused by the increased flexibility of curriculum, the Center of University Entrance Examination has decided to pose a full menu examination including all modules of the selective subjects Math A and Math B.

On the other hand, however, most of the prestigious national universities are not very cooperative with the new CS and have flatly designated two modules to be tested from each of Math A, Math B, Math C, in particular, excluding the computer related modules. This exerts a strong negative influence on SHS, and makes it difficult for SHS to implement the CS as it was intended.

5) *Computers:* Computer-related modules are rarely offered to teach a SHS, although many SHS recognize importance of these modules and the hardware environments are not poor nowadays, probably because teachers are not well prepared, and, as mentioned above and because of exclusion of these modules from the range of mathematics problems at the individual entrance examination to many universities. Nevertheless, a number of conscientions universities have announced to include computer modules to the range of their examinations.

6) *Response of university professors:* Except for those who are particularly concerned with the secondary education since before, university mathematics professors feel that the current CS is too non-systematic to lose the characteristic nature of mathematics, and is inconvenient practically in setting problems of entrance examination. Some of them hate the increased teaching burden caused by the acceptance of students with diverse backgrounds which is a consequence of new CS.

On the other hand, because of the recent issues which they seriously experience in teaching mathematics of the university level, a number of university professors express their support of the underlying idea of the new CS.

§6. Crisis of Mathematics Education

In Japan, youth's disinclination for study of science and technology as well as for study of mathematics has become a serious matter of concern. As for mathematics, on July 2, 1994, presidents of academic societies of mathematics and mathematics education made a public appeal, "Crisis of Mathematical Education in Japan" in order to call for measures and efforts to meet this difficulty. Furthermore, the ICMI national committee of Japan chaired by Prof. S. Iitaka sent a letter on July 15, 1995 to Professor A. Arima, President of the Central Council of Education, requesting to incorporate necessary measures to resolve this serious issue when the Council works out their recommendation to the minister of Monbusho.

6.1. Some symptoms

Particularly in regard to mathematics, the following symptoms of the crisis are observed:

1) *Lowering of scholarship of university students,* remarkable even with engineering students of prestigious universities.

2) *Lowering of quality of learning* is a matter of concern. Children and students opt to avoid mathematical problems which require deeper thinking. Even when they earn some good scores in mathematics, children are poor with verbal problems and students hate problems involving proof.

3) *Decay of popularity of mathematics among élite students* should be noted, although the decrease in number of SHS students who take selective mathematics courses is not drastic yet.

In suffering from students' falling away, mathematics is not alone. Japanese youths with better aptitude prefer, as their majors, fields of literary or social sciences to science and technology, although nobody denies the importance of science and technology in the coming era.

At SHS, physics is learned only by 20% of students, while physics was taken by 80% of students some decades ago. As reasons for this tendency, we may refer:

- Decay in youths of traditional cultural backgrounds like diligence and perseverance.

- Youths dislike sustained efforts which S&T (Science and Technology) requires.

- Freshmen's wish to relax and enjoy after competitive entrance examinations is difficult to realice with S&T.

- Scientists and engineers are not well paid in comparison with bankers and commercial managers. They are unhappy in companies when their knowledge becomes obsolete.

- Facilities and learning environments of S&T in universities are poor.

- Curriculum for science at the secondary level may be too stiff to kill students' fondness of science.

6.2. Demographic factor

The number of 18 year - old in Japan decreases sharply after the peak in 1992.

Number of 18 year - old youths. (Unit = 10,000)

1980	1985	1986	1990	1991	1992	1993	1994	1995	1996
158	156	185	201	204	205	198	186	177	172

1997	1998	1999	2000	2001	2002	2003	2004	2005	2006
167	161	153	151	150	147	141	137	133	130

This decrease in size of this age group has favourable as well as bad influences on school education. For instance, the number of children in a classroom may be reduced. The competition at the entrance examination will be relaxed except for those who aim at very prestigious schools and universities. On the other hand, however, new employment of young and active teachers will become difficult, because the educational budget depends monotonously on the number of pupils and students. Furthermore, universities of medium level may exclude mathematics from their entrance examination in order to attract more applicants who do not like mathematics, and thus discourage mathematics learning.

6.3. Appeal by presidents of societies

As mentioned above, the presidents of the following societies signed the Appeal *"Crisis of Mathematics Education"*: Mathematical Society of Japan (S. Iitaka), Japanese Society of Mathematical Education (T. Uetake), Japan Society for Industrial and Applied Mathematics (H. Fujita), Society of Mathematical Education (K. Yokochi).

Items Suggested in the Appeal are:

1. More school hours, particularly in Junior high schools, must be alloted to mathematics.
2. Ample mathematical literacy must be fostered in all students through enjoyable (not painstaking) approaches.
3. Study of coherent curricula of mathematics with an integral view over all grades and school levels is needed.
4. Active and enjoyable learning of mathematics by students should be promoted with active use of computers.
5. More mathematics teachers with a lively mathematical sense must be brought up and employed.
6. The weight of mathematics at entrance examinations should not be reduced, while improvement of its problem-setting must be done increasingly.

§7. Required Further Efforts

In the coming reorganization of CS, which is to be started during 1996 by forming the Council of Educational Curricula, we have to try to achieve the following:

1. Pursuit of the objectives of the current CS with necessary amendments of the content.
2. More active use of computers and graphic calculators into each topic in mathematics.
3. Review of JHS mathematics, which used to be too uniform with little selective components. We have to re-organize the curriculum so that even in this period of compulsory education, we can foster germs of various abilities of individual students, and on the other hand, we do not force the majority of students to learn too sophisticated topics beyond their aptitude.
4. Re-examination of teaching topics to meet the 5-days (per week) school system.
5. Organize curriculum with ML-MT targets which is properly applicable to the group of stronger (even gifted) students as well as the majority of students, provided that their teachers are qualified and well-prepared.

References

[1] H. Fujita: *The present state and a proposed reform of mathematical education at senior secondary level in Japan,* J. Sci. Educ. Japan, vol. 9 (1985), pp. 39-52

[2] A.G. Howson, B. Wilson and 7 others, *School Mathematics in the 1990s,* ICMI Study Series, 1986, Cambridge Univ. Press.

[3] H. Fujita: *The present state and current problems of mathematics education at the senior secondary level in Japan,* Proc. UCSMP Intern. Conf. on Math. Educ., Chicago (Development in School Mathematics Education around the World, vol. 1), NCTM and UCSMP, 1987, pp. 191-224.

[4] H. Fujita, T. Miwa and J. Becker: *The reform of mathematics education at the upper secondary school (USS) level in Japan,* Development in School Mathematics Education around the World, vol. 2, NCTM and UCSMP, 1991, pp. 31-52.

[5] H. Fujita and F. Terada: *A coherent study of mathematics education for the information age,* Proc. ICMI-China Regional Conf. on Math. Educ., 1991, Beijing, pp. 1-7.

[6] H. Fujita: *New paradigm of applied mathematics; its historical position and projection on mathematics education,* J. Cult. Hist. Math., vol. 3 (1993), pp. 28-33.

[7] H. Fujita: *Principles in organizing the university mathematics curriculum for scientists and engineers,* Proc. SEACME-6, June 1993, Surabaya, Indonesia, pp. 1-11.

ISSUES IN ASSESSMENT: A NEVER ENDING STORY

Peter Galbraith

Let us begin by agreeing that winds of change have been blowing for some time in the world of mathematics assessment and that these winds vary in strength from gentle zephyrs to potential hurricanes. Let us recognise that shifts in emphasis have occurred and are occurring; for example a move away from sole reliance on formal testing; the introduction of so-called coursework assessment involving project work and other activities of an open nature; an increase in the number of countries, states and territories that involve teachers actively in assessment activities; and an increased consciousness that assessment should form an integral part of teaching/learning transactions.

Simultaneously let us acknowledge, in apparent conflict with some of the above, moves towards system wide 'accountability' at various levels of schooling through the agency of national or state mandated tests of mathematical 'ability' or 'competence'. Rather obviously the different 'winds' have sources in belief systems that themselves vary in what they value most.

It seems of doubtful benefit in a paper such as this to discuss the detail of various assessment instruments or methods, existing or developing, or the efficacy or efficiency with which such instruments might be administered, for inevitably any given choice will be outside the current interests of some countries and systems, and hence by definition peripheral to some potential readers. There is an expanding source of reference material that may be consulted with respect to such developments, for example (Niss, 1993(a) and (b); Romberg, 1992; Gifford and O'Connor, 1992; Leder, 1992; Grouws, 1992; as well as a variety of National Reports).

So it is my intention to assume that these or similar, actions, circumstances, methods, and contexts exist in some form in all countries and to attempt to address at a more general level issues and questions that are consequently posed for the mathematical education community.

An international perspective

Recognising that circumstances vary between countries, there do seem to be changes in social, political and educational climates that form a broad backdrop to the assessment saga on a sufficiently global basis as to affect almost all of us.
Acknowledging that any selection is subjective, I will nominate five that seem to me to be illustrative of such movements.

1. Educational opportunities and requirements are being broadened globally - this may involve more children completing primary school, more children undertaking secondary education, more students proceeding to tertiary studies, or changes in the composition of schooling due to policies of positive discrimination on behalf of population sub-groups.

A consequence is a continuing decline in the so-called 'unskilled population', an increase in the level of formal qualifications demanded by employers, and at the global level a developing international trade in qualifications and courses which may be expected to increase through expanded use of the Internet.

Within such societal shifts, assessment is seen as a means of exercising control (Wolf, 1996) through which we find manifested:
- accountability as a public demand particularly in industrialised countries
- monitoring of standards through national and international agencies for social and economic development
- increased linking of teaching with work experience
- increased concern on the part of students, teachers, parents and employers for education to provide an adequate basis for occupational selection.

These moves have locked into the pre-existing interest in international comparisons (FIMS; SIMS, TIMSS) (Robitaille, 1992) involving testing across perceived common standards and supported by more general tracking of societal indicators over time by agencies such as the World Bank and UNESCO.

Nationally 'standards' have become prey to political processes that result in something like the following:

"Standards must be raised so we need assessment based on standards; hence transfer power from schools to central agencies and professional test providers."

Since reliability as a public perception is paramount, it is easier to sacrifice validity, and a way to muzzle resulting critique is to freeze teachers and the mathematics community out of the process. Now it becomes a question of who decides what quality is, and who controls it! - a political question rather than an educational one.

2. There are re-definitions of the assessment agenda that use common terms but with different meanings. For example various 'deconstructed' meanings are given to key words and what these imply for practice. A word such as Accountability can be construed respectively as, following Wolf (1996):

(i)   being able to *explain* (account for) actions; or
(ii)   being responsible *for* some actions; or
(iii)   being responsible *to* someone for actions taken.

These interpretations have substantially different meanings in practice where for example (1) provides for considerable teacher autonomy while (3) can mean the withholding of funds unless prescribed standards and methods (as specified by major stakeholders) are adhered to.

When defining such standards associated with criterion based assessment the construct of transparency must be added to the traditional constructs of validity and reliability suitably re-defined. Transparency refers in particular to criterion targets that aim to ensure that students can see clearly where to go. The more transparent the criteria the better the student should be able to target learning. However following the maxim that 'every silver lining has a cloud' explicit clarification of what is to be achieved also opens the door to challenge, especially in litigatious societies.

3. Issues of 'equality' continue to add unresolved questions to the assessment debate. Some learners, for example through culture and background, are better equipped to engage in 'assessment games' than others so that opportunities are unequal even though public procedures have an air of objective legitimacy. The traditional use of mathematics as a filter (based on some version of faculty psychology), through which mathematics performance continues to be viewed as a proxy for general ability, continues. Given the acceptance of this view society then feels empowered to use assessment as a means of disciplining students, teachers and institutions as argued by Niss (1993(a)) in terms of the carrot/stick approach to assessment. In places where external examinations continue as vestiges of colonial power, Ridgeway and

Passey (1992), the impact of associated social and political beliefs are as strong (or stronger) than pressures for reform deriving from research-based educational outcomes or generative professional wisdom.

4. Conceptions of ability continue to represent a pervasive fundamental conflict among issues yet to be resolved. Beliefs that innate intelligence and aptitude are the determiners of mathematical success continue to exist and sustain fatalistic approaches to mathematics performance. Such beliefs effectively excuse individuals on the one hand from trying as students, and on the other from trying as teachers. That fatalism is alive and well in my own country amongst both teachers and the public was demonstrated all too cleariy through two research studies (Galbraith and Chant, 1990, 1993).

The other aspect of ability attribution that continues as an issue involves the domain specific versus domain general explanation of the development of human talent (Brown and Campione, 1992). If intelligence as the ability to leam is innate, then it does not matter much what kind of testing is used to assess its level, providing it meets conventional notions of reliability and validity - as capitalized by commercial producers of educational tests. If, however, performance can be enhanced by careful teaching then it matters a great deal how the standards are set, how the learning goals are made transparent and explicit, and how the assessment program is matched to the specific leaming goals. Related issues expounded by Brown and Campione (1992) include the amount of guidance provided, rather than the number of trials needed for leaming to appear (a metacognitive rather than a behaviourist position), and the focus of assessment on the effectiveness of current learning rather than on the fruits of past learning. The paper presents one of the more powerful theoretical supports for a dynamic interaction between assessment and instruction, both for learning potential, and for the linking of assessment and instruction as an alliance against the re-ification of test scores into fixed cognitive entities. This theoretical debate continues to underlie activities that at another level appear to be concerned with practice.

5. Forms of reporting progress have increasingly become a focus for innovation. Zarinnia and Romberg (1992) provide seven categories within which assessment outcomes might be reported. In referring to a range of positive or negative side-effects associated with each they draw attention to advantages and distortions potentially deriving from new assessment directions. For example while focussing on process may present mathematics as powerful and active, it may also cause fragmentation in which various processes become ends in themselves rather than as means to an holistic end -no less a fragmentation than has occurred with

a focus on content. Similar analyses in a variety of countries point firmly away from reliance on standardized testing to the use of contextualized evidence obtained from tasks incorporated in regular instruction. This in turn sets an agenda for the re-professionalization of the teaching community in which beliefs about the nature of authentic mathematical activity is a target for change, and a basis for developing exemplars descriptive of quality as a pre-cursor to the development of ways of promoting inter-judge agreement on the quality of student work. These continuing manifestations of the nature/nurture debate impact in various ways on all efforts to change the emphasis in assessment towards learning in context.

A question of interests

The preceding section has sampled some of the events and movements currently engaging the field of Mathematics Education. It is assumed that through our pedagogical and assessment practices we hope to provide for the development of a liberated person in the sense described by Siegel (1980) as one who is "free from the unwarranted control of unjustified beliefs, insupportable attitudes, and the paucity of abilities which can prevent that person from completely taking charge of his or her life". The search for liberty inevitably calls into question the "interests" that are served by concepts and procedures used to control and label the capacities of individuals.

The question of "interests" as it has been applied in Education generally is associated with the 'critical theory' movement from which it has drawn its conceptual basis (Habermas, 1971; Gibson, 1986; Carr and Kemmis, 1986). Three levels of interest have been articulated, viz technical, practical, and emancipatory, and much has been written concerning these in the general teacher education literature, see for example van Manen (1977) and particularly Zeichner and his associates (Zeichner and Liston, 1987; Tabachnik and Zeichner, 1984; Zeichner, 1993).

Technical interests refer to the interest in gaining knowledge for the purpose of efficient and effective application in controlling the environment defined in a broad sense. This may be taken to include the attainment of prescribed educational objectives requiring technical skill, and mastery approaches to learning and assessment provide an exemplar for the achievement of technical interests in mathematics. Technical interests in the eyes of critical scholars are not necessarily bad, however they do not represent the only kind of knowledge to be sought.

Practical interests refer to a conception of action that involves explicating and clarifying assumptions behind alternative actions and evaluating the ultimate consequences of the actions. Actions and decisions are linked to value positions and those who are actors in the system must consider the worth of the various alternatives.

This type of knowledge is concerned with interpretive understanding. However, the subjective meanings embedded in aspects of this knowledge are controlled (limited) by the context in which it is enacted, and hence govern the extent of what can be achieved. Reflection plays a significant role in developing the scope of *practical interests* which might encompass, for example, acceptance of a range of assessment forms as necessary to evaluate different types of valued mathematical activity.

Emancipatory interests refer to issues of justice, equity, and fulfilment, and can only be served by a 'critical approach' that identifies the restrictions referred to above and reveals how they may be eliminated. Thus they offer an awareness of how aims, purposes and possibilities have been repressed and distorted, and what actions are required to eliminate sources of inadequacy or frustration.

It is emphasised that it is distortions that offend this latter viewpoint not the pursuit of other interests as such. For example technical interests may facilitate emancipation through the provision of mathematical power to learners, but they may also disempower through culturally inappropriate methods of assessing and thence accrediting competence.

It is my purpose now to use these conceptions of interests as a lens through which to view contemporary issues in assessment such as were sampled in the preceding section.

Let us take for example the term *accountability* as it might be interpreted within an Education system. If we define this term as meaning being able to explain actions (i.e. account for) we give freedom for teachers and schools to argue for or defend a variety of assessment practices based on corresponding value positions – practical interests at least are provided for. If we define the term *as being responsible for* some action we again locate the power and responsibility with those who design the learning and the assessment. Decisions made must be defensible in terms of the context of operations. If however the term is defined to mean being responsible to someone (or some organization), then there is a major shift in the location of power. This can involve a requirement to carry out a particular educational program with non-compliance punishable by withdrawal of funding. Interests served in this situation are likely to be narrowly technical. Those concerned with practical or emancipatory interests are likewise outraged by this position which is often compounded by their exclusion from the design and rationale of assessment procedures. The former's outrage is essentially intellectual, concerned for the quality of mathematics mandated by the procedures; the latter's outrage extends to encompass the political - concern for students and educational professionals, at the narrowly technical expertise they are offered, and concern that educational decisions have been usurped by ideological expediency.

The point at issue for the profession is that of involvement. At the outset terms like accountability tend to be used as buzzwords in as yet uncrystallised forms. Emancipatory interests would demand that the profession become involved at the outset, while there may still be time to influence the definition ultimately adopted for implementation, and to fight where necessary to overthrow imposed structures and definitions deemed educationally or morally unsound or restrictive.

It is, however, possible for developments generated from a concern for practical or even emancipatory interests to become re-ified in a way that consigns them to technical rationality. Zarinnia and Romberg (1992) sound a timely warning in alerting that the elevation of process categories of performance assessment, introduced for the purpose of increasing the mathematical power of all students, can lead to fossilisation just as restrictive and mind-numbing as content based categories have been deemed to be, e.g. 'working through' or 'writing reasons' can become separate ends in themselves rather than parts of a greater whole.

Perhaps nowhere is conflict of 'interest' more of a continuing issue than in the development of assessment instruments, and in particular those associated with the newer emphases of investigatory work, problem solving, and modelling. However they are otherwise presented, arguments ultimately centre around the location of power. When power has traditionally resided with universities, state or national examining bodies, or test manufacturers, the implications are substantial both in intellectual and monetary terms.

Coursework assessment represents a substantial transfer of authority from external experts to schools and the teaching profession. With the opportunity of taking into account the school context and associated societal factors there is a potential shift in focus away from purely technical interests. Indeed some authors (e.g. Keitel, 1993) have suggested how the opportunity exists to address also wider issues of justice and emancipatory concerns through developing such foci. Not surprisingly some of the most vigorous territorial battles are fought in this domain for the potential power shift is substantial since at least two 'interests' battles must be fought here.

(1) to facilitate a change in 'beliefs' about what constitutes authentic mathematical activity, when past conceptions have been moulded by narrowly defined technical interests.

(2) to support the profession in its transformation into a community of practice: for example through the provision of training in the development of inteijudge reliability in assessing project work - an attribute requiring the same type of professional knowledge and judgment that is currently used in assessing the worth of doctoral theses by the academic community.

Hoge and Colardarci (1989) leave no doubt as to where they believe opposition to such transfer of power lies. Following their survey showing that teachers were, by and large, very good judges of their students' performance, they go on to nominate groups who continue to reject teacher judgments as valid assessment data in the interests of maintaining control over assessment practices.

It is possible to go on to identify conflicting interests in almost every area of the assessment debate. The question is what this does for the advancement of knowledge and process, for awareness and critique at one level can serve to harden and re-ify opposition and defences at another, or can remain simply as critique. One possible path to progress is to adopt a dialectical strategy, that is to specify potential conflicts of interest and subject them to informed rational debate, rather than polarize and entrench opposing viewpoints through verbal attack or to strive for an uneasy but superficial peace. To question rather than condemn is also consistent with the Habermasian approach exemplified in his promotion of the Ideal Speech Situation (Habermas, 1971; Gibson, 1986).

The ideal speech situation (ISS) requires that each individual communication possess four qualities. It should be

(a) comprehensible - e.g. made in a shared language
(b) true, i.e. matching what we perceive as reality
(c) correct, i.e. legitimate within the context of the topic
(d) sincere

Furthermore, the ISS requires that all speakers (or communicators) have equal rights to dispute, assert and question and, by inference, have equal access to relevant knowledge. Put differently, this requires that an ISS be free from domination and, given this condition and genuine goodwill, progress can be pursued by rational argument.

It is not however difficult to identify impediments to this ideal in our debates on assessment, e.g. unequal 'rights of speech' afforded to political voices versus educational voices, administrators versus teachers, academic mathematicians versus professional educators, parent demands versus teacher ideals, competency advocates versus wider mathematical adherents.

How might such an approach work? A simple beginning would involve selecting issues of significance and for each posing questions that direct debate to the intellectual content and power relations represented by identified alternative interests made public. The following examples illustrate the dialectic properties of this approach.

Interests of teachers in developing understanding	vs	Interests of students in achieving grades
Interests of administrators in placating parents	vs	Interests of teachers in using innovative assessment
Interests of schools in meeting league table pass levels	vs	Interests of weaker studen abandoned to enable others to reach that level
Interests of subject department heads in controlling assessment	vs	Interests of teachers in developing best practice
Interests of Universities in maintaining power over school mathematics	vs	Interests of schools in increasing professional autonomy
Interests of employers in prescribing 'basics'	vs	Interests of schools in achieving 'fundamentals'
Interests of Testing Services in selling instruments	vs	Interests of teachers in designing assessment
Interests of the State in competency measures	vs	Interests of the school in quality measures

Such a listing is not intended to imply a "good" versus "bad" characterisation. The purpose in establishing a dialectic is to create an agenda and a forum through which interests may be disclosed and addressed that are often present but not made public. While there is no assurance that this will always work, public declarations of position and the relentless exposure of assumptions, enhance the possibility of progress and render a little less likely the use of vicarious means to avoid confronting issues and the use of managerial methods to overthrow educational goals (Bates, 1984).

This section has been written bearing in mind comments of Marshall and Thompson (1994) that their review of six books on assessment had revealed a plethora of issues and approaches, many criticisms of current practices, but few suggestions for progress. The classification of interests has been introduced as a set of 'spatial coordinates' together with a mechanism (ISS) that provides a structured means for advancing debate on contentious issues - given however a genuine desire to achieve progress on the part of all parties.

A question of scale

Another way of approaching issues is to estimate the extent and type of their impact. Kaput and Thompson (1994) used nautical metaphors to describe the perceived profundity of impact of various aspects of computer technology on mathematics learning.

Borrowing their terminology and adding minor changes of emphasis we obtain the following classification.

Surface wave:	represents procedures and impacts at the level of the individual classroom and school.
Swell:	larger scale and more pervasive so there is impact at the local system level.
Tidal wave:	generated beyond local frames of reference and requiring timescales with larger orders of magnitude.
Sea level change:	fundamental reshaping, analogous to a change in sea level due to global warming.

Using this broad classification we may now assign a range of assessment issues -clearly this contains a substantial element of subjective judgment. At the level of *surface waves* we assign variations of test procedures including the development of contextualized assessment materials such as school-based projects and investigations, and the use of data collection alternatives such as interviews and innovative writing tasks.

At the *swell* level we have the re-conceptualization of concepts like reliability and validity (to encompass notions of transferability and trustworthiness), moves to accept the veracity of and enhance the quality of teacher judgments, and moves to incorporate a range of non-test assessment in certification procedures.

At the *tidal wave* level we look for more pervasive change identifiable beyond the boundary of a local system and might include respectively, the profound change wrought when a formal assessment system is redesigned on the basis that teaching and assessment form an integrated whole; the transforming action of a new epistemological stance (a current example would be constructivism); and the changes wrought as a consequence of some countries' responses to international studies of mathe-matics achievement.

Although tidal influences are profound there may be regions that remain isolated from their effects and for a *sea-level* change we look for uni-directional forces of massive impact and irresistible momentum. It would be a very wise or very foolish individual who felt confident in pronouncing definitively on such issues, so I will merely suggest three which seem at this time to be potential candidates. They are respectively the continuing development of mathematical software and associated technology, the communication properties and potential of the Internet, and an internationalization of notions of competence and standards as a consequence of a developing international trade in qualifications and courses.

This section has attempted to address another difficulty perceived in the assessment debate. The issues we consider and the books we write tend to be important but undifferentiated: better methods of testing computation are considered together with ways to improve the quality of feedback on problem solving, together with the merits and demerits of national and international testing etc etc. The metaphor seems to be J.J. Thomson's plum pudding model of the atom with issues scattered around like currents and raisins in a mass of material labelled assessment.

The nautical metaphor suggests an approach closer to the Rutherford-Bohr model by separating assessment issues into 'energy levels' on the basis of their perceived location and pervasiveness. This is a crude device but it is one way of structuring issues into family groups that may then, if desired, be examined using another set of dimensions such as 'interests' served, or other agreed criteria.

Towards a theory of assessment

As noted above, in their review of six books on assessment, Marshall and Thompson (1994) remark on the feature, common to them all, of identifying what is wrong with current assessment practices. Niss (1993) refers to 'conflicting interests, divergent aims, and unintended or undesired side-effects' characteristic of assessment modes and practices and observes that 'difficulties involved in devising and employing effective, harmonious assessment modes, free from serious internal and external problems seem to be fundamental and universal in nature'. Webb (1992) in summarizing a similar range of developments and concerns calls for a 'specific theory of mathematics assessment within a general theory of educational assessment'.

What are issues relevant to the development of a theory of mathematics assessment as a home within which to locate and extend the plethora of current issues, actions, needs, and beliefs. Three or four years ago I raised the role of basic assumptions about the nature of knowledge in influencing the direction and purpose of mathematics assessment (Galbraith, 1993) and it is not the intention to repeat those arguments here. However nothing has happened in the intervening period to lessen the conviction that basic belief systems are the ultimate determiners of positions (causes), which at another level appear in the form of arguments that refer to the specifics of assessment processes and products (symptoms). To the extent that they underpin the discussion that follows I have summarized basic assumptions of the two approaches to 'knowledge' and 'reality' described by Lincoln and Guba (1990) as characterising respectively the positivist and naturalistic (constructivist) paradigm (see below).

Axioms about	Positivist Paradigm	Naturalistic Paradigm
Nature of reality (ontology)	Single, tangible and 'out there'	Multiple, constructed and holistic
Relationship of Knower to Known	Knower and known are independent	Knower and known are interactive
Possibility of gereralisation	True and context-free generalisations are possible	Only time ad context-bound working hypotheses are possible
Role of values	Inquiry is value-free (fact-value independence)	Inquiry is value bound (fact-value interdependence)

Four philosophical 'realities' relevant to respective ontological positions are identified.

(1)   *Objective reality* - a tangible reality exists and given enough time and sound principles of investigation the reality can be converged upon (even though individual studies may be only approximations).

(2)   *Perceived reality* - a reality exists but it cannot be known fully but only through a spectrum of perceptions. Reality for any individual or group is at most a partial portrait of the whole and capable of different interpretations when considered from different viewpoints.

Positions (1) and (2) agree on the existence of a "real" reality but differ in what they consider to be knowable about that reality.

(3)   *Constructed reality* - defined terms such as "problem", "learner", "examination system" evoke different meanings within individuals. None exist in forms other than those constructed by persons who 'recognise' the term in question. Such constructed realities may indeed match 'tangible entities' quite closely. For example a group of individuals from out of town may agree closely on the scope of actions displayed by a policeman on traffic duty. However this represents a consensus among the observers rather than the discovery of a single true reality. Truth by consensus is the approach consistent with this ontological position.

(4)   *Created reality* - effectively means that there is no reality at ah until it is perceived as a consequence of some action. If stranded by a rockfall on one side of a deep chasm over which the single possibility of escape resides in a damaged footbridge, two possible futures exist side by side. Creation of the reality of survival or doom depends upon the act of testing the bridge as a means of escape.

Positions (3) and (4) share basic assumptions about the nature of 'reality' - viz that it doesn't exist until it is constructed by an actor (3) or is created by a participant (4).

Now with respect to discussions about the principles and practices of assessment we find representations of all four positions. Belief in ability as inherent intellectual endowment independent of context or task continues to support test construction with its corresponding emphasis on reliability of measures as the attribute of paramount importance, a manifestation of position (1). Position (2) attracts adherents who value a range of assessment types as a better means of converging on that elusive concept 'mathematical ability' that nevertheless exists in some absolute form. Non traditional assessment tasks may be utilized but are only to be trusted if set and marked centrally and administered under conditions that in some sense may be described as standard.

Position (3) is the province of those who admit and indeed rejoice in the possibility of equivalent but different contributions to the assessment of quality. A pattern of performance that includes subjective measures of quality, and consensus rating of judges, is characteristic of this position. Verbal statements of criteria and standards must be translated for application across a range of conditions and scholarly consensus represents the only viable basis for agreement. Project work, problem solving, modelling and other forms of extended assessment are valued within this viewpoint as is more conventional testing under certain circumstances. These circumstances however are approved in terms of the purpose of the test (e.g. to check facility with a calculator or assess the level of algebraic skill) and not in terms of some objective measure of mathematical ability supposedly measured by the test score. Project work et al within this view is best marked by the professional most familiar with the students' work (i.e. the teacher) with the latter's expert judgment a consequence of the application of principles characterizing a community of practice and accredited by that community.

Position (4) supports the radical possibility of creating new 'realities' of assessment. In fact this is not as radical as it sounds depending upon the circumstance. An actual example comes to mind of a subject head who introduced a policy that no assessment would be approved that could not be conducted within the time and format of ordinary class lessons. This replaced a scheme whereby schooling was suspended at intervals for the 'exam week'. The new 'reality' was a commitment to the integration of teaching and assessment in the fullest sense, a carefully crafted alternative to the 'objective' model previously in force.

And so to the question of a theory of mathematics assessment. Any theory must rest upon some agreed ontological position and its epistemological consequences. It can safely be asserted that no theory of assessment can be built on a positivist ontology -not because of questions of right and wrong but simply because so many in the mathematics community reject this philosophical stance. If such an approach were to be attempted it would be rejected by large sections of the community and hence could not function as an effective theory. This then brings us to the ontology of the naturalistic (constructivist) paradigm and the situation here is not clear either. By its very nature the constructivist position cannot claim universal interpretations and truths that are a positivist legacy, and must depend upon consensus for progress to be achieved. Here a difficulty emerges because of the many viewpoints, and in the words of Niss (1993) 'conflicting interests, divergent aims, and unintended or undesired side-effects'. Yackel, Cobb and Wood (1992) make an important point when discussing the role of the teacher in a constructivist classroom. In pointing out that teacher and student roles are not symmetric they remind us that 'it is the teacher who expresses his/her institutionalised authority in action to help students develop an understanding of what is, and what is not, an acceptable mathematical argument'.

And here is our dilemma. Yackel et al are referring to the learning of mathematics: a disciplined body of knowledge for which agreed norms and practices have been established and accepted by its community of scholars. We have as yet no such agreed precepts and principles for assessing the quality of that closely related yet distinct property of mathematics performance. Indeed we are in the process of trying to establish them.

It seems that we are collectively engaged in an activity much more profound than that which occurs in many classrooms allegedly run according to constructivist principles. It is ironic that in many such classrooms there is encouragement to interpret, construct, and re-construct mathematics; indeed to treat everything (except one) as a candidate for constructivist action. "You (the student) are encouraged to question, interpret and reconstruct everything except the method by which I am teaching you."

The teacher in constructivist mode is still in control in an ultimate sense supported by the impressive edifice of mathematical knowledge from which to draw (while granting that many enriching uncertainties occur in probing new directions of content and process).

I suggest that a major reason why a theory of assessment is so elusive is that the whole mathematics community is engaged in an exercise in construction more profound than that occurring in any classroom. It is endeavouring to construct an edifice of assessment while lacking disciplinary consensus on what particular building materials should go into the cbnstruction. That is, it does not have an established agreed knowledge base to which to appeal - for that is part of the construction in progress. We are attempting to build in a few short years structures parallel to that which took centuries to construct, test, and re-construct for the discipline of mathematics.

To use an analogy from the History of Mathematics to describe our progress towards a theory of assessment, we have been growing through our 'Babylonian and Egyptian' periods. The pragmatic needs of assessment have seen us engineer and refine instruments and methods for application in a variety of practical circumstances, and doing the practical job required has been a sufficient end. We are now attempting to enter our 'Greek' period, to set out practices within a theoretical framework that will simultaneously provide a quality test for our methods, and a springboard for further development.

It is imperative that we retain all parties and viewpoints in the dialogue if some consensual agreement is to be achieved, and for this we need to adopt a global view that transcends our own particular national or local context. Withdrawal from debate and discussion will be as detrimental to the ultimate purpose as a student refusing to participate in the classroom construction of knowledge.

If I treat discussions involving external examinations as irrelevant on the grounds (true) that these are not part of my State's assessment practices, how am I different from a student insisting that every mathematical topic of study should be of personal relevance to him/her? If I reject project work out of hand as valid assessment what distinguishes my approach from a student who refuses to participate in a group? If I, attempt to suppress the analysis of power relationships implicit in an assessment program because I prefer things as they are, how can I require students to engage in mathematical activity beyond their preference for say basic computation?

In other words the kind of involvement we as teachers require of our students as participants in knowledge. construction, we need to require of ourselves in building a foundation on which a theory of assessment might be erected. Perhaps indicative of our pre-theory phase is the existence side by side of procedures that on examination appear to rest upon quite different and conflicting assumptions. Assessment in tertiary mathematics embraces both common timed examinations for large classes and the PhD model of research assessment. The first is commonly argued for on the basis that everyone should be tested under common conditions to enable relative ability to be revealed - a positivist position. Suggestions that PhD students should research the same topic or be subject to uniform conditions are too ludicrous to be even thought about. The PhD model embraces the constructivist position recognizing that quality has a variety of manifestations and may be assessed by the consensual agreement of experts in the field. A theory of mathematics assessment must address such issues among the others.

It has been argued that our community of practice yet lacks an agreed ontology on which to construct a comprehensive theory of assessment. In seeking this goal it is useful to consider issues within frameworks structured around questions of 'space' and 'time'.

The Habermasian dimensions of technical, practical and emancipatory interests provide one means of examining assessment in relation to its purpose and impact across 'space', i.e. with respect to individuals, groups, and societies.

Nautical metaphors provide a means for separating issues in terms of their perceived impact and hence a means of re-organising priorities and expectations. Such frameworks aim to facilitate analysis and discussion at a level beyond the mechanics of particular assessment methods.

Ultimately the way we agree to view 'reality' or 'genuine mathematics' or 'true mathematical ability' will be definitive as a basis for a theory of assessment. Present evidence suggests that we are in the process of a giant exercise in social constructivism within which premature closure will inhibit the ultimate achievement of a theory. Within this activity two approaches threaten to inhibit our collective progress. These are respectively withdrawal from debate on the grounds of incommensurability of ideas, and comfortable living within a restricted community of like minds.

References

Bates, R.J. (1984), *Educational versus Managerial Evaluation.* In P. Broadfoot (Ed.), Selection Certification and Control: Social Issues in Educational Assessment, 127-143. New York: Falmer Press.

Brown, A.L. and Campione, J.C. (1992), *Interactive learning environments: A new look at assessment and instruction.* In B.R. Gifford and M.C. O'Connor (Eds.), Changing Assessments: Alternative Views of Aptitude, Achievement, and Instruction. Boston; Kluwer Academic.

Carr, W. and Kemmis, S. (1986) *Becoming Critical: Education, Knowledge and Action Research.* New York: Falmer Press.

Ferguson, P. (1989), *A Reflective Approach to the Methods Practicum,* Journal of Education for Teaching, 16, 1, 29A3.

Galbraith, P.L. (1992), *Paradigms, Problems and Assessment: Some Ideological Implications.* In M. Niss (Ed.), Investigations into Assessment in Mathematics Education: An ICMI Study, 73-86. Dordrecht: Kluwer Academic Publishers.

Galbraith, P.L. and Chant, D. (1990), *Factors Shaping Attitudes to School Mathematics: Implications for Curriculum Change.* Educational Studies in Mathematics, 21, 4, 299-318.

Galbraith, P.L. and Chant, D. (1993), *The Profession, The Public and School Mathematics,* in W. Atweh, C. Kones, M. Carss, G. Booker (Eds.), Contexts in Mathematics Education, 267-274. Brisbane: MERGA.

Gibson, R. (1986), *Critical Theory and Education.* London: Hodder and Stoughton.

Gifford, B.R. and O'Connor, M.C. (Eds.) (1992), *Changing Assessments: Alternative Views of Aptitude, Achievement and Instruction.* Boston: Kluwer Academic.

Grouws, D.A. (Ed.) (1992), *Handbook of Research on Mathematics Teaching and Learning,* New York: Macmillan.

Habermas, J. (1971), *Knowledge and Human Interest.* Boston: Beacon Press.

Hoge, R.D. and Colardarci, T. (1989), *Teacher based judgments of academic achievement: A review of literature,* Review of Educational Research, 59, 297-313.

Kaput, J.J., and Thompson, P.W. (1994), *Technology in Mathematics Education Research:The first 25 years in the J.R.M.E.* Journal for Research in Mathematics Education, 25, 2, 209-218.

Keitel, C. (1993), *Implicit Mathematical Models in Practice and Explicit Mathematics Teaching by Applications.* In J. de Lange, C. Keitel, I. Huntley, and M. Niss (Eds.), Innovation in Mathematics Education by Modelllng and Appilcations, 19-30.London: Horwood.

Leder, G.C. (Ed.) (1992), *Assessment and Learning of Mathematics,* Melbourne, ACER.

Lincoln, Y.S. and Guba, E.G. (1990), *Naturalistic Inquiry.* Newbury Park: Sage.

Marshall, S. and Thompson, P.W. (1994), *Assessment: what's new and not so new* -A review of six books, Journal for Research in Mathematics Education, 25, 2, 209-218.20

Niss, M. (Ed.) (1993a), *Investigations into Assessment in Mathematics Education: An ICMI Study.* Dordrecht: Kluwer Academic Publishers.

Niss, M. (Ed.) (1993b), *Cases of Assessment in Mathematics Education: An ICMI Study.* Dordrecht: Kluwer Academic Publishers.

Ridgeway, J. and Passey, D. (1992), *An International View of Mathematics Assessment through a glass darkly,* in M. Niss (Ed.), Investigations into Assessment in Mathematics Education, 57-72, Dordrecht: Kluwer Academic Publishers.

Robitaille, D. (1992), *International Studies of Achievement in Mathematics.* In D. Grouws (Ed.), Handbook of Research on

Mathematics Teaching and Learning, 687-709. New York: Macmillan.

Romberg, T.A. (Ed.(1992), *Mathematics Assessment and Evaluation: Imperatives for Mathematics Educators.* Albany: State University of New York Press.

Siegel, H. (1980), *Critical Thinking as an educational ideal.* Educational Forum, 45, 7-23.

Tabachnik, B.R. and Zeichner, K.M. (1984), *The impact of student teaching on the development of teacher perspective,* Journal of Teacher Education, 35, 28-42.

Van Manen, M. (1977), *Linking Ways of Knowing with Ways of Being Practical,* Curriculum Inquiry, 6, 3, 205-228.

Webb, N.L. (1992), *Assessment of Students' Knowledge of Mathematics: Steps Toward a Theory.* In D.A. Grouws (Ed.), Handbook of Research in Mathematics Teaching and Learning, 661-686. New York: Macmillan.

Wolf, A. (1996), *Setting Standards in Educational Assessment: Basis for Consensus? Focus for Dissent?* Keynote address, Assessment Conference, Graduate School of Education, University of Queensland, March.

Yackel, E., Cobb, P., and Wood, T. (1992), *Instructional Development and Assessment from a Socio-cultural Perspective.* In G.C. Leder (Ed.), Assessment and Learning of Mathematics. Melbourne: ACER.

Zarinnia, E.A. and Romberg, T.A. (1992), *A Framework for the California Assessment Program to report Students' Achievement in Mathematics.* In T.A. Romberg (Ed.) Mathematics Assessment and Evaluation: Imperatives for Mathematics Educators, 242-284. Albany: State University of New York Press.

Zeichner, K.M. (1993), *Traditions of Practice in US Pre-service Teacher Education Programs,* Teaching and Teacher Education, 9,1,1-13.

Zeichner, K.M. and Liston, D.P. (1987), *Teaching Student Teachers to Reflect,* Harvard Educational Review, 57, 1, 23-48.

A SOJOURN IN MATHEMATICS EDUCATION

Solomon Garfunkel

This is a personal article. It relates one person's passage into the professional world of mathematics education. It is a story that I tell here, not so much to enhance my own cult of personality, but to give some historical developments in a context I know and hopefully (some day) will come to understand. As with all personal stories it's somewhat difficult to know where to begin. But for want of a better alternative, I'll start with my first full-time job.

I received my Ph.D. in mathematical logic from the University of Wisconsin, Madison in 1967 and at the ripe old age of 24 began my academic career as an instructor at Cornell. On my first day, the chairman of the mathematics department, Alex Rosenberg, invited me in for a chat. Alex was in many ways the ideal chair of a math department. He treated everyone alike, from instructor to full professor. His rabbinical demeanor certainly helped.

While I can't remember his exact words, his fatherly speech went something like, "I hope that you are a good teacher. We want good teaching here at Cornell.

But if you think for one second that anything you do in front of the classroom will have anything to do with whether you eventually get tenure here, you are mistaken. I don't say that this is how things should be; but this is how things are. So, if you ever have to make a choice between working on your research or preparing for a course, and what you care about is staying here, then work on your research."

I was shocked, truly shocked. I saw myself as an adequate researcher, but I knew how much I wanted to teach. I went home and wrote a handwritten (olden days) letter to John Gardner, then the Secretary of Health, Education, and Welfare saying in effect that the gods must be crazy. To my surprise he wrote back. Essentially he told me to work hard, get tenure, and then try to destroy the system from within. And more or less, with many twists and turns, that is what I've tried to do.

I spent three years at Cornell as instructor and assistant professor and then moved to the University of Connecticut at Storrs. At Cornell I had met and become friendly with a biochemist who went to work at M.I.T. at the same time I moved to Connecticut. He was working at a place called the Education Research Center, a sort of curriculum development lab where people had funny titles like senior research scientist. ERC was directed by Jerrold Zacharias.

For those of you unfamiliar with that name, Zach, as everyone called him, was a research physicist of great renown who had pioneered work in physics education in the post-Sputnik era. NSF was rumored to measure grants in Zachs (supposedly 250K dollars per).

At any rate, when I went to visit my friend the biochemist, he introduced me to the people working on mathematics curriculum development. I should note that at that time (the early 70's) almost all NSF grants were at the undergraduate level. So the math group was working on calculus reform, although they didn't call it by that name. The nature of the reform was applications. There was after all a strong bias towards physics and physical applications at ERC. Their overriding philosophy was that for the vast majority of students the only practical way to motivate their study of calculus was to show them early on what calculus was used for. Believe it or not, this was considered an extremely radical position back then.

As I watched people create bubble accelerometers, make wine from grape juice, and slide cars down inclined planes, I was hooked. After all, I was a logician. My training had been as pure as the driven snow. This stuff was brave new world. And more importantly, I recognized the truth behind the basic premise, namely that we could not teach all students with the same assumptions we used for majors. So, I began commuting one day a week from UConn to M.I.T. and working with the math group. I should note that there was a fair amount of pedagogical experimentation as well - programmed learning, mastery learning, hands-on group activities, etc.

At any rate, I brought it all to UConn, running experimental section after experimental section. To be honest, this work was not greatly appreciated.

To be fair, they hired a research logician and it was becoming increasingly clear they got a naive, but energetic math education novice. After surviving a rather bitter tenure fight, I found myself devoting all of my time to curriculum development. And a funny thing happened. I started to have some ideas, to write them up as proposals, to talk to funders, and to have some of those proposals funded. I was a grantee.

In 1976 I co-authored the Undergraduate Mathematics and its Applications (UMAP) grant proposal to the National Science Foundation (NSF). This grant had two goals. The first was to produce, through a user/developer network, a body of modules which taught specific mathematical topics through their contemporary applications. The second was to create an organization which could continue that effort after federal funding was terminated. After all, it was clear that there was no fixed body of modules that could cover all of the applications and models. Moreover, the network of authors, reviewers, field-testers, and users was as much about staff development as materials development - and the need for staff development doesn't go away. I called this mythical organization, COMAP, the Consortium for Mathematics and its Applications.

For the next four years COMAP remained a mental construct, while work on module development proceeded apace. In December of 1980 we formally incorporated and applied for tax-exempt status, which was granted. I need to back up one step. In 1976, soon after NSF funded the UMAP project, the math group at ERC moved to the Education Development Center (EDC). The reasons for that move had mostly to do with Zach's relationship to M.I.T. (which I was much too junior to know about at the time). However, EDC was a friendly home, with many exciting curriculum projects going on in math and science, and a staff of people connected to several Boston area colleges. The UMAP project flourished at EDC and we were able to produce a good many modules and to found the quarterly UMAP Journal.

Fast forward to the fall of 1981. I had a sabbatical coming up and UConn was still quite unhappy with my decision to focus my efforts on math education.

To be fair, I doubt that I could still do any research in logic by that time.

At any rate, I decided to spend the year in Boston and see if COMAP could become more than a paper corporation; for while we were incorporated, all of our funds and administration went through EDC.

In October of 1981 we wrote the proposal to the Annenberg/CPB Project which became our first television course - For All Practical Purposes. For those of you who may not remember, 1981 was the year that the NSF science education budget went almost to zero as Ronald Reagan's administration took hold. While there were still funds in the UMAP grant, the future for NSF funding was incredibly bleak. The cutbacks were so severe that essentially all of the staff at NSF had left or been reassigned. For COMAP's future, the Annenberg moneys were a lifesaver. we received co-funding from the Carnegie Corporation of New York and the Alfred P. Sloan Foundation. After a fair amount of contract negotiations, the actual award was made at the end of summer 1982.

UConn of course had asked me about my plans well before. But the announcement that our proposal was successful had come in by that time and I requested a leave without pay. It was quickly granted. I suspect that they were just as happy not to have me on campus, my replacement was cheaper, and they didn't want to lose the line. By February of 1983, with the Annenberg/CPB grant in hand and the last year of the UMAP grant funds we decided to leave the nest.

We rented office space in Lexington, MA, bought some accounting software and took the independence plunge.

Those first few years were a true struggle to survive. We learned the hard way about taxes, social security, retirement plans, auditors, etc. We also had a crash course in television production. But to be honest, it was great fun. COMAP was a labor of love in the best sense. Then came 1984. In '84 moneys started to come back to the NSF science education budget. But interestingly, the funds were pretty much all earmarked at K-12 education.

This was hardly an accident. It was a direct result of "A Nation At Risk", the first of a series of reports detailing the deficits in the U.S. educational system and student performance.

Well, what could be more natural than HiMAP, a module project designed for high school teachers? By the time the HiMAP project was funded, the theorem was proven. COMAP could and would work. For All Practical Purposes was a great success. The accompanying text sold almost 50,000 copies in its first three year edition. We soon received two more Annenberg/CPB grants - Against All Odds and In Simplest Terms, telecourses in statistics and college algebra.

A number of additional NSF grants followed including GeoMAP, HistoMAP, and most importantly ARISE.

The ARISE project represents a culmination of our efforts on the high school scene. We have produced many sets of modular materials at the secondary level for both teachers and students. But ARISE is meant to be a comprehensive curriculum, grades 9-11 (and some day 12, NSF willing). We have always been on the outside looking in, telling instructors what they could do, and showing them with exciting pieces of curriculum. But ARISE is truly different. NSF has said to us, ok you win, we believe. Now go and write a complete high school curriculum. Teachers want to know what to do Monday morning - tell them.

This has been our most complicated project to date. Five years have gone into the effort, with a writing team of over twenty high school teachers (and a few of us college types, including Henry Pollak). This fall, our first ARISE text will be on the market. It's both exciting and scary. After all, we've changed the content, the pedagogy, the technology, and the assessment. It is extremely hard to know how the community will react. In some ways, though, that is the joy of working at COMAP. We push the edge of the envelope. We create new materials for new courses. So far we have been extraordinarily lucky. Our materials have been well received and helped to generate a revenue stream which keeps us in business.

But no one can time markets, and some ideas may simply not work or may be too far ahead of the curve. That's all right; someone has to be there stirring the pot, trying new things.

The real joy of COMAP is the people I work with. I honestly believe that they are the finest mathematicians and educators in the country. And they are truly too numerous to mention. From Joe Malkevitch who believed in the idea of COMAP and helped to found the organization with his ideas and his writings to David Moore, who worked on his book as he worked on the programs for Against All Odds to Joe Blatt who was our executive producer on the telecourses, to Frank Giordano who has helped make the Mathematical Contest in Modeling a fixture on our college campuses, to Landy Godbold who has worked tirelessly as project director for ARISE, I have had the privilege and honor to be their colleague.

Moreover, COMAP was the right idea at the right time. There is simply an enormous amount of talent and expertise in american classrooms. There are untold numbers of faculty at all levels ready and willing to write, review, field-test and try out new materials because they are truly dedicated to their students. COMAP opened up an avenue for the expression of that talent. COMAP is proof that some ideas are simply better than the people that have them.

ON CULTURE AND MATHEMATICS EDUCATION IN (SOUTHERN) AFRICA

Paulus Gerdes
Departamento de Matemática
Universidade Pedagógica (UP), Maputo, Mozambique.

To introduce the theme of culture and mathematics education in a multicultural African context, I should like to present a recent testimony by Salimo Saide, one of the mathematics teacher graduates from Mozambique's 'Universidade Pedagógica'.

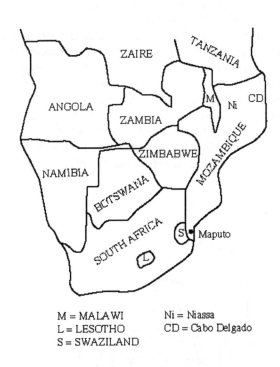

M = MALAWI   Ni = Niassa
L = LESOTHO   CD = Cabo Delgado
S = SWAZILAND

Map of Southern Africa

Testimony by Salimo Saide

"I was born June 20, 1965 in Lichinga, capital of the northern Niassa

Province (see Map of Southern Africa). There I went to primary and secondary school. From 1985 to 1987 I took part in a teacher education program. From 1987 to 1991 I taught Mathematics and Physics at the secondary school of Pemba, capital of the Cabo Delgado Province. In that province I coordinated the local Mathematics Olympiads. In 1991 I came to the capital Maputo in the south to continue my studies and in 1996 I concluded my 'Licenciatura' in Mathematics and Physics at the 'Universidade Pedagógica'.

In 1977 I had the opportunity to read a book written by the priest Yohana, entitled "Wa'yaowe", that means "We the Yao people". It opened a whole new horizon for me. I was lucky to be able to read and write Yao – in school only Portuguese is taught. During my whole youth I loved to read more in Yao, but there did not exist any opportunity. When I came to the national capital Maputo to continue my studies, I thought my dream had died. However, when I took part first in a voluntary "circle of interest" on mathematical elements in African cultures and then in the optional course "Ethnomathematics and Education" my dream started to live again. I found a strong link between mathematics and the art of my grandparents. My participation let me feel returning to my land, let me remember my grandmother, her decorated mats and baskets, and her beautiful "nembo" – tattoos (see Figure 1) and pot decorations (see Figure 2). The idea "caught" me and during my holidays I made three field trips to Niassa to study the geometry of ceramic pot ornamentation. Now after having finished my university program, I hope to return definitively to my land, to con-

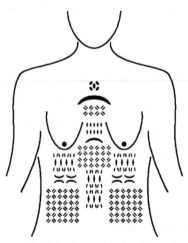

Example of a "nembo" tattoo
Figure 1

tinue my research and to teach mathematics integrating the "nembo" of the Yao people into it." [1]

It was not easy for Salimo to realize his fieldwork. Sometimes it took him various encounters on several successive days to win the confidence of the old female pot makers, as they did not understood easily why a young man, speaking with the accent of someone educated in the cities, could be interested in their nowadays downgraded and disappearing female art and craft of pot decoration; why would he be interested to see their tattoos when the churches, both Christian and Islamic, have been combating tattooing so strongly? However, once he won their confidence, they were happy to speak about their craft and art, and about how they learned it, to discuss with the student alternative ways of reviving, of valuing their symbolic language, their knowledge, wisdom, and creativity. For instance, it was suggested to decorate 'capulanas' – square woven cloths worn by the women around their middle – with ceramic "nembo" and T-shirts with tattoo "nembo".

Through their fieldwork, students like Salimo came also to grasp with 'out-of-school' learning processes: from individual learning by imitating and copying or by trying and experimenting, learning through guidance from older family members or friends, to collective learning environments among children from the same age group. Through their fieldwork, they understood better how important social and cultural factors like interpersonal relationships, family context, opportunity, needs, and motivation are in stimulating or blocking what, how, and what for something like a craft is learned. The results of making decorated pots, baskets, etc. may seem similar; the learning processes involved may be very distinct. This field experience reinforced the students' reflection on what school mathematics education might learn from 'out-of-school' learning processes.

Teachers like Salimo – who as students voluntarily took part in 'clubs' and optional courses related to culture and mathematics education – return, well motivated, to their home provinces, determined to work as mathematics teachers in such a way that it is both useful for their people and dignifying to its cultural heritage.

---

[1]   S. Saide, Sobre a ornamentação geométrica de panelas de barro por mulheres Yao (Província de Niassa), in: P. Gerdes (Ed.), *Geometria e Artesanato em Niassa e Nampula*, UP, Maputo (in press)

 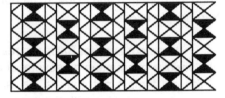

Two examples of "nembo" strip decorations on pots
Figure 2

On Culture, Education, and the Development of Africa

Well-known African politicians, historians, scientists, and educators alike have lately stressed the importance of cultural factors for Africa's development in general and education in particular.

The South Commission, led by the former President of Tanzania, J. Nyerere, criticizes in its report, *"The challenge to the South"*, [2] development strategies that minimize cultural factors, as such strategies only provoke indifference, alienation and social discord. Development strategies "have often failed to utilize the enormous reserves of traditional wisdom and of creativity and enterprise in the countries of the Third World" (p.46). Instead, the cultural wellsprings of the South should feed the process of development.

In the book *"Educate or Perish: Africa's Impasse and Prospects"* [3] the historian J. Ki-Zerbo explains that today's existing African educational system is generally still rather "unadapted and elitist" and "favors foreign consumption without generating a culture that is both compatible with the original civilization and truly promising". "Too often, schools alienate children from their social environment" (p.69). What is necessary is "a new educational style which focuses the whole variety of approaches on the objective of Africanization, especially by integrating the natural and cultural environments into the educational process, along with productive work..." (p.91, italics pg).

---

[2] J. Nyerere (Ed.), *The challenge to the South – Report of the South Commission*, Oxford University Press, Oxford, 1990, 325 pp.

[3] J. Ki-Zerbo, Educate or Perish: Africa's Impasse and Prospects, UNESCO-UNICEF, Dakar / Abidjan, 1990, 109 pp.

In *"African Thoughts on the Prospects of Education for All"* [4] African peoples' cultural identities (including the awareness of these identities), are seen as the springboard of their development effort (p.10). It is stressed that Africa needs culture-oriented education, that would ensure the survival of African cultures, if it emphasized originality of thought and encouraged the virtue of creativity. Scientific appreciation of African cultural elements and experience is considered to be "one sure way of getting Africans to see science as a means of understanding their cultures and as a tool to serve and advance their cultures" (p.23).

On Mathematics, Education, Culture, and History

African countries face the problem of low 'levels of attainment' in mathematics education. Relatively few students pursue university programs with a strong mathematical component. Math anxiety is widespread. Many children (and teachers too!) experience mathematics as a rather strange and useless subject, imported from outside Africa; as something that exists only in schools.

In his editorial "Mathematics and Africa",[5] T. Isoun, former Vice-Chancellor of Rivers State University of Science and Technology in Nigeria and first editor of "Discovery and Innovation" – the scientific journal of the African Academy of Sciences –, remarks "The way mathematics is taught in primary and secondary schools in Africa, appears to turn off many bright young men and women" (p.6). Therefore, there is "need for mathematicians in Africa to write textbooks to reflect our cultural background, and ensure that mathematics is firmly grounded within our environment" (p.6). The cultural-scientific heritage of the continent may constitute a source of inspiration. Surely "any inspiration we gather from the African past must be used to enable the peoples of Africa to participate in the generation, advancement and use of the scientific and technological enterprise. Mathematics, as a cultural, artistic, humanistic, as well as scientific and technological enterprise, will serve as a key to the full participation of the continent" (p.4). The African Academy of Sciences launched its program on science and culture in 1992. The African Mathematical Union Commission for the History of Mathematics in Africa (AMUCHMA), formed in 1986, stimulates research in the history of mathematics in Africa and promotes the dissemination of research findings[6] in African universities

---

4   *African Thoughts on the Prospects of Education for All*, UNESCO-UNICEF, Dakar / Abidjan, 1990, 193 pp.

5   T. Isoun, Mathematics and Africa, *Discovery and Innovation,* African Academy of Sciences (P.O.Box 14798), Nairobi, 1992, Vol.4, No.1, 4-6

6   For an overview, see P. Gerdes, On Mathematics in the History of Sub-Saharan Africa, *Historia Mathematica*, New York, 1994, Vol.21, 345-376

and teacher education colleges.[7] Present chairman of the African Mathematical Union Commission on Mathematics Education (AMUCME), M. El Tom from Sudan, singled in a recent report to the Third World Academy of Sciences[8] ethnomathematical-educational research and experimentation as a noteworthy exception and necessary activity in a context where most African countries attempt to imitate major curriculum reforms in the West. [9]

An ethnomathematical research perspective [10]

Defined as the cultural anthropology of mathematics and mathematics education, Ethnomathematics is a relatively new field of interest.[11] The view of Mathematics as "culture-free", as an "universal, basically aprioristic form of knowledge" has been dominant internationally. And a reductionist tendency tended to dominate mathematics education, implying on culture-free cognition models.[12]

At the end of the 1970s and beginning of the 1980s, there developed internationally a growing awareness among mathematicians of the societal and cultural aspects of mathematics and mathematical education. It is in that period that U. D'Ambrosio (Brazil) proposed his ethnomathematical program as a methodology to track and analyze the processes of generation, transmission, diffusion and institutionalization of (mathe-matical) knowledge in diverse cultural systems. In his view one should compatibilize cultural forms, i.e. "...the mathematics in schools shall be such that it facilitates knowledge, understanding, incorporation and compatibilization of known and current popular practices into the curriculum.

---

7   Readers interested in receiving the AMUCHMA Newsletter may send their request to the author.

8   M. El Tom, The present Status of Mathematics and Mathematics Education in Africa, (unpublished) report presented to the Third World Academy of Sciences, Triest, 1995

9   Readers interested in receiving the AMUCME Newsletter may contact AMUCME Secretary, Prof. Cyril Julie, Department of Didactics, University of the Western Cape, Private Bag X17, Belville 7535, South Africa

10   For an overview see P. Gerdes, Ethnomathematics and mathematics education: an overview, in: A. Bishop, K. Clements, C. Keitel, J. Kilpatrick, C. Laborda (Eds.), *International Handbook on Mathematics Education*, Kluwer, Dordrecht, 1996 (909-943)

11   Analyzing the contents of "Tanbih al-albab" by the Maghrebian mathematician Ibn al-Banna (1256-1321), A. Djebbar considers several parts of it as related to ethnomathematics. See A. Djebbar, *Mathematics in the medieval Maghreb*, AMUCHMA Newsletter, Maputo, 1995, No. 15, 3-42 (p.19)

12   Cf. U. D'Ambrosio, *Etnomatemática: raízes socio-culturais da arte ou técnica de explicar e conhecer*, UNICAMP, Campinas, 1987, p.80

In other words, recognition and incorporation of ethnomathematics into the curriculum". [13]

Short overview of research on culture and mathematics (education) in Africa

A rather isolated forerunner of reflections on culture and mathematics education in Africa, was O.Raum, whose book "Arithmetic in Africa" appeared in 1938.[14] Two already classical studies, published in the USA, dealt with mathematics (learning) and African culture: "The New Mathematics and an Old Culture – A Study of Learning among the Kpelle" (1967)[15] and Zaslavsky's "Africa Counts" (1973).[16]

One of the first Africans to organize research in the field of mathematics education and culture, is S. Touré – former Secretary-General of the African Mathematical Union, and today's Minister of Higher Education and Research of Côte d'Ivoire – who introduced in 1980 a research-seminar on "Mathematics in the African socio-cultural environment" at the Mathematical Research Institute of Abidjan.[17] The seminar is now directed by S. Doumbia. One of the interesting themes analyzed by her and her colleagues is the mathematics of traditional West-African games and its use in education.[18] In the series of mathematics textbooks for secondary

---

13 U. D'Ambrosio, *Socio-cultural bases for mathematics education*, UNICAMP, Campinas, 1985, p. 71. Cf. also U. D'Ambrosio contribution to ICME8 (RL5) in which he analyzes various dimensions of ethnomathematics: mathematical, socio-political, epistemological, holistic, ethical, and pedagogical: Ethnomathematics: where does it come from and where does it go?, *Proceedings ICME8,* Seville (in press)

14 O. Raum, *Arithmetic in Africa*, Evans Brothers, London, 1938, 94 pp.

15 J. Gay & M. Cole, *The New Mathematics and an Old Culture – A Study of Learning among the Kpelle*, Holt, Rinehart & Winston, New York, 1967, 100 pp.

16 C. Zaslavsky, *Africa Counts: Number and Pattern in African Culture*, Prindle, Weber and Schmidt, Boston, 328 pp. (paperback edition: Lawrence Hill, Brooklyn, NY, 1979); Hungarian translation: *Africa Szamol*, Gondalet, Budapest, 1984; French translation: *L'Afrique compte! Nombres, formes et démarches dans la culture africaine*, Éditions du Choix, Argenteuil, 1995.

17 Cf. S. Touré (Ed.), *Mathématiques dans l'environnement socio-culturel africain*, IRMA, 1984

18 See e.g. : S. Doumbia & J. Pil, *Les jeux de cauris*, IRMA, Abidjan, 1992, and: S. Doumbia, 'L'expérience en Côte d'Ivoire de l'étude des jeux traditionnels africain et de leur mathématisation', in *First European Summer University Proceedings: History and Epistemology in Mathematics Education*, IREM, Montpellier, 1995, 549-556

and high schools in francophone African countries, coordinated by S.Touré, it is tried to incorporate elements from diverse African socio-cultural environments.

Since the beginning the 1980's, the Ahmadu-Bello-University (Zaria/Bauchi, Nigeria) has been very active in doing ethnomathematical research, e.g. on the mathematics used by unschooled children and adults in daily life, and the possibilities to embed this knowledge in mathematics education. S. Ale does research on the mathematical heritage of the Fulbe (Fulani) and the possibilities to construct a curriculum that builds upon this heritage and fits the needs of the Fulbe people.

Among a whole series of research projects, all over the continent, on spoken and written numeration systems, and their role in education, A. Kane's – today Senegal's Minister of Culture – profound study on "The spoken numeration systems of West-Atlantic groups and of the Mandé", may be singled out.

Southern Africa

From the surviving San hunters in Botswana, H. Lea and her students at the University of Botswana have collected information. Her papers describe counting, measurement, time reckoning, classification, tracking and some mathematical ideas in San technology and craft. The San developed very good visual discrimination and memory as needed for survival in the harsh environment of the Kalahari desert. In "Common threads in Botswana" suggestions are included about the use of baskets, hair braiding, and weaving designs in mathematics education. K. Garegae-Garekwe concluded a masters thesis on "Cultural games and mathe-matics teaching in Botswana", and continues her research with an analysis of patterns on floors, walls, pots, basket weaving, knitting, etc. among the Tswana and possibilities to use them in mathematics education.

D. Mtetwa (University of Zimbabwe) started a research project on "Mathematical thought in aspects of Shona culture" and is also interested in the ethnography of children and its implications for mathematics education. B. Seka (Tanzanian Institute for Curriculum Development) experiments with the tradition of story telling as a didactical means in mathe-matics teaching.

The Association for Mathematics Education in South Africa (AMESA) organized at its first national congress in 1994 a round-table on ethnomathematics and education. In the same year AMESA formed a study group on ethnomathematics coordinated by D. Mosimege. Mosimege (University of the North) is preparing a Ph.D. dissertation on the exploration of string figures and traditional games from the north of South Africa in mathematics education. W. Millroy conducted an ethnographic study as an apprentice carpenter in Cape Town, to document the mathematical ideas that are embedded in everyday woodworking activities of a group of carpenters.

Mozambique

Ethnomathematical research started in Mozambique in the late 1970's. Several books have been published by the author in the context of Mozambique's Ethnomathematics Research Project. Among them are: "Culture and the awakening of geometrical thinking"; "Ethnogeometry"; "Living mathematics: Drawings of Africa" (see Figure 3); "Lusona: Geometrical recreations of Africa"; "Ethnomathematics: Culture, Mathematics, Education"; "African Pythagoras. A Study in Culture and Mathematics Education"; "Sona Geometry: Reflections on the Tradition of Sand Drawings in Africa South of the Equator" (Vol.1: Analysis and Reconstruction; Vol.2: Educational and Mathematical Exploration; Vol.3: Comparative Analysis); "Sipatsi: Technology, Art and Geometry in Inhambane" (see Figure 4); "Ethnomathematics and Education in Africa"; "Women and Geometry in Southern Africa: Suggestions for further research"; "Lunda Geometry — Designs, Polyominoes, Patterns, Symmetries".

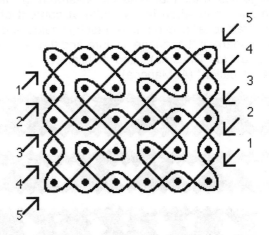

Exploring a traditional sand drawing to reflect about arithmetical sums
Figure 3

Since the end of the 80's more lecturers and in particular young lecturers became interested in and started ethnomathematical research. So far, two collective works have been published. "Numeration in Mozambique" presents a reflection on culture, language and mathematics education. It includes studies on African systems of numeration (P. Gerdes & M. Cherinda), written and oral on spoken numeration systems in Mozambique, popular counting techniques (A. Ismael & D. Soares), comparative tables and maps on numeration (A. Mapapá & E. Uaila), and on spoken numeration and the learning of arithmetic (J. Draisma). In "Explorations in Ethnomathematics and Ethnoscience" is presented a collection of papers written by various lecturers at the 'Universidade Pedagógica', both based in Maputo situated in the South of Mozambique and in Beira in the central Sofala Province. The ethnomathematical papers reflect on some mathematical ideas involved in basket and mat making in the North of the country (A. Ismael), on languages and mental calculation (J. Draisma), on popular counting practices all over Mozambique (D. Soares & A. Ismael), symmetries on gratings in Maputo city (A. Mapapá) and on decorations of spoons in Sofala (D. Soares) and the southeastern Inhambane Province (M. Cherinda). Soon to be published are two more collective works: "Further explorations in Ethnomathematics and Ethnoscience in Mozambique" and "Geometry and Craft in Niassa and Nampula".

At this moment several Ph.D. theses in the field of culture and mathematics education are in progress: "Exploring basket and mat weaving in the mathematics classroom" (M. Cherinda); "Ntchuva and other Mozambican games in the mathematics classroom" (A. Ismael); "Gender and mathematics education in the cultural context of Mozambique" (S. Fagilde); "Traditional house building technologies and the teaching of Geometry" (D. Soares); "Language, culture and the teaching of Arithmetic in Mozambique" (J. Draisma); and "Children's games and toys in mathematics education" (A. Mapapá).

Example of woven band strips on 'sipatsi' handbags
Figure 4

Conclusion

Notwithstanding the research already realized, ethnomathematical-educational experimentation and, generally, the study of possible educational implications of ethnomathematical research, both internationally and in Africa, are still relatively in the beginning. In order to experiment a basic and radical assumption, namely that – in the words of A.Bishop – "all formal mathematics education is a process of cultural interaction, and that every child (and teacher, pg) experiences some degree of cultural conflict in that process", has to be taken into account. Established theoretical constructs of mathematics education are not based on this assumption. Generally ethnomathematical research findings oblige to reflect about fundamental mathematical-educational questions: Why teach mathematics?, What and whose mathematics should be taught, by whom and for whom?; Who participates in curriculum development?; How to organize the school practices in order to minimize the effects of the possible disruptive relationships between home and school culture and mathematics?

In the case of Mozambique, and maybe more generally in Africa, a fundamental objective of ethnomathematical research consists in looking for possibilities to improve the teaching of mathematics by embedding it into the cultural context of pupils and teachers. A type of mathematics education is intended that succeeds in dignifying and valuing the scientific knowledge inherent in the culture by using this knowledge to lay the foundations to provide quicker and better access to the scientific heritage of the whole of humanity.

A NEW ROLE FOR CURRICULUM DOCUMENTS - FROM GUIDELINES TO PRODUCTION PLANS?

Gunnar Gjone

RECENT EDUCATIONAL REFORMS

During the 1980s most industrialized countries have carried through extensive reforms in education. There are two characteristics in these reforms that should be stressed.

One dominating element is that the reforms are directed towards greater decentralization, that is a shift in decisionmaking from central level to the periphery. There are exceptions to this picture, but these exceptions are countries with an already strong decentralized system. The other element visible in the reforms are the stressing of management by objectives.
(Utbildningsdepartementet (The Swedish Ministry of Education), 1992, p.117. Translated by the author)

It is the second element, mentioned by the Swedish Ministry of Education that is our concern: Will a strong focus on management by objectives fundamentally change mathematics education? How is this management model related to the present situation of mathematics education?

To get knowledge on the state of education in a country, it has been a long tradition to compare with other countries. Projects in comparative education have also been used to investigate broad trends in international education. In this article we will consider the recent developments in some countries. Our first concern, however, is that the development in many countries are subject to comparisons with other countries, and this also influence the development in education in the countries studied.

THE CHANGING ASPECTS OF COMPARATIVE EDUCATION AND THE SEARCH FOR EFFICIENCY
From visits to statistics, or from qualitative to quantitative approaches

Comparative education is an active field among mathematics educators today. As mathematics educators have come to realize the international character of problems in their field, we have seen several projects where comparisons are made between programs and countries.

Comparative education is nothing new. The dominant form in earlier times was educators visiting other countries, making observations - or perhaps working there for some time, and then return to their home country with new ideas and knowledge. Such visits go far back, even to antiquity. A more systematic comparison is of a later date. Sjöstedt and Sjöstrand (1952) observed that increased activity in comparative education as a rule followed major conflicts.

They observed three periods of special activity in comparative education. The first they found after the Napoleonic wars, the second after the first world war, and the third after the second world war. In the first IEA[1] study (Husen, 1967) this fact is also presented, and the reasons discussed:

As all who have followed events on the educational scene know, there has been an upsurge in comparative education since the end of World War II. ... The more we have recognized education as an investment in human resources and as an instrument for bringing about economic growth and social change, the stronger has been the need to investigate the roots of the educational systems of which the world around us shows such a striking diversity. (Husen, 1967, p.19)

But where the earlier forms of comparative education were qualitative studies, we have since the mid 1960s seen qualitative studies increasingly being replaced by more quantitative studies. The most wellknown such studies are the IEA studies. A strong focus of these studies has been testing of students, but there has also been a qualitative element in these studies, comparing curricula, textbooks as well as other elements of the educational system.

In recent years we have seen a large number of comparative studies. We can mention here the IAEP[2] studies. In the second study in 1990-91, a total of 20 countries participated in surveying mathematics and science performance of 13 year old students.

Another study to mention is the Exeter - Kassell study. This study not only included England and Germany, but Scotland, Hungary and Norway as well. A special feature of such comparative projects has been the media coverage in some countries: Results from the Kassell-Exeter project were presented in the Times, London, with the headlines: *Britain gets a minus in maths* (The Sunday Times, 14 May 1995).

Results from international comparison tests in reading/writing have been presented in the newspapers for some time. Comparisons and status

---

[1] IEA - International project for the evaluation of Educational Achievement
[2] IAEP - The International Assessment of Educational Progress

reports concerning mathematics education have also been covered extensively in the newspapers. The United States is involved in several international and national projects where the goal is to "measure" the state of American education. "The Nations Report Card" NAEP[3] is an issue presented yearly in newspaper articles.

It seems that in some countries there are comparisons that get extensive media attention. In the United Kingdom there seems to be strong interests in comparing results with continental Europe (Prais, 1995). In the US there is a comparison with Japan, but also with the rest of the world. The notion "world class (mathematics) education" has been used from time to time to denote the goal for mathematics education in the United States - but it is not clear what the formulation means.

However, if we look at the situation in Norway, up to the early 1990s, we have been somewhat reluctant to compare our mathematics education with other countries, a notable exception being a more qualitative comparison with Sweden. The situation in Sweden has been somewhat different. Sweden participated in the Second International Mathematics Study (SIMS)[4] . It should be added that as a result of that study a large effort to reform mathematics education in Sweden was launched. We will most likely see a change in this situation for all the Nordic countries, since now most Nordic countries are participating in TIMSS[5] .

Another type of investigation which is qualitative, but not comparative, is an OECD evaluation of educational policies of various countries. In this type of evaluation, a group of experts travels quite extensively, visiting schools and school-authorities, as well as colleges and universities, e.g. in Norway. The report is a feedback to the Norwegian authorities on the impressions of the experts, who - in the Norwegian study - were from Ireland, Sweden and England. Important features of this evaluation were management and control at all levels of the school system, but some issues also considered the content of school subjects. These studies were clearly focused on the efficiency of the educational system in a country.

A feature of several more recent comparative studies has been the notions "effective" and "efficient". The volume examining data from the IEA Second International Mathematics Study (SIMS/SISS) had the title: "In Search of More Effective Mathematics Education". The notion "effective" is referred to in the index, but it is not given a descriptive definition in the

---

3 NAEP -The National Assessment of Educational Progress

4 SIMS/SISS - The Second International Mathematics/Science Study

5 TIMSS - The Third International Mathematics and Science Study

sense of Israel Sheffler (Scheffler, 1960). In a study, relating also to the second IEA study (Westbury, 1989) another similar notion is used: yield (due to Neville Postlewaite).

In the document laying the foundation for the third international study, efficiency is not mentioned explicitly, but various other similar notions are being used, conveying a more neutral connotation. The aims behind this type of comparative studies are outlined by David Robitaille and Cynthia Nicol:

In addition, such studies provide valuable international perspectives for current national discussions and debates on development of efficient, effective, and qualitative mathematics education. (Robitaille & Nicol, 1994, p.403)

To strive for more effective and efficient mathematics education has been a goal for a long time in educational management, but it is not always clear what is meant by these words. In the report from the OECD experts on Norwegian education, effective education is linked to the use of resources and results, but again the concept results is not given a clear (descriptive) definition. We will conclude that comparative education has a double role: On the one hand it provides methods to study the development in a country compared to other countries, on the other hand it might strongly influence the developmetn within a country, with aiming towards larger efficiency.

What then should we mean by more effective and efficient education?

MAKING EDUCATION EFFICIENT

Efficient (effective) education is nothing new. It was in the forefront of discussion in the new math movement. In Bruner (1960) Bärbel Inhelder discussed over several pages the question if students can accelerate through the (Piagetian) stages of development.

Overview of trends

What is meant by more efficiency in education? Trying to look into this question, we find that some elements are often mentioned: resources, results, quality, and evaluation - to mention some. Concerning efficiency, important factors are the relationships between these elements. What results - and with what quality - can be obtained with given resources, and how can we evaluate the quality of the product?

The search for efficiency has been performed on all levels - from the central school authorities to teachers and students in the classroom. These questions have also been in the forefront concerning governement funded research. There is a clear parallell between education and research in this respect. We will come back to this relation at the end of the article.

An important element in Norway's school reforms was the relationship between money for education provided by the parliament, and the "output". "Output" is in this context taken to mean the performance of the students (on national tests).[6] The relationship between economy and education is important today, and has been given much consideration by educators and administrators. One such special case - that has been much debated in several countries is comprehensive education.

The case of comprehensive education

Comprehensive education is a term usually linked to secondary education. In the United States the following formulation has been taken as a definition:

It is called comprehensive because it offers, under one administration and under one roof (or series of roofs), secondary education for almost all the high school age children of one town or neighborhood. ... It is responsible for educating the bright and the not so bright children with different vocational and professional ambitions and with various motivations. (John W. Gardner in the foreword to (Conant, 1959)).

The term comprehensive education can also be used in a more general sense. In Scandinavia the corresponding term "enhetsskole", is used to denote a school system where all children in a district are taught together for a large part of their education. Comprehensive education is moreover not an absolute entity, there are degrees of comprehensiveness.

In March 1996, a matter concerning education was on the front page of several English newspapers. The reason was statements that the labour shadow government had made concerning comprehensive education. From a tradition of fully supporting an extensive form of comprehensive education, newspaper articles stated that some changes were underway in the labour party - not favoring comprehensive education to the same extent anymore. In the debate and articles that followed the initial article we find:

---

6 In Norway, in contrast to the United States, little is stated in official documents on what is meant by output and results.

Mr. Blubkett called for more setting by ability more specialization and a greater emphasis on vocational alternatives to a narrowly academic. curriculum (The Daily Telegraph, February 28, 1996)

The Office for Standards in Education said many schools were not even aware of the targets, which were launched five years ago in an effort to increase skill levels throughout the workforce and strengthen international competetiveness. ... Heads were concerned that the targets were nearly always promoted in relation to increasing Britain's industrial and commercial competitiveness. (The Daily Telegraph, March 5, 1996)

It was thought provoking to read this short and intense newspaper sequence, before other news again would dominate the front pages. In all the Nordic countries we have a well established comprehensive education. In Norway, with the present school reforms, we moreover have extended compulsory education from 9 to 10 years, and in addition all students will have the right to 3 years of further education after the first 10 years.

The issue of comprehensive education has an obvious link to efficient (mathematics) education. The discussion on comprehensive education has come up in several countries from time to time, e.g. also the German discussion on Gesamtschule, in the 1970s and 80s. An argument in such discussions has often been that comprehensive education might not be very efficient and competitive in the international marketplace.

In some countries this has lead to a search for models on how to manage education. In some countries models have been found in the private sector (models for production and control). This has - in most cases - not been explicitly stated. One exception, however, is the Swedish government. Following the quote in the introduction to this article it is stated that:

The kind of management by objectives that has developed has elements and knowledge from management of other types of systems, especially from private sector. ... As time goes, management by objectives in education has found it's own form. (Utbildningsministeriet, 1992, p.117)

It is interesting to note that the Swedish ministry is stating this relationship explicitly. However, it is not clearly explained what this "own form" is. To find out what is usually meant by the concept *management by objectives* we will look to management literature on organizational theory.

MANAGEMENT BY OBJECTIVES (MBO)

We will present the introduction to a chapter on management by objectives from a Norwegian textbook in organizational theory. This passage is not written for school systems, but could easily be applied to such systems as well:

Management by objectives from the leadership is that an upper instance manages by giving a message about a wished result and sets frames of resources. The subordinate unit is free to choose how and by which means the objectives should be reached. In addition to stating the objectives the reporting of results is the central element in management by objectives.

Objectives, have in this context, two different functions on two different levels. On the one side it gives subordinates a goal (objective) to reach for. On the other side management by objectives is a tool for an upper instance to evaluate their subordinates. (Flaa, et al., 1995, p.118. Translated by the author)

The mechanisms of MBO are also presented in a diagram and discussed :

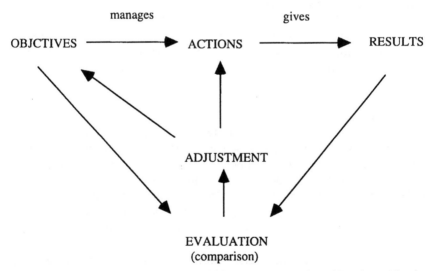

(Figure 1: From Flaa et.al.,1995, p.121. Translated by the author)

In the book we also find a discussion of MBO in public sector which is especially relevant for education. A thorough discussion of prerequisites for MBO is presented, as well as parts of the Norwegian discussion.

Relating this to education, we find that management by objectives can be introduced at several levels: It can be introduced in the classroom, but also at school level, hence the present interest in "school evaluation". We also find "program evaluation", as well as projects to "evaluate" several aspects of the school organization.

The Norwegian philosopher Hans Skjervheim, has introduced the two notions:
(1) MBO as a *system*, and (2) MBO as a method. (Flaa et al, 1995, p.122)

MBO as a *system* means that this way of management is introduced at all levels. In a sense reality is adjusted to the model. Reality is simplified and delimited. One concentrates on concrete and restricted objectives (aims). MBO as a *method* is a more pragmatic use of the management model - the model is adjusted to reality. Taking into account the wealth of evaluation procedures now being used in education, it seems that it is MBO as a system we see developing in education. An important element of *education*   (German: *Bildung*) is in danger of being lost using management by objectives as a system. *Education* in this sense has more elements than can be regulated by an MBO model.

In Flaa etal. (1995) there is also a discussion of the use of MBO in the public sector. Two reasons are given for this use: (1) Use for political control; (2) Use to increase efficiency, to get more and better results

The authors also outline possible conflicts that may arise between the different levels of management if the objectives are very precisely stated. They argue that conflicts may seemingly be avoided by stating vague objectives, but that this will introduce new conflicts at different levels. In education, the formulation of broad and general goals and objectives on a high national level, might introduce conflicts when one seeks to make these concrete, say for a subject like mathematics. As a consequence, to avoid this situation, we find, that very precise objectives (targets) are being formulated at a national level in several countries.

Student assessment is also given broad attention in the process. Students' performance on tests can be seen as the outcome of education. An international study like TIMSS focuses on this dimension. We will come back to student assessment later in this article.

What are the consequences of this "philosophy" of education found in the curriculum materials that are prepared for school systems? If we look at curriculum material, constructed in the present reform wave, can we find reflections of the elements in the diagram presented above (Figure 1)?

Curriculum documents

Curriculum documents are reflecting the educational ideas of a country, "carries a message about a system" (Howson, 1991). Authorities have, for a long time, shown faith in the role of formal curriculum documents. (This faith, however, has not been shared by the (mathematics) education community in general, e.g. the popularity of the notion of the so-called hidden curriculum.) MBO has lead to some important changes in curriculum documents. There is a marked change in the formulation of aims for education in some countries. Formulations of the targets are moreover constructed to address an objective that can be easily assessed. As an illustration let us look at an example from Norway (upper secondary mathematics education, grade 10):

TARGET 7: Functions

Pupils should become familiar with the function concept and learn to draw graphs with and without IT aids. They should be given a first introduction to the derivation concept and be made familiar with it by means of simple examples.

Main points:
Pupils should

...
7c be able to find the points of intersection of curves both by calculation and by means of graphs.
(Norwegian Ministry of Education, Research and Church Affairs, 1994)

It is interesting to compare today's language of education found in curriculum documents, with the language used some years back.

The language of education - revisited

In his well known book *The Language of Education* (Sheffler, 1960) Israel Scheffler lists some words and formulations related to education: "knowing", "learning", "thinking", "understanding" and "explaining" (p. 8). He adds a few more "mental discipline", "achievement", "curriculum", "character development", and "maturity" (p. 9). If we were to write down such a list from some curriculum documents written today, would we find the same words and formulations for inclusion on a list? Would it not contain word such as "assessment", "evaluation", "quality", "standards", "(attainment) targets", "aims" - perhaps "outcomes" and "results", would be listed as well. We could ask if this set of words, also to be found in other areas of society like production and management, signifies a new view and role for education?

As seen from form the diagram on MBO above (Figure 1), *evaluation* played a crucial role in the process. Let us try to relate evaluation/assessment in (mathematics) education, to the MBO model.

A ROLE FOR ASSESSMENT

Assessment of students has traditionally had several aspects:
• the information aspect, giving information to the student, the parents, the teacher, the school system
• the motivational aspect: to motivate students (and teachers)
• the selection aspect: to select students for further advance through the educational system
However, using the diagram above (Figure 1) we might see student assessment in the MBO model in a somewhat different perspective from what is usually the case. Below we will present a revised diagram focusing on assessment of students in education in an MBO model. The categories have been given slightly different names, to be closer to "the language of education" being used today:

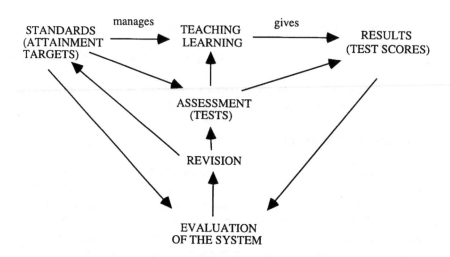

(Figure 2)

The diagram focuses on the importance of assessment (tests) in MBO. The testing system in some countries like Norway and the United Kingdom fits very well into this model. It has been a well known "fact" in education, that assessment (tests) has a strong influence on the teaching-learning process. In this diagram we try to show that in the MBO model it will have a central position in managing education (the teaching-learning process).

In this discussion focus has been on centralized systems, like we find in the Scandinavian countries. However, the elements would be found in many decentralized systems as well. It might be, like in the United States, that there are various instances being responsible for the various parts, such as curriculum and (some form) of testing within the system. I will argue that the model is valid also for countries like the United States.

A first conclusion

Will using this model for education bring changes to the system? The answer will be depending on the educational tradition.

The central element in the model is assessment and testing. Linked to this is the formulation of goals, standards or targets. The important relation to realize is that in such a model, one seeks to formulate quite specific targets for student performance at some level, in mathematics.

In some countries this will mean a major change, since testing/assessment within the system in a comprehensive type of education, will have a different function from the one presented in the diagram (Figure 2). We will use this diagram to show how different countries have different traditions in education, and that they are moving in a direction of a more complete MBO model.

In the United States there is a strong tradition of testing, and looking at the result of tests (the right side of the diagram). Recently we have seen advances in the process of establishing more precise standards (or benchmarks) at national and hence at state level. (NCTM, 1989; AAAS,1993)[7] In England, with *the National Curriculum* they seem to try to adapt to all elements of this model in one step, starting from a very decentralized system.

We will also note that the model we have presented for MBO in education is a variation of the general MBO model (Figure 1). We will therefore challenge the opinion in the Swedish document cited above, that

---

7 NCTM - National Council of Teachers of Mathematics
  AAAS - American Association for the Advancement of Science

there is an "own form" of MBO for education. We argue that it at most will be minor adjustment to the general model.

We will also argue that the change of the "language of education" (in the spirit of Sheffler), signifies a deeper change in the same direction, in the state of educational philosophy.

The model of management by objectives depends on goal formulations to be quite specific. The question if it is reasonable to give such specific formulations of goals in mathematics education, is an important question. On the one hand mathematics is often presented and thought of as a strong hierarchical discipline, which would be ideal for a structure of attainment targets. However, this view is not the only possible of mathematics for education.

MANAGEMENT BY OBJECTIVES IN MATHEMATICS EDUCATION

Mathematics in school is closely related to some other areas. We will here consider some of these areas: mathematics, development of mathematical knowledge, and the research discipline of mathematics education (didactics of mathematics).

The nature of mathematics

The structure of mathematics as a deductive system is - in some sense - well suited for MBO. It is possible to formulate a hierarchy of attainment targets, e.g. the National Curriculum in England.

Such a hierarchical view of mathematics, however, is being challenged by many mathematics educators. Activities like investigations, explorations, and problem solving do not fit the structure as well as facts and skills do. The following quote expresses what many mathematics educators see as important:

As a matter of fact, we want students to understand that mathematics is, essentially, a human activity, that mathematics is invented by human beings. The process of creating mathematics implies moments of illumination, hesitation, acceptance, and refutation; very often centuries of endeavors, successive corrections and refinements. We want them to learn not only the formal. deductive sequence of statements leading to a theorem, but also become able to produce, by themselves, mathematical statements, to build respective proofs, to evaluate not only formally, but also intuitively the validity of mathematical statements. (Fischbein, 1994)

With this view of mathematics - and hence of school mathematics - it is problematic to construct a structure of precise attainment targets. Moreover, a step by step process implicit in such a structure of targets is not the only possible process of building competence in mathematics. This view of building competence has been realized in other subjects as well as mathematics. Some interesting models in teaching reading, writing and mathematics, of what is called cognitive apprenticeship are presented and discussed in (Collins, et al., 1989) [8]

An important type of consideration in education is how knowledge is developing in the individual. Constructivism in one form or another has a strong influence in the mathematics education community.

The nature of learning (knowledge development)

There are various forms of constructivism, but they all have some common elements. One element present in most forms of constructivism is the following: *Knowledge is constructed actively by the individual, it is not passively received.* (e.g. Kilpatrick, 1987). How does a constructivist view of the teaching-learning process correspond to the MBO philosophy?

With a constructivist view of the teaching-learning process, there must be a freedom of interpretation and choice for the teachers:

Using their own mathematical knowledge, mathematics teachers must interpret the language and actions of their students and then make decisions about possible mathematical knowledge their students might learn. (Steffe, 1990)

There will be a problem with teachers' freedom to choose if the targets are very precise, and issued at classroom level. One might argue that this is not the case in most school systems today, but the combination of extensive use of tests linked to targets will clearly have consequences for the teacher.

---

8   I would here like to add a personal observation. There are many similarities between mathematics and music, and between learning mathematics and learning to perform music. To learn to play a piano, was considered a step by step process, building up from simple exercises to more and more complicated tasks. A lot of "meaningless" exercises were necessary to advance through the levels of playing the piano. This was my experience when learning to play. When my daughter started piano lessons, she was going almost directly to playing melodies. Music was "in context". The"meaningless" exercises were introduced late when/if needed. I notice today that my daughter has more confidence in playing piano than I have.

Research in mathematics education

Education and research are two areas that in many countries are managed and funded by the government. What we have seen, e.g. in Norway in later years, are attempts by the authorities to manage research in the same way as outlined above - management by objectives.

The restructuring of government funded research has been an issue in Norwegian research administration. The establishement of new councils and units for administrating research has gone on for some time. The driving force has been efficiency of research - more results for the resources. These attempts have been argued against by researchers doing basic or fundamental research.

A Norwegian philosopher and scientist, Nils Roll Hansen, has argued that basic research does not contribute to solve the problems in society, but rather it helps formulate the problems (Roll Hansen, 1995). Basic research is in this respect not very efficient, not very economical to use this term.

Would this not be the case for much research in mathematics education? Mathematics education research has a tradition of close ties with practice - the teaching learning situation in classrooms. However, there is also a sizeable amount of what could be termed as basic research, seeking to formulate fundamental questions. Much of what is developed concerning knowledge development (e.g. constructivism) is also not directly applicable in the classroom. There would be a very different situation for mathematics education research if the model MBO should be used to manage research in the field.

CONCLUDING REMARKS

If we consider the reasons for MBO stated in (Flaa et.al., 1995) there would be several different functions for use of MBO in education:

(1) Objectives are formulated for the teachers and students to reach for,

(2) MBO will be a tool for school authorities to evaluate teachers and students,

(3) To increase efficiency.

There is a long tradition of setting aims or objectives in education. As Diane Ravitch argues (Ravitch, 1995), "standards" were used in the

United States in the 19th century. Also, the strict criteria of minimum competency that were used in some countries, could also be considered as part of the same philosophy. Few would argue that there are need for aims in education. However, what is new in the more recent development, is the structured approach to MBO in education. Large efforts in many countries now go into formulating very precise targets/standards for education, and systems of testing are being developed to go along with the targets. The consequences are that school subjects are presented as a set of "targets" or "standards". Students' performance on "targets" will be the "outcome" or "results" of education. For school authorities to evaluate the system (teachers and students), they would look to results.

Again, few would argue that good results are "good", but there are several problems: Is it possible to state precisely the type of objectives wanted in mathematics? There will be a danger of having skill related objectives - that are easy to assess. With the responsibility on how the objectives are attained in the end, solely on teachers and students, drill and practice activities might dominate classroom instruction.

There is also an obvious link to efficiency in education, which we have tried to show is a problematic concept. In MBO economic priorities will have to be decided in the "lower levels" of the system. Hence using MBO is also a way for school authorities to limit resources, but insisting on the same objectives being attained. It is a question if school systems can - or should - function like corporations in such cases.

Is it possible for us - with our market economy thoughts penetrating all layers of society - to think of alternatives to the MBO model? An essential factor of an alternative would be to give more freedom to teachers, and at the same time having the school authorities take a more direct responsibility in the teaching learning process.

References

AAAS (1993) *Benchmarks for Science Literacy.* New York/Oxford: Oxford University Press.

Bruner, J. S. (1960) *The Process of education.* Cambridge, MA: Harvard Univ. Press.

Collins, A., Brown, J.S. & Newman, S. (1989) Cognitive Apprenticeship: Teaching the Crafts of Reading, Writing, and Mathematics. In Resnick, L. (Ed.) *Knowing, Learning, and Instruction.* Hillsdale, NJ: Erlbaum.

Conant, J.B. (1959) *The American high school today:* a first report to interested citizens. New York: Mc Graw Hilll.

Fischbein, E. (1994) The interaction between the formal, the algorithmic, and the intuitive components in a mathematical activity. In Biehler, R. et. al (Eds.) (1994) *Didactics of Mathematics as a Scientific Discipline.* Dordrecht: Kluwer Academic Publ.

Flaa, P., Hofoss, D., Holmer-Hoven, F., Medhus, T. & Rønning, R. (1995) *Innføring i organisasjonsteori.* (Introduction to Organisation Theory). Oslo: Universitetsforlaget.

Howson, G. (1991) *National Curricula in Mathematics.* Leicester: The Mathematical Association.

Husen, T.(ed.) (1967) *International study of achievement in mathematics; a comparison of twelve countries.*
Stockholm: Almquist & Wicksell.

Kilpatrick, J. (1987) What Constructivism might be in Mathematics Education. In Proceedings of the 11th International Conference on the *Psychology of Mathematics education, Vol 1.* Montréal: Psychology of Mathematics Education.

NCTM (1989) *Curriculum and Evaluation Standards for School Mathematics. Reston, VA:* Author.

Norwegian Ministry of Education, Research and Church affairs (1994) *Upper Secondary Educaion in Norway. Structure and Excerpts of foundation Course Curricula.* Oslo: Author.

OECD; Norwegian Ministry of Church and Education; Norwegian Ministry of Culture and Science (1989) OECD-*vurdering av norsk utdanningspolitikk. Norsk rapport til OECD. Ekspertvurdering av OECD.* (OECD Evaluation of Norwegian Educational Policy. Norwegian Report to OECD. Expert Evaluation Performed by OECD). Oslo: Aschehoug.

Prais, S. (1995) Improving SchoolMathematics in Practice. In The Gatsby Charitable Foundation (1995) *Proceedings of a Seminar on Mathematics Education.* London: Author.

Ravitch, D. (1995) *National Standards in American Education.* A Citizens Guide.
Washington, DC: Brookings Institution Press.

Robitaille, D. & Nicol, C. (1994) Comparative International Research in Mathematics Education. In Biehler, R. et.al. (Eds.) *Didactics of Mathematics as a Scientific Discipline.* Dordrecht: Kluwer Academic Publ.

Roll Hansen, N. (1995) "Effektivisering" av norsk forskning? *Aftenposten* Feb. 8th (Oslo newspaper).

Scheffler, I. (1960) *The Language of Education.* Springfield: Thomas.

Sjöstedt, C.E. & Sjöstrand, W. (1952) *Skola och undervisning i Sverige och andra länder; en jamförande översikt.* (Schools and education in Sweden and other countries; a comparative overview). Stockholm: Natur och kultur.

Steffe. L. (1990) Mathematics curriculum design: A constructivist perspective. In L. Steffe & T. Wood (Eds.) *Transforming children's mathematics education: International perspectives.* Hillsdale, NJ: Lawrence Erlbaum.

Utbildningsdepartementet (Swedish Ministry of Education) (1992) *Skola för bildning.* (Schools for education).

SOU 1992:94. Stockholm: Author.

Westbury, I. (Ed.) (1994) *In search of more effective mathematics education.* Norwood, NJ: Ablex.

WHAT RESPONSABILITY DO RESEARCHERS HAVE TO MATHEMATICS TEACHERS AND CHILDREN?

Kathleen Hart, Director Shell Centre,
Nottingham University

Research in mathematics education is mainly carried out by students working towards higher degrees. They are essentially apprentices. Research by professionals, designed to answer wider more significant questions must be for longer periods and needs external funding so that it can be pursued full-time.

There are different viewpoints on what constitutes research, as witnessed at the ICMI Conference "What Is Mathematics Education Research" in Maryland, 1994, the report of which is expected soon. In 1989 in Paris a discussion group of the Psychology of Mathematics Education Conference agreed that research in mathematics education should contain the following:

1.   There is a problem.
2.   There is evidence/data.
3.   The work can be replicated.
4.   The work is reported.
5.   There is a theory.

My position is that research should at least contain all these.

Research and Evidence

For whom is research carried out? My point of view is that researchers in mathematics education should be trying to answer classroom questions concerned with teaching and learning mathematics. We know very little about how humans, especially children learn mathematics, how to teach effectively, what is the most advantageous order in which to present topics, etc, etc. These are questions of importance to millions of children and their teachers.

The responsibility for informing teachers carries with it the need to provide evidence that is sufficiently full and convincing for teachers to accept. Teachers in turn have the responsibility of looking at evidence carefully and then making decisions on its acceptance not letting prejudice and beliefs cloud their judgement.

The National Curriculum of England

In the United Kingdom we have had the same political party in power for 16 years. There is no child in British schools who has known or been educated under any other government. We have had at least 16 'Education Reforms' and each has been far-reaching and enforced immediately by law. Since 1988 there has been a National Curriculum instituted in England (a different one is implemented in Scotland). Britain never had such a curriculum before, although there always was considerable unity because of the united advice from an independent inspectorate, national school leaving examinations and a choice made by the majority of schools to use the same textbooks. Since 1988 Mathematics has been one of the three 'Core' subjects in the school curriculum to be studied in state schools during the ages of compulsory schooling (5-16 years). Private schools do not need to follow the contents of the National Curriculum. The contents of the mathematics curriculum are listed in 'levels' (there were ten but there are now eight). The set of levels provides a progression of mathematical topics which are supposed to match the development of children. The first set of level descriptions was very detailed, drawn-up by a committee of mathematics educators. These persons placed considerable emphasis on using and applying mathematics, thus showing what they valued. The curriculum has been changed three times by others since then and is now composed of four topic strands rather than 14. It still contains a strand called "Using and Applying Mathematics".

Testing

Tied to the content of the National Curriculum is the legal requirement for the schools to test their pupils with statutory externally written (and marked) tests at the age of 7, 11 and 14 years. There are national school-leaving tests at age 16 years, set by private examination boards. Additional to the statutory tests teachers are required to give their own assessments. Parents are important recipients of this information and every home in the country has received a copy of the "Parents Charter" which says the following:

Pupils will be tested in the core subjects in English, maths and science at about the ages of 7, 11 and 14. The tests are designed to be easier for teachers to manage than they were in the past. But they will still be challenging. They will show what pupils are able to do at the key stages of their time at school. They will help you to know how your child is doing. And assessing pupils against national standards will be made easier for teachers.

(Parents Charter 1994)

In the absence of multiple items to exemplify the rather general descriptions of the national curriculum we now have, the tests are used to interpret the meanings and requirements. They have as well become instruments which record a) the achievement of children, b) the effectiveness of the teaching in delivering the contents of the curriculum and c) keep teachers and schools 'in line'. Notice that schools are to improve through no extra training, provision of materials or RESEARCH but simply through fear of what test results might bring.

The inevitable 'teaching to pass the tests' has of course become apparent and the Review of Assessment and Testing published by the School Curriculum and Assessment Authority (1995) admits that schools are narrowing the range of questions children are given.

Expectations

In the first version of the Mathematics Curriculum (1989) it was stated that during the key stages 5-7 years, 7-11 years, 11-14 years and 14-16 years the content of school mathematics would encompass the following levels:

		Mathematics Levels
(5 - 7 yr)	KS1	1 - 3
(7 - 11 yr)	KS2	2 - 6
(11 - 14 yr)	KS3	3 - 8
(14 - 16 yr)	KS4	4 - 10

It is expected that the attainments of the great majority of pupils at the end of key stages will fall within the specified ranges of levels.

(Mathematics in the National Curriculum 1989)

More important was the statement of expectations held concerning pupils' performance.

In formulating the statements of attainment which define the levels, the working assumption, which will need to be tested in practice, has been that pupils should typically be capable of achieving around levels 2, 4, 5/6 or 6/7 respectively at or near the reporting ages of 7, 11, 14 and 16. The levels at the outer limits of the ranges will be achieved by a minority of pupils only.

(Mathematics in the National Curriculum 1989)

Since 1989 the content of the levels has changed, for example the subject 'Vectors' no longer appears BUT the expectations are the same. This has given rise to the continued harassment of English mathematics teachers by the media with headlines such as:

England's maths wins yet another brickbat

Primary maths in trouble

The 'expected' levels with no research to show whether the expectations are all reasonable have become the standards by which schools succeed or fail. At age 11 years the expected performance is success at level 4 or higher. The highest scoring English geographic region had 58 per cent of its eleven year olds reaching this score. Perhaps the expectations were wrong. Our politicians do not consider this; they declare English children have failed. Nobody declares we need to redefine the expectations because that would be tantamount to saying 'standards' should be lowered. This word 'standards' is usually based on myth e.g. (1) "In the past everybody could calculate their shopping bill"; (2) "Everybody in my class could do long division". Not true! You only have to read reports of school mathematics 50 years ago to realise how little has changed. This is not a cry for complacency but a request for a thorough investigation of what it is we are trying to preserve. There are people who think a good standard is preserved when 60 per cent of the candidates in an examination fail. This is surely a terrible waste of human resources - failure is not motivating for any learner.

Myths and Folklore

Over the last 30 years mathematics educators have espoused many causes but done little to show whether these 'good ideas' work with an ordinary class. We have said "using bricks are good things in the primary school". We had no research evidence of the circumstances in which the manipulatives might aid learning and when children still did not add fractions successfully we said 'the bricks have not been used enough'. Teachers knew better. Manipulatives are not the miracle products we pretend. Perhaps the bricks are made of coloured wood. Why should two pieces of pink wood and one of green lead the child to solve 2x - 5 = 17? There is a very large gap between these two statements, one in wood and the other in symbols. As I have quoted before of a child I interviewed, who showed great sense when I asked whether the concrete aids used by her class in learning subtraction with decomposition and the symbolic subtraction she was doing in her book were connected. "Sums is sums and bricks is bricks".

We have told teachers that part of their work is to write the materials for their class. We have not thought how difficult (and different) it is to write mathematics text and questions. Why should teachers be good authors? It should be enough that they be good teachers. Two of my students at the Shell Centre, Beth Moren and Dora Santos have been researching teachers' use of textbooks. Let us not suppose that teachers have stopped using mathematics textbooks (as is shown by the survey of Johnson and Millett, 1996)

Table 1   Proportion of pupils' mathematics work done from a commercial scheme (question 15) (%)

	n	0	1 - 5	6 - 20	21 - 50	51 - 80	>80
KS1	215	11	15	19	23	27	6
KS2	282	4	6	7	24	49	10
KS3	237	4	4	5	8	41	38

KS1 - 7 yr
KS2 - 11 yr
KS3 - 14 yr
(Implementing the National Curriculum (Johnson & Millett))

Teacher-trainers and advisers have often been heard to say 'you should dip into a textbook, do not follow it page by page'. "Slavishly" is sometimes added, gratuitously. This really appears to be strange advice when one considers that the author of the book has presumably sequenced the content so that it made sense and in order to address prerequisites. "Dipping-in" destroys this sequence. If a teacher was seeking examples to illustrate or extend material already available, then the textbook may be being used for a purpose not intended by the author but better served by lists of examples/word problems.

We have started some research on styles of using printed material in mathematics classrooms. Initially with one student's PhD work in which secondary school mathematics teachers are observed in class. The teachers are also interviewed and asked how the material has been chosen. Is there a set of textbooks chosen by the department? What part was played in the choice by this individual? The observations are for a number of reasons for example:

a) to ascertain whether a new topic is introduced by the teacher or by the child reading the textbook.

b) How close to the book is the teacher's introduction?

c) Do the examples that follow match it?

d) How do the children use the material?

e) How close to the teacher's objectives for a lesson (or series of lessons) is the class performance? In other words "How effective is the teaching?"

The simple recognition of different styles of textbook use should allow teacher-trainers the opportunity to discuss what is likely to be the principle teaching aid with future teachers. It should be possible to suggest a variety of styles amongst which the young teacher could choose and which might be adapted for individual needs.

What is in textbooks is often decided by an editorial assistant working in the publishing house and not one who necessarily knows anything about teaching or mathematics. The author might have considerable control over the words and exercises in the textbook but little influence on the illustrations. Modern mathematics textbooks are full of illustrations. These are not diagrams or graphs which might be considered to be part of the content of mathematics but pictures showing "real-life contexts" and meant to be informative and motivating. The quality of the drawing is often poor and the scene depicted is often irrelevant or more dangerously it is inconsistent with the information given in the text. Children make the best effort they can to cope with the printed page (we teachers do not explain how to use a textbook) and sometimes the child-rule is to ignore all pictures. Textbooks are very important in children's mathematical lives but we know very little about how they might be produced to achieve greater effectiveness.

Conclusion

This paper based on a lecture given in Seville is a cry for more research. The citizens of our countries should be demanding evidence of benefit before their children are subjected to yet one more education reform. Our teachers should be demanding research before they try out yet one more 'good idea' and we, the professionals should be making our presence felt. Decisions on what is given to children in the name of mathematics, are being taken by amateurs.

MATHEMATICS AND COMMON SENSE

Geoffrey Howson

Let me begin by explaining what prompted my current interest in this topic, and also by emphasising that here I shall be presenting very much a personal view, and not a survey of all recent writings, such as the report of a meeting held in Berlin on this subject (*Keitel et al, 1996*) or the chapters in a forthcoming volume written by members of the Basic Components of Mathematics Education for Teachers project (Hoyles, Kilpatrick and Skovsmose, to appear).

About three years ago I became involved in two pieces of work: one was linked with the Third International Mathematics and Science Study and involved the study of Grade 8 texts drawn from eight different countries (Howson, 1995); the other was part of the BACOMET group's investigation of "meaning" within mathematics education. One important aspect of the latter was the way in which we help students to construct not only "meaning" for concepts, but also to provide "meaning" for their study of mathematics itself.

With one exception, the authors of the texts I considered all sought to supply "meaning", in both senses, through the use of real world examples and the obvious utility of the subject. Moreover, it seemed mathematics was to be viewed as a specialised form of "common sense" and the various approaches appeared to be based on the principle that all we are doing in school mathematics is trying to codify common sense and to extend commonly held notions. (The one exception was a book which still showed the influence of the 1960s French approach to mathematics teaching. It laid considerable stress on algebraic structures introduced in a "semi-formal" way, although now tempered by reference to a number of "motivatory" real-life examples. That textbook, however, was in the process of being superseded.) Even more recently, I have seen various materials which have placed less emphasis on the "real world" and more on mathematical "activities", some of which were quite abstract. Yet even these texts appeared to assume that the use of common sense would lead to the desired mathematical outcomes, and, because of their lack of emphasis on definitions, facts or skills to be learned, that the aim of the teaching was to develop a kind of specific mathematical common sense which could then be applied to any mathematical problem.

Now it is important to emphasise at this point that I should not want entirely to abandon such approaches, particularly in the early years of education. However, my study of the Grade 8 texts alerted me to the tensions which will naturally arise if the shortcomings and possible dangers of such an approach are not recognised.

My aim, then, is to look at some of the interactions between mathematics and common sense - for we are not talking of an interface, the two are not disjoint; to consider the implications for the ways in which we both think about mathematics and also teach it; and to cause us to re-examine certain ideas, beliefs and teaching practices.

First let us begin with a dictionary definition of "common sense":

Common sense: average understanding; good sense or practical sagacity; the opinion of a community; the universally admitted impressions of mankind (Chambers' *Twentieth Century Dictionary*)

We see immediately, then, that "common sense" is far from being a scientific term: it is a vague, culturally dependent, but nonetheless extremely valuable concept. In essence, it provides us with a means to talk about mathematics, and with a rudimentary, one-way form of logical reasoning. Normally, "use your common sense" is a call for someone to come to a conclusion or devise a course of action based on local knowledge, past experience and simple reasoning. Common sense is distinguished by the way in which it depends upon evidence, accepted truths and conventions, and upon "innate" operating systems of perception, meaning and understanding. There is no doubt that it provides a powerful tool for survival in social life. It cannot be denied, then, that "common sense" is something which educators must try to develop in students and, conversely, something on which we must draw in our teaching.

But common sense is not just something which can aid mathematics learning, it can be seen as the foundation upon which mathematics is erected. In his "China Lectures" (1991), Freudenthal asks whether or not common sense is not the primordial certainty: the most abundant and reliable source of certainty within mathematics. He goes on to point out the extent to which number and elementary geometry (eg, ideas of similarity) are grounded in common sense. The significance of this to me is as great as the implications of common sense for mathematics teaching. Many of you will be familiar with, at least, the title of Morris Kline's book, *Mathematics: the loss of certainty,* and will know of the implications of

Gödel's work. I am certain that much will be made of this in other talks at this Congress. Nevertheless, such findings have not led to a loss of faith, changes in practice, or to an increase in neuroticism, within university mathematics faculties. The brilliance and significance of Gödel's work is readily acknowledged, but essentially mathematicians take refuge not in their axiom systems, but in the nesting of logical models which, for example, rest the consistency of hyperbolic geometry upon that of the natural numbers, and these, as Freudenthal remarks, are firmly grounded in common sense - the ultimate basis for the mathematician's confidence in what he or she is doing. I shall return to such matters, including questions of "fallibility", later in my talk.

In reading the Grade 8 texts, I became aware of how these, in many countries, represent a "fault line" so far as arguments based on common sense are concerned, for it is at this level that many countries introduce the multiplication of negative integers. Here, probably for the first time at a school level, the link between common sense and mathematics breaks down. Negative numbers have caused difficulties to more than Grade 8 students. For example, in the late 1700s and early 1800s, many in England still looked upon such numbers with considerable misgiving. Indeed, in 1796, Frend, a Cambridge mathematician, produced an algebra text in which he avoided their use. He argued that "multiplying a negative number into a negative number and thus producing a positive number" finds most supporters "amongst those who love to take things upon trust and hate the labour of serious thought", for "when a person cannot explain the principles of science without reference to metaphor, the probability is that he has never thought accurately upon the subject"[1] . Frend's son-in-law, the better-known mathematician, De Morgan, was to write in his *On the Study and Difficulties of Mathematics* (1831) that "the imaginary expression $\sqrt{(-a)}$ and the negative expression -b ... are equally imaginary *as far as real meaning is concerned* (my italics). [One] is as inconceivable as [the other].[2] "

---

1 Frend was removed as a tutor from Cambridge, not because he lacked belief in negative numbers, but because of his unorthodox religious beliefs: as a Unitarian, he did not believe in the Holy Trinity. He was later banished from the university when he publicly denounced the war against France. Cambridge was prepared to tolerate mathematical unorthodoxy, but not religious or political dissent.

2 In the early 19th century negative numbers were referred to by many English authors as "imaginary numbers". Nowadays, see below, negative integers have become part of "local knowledge", thus adding weight to Paul Langevin's claim that "the concrete is the abstract made familiar by usage".

Frend's objections to negative numbers were essentially based on common sense: how could multiplication of two of these mysterious objects yield something with which he was familiar - something which was part of common sense? Many other examples illustrate what happens when the links between mathematics and common sense break down. When Gauss suppressed his findings on hyperbolic geometry because, as he wrote, he feared the shrieks which they would elicit from the Boeotians (a Greek tribe traditionally considered dull-witted), he surely meant that many of his fellow mathematicians would reject, as an affront to their common sense, the assumption that given a point and a line in the plane then there could possibly be more than one parallel to the line through that point. Du Bois-Reymond objected to Cantor's set theory because "it appears repugnant to common sense" (1882, quoted in Kline, 1972, p. 998). Clearly, the theory of infinite sets **does** contradict common sense. Let us take a simple example. Suppose there are footballers on a field, some in red kit and some in indigo. If I ask them to form a line according to the rule that between every two in red there must be one in indigo, and between every two in indigo one in red, and then note that the line begins and ends with a person in red, common-sense tells me that there is one more person in red than in indigo. But what happens on the number line in the closed interval 0 to 1? The interval begins and ends with a rational. Between every two rationals there is an irrational and between every two irrationals a rational. But there are not more rationals than irrationals: indeed the number of rationals is insignificant compared with that of the irrationals. What has happened to common sense? Other such examples exist outside of set theory, but there is not time to give them here.

Mathematics should not be confused with, or constrained by, common sense. The latter, if it is to become genuine mathematics, must be systematised, organised and, if necessary, formalised. Arguments must be based on more than that elementary logic and inferential reasoning which underpin common sense. These seemingly obvious remarks can create problems for the textbook author or curriculum developer. Let us take one simple example based on exercises to be found in one of the series I studied. Students were provided with photographs and asked, on the basis of the plans provided, to identify the church photographed, or, using a town plan, to say from which point a particular photograph was taken. These I see as useful activities to develop "spatial awareness" (whatever that means!), which mathematicians will wish to draw upon. Yet in these sections the textbook had no "kernels" to offer, that is, no mathematical definitions, results or procedures which students might identify, learn or follow, or which might help them to crystallise what they had learned into a usable form.

Opportunities were provided for students to use their "common sense", presumably in order to develop this further. It was hoped that in so doing they would also develop desirable, idiosyncratic traits. However, the logicality and systematics which lay behind these were never discussed or assessed. Is this the best which we as mathematics educators can offer? Strangely enough, 1960s textbooks carried within them a language of systematisation that might be applied to this problem. Looking at a town plan we could consider the set of all points from which, say, the spire of St Peter's church would appear to be on the left of that of St. John's. Consideration of the intersection of various such sets would lead to the desired answer. In the 1960s such context-based questions were rarely, if ever, set. In the 1990s there is a danger that context and a dependence upon common sense are driving out mathematics. There is a nice balance to be observed. We have to build upon common sense, but we need to demonstrate that, unlike common sense, mathematics relies upon the structuring, organisation and sharing of knowledge, experiences and techniques.

Already, then, we begin to see certain problems arising in connection with "mathematics and common sense".

(a) Although founded upon common sense - ie, the "universally admitted impressions of mankind" - mathematics is more than common sense. Indeed, the latter can be a constraining force on the learning, comprehension and development of mathematics.

(b) In our mathematics teaching there will frequently be a need for us to develop our students' "common sense" (ie, bring a student up to "average understanding" as in the example just cited on spatial awareness) in order for him or her to make progress in mathematics. This may be a legitimate part of mathematics education, although perhaps scarcely qualifying as "mathematics". Moreover, children from different social communities will bring with them different types of "common sense", for this is not a universal constant: indeed, it has been described elsewhere as "local knowledge". Discussions of "ethnomathematics" might well gain, then, by focussing more on the issue of the common sense peculiar to a particular society.

There is a great need to recognise and build upon such "local knowledge" and to be aware that such knowledge is never static - changing social contexts ensure that there are new mathematical entries and omissions. Textbook writers have, to some extent, recognised this and, for example, most of the books I studied made use of the fact that weather forecasts on television have now made most children from non-tropical countries very familiar with negative numbers. These are now part of "local knowledge", although the operations on them are not. But many opportunities would still seem to be lost. One of the most interesting national reports to come out of the Second International Mathematics Study described how in one developed country teachers had great difficulty in forecasting which items their students could answer successfully. All too often they expected failure simply because they had not yet taught the topics: in fact students were able to answer the questions from what had become "local knowledge". To take an example from another country: when the English National Curriculum was devised in 1988, scientific notation was thought appropriate to be learned by only about half the students by age 16. Yet, again, SIMS had shown that in 1981 almost 40% of English 13-year-old students answered an item on that topic correctly. Whether they had learned it in science lessons, in mathematics, or simply by playing around with a calculator or computer, I do not know - but for them it had become "local knowledge". I look forward to the publication of the results of the Third International Mathematics and Science Study in order to see how 13 year-olds in those countries which have not taught probability or, in some cases, devoted much time to the graphical representation of data, perform on such items. My suspicion is that the elementary aspects of these topics are fast becoming "local knowledge" amongst young adolescents.

We all know that it is wrong for teachers to assume that "what has been taught has been learned", but it is equally dangerous to assume also that "what has not been taught is not known". An immediate consequence is, of course, the influence of the student's social background - for this automatically defines the "local knowledge" associated with the student.

(c) Mathematicians as "a community" have their own brand of "common sense". A major aim of mathematics education is to develop this type of common sense in students - to add to what they consider to be normal mathematical behaviour, to develop that knowledge and those methods of thinking which are often ascribed to "(mathematical) common sense". Does, for example, "It is obvious that ...", really mean: " given my knowledge of mathematics, it is (mathematical) common sense that ..."? (Perhaps one should add a note here concerning the differences between "the mathematician's common sense" and those other two useful, but ill-defined terms, "intuition" and "insight". I remember being embroiled in arguments about the meanings of the last two terms over twenty years ago - and the meanings attached to them are still largely idiosyncratic. However, I believe "intuition" is like "common sense" in that it is based on local (although frequently highly professional) knowledge and experience - but I do not see its results being derived even by the simplistic logic utilised in "common sense". On the other hand, "insight" goes far beyond "common sense" in demanding an appreciation of the structure of the problem or of the mathematical topics involved.)

(d)   If the Greeks (in the case of irrational numbers), and mathematicians such as Frend and Lazare Carnot (negative numbers), and Du Bois-Reymond (set theory) had difficulty in accepting new ideas which contradicted their "common sense" views, then it should not surprise us if our students have problems.

All these points would repay much more detailed study. In particular there would seem to be close links between "mathematics" and "common sense" in what Skovsmose, following Bourdieu, has described as different "spheres of practice", whether these refer to the arithmetical practices of Brazilian street children or to the activities of professional research mathematicians. The aim of developing specific mathematically-oriented common sense within a particular sphere of practice, as in the case of the example just given on spatial awareness, is, of course, present in the writings of, for example, Greeno (1991) on number sense, Eisenberg (1992) on function sense, and Arcavi (1994) on symbol sense. We note, however, the difficulty of expressing specific objectives, ie, the desirable "senses" to be developed, in those simplistic, knowledge-based terms which fit happily in national curricula for mathematics.

All of us present will no doubt be able to call on personal experiences in which the difficulties mentioned in (c) and (d) arose. Certainly, they were clearly present in the case of a university student observed on video by the BACOMET group. When asked, in a course on linear spaces, to prove that there can be only one zero vector, his reaction was that this was "common sense". This inference appeared to be based on the study of a particular geometrical representation of a vector space and he saw no reason to apply reasoning other than that associated with common sense. The student's difficulties seemed also to be reinforced by the request that he should "prove" something. For does the concept of proof have any standing within "common sense" or is it lodged firmly within mathematics? This latter problem arose also in relation to the Grade 8 texts I studied, for two countries attempted to introduce the notion of formal geometrical proof at this level. Although both texts had many good features, nevertheless there seemed to be a marked and largely unexplained and unmotivated jump from the "common sense" approach which had characterised the books up to that point and the more formal notions of the proof sections.

Another video seen at the same time showed a similar problem, hinging on a limited representation, but this time arising in the primary school. This concerned fractions discussed in the context of the ubiquitous pizza. Did 4/4 equal 5/5? One child supplied the required response, but another actually *used* her common sense and argued correctly that a pizza divided into four equal parts was not the same as one divided into five. The former would be useless should five children wish to share it! Of course such subversive reasoning had to be corrected! But the child was right. It has to be an odd equivalence relation which treats many real-life, or common sense, situations as equivalent. Someone tying a parcel will need a lot of convincing that 100 pieces of string each 1 cm long are equivalent to one piece of one metre in length. Abstract mathematical equivalence relations do not always translate sensibly into real life terms.

There is no easy way to teach fractions, but that which leaned too heavily on pizzas had probably resulted in at least one girl believing that mathematics teachers could be very selective when deciding what comprised "common sense". I am not here offering a solution to this difficult problem, but unless we recognise its existence, we are unlikely to make significant headway towards its solution.

There comes a time in mathematics when the constraints of common sense must yield to the demands of structure - whether this accompanies the introduction of new types of number and the operations upon them, or of algebraic and topological structures per se. In some ways this parallels developments in the foundations of mathematics, from Frege, who attempted to build mathematics upon the foundations of a "common sense" logic, to those of Hilbert and the development of formal systems. Thus, for example, in 1919, Hilbert stressed that the concepts of mathematics were built up "systematically for reasons that are both internal and external" (quoted in Rowe, 1994). Common sense, supplies "external" motivation, but we must look to mathematics for the internal reasons.

It will never be easy to make the change from a view based on common sense, to one which takes into account the internal structure and demands of mathematics. However, attempts to disguise the need for this transition will almost invariably lead to confusion in the minds of students and teachers.

Certainly, I felt that none of the textbooks I studied provided a satisfactory introduction to the multiplication of integers. As I have already mentioned, one approached the subject from the "internal" standpoint of algebraic structure, but in such a way as to make little sense either to an eighth grade student or a mathematician. Other texts tried to make the result "convincing" through a variety of approaches: for example, by an appeal to the authority of a calculator; by a weird fable which ignored the laws of physics and, like several other approaches, essentially fudged the mathematical issue by taking the product of two different representations of the integers; or by assuming that the result followed by applying common sense to the extension of numerical patterns (see Howson, to appear, for further details). It was interesting to compare these approaches with two from the 1930s. The first, told by the poet, W.H. Auden, was by being made to memorise:

> *Minus times minus equals plus.*
> *The reason for this we need not discuss.*

which had at least the virtues of honesty and being easy to remember. The second, more serious example, concerns the advice given by the schoolteacher, C.V. Durell, in his 1931 book, *The teaching of elementary algebra*. What was most frightening was that I could not detect in any of the modern texts the pedagogical and mathematical understanding shown by Durell [3]. It would seem to be a serious criticism of mathematics education

---

[3] Durell stressed history as strong evidence of the difficulty of the concepts involved and remarked that the introduction of negative numbers had, in recent years, tended to be delayed as a result of the underlying theory and difficulties being better appreciated. He, himself, strongly believed that "it is inexcusably wrong to teach pupils to use symbols to which they attach no meaning". One consequence of this was his wish to distinguish between a signed negative number and the operation of subtraction on unsigned numbers. (Only one of the texts I studied did this.) The approach he suggested for the introduction of directed numbers and for addition and subtraction are those most favoured today: temperatures, gain and loss, etc. Here, however, he wished emphasis to be placed on the fact that "the 'rules of signs' are definitions which have been framed to establish correspondences between similar processes in different number systems. The question of proof does not arise here, though it does so in connection with the consequences of the rules, but [such work] is for specialists". On multiplication, he suggested beginning with consideration of repeated addition, eg $(-5) \times 3$.

"This does not prove that $(-5) \times 3 = -15$; it would merely make matters very awkward if it were not so, and suggests what kind of definition is most useful." Further justification for a definition is sought through contextualised examples. Here we want to substitute negative numbers into physical formulae which involve products. Durell suggested simple equations arising in kinematics and, for example, temperature rising at a steady rate in a boiler. He then suggested that students be asked to supply interpretations of these formulae when none, one or two of the variables have negative values. And so his advice proceeded.

and of mathematics educators that in over 60 years we seem to have made no progress in our thinking on how a key topic to be found in the curriculum of every country, namely the multiplication of negative numbers, should be taught.

We have already seen some of the problems which arise when we do not distinguish clearly enough between the world, and our common-sense conceptions within that, and the abstract model of it which we form within mathematics. In his *Pathway to Knowledge* (1551), Recorde tackled this problem head on:

> A point [the spelling has been modernised throughout this extract] or a prick is named of geometricians that small and insensible shape which hath in it no parts, that is to say, neither length, breadth or depth. But as the exactness of this definition is [more suited] for only theoretic speculation, than for practice and outward work (considering that my intent is to apply all these principles to work) I think it [more suitable] to call a point or prick that small print of pen, pencil or other instrument which is not moved nor drawn from the first touch. ...

Similarly when defining a line he was led to observe how geometers "in their theories (which are only mind works) do precisely understand these definitions". Whether Recorde shared our appreciation of the distinction which he drew between the abstract nature of the geometer's system and the artisan's real world of which it is a model is, of course, doubtful. Nevertheless, it demonstrates the care with which he approached his task. Perhaps at the other extreme to Recorde, in so far as it confuses abstract mathematics with the real world, is an example I saw recently which sought to bring sense to irrational numbers through contextualisation. It was a proposed test item which described a clock having a minute hand of $\sqrt{5}$ cm and an hour hand of length 2 cm. The students were asked to state whether the distances between the tips of the two hands at 12, 6 and 9 o'clock were rational or irrational. The question demonstrates a degree of bizarre ingenuity. The outcome, however, is more irrational than the numbers involved. Irrational numbers are not measuring numbers in the real world - indeed it is difficult to imagine what an irrational measurement could mean in physical terms. What degree of accuracy is reasonable in a measurement? What clock has its minute and hour hands moving in the same plane? This example, then, provides us with a misguided attempt to supply meaning - driven not by the demands of mathematics, but by a belief that meaning and motivation must be provided through "real-world(!)" contextualisations. We note also not only a reluctance to move into what Recorde calls the geometer's system, in which the diagonal of a square of side 1 has length root 2, but an utter confusion between the real world, and measurements within it, and that of formal geometry. Let me give another example. In England it is now common to "motivate" and add "reality" to mathematics by always placing geometrical problems in the "real world" of measures. So a question such as "is a triangle with sides 12, 12 and 17 right-angled?" would be replaced by "is a triangle with sides 12 cm, 12 cm and 17 cm right-angled?" However, there are enormous differences between these two questions. The answer to the first question is a straightforward "No". The second question is much more difficult - what, in the real world do we mean by "12 cm long" or "right angled"? The obvious answer this time is "more or less"; but it is not simple to calculate the probability and this will depend upon what assumptions are made en route.

Such confusion is not only to be found in school texts. I see it, for example, in some of the writings about the "fallibility" of mathematics. Many of you will be familiar with the problem of adding together two numbers, A and B, say, each some 60 or so digits in length and constructed using only the digits 1 and 7. One writer asks the question: "[Since] we have no certain answer by which to check or verify [this addition]... what are we left with, as far as certainty in mathematics goes?" (Lerman, 1994, p. 203) Again, this to me would seem to confuse the problems caused by doing mathematics in the real world and those inherent to mathematics itself. If A + B is not uniquely defined, then we can all go home and abandon the teaching of mathematics. Physical limitations may prevent my adding the two numbers together correctly, and might cause me to have doubts about the validity of a proof which hinged on that calculation being correctly done (although I find it hard to envisage how such a proof might arise). However, I am certain that A + B is even and that AB is odd - and of other similar results. To dismiss "certainty" because of our human limitations would seem to me to be only one step on from Lewis Carroll's:

> "What's one and one and one and one and one and one and one and one and one and one?", [asked the White Queen].
> "I don't know", said Alice, "I lost count".
> "She can't do Addition", the Red Queen interrupted.
>
> *(Alice through the Looking Glass,* 1871)[4]

---

[4] Lewis Carroll's allusions normally had a serious point. A colleague suggested that here he might have been influenced by thoughts on Peano's "successor" notion, but since Peano did not publish his axioms until 1892, I think this unlikely. Could it be that, in the section from which this excerpt was taken, Carroll was poking fun at the simplistic way in which student attainment and teacher effectiveness were being measured following the establishment of the "payment by results" scheme in 1862 (see, eg, Howson, 1982)? If so, one can only wonder what Carroll would have made of educational developments in England since 1988!

However, this is in some ways taking me away from my main theme. Let me finish, then, by summing up some of the points I wish to make.

First, our mathematics teaching, like mathematics itself, must be founded upon common sense.

However, as we have observed, common sense is a vague and unstructured notion: we must ensure that students see mathematics not merely as an extension of common sense, but as a structured, organised discipline that builds upon accepted, shared results and techniques.

Sooner or later, the "shared" results and techniques of mathematics transcend common sense. It is necessary to be aware of this and to ensure that students are properly prepared for this shift and that the transition is achieved honestly - that they are not misled by half-truths.

Common sense is rooted in everyday experiences: when we make use of common sense in our teaching we must appreciate that there are significant differences between this world and that which mathematicians have created. Care must be taken to ensure that students do not become confused by this.

References

Arcavi, A., 1994, "Symbol sense:Informal Sense-making in Formal Mathematics", *For the Learning of Mathematics*, **14** (3), 24-35

De Morgan, A., 1831, *On the Study and Difficulties of Mathematics*, London

Durell, C.V., 1931, *The Teaching of Elementary Algebra,* Bell

Eisenberg, T., 1992, "On the development of a sense for functions", in Harel, G. and Dubinsky, E, (eds), *The Concept of Function: Aspects of Epistemology and Pedagogy*, MAA Notes, Vol 25, Mathematical Association of America, 153-174

Freudenthal, H., 1991, *Revisiting Mathematics Education* (*The China Lectures*), Kluwer

Greeno, J.G., 1991, "Number sense as Situated Knowing in a Conceptual Domain", *JRME*, **22**, 170-218

Howson, A.G., 1982, *A History of Mathematics Education in England*, Cambridge University Press

Howson, A.G., 1995, *Mathematics Textbooks: a comparative study of Grade 8 texts*, Pacific Educational Press

Howson, A.G., to appear, *"'Meaning' and School Mathematics"* in Hoyles, C., Kilpatrick, J. and Skovsmose, O.

Keitel, C, et al, (eds), 1996, *Mathematics (Education) and Common Sense,* Free University, Berlin

Kline, M., 1972, *Mathematical Thought from Ancient to Modern Times,* Oxford University Press

Kline, M., 1980, *Mathematics: the Loss of Certainty,* Oxford University Press

Rowe, D.E., 1994, *"The Philosophical Views of Klein and Hilbert",* in Chikara, S. *et al (eds), The Intersection of History and Mathematics,* Birkhäuser, 187-202

Lerman, S., (de), 1994, *Cultural Perspectives on the Mathematics Classroom,* Kluwer

THE CHANGING FACE OF SCHOOL ALGEBRA

Carolyn Kieran
Université du Québec á Montréal
Canada

Traditionally, school algebra has been associated with literal symbols and the operations that are carried out on these symbols. But for the past decade or so, this vision of school algebra has gradually been widening to encompass activities and perspectives that were not previously considered part of algebra. The broader term, algebraic thinking, is being employed more and more often as a vehicle for describing the kinds of encounters students are having with algebra. This paper examines a couple of these newer perspectives in the light of a distinction between algebra and algebraic thinking, discusses some recent research that shows what we might expect from these approaches, and offers a suggestion as to the direction in which we ought to be heading.

1. ALGEBRA VERSUS ALGEBRAIC THINKING
1.1. ALGEBRA

In order to distinguish algebra from algebraic thinking, let's begin with what I believe to be a fairly widespread definition of what has traditionally been meant by algebra, at least elementary algebra: Algebra is a tool whereby we not only represent numbers and quantities with literal symbols but also calculate with these symbols. Thus, in North America at least, school algebra has been viewed as the course in which students are introduced to the principal ways in which letters are used to represent numbers and numerical relationships--in equations as unknowns and in expressions of generality as variables--and to the corresponding activities involved with these uses of letters--mainly equation solving and expression simplification. In this paper, school algebra is taken to be synonymous with elementary algebra.

Implicit in this definition of school algebra is both the "acting upon" (or "actions") and the "objets" themselves. We might ask ourselves at this point whether there are specific algebraic objects. For example, are the objects of algebra different from the objects of, say, calculus? Some would say "yes": "In the calculus, differentiation and integration are perhaps most readily thought of as operations on functions as entities" (Schwartz &

271

Yerushalmy, 1992, p. 266). In other words, the functional expressions that are the objects of the operation of differentiation are viewed as entities rather than as sequences of operations (see also Sfard, 1991). Others, possibly a majority, might say "no," that the expressions that are the objects in calculus have the same form as the expressions that are the objects of school algebra, even though they might be interpreted differently and have other referents. In line with this perspective, there are no distinct objects in algebra, thus making algebra an all-purpose tool, handy in more than one mathematical domain. But then are the activities of algebra different from the activities of, once again, calculus? Many would be of the opinion that the basic activities of algebra--simplification and equation-solving--can be distinguished from the basic activities of calculus--differentiation and integration--even though the former activities are clearly engaged in when doing calculus.

Let us at this moment look a little more closely at these tool-based activities of algebra. We can view them as being of different types. First, there are what we might call the *generational* activities. These involve the generating of expressions and equations that are the objects of algebra, for example, equations containing an unknown that represent quantitative problem situations (see, e.g., Bell, 1995), expressions of generality from geometric patterns or numerical sequences (see, e.g., Mason, 1996), and expressions of the rules governing numerical relationships (see, e.g., Lee & Wheeler, 1987). Another way of looking at these generational activities is from the perspective of translating, that is, translating a situation into an algebraic representation--however, the use of the term translation suggests a fidelity with respect to maintaining all the information of a situation, which is clearly not the case in algebra. Then, there are the *transformational*, rule-based activities of algebra, for example, collecting like terms, factoring, expanding, substituting, solving equations, simplifying expressions, and so on. Much of this activity is concerned with equivalence and the preservation of essence despite the apparent transformation of form. And lastly there are the *global, meta-level, mathematical* activities for which algebra is used as a tool but which are not exclusive to algebra and which could be engaged in without using any algebra at all, such as, problem solving, modeling, finding structure, justifying, proving, and predicting (Kieran, 1.997). In these latter activities, the algebraic representations that have previously been generated or manipulated are interpreted or closely examined so as to provide insights into, for example, the underlying mathematical structure of a situation or to yield answers to specific or conjectural questions. The case could be made that, since these latter activities are not restricted to the algebraic domain, they are, in fact, not part of algebra. But attempting to divorce these meta-level activities from algebra removes any context or need that one might have for using algebra.

This, in summary, we have these three types of algebraical activities- the generational, the transformational, and the global, meta-level -all of which I will be referring to again and again in this paper.

Another lens with which to view the activities of algebra is that of *mathematical doing* versus *mathematical thinking*. We are clearly "doing" mathematics when we are engaged in any of the above activities. But the question of whether we are "thinking" mathematically is more problematic. If we look first at the generational and transformational activities of algebra, Love (1986) has described the kind of thinking that is entailed as follows:

> Algebra is now not merely "giving meaning to the symbols," but another level beyond that; concerning itself with those modes of thought that are essentially algebraic--for example, handling the as yet unknown, inverting and reversing operations, seeing the general in the particular. Becoming aware of these processes, and in control of them, is what it means to think algebraically. (p. 49)

For experts, much of the transformational activity can become quite automated. Once one makes the transformation rules one's own, the algorithms of algebra can be executed, in a sense, without thinking. Wheeler (1989) has pointed out that this is, indeed, one of the main advantages of working in the symbolic system of algebra. This is the power of algebra! One need not be thinking of, for example, the operations one is carrying out or the referents of the expressions. In fact, once one has generated the expressions or equations (or has been provided with them) and knows what one's goal is, they can be treated in an almost mindless fashion. But not quite! We have all seen students who in trying to solve equations or simplify expressions knew the techniques, but kept going in circles (Wenger, 1987), not having a sense of where they were going or when they should stop. For these latter students, even the doing was not under control. Boero (1993) has discussed this issue in terms of anticipation, that every algebraic manipulation contains an anticipatory element, a sense of the direction in which you want to be going and of what the desired expression will look like once you get there. Pimm (1995) has remarked that the development of this sense of anticipation can provide an alternative to the "blind" manipulation that is so often found in beginning algebra students. Thus, even the doing of algebra, for it to be successful, must involve a particular kind of thinking.

But what about the global, meta-level activities of algebra, or more precisely those special activities in which algebra can be used as a tool (e.g., problem solving, proving, etc.)? These are usually considered the arenas of higher-plane mathematical thinking. Examples of the kinds of thinking engaged in with respect to some of these activities is one of the topics of this paper. But, before going further in a discussion of these meta-level activities and their role in the changing face of school algebra, I wish to shift gears slightly and address a broader question, one that involves a different interpretation of the term algebraic thinking.

1.2. ALGEBRAIC THINKING

In all of the activities described above, the view of algebra has been limited to a very narrow and quite traditional perspective, that involving letter-symbolic representations and an implicit set of numerical references--sometimes referred to as "generalized arithmetic" (see also Kieran, 1989). In this regard, Bell (1996) reminds us that there are several other algebras, each involving its own objects and actions, such as, "geometric algebras in which the elements are geometric transformations and the (single) operation is function composition" (p. 173) and "Boolean algebra, where the letters may denote propositions, and the operations are *and* and *or*" (p. 174). However, these have rarely been the domain of school algebra. My aim is not to move in this direction, but rather to enlarge our view of what might be considered algebra by including a broader range of algebra-related tools, with the purpose of ultimately arriving at a much wider vision of what we deem to be the content of school algebra.

Up until very recently, we have privileged the letter-symbolic in our representations of numerical relationships. But, with the advent of computer technology, we now have open to us several other means of representing such relationships and of operating on these relationships in ways that can be seen to be somewhat analogous to the generational and transformational activities of algebra described earlier. And since the relationships that are underlying these alternate representations are still numerical, it seems appropriate that these other representations and our thinking about them and with them be included in the domain of algebra, even if they look different from the representations that we are used to considering as part of algebra.

When viewed from this perspective, algebra does not require the letter-symbolic form. From now on, when I employ the term algebraic thinking, I am referring to a broader range of representations that nonetheless includes at times the letter-symbolic. This enlarged view of algebra is called algebraic thinking to distinguish it from traditional elementary algebra. Thus, algebraic thinking can be defined as the use of any of a variety of representations in order to handle quantitative situations in a relational way. Once the representation has been generated, it can be operated upon according to certain transformational rules related to the particular representation being used, within the context of global, meta-level mathematical goals, just as was the case with the activities of purely letter-symbolic algebra.

From a pedagogical angle, the non-letter-symbolic representations and their transformations can be used to make contact with or give meaning to the letter-symbolic representations that are traditionally involved in algebraic activities. Thus, algebraic thinking can be interpreted as an approach to quantitative situations that emphasizes the general relational aspects with tools that are not necessarily letter-symbolic, but which can ultimately be used as cognitive support for introducing and for sustaining the more traditional discourse of school algebra. This supporting use of non-letter-symbolic representations is not, however, meant to suggest that the primary value of these alternate representations is pre-algebraic; in the perspective being discussed here, they are considered full-fledged ongoing objects of algebraic activity. In view of my earlier remarks on mathematical thinking and doing, and how in the algebraic activities of generation and transformation, the thinking of experts often becomes routinized to an anticipatory kind of thinking, this new perspective on algebra and its being named algebraic thinking does not imply that it is at a higher level of thinking than that of traditional algebra. Perhaps it would have been simpler to redefine algebra than to create something new called algebraic thinking; but the term algebra already has so much baggage associated with it.

In the international mathematics education community, the development of algebraic thinking has recently received a great deal of research interest. Different approaches aimed at making algebra meaningful for students have been proposed which combine the use of various representations for expressing quantitative relationships and an emphasis on global, meta-level activities. Two examples of such approaches will now be presented, each of them giving priority to the meta-level activity of problem solving. In fact, of all the global activities mentioned above for which algebra has been used as a tool in schools, the one that has received the most attention in the newer approaches is that of problem solving. As is also typical of many of these new approaches, the computer plays an important role. In both examples of algebraic thinking to be described, it will be seen that the three-fold nature of the activities engaged in parallels that noted earlier for traditional algebra. More detailed information on these two approaches and others--

approaches that illustrate how the face of school algebra is indeed changing and is being widened to include algebra-related tools--can be obtained from Bednarz, Kieran, and Lee (1996).

2. TWO OF THE NEWER APPROACHES TO SCHOOL ALGEBRA

Problem solving has always been a part of school algebra; in fact, problem solving is at the heart of the historical development of algebra. But the way in which problem solving has generally been treated in traditional algebra courses is as a vehicle for applying the most recently learned symbolic form or technique. Problem solving itself has not until recently been taken very seriously in school algebra. However, during the last decade or so, several countries have shifted the emphasis in their algebra curricula from manipulation techniques to the pursuit of solving problems. The accent has moved from the typical transformation activities to the more global, meta-level activity of problem solving. A first example that illustrates some of the newer facets of this perspective on problem solving, in particular the kinds of thinking that are engaged by the use of a non-traditional algebraic representation and its related transformations, is drawn from the work of Rojano and Sutherland (1992, 1993; see also Sutherland & Rojano, 1993). Central to these new approaches to school algebra are the countless research findings related to the difficulties that students have typically encountered in the study of algebra.

2.1. A SPREADSHEET APPROACH

Rojano (1996) has argued that "trial and error, together with other strategies considered informal and which are found in students beginning the study of algebra, are indeed a real foundation upon which the methods or strategies of algebraic thought are constructed" (p. 137). This conviction, along with the large body of research evidence showing the inability of many students to achieve an integration of their problem solving and symbolic manipulation domains of knowledge, led Rojano and Sutherland to approach problem solving by the alternate avenue afforded by spreadsheet computer environments. Thus, students' own strategies are put into play in an environment that helps them symbolize their informal procedures for the problem.

In the following extract that describes the algebraic thinking activities involved in spreadsheet work, 10- and 11-year-old children had been attempting the problem: "In a rectangular piece of land the length is 4 times the width. The perimeter is 280 meters. What is the area of this piece of land?"

Throughout the spreadsheet word-problem sequence, pupils were taught a spreadsheet-algebraic approach (algebraic because it involves working from the unknown to the known; see Figure 1). The unknown is represented by a spreadsheet cell (this might be called x in an algebraic solution). Other mathematical relationships are then expressed in terms of this unknown. When the problem has been expressed in the spreadsheet symbolic language, pupils then vary the unknown either by copying down the rules or by changing the number in the cell representing the unknown (in a paper and pencil algebra approach, this would be the equation-solving part). In the figure below, the spreadsheet formulas are shown in order to present the pupils' solution processes. However, once the formula is entered into the spreadsheet, a number is automatically computed and a table of numerical values is produced (although the user can ask to view the formulas). (Rojano, 1996, p. 141)

	A	B	C	D
1		WIDTH (CM)	LENGTH (CM)	PERIMETER (CM)
2		25	= B2 * 4	= (B2*2) + (C2*2)
3		= B2 + 1	= B3 * 4	= (B3*2) + (C3*2)
4		= B3 + 1	= B4 * 4	= (B4*2) + (C4*2)
5				
6				
7		rule copied down	rule copied down	rule copied down

Figure 1.

One of the features that distinguishes this approach from traditional school algebra is the absence of standard algebraic symbolism; the representation used is the spreadsheet-symbolic. Nevertheless, the strategies used for solving this and other similar quantitative situations are not unlike those called into play in more typical algebra environments in which the student begins by identifying the variables and then decides on the relationship among the variables. Rojano (1996) points out the critical aspects of algebraic thinking that are favored in this approach: "The spreadsheet environment supported pupils in moving from thinking with the specific to the general, both in terms of the unknown and of the mathematical relationships expressed in the problem" (p. 144). Thus, the algebra-like tools of the spreadsheet environment are assumed to engage mental processes that are similar to those used in the more traditional algebra environment, but which are made more accessible due to the spreadsheet's unique modes of representation and transformation.

Rojano and Sutherland have also employed this same problem-solving oriented, spreadsheet method to help students who have been experiencing difficulty with the algebraic symbolism of more traditional approaches to school mathematics. The example given here was recounted by Sutherland (1993) in her story of a student named Jo. As was also the case with several of her 14- and 15-year-old peers, Jo had had some previous experience with algebra, but, as Sutherland points out, disliked mathematics and had performed very poorly on the algebra test and interview at the beginning of the study. She viewed algebraic symbols as letters of the alphabet and considered the numerical values of these letters to correspond to their position in the alphabet. During the 4-month study (one lesson per week), Jo learned how to use the spreadsheet to solve problems such as the one provided above in the Rojano excerpt. At the end of the study, Jo was given the following problem to solve (with no computer present):

> 100 chocolates were distributed to three groups of children. The second group received 4 times as many chocolates as the first group. The third group received 10 chocolates more than the second group. How many chocolates did the first, the second, and the third group receive? (p. 22).

She drew a spreadsheet on paper and showed in her written solution "the way in which the spreadsheet code was beginning to play a role in her thinking processes" (p. 22).

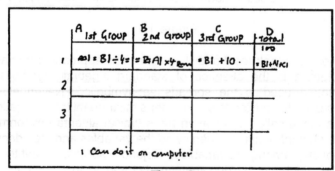

Figure 2.

When subsequently interviewed, Jo was asked, "If we call this cell X what could you write down for the number of chocolates in the other groups?" (p. 22). She wrote down the following, which shows that she was now able to represent the problem using the literal symbols of algebra:

=X	=X x 4	=X x 4 +10

In closing, Sutherland points out that "working with a spreadsheet can help pupils develop algebraic ideas which they can also use in a paper setting" and concludes that "the transfer from spreadsheet to traditional algebraic symbolism is not as difficult as many people have predicted" (p. 22).

2.2. A GRAPHICAL, FUNCTIONAL APPROACH

The previous example focused on using the spreadsheet symbolism and methods both for initiating students into the realm of algebraic thinking and for bridging with the literal-symbolic representations of traditional algebra. In the example that follows, functional graphical representations and the operations that can be carried out with these graphs are used as a foundation for approaching algebraic symbolism and its transformations. The central idea here is that students develop (a) algebraic symbols as a means for describing the functions represented by the graphs and (b) algebraic manipulations as a means for recording operations with the graphs of these functions. The meta-level activity that provides the context for these algebraic thinking activities is once again problem solving, but with two additional emphases that distinguish it from some other problem-solving approaches.

First, there are various criteria that may be used to select the types of problems that can be presented to students in a problem-solving approach, for example: (a) traditional categories such as age problems, distance-rate-time problems, mixture problems, and so on; (b) problems borrowed from the physical modeling sciences such as population growth problems; (c) problems based on situations according to their class of function. The algebraic thinking approach being described in this section focused on problems that were selected according to their function family. This functional orientation provided a means of unifying problem situations and of connecting them with their corresponding graphical, tabular, and literal symbolic representations. One of the complaints often heard with respect to traditional algebra is that students never make the links between the work they do with the literal symbolic representations and their later experiences with graphs of functions; this functional approach attempted to overcome such weaknesses and to help students see a larger picture. Significant attention was given from the outset to graphical representations and the important role played by the parameters.

Second, when solving problems in a traditional algebra environment, the letter in the equation representing the problem to be solved is viewed as an unknown. In some of the newer problem-solving approaches that do not involve equations--at least not at first--the distinction between unknown and variable is blurred. In the functional approach that we are now looking at, the initial emphasis is on representing the situation graphically before searching for the problem solution. Thus, the literal symbols that are developed in order to describe the graphically-represented function are interpreted more as variables. It is when the function is examined with a view to answering some specific question that the notion of unknown might enter. (Note that the spreadsheet-symbolic representation that was just seen also tends to blur the unknown-variable distinction.)

In this functional approach, which was developed in collaboration with my fellow-researcher Anna Sfard, the computer software *Math Connections: Algebra II* (Rosenberg, 1992) was used in conjunction with paper-and-pencil work. Over the course of 30 lessons, the 12- and 13-year-old students soon learned, for example, how to look at a linear graph, directly read from it the slope and y-intercept, and generate a story and literal-symbolic expression that would fit the observed properties. One of the classroom tasks that led to this kind of thinking was the Snowfall Problem, taken from Lesson 11, and provided in Appendix 1 certain physical phenomena associated with falling snow, such as compacting, etc., have been ignored in this introductory problem.

The students also learned to add functional expressions by adding the graphs of two linear functions. One of the problem situation that provided the initial motivation is excerpted here from Kieran (1994):

Two brothers have savings accounts in the bank. When they opened their accounts, they each had a lump sum to deposit; this amount was to be increased by regular deposits of their allowances. The two given graphs represent how their accounts have grown each month. If they had opened only a joint account from the beginning, what would the graph look like?

After the sum-graph was generated by means of adding the corresponding vertical lengths of the two given functions (--see Figure 3), the students were asked to give the expression for the sum-function directly from its slope and y-intercept. the expressions for the two given lines had not been provided to the students One pair of students, after they had written down the expressions for the two lines, soon noticed that they would get the same expression by merely adding together the slopes and intercepts of the two original functions. After this shortcut had spread throughout the class, the students next worked with the multiplying of a function by a constant, also done initially by means of Cartesian graphs.

They could now simplify any combination of linear functions into canonical form. Thus, equations such as *3x + 4 - 2 - 7x + 6(x + 5) = 2(3 - 4x) - 14* could be solved graphically by first "adding both the slope and intercept terms on each side" to obtain the canonical form of each expression, and then graphing the two functions being compared by means of the slope and y-intercept terms of the two expressions, in order to find the value of x for which the two functions were equal. During the 30 lessons of the study, students were not introduced to the solving of equations by algebraic manipulation.

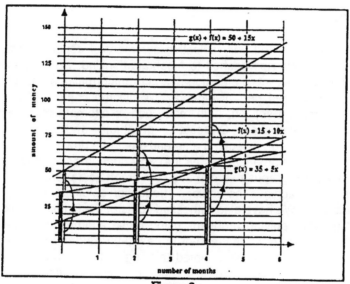

Figure 3.

One month after the above study had been carried out, several students were interviewed on an individual basis. Following is an extract from the interview with the student, Nat:

Interviewer: Can you solve 7x + 4 = 5x + 8?

Nat: Well, you could see, it would be like start at 4 and 8, this one would go up by 7, hold on, 8, 8 and 7, hold on, no, 4 and 7, 4 and 7 is 11. ... They'd be equal, like, 2 or 3 or something like that.

Interviewer: How are you getting that 2 or 3?

Nat: I'm just like graphing it in my head.

That Nat had learned to "graph in his head" by means of the parameters is quite impressive. The value of graphical representations as a foundation for the letter-symbolic was noticed by the classroom mathematics teacher, Bob, who was involved in our research project and who compared these students with others whom he had taught in the past with more traditional approaches. He said:

> They now have a visual tool to both think with and to talk with. With my past students, I often noticed that their algebra never seemed to have a handle. ... We all have different ways of understanding and of seeing things. But for many people, if you can picture something, it's much easier to understand.

3. DISCUSSION

In this brief and very selective summary of aspects from only a couple of the new approaches to algebraic thinking, we have seen two different examples of generational and transformational activities not normally considered part of algebra. Within the context of the global activity of problem solving, both made use of alternate representations (spreadsheet-symbolic; Cartesian graphic) and their related transformations (e.g., extending a spreadsheet rule down a column rather than substituting numerical values into an equation or manipulating that equation; adding graphs to arrive at a sum graph as a precursor to adding expressions) to achieve the analogs of equation solutions and expression simplifications. We have also witnessed some of the kinds of thinking that can occur while solving problems using these alternate algebra-related tools--from the informal, trial-and-error based thinking of the spreadsheet environment to the visually-oriented thinking of the graphical, functional environment. Several other illustrations of facets of algebraic thinking approaches could have been provided, such as, setting up a program of some situation in a computer language, say Logo, and running it with varying inputs, to obtain certain pieces of information in the form of output and then examining this output in order to find, for example, a problem solution or some structural pattern. In presenting these examples, I have attempted to interweave the two features--alternate representations and significant meta-level contexts--that have both tended to characterize the new face of school algebra, a subject area that is increasingly being referred to as algebraic thinking. Even though the use of computer as tool figured prominently in the given examples, in some of the new problem-solving oriented approaches to algebraic thinking it does not figure at all.

The testimony provided by Jo, Nat, and Bob suggests that these new approaches do indeed have a lot to offer. But as with any reform, finding a middle-ground is not always easy. In some national curricula, the pendulum has swung completely to the other side. In attempting to eliminate or at least greatly reduce the meaninglessness of past traditional algebra curricula, some have gone too far. The search for meaning and the consequent suppression of symbolism in, for example, the United Kingdom have led to a situation where most students now do hardly any symbol manipulation (Sutherland, 1990). In various countries, problem solving--by whatever means--has all but replaced traditional algebra. The hope was that, in focusing on understanding, the techniques would take care of themselves. But it has not happened (Artigue, cited in Lee, 1.997). Without a developed feel for the literal-symbolic representation, tasks that touch upon the class of activities related to finding structure, justifying, and proving--activities for which algebra is well suited and which have always been difficult in any case for algebra students (see, e.g., Figure 4)--are now quite beyond their reach. These students have little or no access to the power of symbol manipulation and to the role it can play whenever they want to get at the "why" of a mathematical phenomenon.

---

1. A girl multiplies a number by 5 and then adds 12. She then subtracts the original number and divides the result by 4. She notices that the answer she gets is 3 more than the number she started with. She says, "I think that would happen, whatever number I started with." Using algebra, show that she is right. (Lee & Wheeler, 1987)

2. Take three consecutive numbers. Now calculate the square of the middle one, subtract from it the product of the other two. Now do it with another three consecutive numbers. Can you explain it with numbers? Can you use algebra to explain it? (Chevallard & Conne, 1984)

Figure 4.

I began this paper with the aim of presenting some of the new ways in which the picture of school algebra is changing and of encouraging all who have not yet begun to do so to consider viewing school algebra from this wider perspective called algebraic thinking. But I have also just shared with you what I believe to be some of the recent excesses of this movement. Thus, I would like to conclude on a cautionary note. I am suggesting that the manipulative side of algebra not be thrown out. To my mind, we are doing ourselves and our students a great disservice if, in embracing the new algebra-related tools for expressing and handling numerical relationships, we completely eliminate the original algebraic tool. The content of school algebra is changing. It had to change. It is being enlarged--and I emphasize the word enlarged--to include alternate representations and their related transformations. In encompassing what we are calling algebraic thinking, it may look at times quite different from traditional algebra. But algebraic thinking should not be a weaker resource than what we had before. For those "algebra" curricula that have all but eliminated symbolic manipulations, it is time, in my view, for the pendulum to swing back to a more middle ground--but not a return to curricula of the past that were exclusively oriented toward symbol manipulation; nor do we have to do as much of the manipulation as we used to do. In fact, there is less time for it; but, in the process of adopting these new approaches, the symbolic work has been made more meaninful than in the past.

The changing face of school algebra strikes a balance. It puts greater emphasis on a context of global meta-level activities and accommodates alternate representations with their related transformational activities, but still keeps the power of algebra. Freudenthal (1983) once remarked that "even if the formalism functions reasonably, the teacher or the one who defines the instruction should avail himself of each opportunity to return to the source of the insight [underlying the formalism]" (p. 469). This suggests not only that it is possible to combine the traditional literal-symbolic with non-traditional representations and operations, but also that it is important to do so. Without falling back into the traps of the past, we must continue to make significant room for the literal-symbolic in the content of school algebra. After all, many of us even enjoy working with it and appreciate its power. I am reminded here of a remark made by one of the 12-year-olds involved in the study on the Graphical Functional Approach. After solving an equation graphically during his post-study interview, he was shown for the first time how to solve an equation by algebraic manipulations. When he saw how he could arrive at a precise solution that had been only more or less correct in the graphical environment, and which had taken a fair bit of time to arrive at, he exclaimed with delight: "There is the solution--on a silver platter!

ACKNOWLEDGMENT

The research project of Kieran and Sfard, a part of which was briefly described herein, was made possible by a grant from the Social Sciences and Humanities Research Council of Canada (grant # 410-93-0605).

References

Bednarz, N., Kieran, C., & Lee. L. (Eds.). (1996). *Approaches to algebra: Perspectives for research and teaching.* Dordrecht, The Netherlands: Kluwer.

Bell, A. (1995). Purpose in school algebra. In C. Kieran (Ed.), New perspectives on school algebra: Papers and discussions of the ICME-7 Algebra Working Group (special issue). *Journal of Mathematical Behavior, 14,* 41-73.

Bell, A. (1996). Problem-solving approaches to algebra: Two aspects. In N. Bednarz, C. Kieran, & L. Lee (Eds.), *Approaches to algebra: Perspectives for research and teaching* (pp. 167-186). Dordrecht, The Netherlands: Kluwer.

Boero, P. (1993). About the transformation function of the algebraic code. In R. Sutherland (Eds.), *Algebraic processes and the role of symbolism* (papers of a working conference). London: Institute of Education.

Chevallard, Y., & Conne, F. (1984). Jalons à propos d'algèbre. *Interactions Didactiques, 3*, 1-54 (Universités de Genève et de Neuchâtel).

Freudenthal, H. (1983). *Didactical phenomenology of mathematical structures.* Dordrecht, The Netherlands: Reidel.

Kieran, C. (1989). A perspective on algebraic thinking. In G. Vergnaud, J. Rogalski, & M. Artigue (Eds.), *Proceedings of the 13th International Conference for the Psychology of Mathematics Education* (Vol. 2, pp. 163-171). Paris: G. R. Didactique, Laboratoire PSYDEE.

Kieran, C. (1994). A functional approach to the introduction of algebra: Some pros and cons. In J. P. da Ponte & J. F. Matos (Eds.), *Proceedings of the 18th International Conference for the Psychology of Mathematics Education* (plenary address, Vol. 1, pp. 157-175). Lisbon, Portugal: PME Program Committee.

Kieran, C. (1997). Mathematical concepts at the secondary school level: The learning of algebra and functions. In T.Nunes and P. Bryant (Eds) *Learning and teaching mathematics: An International perspective* (pp.133-158) Hove, U.K.: Psychology Press.

Lee, L. (1997). *Algebraic understanding: The search for a model in the mathematics education community.* Unpublished doctoral dissertation. Université du Québec à Montréal.

Lee, L., & Wheeler, D. (1987). *Algebraic thinking in high school students: Their conceptions of generalisation and justification* (research report). Montréal, Canada: Concordia University, Mathematics Department.

Love, E. (1986). What *is* algebra? *Mathematics Teaching, 117*, 48-50.

Mason, J. (1996). Expressing generality and roots of algebra. In N. Bednarz, C. Kieran, & L. Lee (Eds.), *Approaches to algebra: Perspectives for research and teaching* (pp. 65-86). Dordrecht, The Netherlands: Kluwer.

Pimm, D. (1995). *Symbols and meanings in school mathematics.* London: Routledge.

Rojano, T. (1996). Developing algebraic aspects of problem solving within a spreadsheet environment. In N. Bednarz, C. Kieran, & L.

Lee (Eds.), *Approaches to algebra: Perspectives for research and teaching* (pp. 137-146). Dordrecht, The Netherlands: Kluwer.

Rojano, T., & Sutherland, R. (1992). *A new approach to algebra: Results from a study with 15 year old algebra-resistant pupils.* Paper presented at Cuarto Simposio Internacional Sobre Investigación En Educación Matemática/ PNFAPM, Ciudad Juárez, México.

Rojano, T., & Sutherland, R. (1993). Towards an algebra approach: The role of spreadsheets. In I. Hirabayashi, N. Nohda, K. Shigematsu, & F. Lin (Eds.), *Proceedings of the 17th International Conference for the Psychology of Mathematics Education* (Vol. I, pp. 189-196). Tsukuba, Japan: PME Program Committee.

Rosenberg, J. (1992). *Math Connections: Algebra II* [Computer software]. Scotts Valley, CA: WINGS for learning.

Schwartz, J., & Yerushalmy, M. (1992). Getting students to function in and with algebra. in G. Harel & E. Dubinsky (Eds.), *The concept of function: Aspects of epistemology and pedagogy* (MAA Notes, Vol. 25, pp. 261-289). Washington, DC: Mathematical Association of America.

Sfard, A. (1991). On the dual nature of mathematical conceptions: Reflections on processes and objects as different sides of the same coin. *Educational Studies in Mathematics, 22,* 1-36.

Sutherland, R. (1990). The changing role of algebra in school mathematics: The potential of computer-based environments. In P. Dowling & R. Noss (Eds.), *Mathematics versus the National Curriculum* (pp. 154-175). London: Falmer Press.

Sutherland, R. (1993). Symbolising through spreadsheets. *Micromath, 10*(1), 20-22.

Sutherland, R., & Rojano, T. (1993). A spreadsheet approach to solving algebra problems. *Journal of Mathematical Behavior, 12,* 353 383.

Wenger, R. H. (1987), Cognitive science and algebra learning. In A. H. Schoenfeld (Ed.), *Cognitive science and mathematics education* (pp. 217-251). Hillsdale: NJ: Lawrence Erlbaum.

Wheeler, D. (1989). Contexts for research on the teaching and learning of algebra. In S. Wagner & C. Kieran (Eds.), *Research issues in the learning and teaching of algebra* (pp. 278-287). Reston, VA: National Council of Teachers of Mathematics; Hillsdale, NJ: Lawrence Erlbaum.

APPENDIX 1 SNOWFALL PROBLEM

EXPLORING LINEAR FUNCTIONS
EXPRESSIONS AND GRAPHS

> One day in January, a corner of the school yard had 60 cm of snow. It began to snow, and continued all day at a rate of 5 cm per hour. The height of snow in the corner of the yard is a function of time.

(1)   Write the algebraic expression which tells how to calculate the height of snow at any time. Use the variable t (or x) to represent the time in hours.

(2)   **Underline** the part of the expression that shows how fast the snow was falling.

(3)   **Circle** the part of the expression that shows the height of the snow at zero hours.

(4) At the computer, Copy from Floppy the file LINEAR (11.1).
Enter your expression into the first expression box and click so that the computer will plot the graph.

Copy the computer graph here (use a ruler, and be accurate). Put a ☐1☐ at the right end of the line.

(5)   **Circle** the part of the graph which shows the level of snowfall at zero hours.

(6)   **Explain** how the graph shows the rate of snowfall:

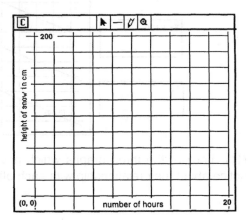

> Meanwhile, across the street from the school, there was a deep snowbank of 120 cm at the beginning of the day. The snow fell at the same rate (5 cm per hour) on this side of the street as it did at the school.

(7) Write the algebraic expression for this story:

(8) Type this expression into the second expression box, and draw the line that represents this story on the graph on the previous page. Put a ②at the right end of the line.

How does the graph show the height of snow at zero hours?

How does the graph show the rate of snowfall?

Someone had shovelled the sidewalk by the side door of the school early in the morning, so it was bare when the snowfall began.

(9) Write an expression for this story:

(10) Enter your expression into the third expression box in the computer, and have the computer graph it. Copy the graph onto the graph on the previous page. Put a ③at the right end of the line.

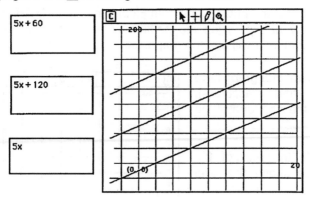

(11) Look at the three graphs which have been plotted. What do you notice about their relationship with each other?

How can you explain this?

Look at the three expressions for these lines.
How are they the same?

How are they different?

(12) Click on the first line that the computer drew. It is connected to the first expression box. You will see small black squares on the line. Put the mouse on the square which is on the vertical axis, and slide the line up and down. Release the mouse, and look at the new expression for the line (in the first expression box). Do this a couple more times.

What part of the story changes when the line slides up and down?

What part of the expression changes when the line slides up and down?

Predict what the expression would be if you slid the line to 500 on the vertical axis. Write the expression here:

Predict what the expression would be if you slid the line to -30 on the vertical axis. Write the expression here:
(13) Click on the second line that the computer drew. This time, put the mouse on the square which is at the right part of the line, and move the mouse. Don't forget to see what changed in the expression box. Do this a couple more times.

How does the line change? (also tell what stays the same)

How does the expression change each time?

What part of the story will change?

(14) Clear the graph window by clicking on⬚C⬚at the top left corner. In the first expression box, enter the first expression that you used (on page 47). Click to have the graph drawn.

Click on the line and move it so that it shows a rate of snowfall of 10 cm per hour.

Write the new expression:

Draw the new line on this graph, and mark it with a ⬚4⬚.

(15) Move the line so that it shows not a snowfall, but a melting rate of 5 cm per hour. Write the new expression:

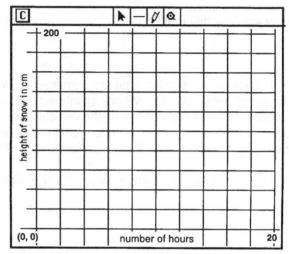

How does the expression show that the snow was **melting**?

Draw the new line on this graph and mark it with a ⬚5⬚.

(16) Move the line so that it shows that the snow neither fell nor melted - the height of snow stayed the same.

Write the new expression:

How does the expression show the rate of change in height of snow?

Draw the new line on the graph and mark it with a ⬚6⬚.

(17) Look at the three lines that you have drawn. What do you notice about their relationship to each other?

Look at the three expressions for these lines. What is the same?

What is different?

ON SOME ASPECTS IN THE TEACHING OF MATHEMATICS AT SECONDARY SCHOOLS IN SWITZERLAND

Urs Kirchgraber
Department of Mathematics
ETH-Zürich, Switzerland

1 Introduction

In this paper I would like to discuss one aspect of teaching which seems to reflect a change in the way Mathematics is taught at the Swiss Gymnasia: *Individualization.*

"New Math" didn't have as significant an influence in Switzerland as elsewhere. This holds true in particular for the non-French speaking part of the country. But even without this disappointing experience it was noticed eventually that teacher-driven instruction with its high frequency pingpong of quick questions and short answers was not truly successful in forming mathematically educated students.

A decade ago Karl Frey became Professor of Didactics and Pedagogy at ETH. Frey, among many other things, pointed out the weaknesses of the traditional teaching style, e. g. that on the average only the top 30% of a class participate in the game. In his lectures Frey proposes a variety of alternative teaching formats, which were not widely known to Gymnasium teachers in Switzerland before. They all have in common that the student's activities are considerably enhanced and they foster his responsibility for his learning processes. We will discuss some of these schemes in the next three sections of this paper. In Section 4 we introduce some remarkable and somewhat related ideas by P. Gallin and U. Ruf, two Swiss Gymnasium teachers. The last section contains a few remarks on the impact of technology.

2 Puzzles

Frey's alternative teaching schemes have meaningful German names. In some cases it is somewhat difficult to provide reasonable

English translations. I will use the German terms and try to explain what they mean. Here are five of these methods

Puzzles
Werkstattunterricht
Lernaufgaben
Fallstudien
Leitprogramme

I will not discuss Werkstattunterricht nor Lernaufgaben, but briefly describe puzzles. The goal of the *puzzle technique* is that pupils make an attempt to explain a piece of Mathematics to their fellow students. A suitable topic is divided into four parts: A, B, C, D. One quarter of the class first works on part A, another quarter on part B, etc. Once the members of each group have made themselves experts in their parts, they are regrouped in such a way that each new group consists of four experts representing the four parts of the topic. The task then is that each expert teaches his fellow students.

I do not want to discuss this technique in any detail. However I would like to mention that a number of our teacher students designed various puzzles for the use at the Gymnasium. I used the method myself with a small group of upper undergraduate University students. The topic was the famous Poincaré-Birkhoff-Smale theorem on chaos. One group of students worked on stable and unstable manifolds, another on the so-called shadowing lemma and the third one on properties of the Bernoulli shift. This took place at a Math Camp. Two and a half days were needed to prepare the students, the presentations covered a bit more than a day. The students enjoyed this experience, as we know from spontaneous reactions as well as from a questionnaire.

3 Case Studies (Fallstudien)

Case studies, or Fallstudien as we call them in German, have a long history. They were introduced early in our century at the Harvard Business School. *The principal goal is that students learn to deal with highly complex and open situations.*

It appears difficult to construct case studies in Mathematics. Nontheless Albert Gächter, who teaches Mathematics at a Gymnasium in

St. Gallen, succeeded in designing six case studies in Mathematics for Gymnasium students of grade 11 and 12. Gächter's work was part of a larger endeavour conducted by K. Frey and supported by ETH's Vice President for Research R. Hütter.

The Titles of Gaechter's Fallstudien are

- What degree of precision is appropriate?
- QED!
- Recursion
- Shape and Number
- Algorithmic Geometry
- Computer Games

Here are some features of these Fallstudien with special emphasis on the first example. A case consists of a number of *documents and a few key questions.* The Fallstudie on precision contains among other material an article by H. Freudenthal entitled "Wie genau ist die Mathematik", a paper by G. Schierscher on computer arithmetic, a section from the book "Descartes' Dream" by P. Davis and R. Hersh, and excerpts fom A. Wittenbergs "Bildung und Mathematik". None of these articles was written for eleven grade students. The material is in fact fairly demanding. Nonetheless, working in small groups the students can gain some insight by studying these papers and by addressing the following questions:

a) What factors determine an appropriate precision of a result?
b) Precision - a virtue?
c) Fallacies with Computer numbers?
d) Why Irrationals?

Working on a Fallstudie is apparently quite different from other forms of instruction. The material is *not* divided into small and easily digestable pieces. There is no unique answer to a given question. There is room for discussions. Participants may come to different conclusions.

A Fallstudie covers 5 - 10 lessons. The Fallstudien experts recommend one or two Fallstudien per year.

4 Leitprogramme

I will discuss Leitprogramme in some detail, because this was a major project recently, again conducted by K. Frey.

Leitprogramme are based on what is ·called *Kellerplan techniques and on the Bloom Mastery Learning Principle.* A Leitprogramm is dedicated to an important subject of some field. It is a booklet, some 50 to 100 pages long, say. It is handed out to each student at the beginning of the working period with the Leitprogramm. It covers the material for a month's work or so. All relevant information is contained in the Leitprogramm.

A Leitprogramm consists of a basic part, compulsory for all students, which we call the *Fundamentum*, and an optional part for fast learners. This part is called the Leitprogramm's *Additum.* At the beginning of the Leitprogramm and at the beginning of each Chapter a brief and nontechnical overview of the subsequent material is offered, and the goals to be achieved are stated. One of the key parts of a Leitprogramm is a very thoughtfully-designed, well-written exposition of the scientific contents. Another important ingredient of a Leitprogramm is the following. The text is interspersed with a reasonable number of *problems,* some routine, some challenging. Their solutions are included.

At the end of each Chapter there are *two sets of problems.* If the reader is successful with the first set she is ready for the Chapter test. Otherwise the Leitprogramm offers her some advice on what to do next and she will return to the second set before taking the Chapter test. The Chapter test may be a brief discussion between the student and the teacher or some tutor, or it may be a written test. *The key point is: The student must not go on to the next Chapter before there is evidence that he or she has mastered the previous Chapter.* Mastery learning in the sense of Bloom means that 80 to 90% of a class master 80 to 90% of the material.

A Leitprogram seems to have a number of advantages compared to the conventional teaching style in the classroom. One of the most important aspects is that *the student controls the speed of his learning process himself:*

• Slow students are not pushed too much. They may read additional explanations provided by the Leitprogramm if they wish to do so.
• As to the solutions of the problems, the author of a Leitprogramm may offer various options: results, hints and comprehensive descriptions.
• If a student gets confused in the traditional classroom dialogue he is lost and gets frustrated. A group tends to exert some pressure on its members in an interaction process. All this is eliminated.

• Fast learners are not bored because the Additum offers complementary material, possibly a variety of different and challenging options.
• It is the student's responsibility to decide if and when he is ready for the Chapter test. Some students will show up soon, after half an hour say, others may take the test the next day only, etc.

A basic goal of the Leitprogramm technique is that students get started reading scientific texts. Reading combined with problem solving fosters the student's attention and enhances his own activity.

The Leitprogramm technique bears some similarities with Programmed Instruction and Computer Assisted Learning. Indeed the following are features common to both methods

• The material is carefully prepared
• The goals towards which the student is working are stated expli-i citly and the material is organized accordingly
• The progress of the learning process is checked repeatedly

On the other hand there are major differences as well:

• A Leitprogramm is much less compartmentalized; the steps are considerably bigger; the reader is guided to make some disco-veries on his own
• A Leitprogramm is more entertaining because of working at times with a partner; because of small experiments that may be part of a task, etc.
• At least some of the tests are personalized.

There is statistical evidence that Mastery Learning improves success at learning. Kulik et al. [1] in a paper published in 1990 state that the improvement due to Mastery Learning in Mathematics is 0.5 standard deviations, if compared to classical instruction. Frey concludes that the Leitprogramm method which combines the Mastery Learning technique with supplementary devices is even more promising.

Between 1991 and 1995 a group of didacticians from various fields at ETH made an attempt to implement the Leitprogramm technique. The fields involved were Biology, Chemistry, Geography, Mathematics and Computer Science and Physics. The goal was to produce Leitprogramme for the use at the Gymnasium, a few in each discipline.

I will focus on the Leitprogramme in Mathematics and Computer Science now. During the 4-year period quite a number of Leitprogramme on a variety of topics were written, first by students of Mathematics' teaching. The more promising ones were discussed with experienced Gymnasium Mathematics teachers, revised, tested in classrooms, thrown away, replaced by completely new versions, again tested, etc.

At the 1995 Swiss Annual Meeting on Mathematics Education organized by ETH and the Swiss Mathematical Society, four Leitprogramme, three in Mathematics, one in Computer Science were presented. The titles of these Leitprogramme are:

Solving Quadratic Equations
If you need a Loan you better know your Mathematics!*
Solving Systems of Linear Equations
Recursive Programming*

The main Authors were: M. Adelmeyer, M. Bettinaglio, J.P. David, W. Hartmann and the Author. I will describe some features of the third of these Leitprogramme. (Versions of the second and fourth one, are available on the Web. The address is http:/educeth.ethz.ch/mathematik/)

The Leitprogramm on Linear Systems is suitable for the ninth grade students; an abbreviated version can be covered in 12 hours, the full version requires 20 hours approximately.

Of course we try to convey that studying systems of linear equations is a great topic! In the first Chapter we indicate that this subject has a very long tradition, by quoting some famous problems from Babylonian, Egyptian and Chinese sources. At the same time we demonstrate that linear systems are a subject of current interest as well by referring to various technical applications. In particular we hint at Computerized Tomography, a subject introduced in more detail later on in the Leitprogramm.

In the second Chapter we use a sequence of carefully chosen 2-dimensional systems to let the students discover the so-called substitution method. And of course we ask them to generalize the algorithm to higher dimensions. As I pointed out before, the material was tested a number of times before it was presented at the 1995 meeting. The students were asked to give their comments. As to the way we guide our readers to discover the substitution method, one student wrote: *"Das Vorgehen auf p. 19 ist super. Man kann versuchen ein System von drei Gleichungen von drei Unbekannten zu lösen. Wenn einem dies nicht gelingt, dann gibt es Aufgaben bei denen man einen 'Startschubs' bekommt. Nachher kann man noch einmal die andere schwierigere Aufgabe versuchen."*

The first two chapters, together with the final chapter on Computerized Tomography, make up the short version of this Leitprogramm.

Chapters 3 and 4 are devoted to theoretical and algorithmic aspects of linear systems. In Chapter 3 we discuss linear systems with no or infinitely many solutions.

Chapter 4 starts with a brief introduction to the history of computation and the use of computing machines. In particular we mention Eduard Stiefel (1909-1978), a Swiss Mathematician. He was a famous topologist when he moved to Computer Science and Applied Mathematics after World War II. He rented Konrad Zuses' famous Z4 machine and at the same time he guided a group of young scientists in constructing the first electronic computer in Switzerland. The main mathematical theme of the chapter is Gaussian elimination. In this connection we also discuss output provided by Texas Instruments' TI 85, a graphical calculator by now widely used at Swiss Gymnasia. Of course we count the number of operations of the Gaussian procedure and relate it to the speed of computation of various computer facilities.

As mentioned before, the final chapter is devoted to an introduction to what is called Computerized Tomography. We have two modest goals here. First, we want our students to understand the basic difference beween classical X-ray photographs and image-sections obtained by Computerized Tomography. Second, we want the readers to see how Computerized Tomography relates to linear systems. To this end we use a very simple mathematical model.

The tests with this Leitprogramme revealed that Computerized Tomography is considered to be a fascinating subject by most pupils. Once, however, a girl showed very strong emotional reactions: somebody in her family had died of cancer.

This concludes the remarks on the Leitprogramm on linear systems.

The four Leitprogramme were offered to the schools at a low price. More than 100 Gymnasia have purchased a set. If a School owns a set, it is entitled to produce as many copies as needed to use the Leitprogramme in class.

At this point, unfortunately, we do not have an overview as to what extend our Leitprogramme are used in practice and how successful they are.

For more information on the Leitprogramme in Mathematics and Computer Science, see [2].

4 Some ideas of P. Gallin and U. Ruf

There is no institutionalized basic research in Didactics of Mathematics in Switzerland. Yet there are remarkably many highly imaginative Gymnasium Mathematics teachers who make substantial contributions. I will make an attempt to briefly introduce some ideas of Peter Gallin and Urs Ruf. Gallin teaches Mathematics, while Ruf teaches German Language and Literature at the Gymnasium in Wetzikon, near Zurich. This latter fact is probably a surprise. It turns out that the combination of these two disciplines is particularly significant. I will not elaborate this point more fully. What is relevant here, is that Gallin and Ruf developed an approach which puts forward the idea of individualization more than any other scheme I know of.

My remarks are based on personal discussions with Ruf and Gallin and on their publications, in particular on an article entitled *Sprache und Mathematik in der Schule, ein Bericht aus der Praxis* [3] .

What makes you go? Under what conditions do you work like mad? One possible answer is: If you are driven by an idea. This idea may be vague at the beginning. But if you are fascinated by your idea, it makes you go. Such an idea is called *Kernidee* by Gallin and Ruf. Kern means Kernel, Germ. Key idea is a suitable translation.

Kernideen are very personal. An idea may be a Kernidea for one person, while it is not for someone else. Everybody has plenty of Kernideas. A pupil in particular has a microcosmos of personal Kernideas. The critical question according to Gallin and Ruf is: can we stimulate them to generate Kernideas in Mathematics, in a certain framework, on a particular subject?

What makes Mathematics teaching so difficult? Why is the success so limited? According to Gallin and Ruf there are two worlds involved, so to speak: the learner's world, his conceptions, his private views, his feelings. And the mathematical cosmos with its network of notions, ideas and procedures. Gallin and Ruf use the word *singular* to characterize the learner's individual world, while they speak of the *regular* world of Mathematics. In their understanding it is decisive that an individual traces his way from his singular world into the regular world of Mathematics. A gentle transition is needed. In one of their papers they use a schematic representation with a triangle. The vertices represent the *task,* its *solution* and the *person.* The edges indicate activities: *to solve, to explore, to comprehend.* Gallin and Ruf advocate the detour via the "Ich" (I), which in their view is not at all a detour but a conditio sine qua non for successful learning and comprehension.

Kernideas permit a global view of a problem from the very beginning, even if it is vague. This contrasts with what happens in traditional teacher-driven classroom instruction. Gallin and Ruf again use a metaphoric representation with a geometric object to illustrate the difference. To describe the traditional scheme they use a sequence of growing segments of a cone. In such an approach the clue is revealed only at the very end. Only when the very last piece is added the cone emerges. The approach via Kernideas on the other hand is represented by a sequence of gradually growing cones. At the start there is a very tiny cone only, yet it is a cone! As it grows, a more and more complete picture develops.

It is obvious that the second approach reduces pressure and stress, for both pupils and instructor. At whatever moment a pupil stops working, he or she has gained a certain amount of insight into the subject, while in compartmentalized learning the effort pays off only if all segments fit together.

To implement their ideas Gallin and Ruf propose what one can call the method of *Reisetagebuecher.* A Reisetagebuch is a kind of mathematical diary. Reise means travel, journey. Tagebuch means diary. A Reisetagebuch in the sense of Gallin and Ruf is a note-book. The pupils write down their thoughts using their own words. They express themselves in their singular language, so to speak. They comment on their ideas. They may express their feelings. The process of writing slows down the process of thinking. This is intended. Writing is like walking in the world of thoughts. Very slowly the landscape of thoughts becomes familiar. An idea may emerge. It may gradually grow. It may 'Gestalt annehmen', as we say in German. To explore, to test an idea, a pupil has to work hard. He or she may have to make an awful lot of computations. Because she is driven by her Kernidea she is willing to carry out all these tedious computations. She is not bored because she is experimenting rather than practicing. Or as Heinrich Winter would put it: "Es wird entdeckend geübt und übend entdeckt."

The instructor reads the students' Reisetagebuecher regularly. He comments on the students' texts. By a thought-provoking remark he helps the pupil to clarify his ideas or to change his direction of thoughts somewhat, and he encourages him to continue his work. The advantages of this scheme are obvious. The pupil gets a highly individualized response because his line of thought is available in written form and the instructor is not urged to react instantanously as in a classroom dialogue. It is obvious as well that the scheme allows very easily the instructor to value and evaluate the pupil's individual learning process.

In their publications, the authors offer a number of excerpts from various Reisetagebücher of pupils, together with descriptions of the underlying situations. A particularly illuminating example is the one on the ordering of fractions, a topic in grade 7. The Kernidea here is to study the hierarchy of gears of a bike. Mathematically the key step is the determinaion of the smallest common multiple of the denominators. Two excerpts are presented. Literally speaking Astrid, does not succeed in solving the problem. From her report it is quite obvious, however, that she understands the clue, and although she cannot deliver the answer, on her way she demonstrates a surprising maturity in dealing with a problem that is hard for her. Ueli on the other hand handles the mathematics without difficulties and very clearly realizes that the obvious ordering of the gears, which presents itself naturally in the mechanism, so to speak, is not the one of interest here. Both pupils, each within his or her capability, have done a very good job.

Ideas similar to the Reisetagebuch technique have apparently been developed elsewhere as well. A study by A. McCrindle and C. Christensen entitled "The impact of learning journals on metacognitive and cognitive processes and learning performance" - in connection with a first-year University biology course - reveals, among other results, an effect size of 0.8.

5 Concluding remarks: Impact of Technology

I conclude with a few remarks on the impact of technology. As mentioned earlier, graphing calculators, in particular TI's 85 are widely used in Swiss Gymnasia. A booklet [5] entitled "Mathematik sehen, Graphikrechner im Unterricht" by M. Bettinaglio, W. Hartmann and H.R. Schneebeli , all three teaching Mathematics at the Gymnasium in Baden near Zurich, offers a collection of very nice applications and convincingly demonstrates how graphic tools can influence the teaching of Mathematics.

Computer Algebra Systems are now moving into the classroom as well. First experiments with the TI 92 are under way. Yet the TI 92 is considered to be a transitional product with more powerful follow up machines to be available soon.

As to Computer Software: Cabri Geometre is widely used. Moreover, there are two products worth mentioning: the program 3D-*Geometer* by H. Klemenz, suitable for Macintosh, and *Geometry* by E. Holzherr and R. Renner for IBM-type machines. Both programs support the teaching of three-dimensional geometry, they permit to represent basic geometric objects and to perform constructions. Klemenz teaches at the Gymnasium in Wetzikon, while Holzherr is at a Gymnasium in Lucerne, Renato Renner was his pupil when their program was first developed. For further information contact the Author.

References

[1] C.-L. Kulik, J. A. Kulik and R. L. Bangert-Drowns: *"Effectiveness of mastery learning programms: a meta analysis"*, Review of Educational Research 60 (1990) p. 265-299.
[2] U. Kirchgraber, W. Hartmann, M. Bettinaglio, M. Adelmeyer, J.P. David, and K. Frey: *"Und dann und wann ein Leitprogramm"*, to be submitted to Zentralblatt fuer Didaktik der Mathematik (ZDM).
[3] P. Gallin and U. Ruf: *"Sprache und Mathematik in der Schule, ein Bericht aus der Praxis"*, Journal fuer Didaktik der Mathematik (JDM) 14 (1993) p. 3-34.
[4] A. McCrindle and C. Christensen: *"The impact of Learning Journals on metacognitive and cognitive processes and learning performance"*, Learning and Instruction 5 (1995) p. 167-185.
[5] M. Bettinaglio, W. Hartmann and H.R. Schneebeli: *"Mathematik sehen, Graphikrechner im Unterricht"*, Sabe 1994.

SOME CONSIDERATIONS ON PROBLEMS AND PERSPECTIVES OF INSERVICE MATHEMATICS TEACHER EDUCATION

Konrad Krainer, Klagenfurt, Austria

1 Inservice teacher education as a complex field

Inservice teacher education, *which focusses on teachers' personal and professional development,* is seen as a major intervention to improve the *quality of education* on different (but closely interconnected) levels: the quality of students' learning, the quality of teachers' work, the quality of schools, the quality of an education system, or the quality of interaction between the education system and the society as a whole. However, due to different contexts, different people (students, teachers, parents, mathematics educators, etc.), institutions (school boards, political parties, unions, universities, ministries, etc.) and countries have different understandings on how to improve the quality of education. Therefore it is not surprising that *conflicting expectations* on inservice teacher education are expressed by different sides (see e.g. Krainer, 1994b; Cooney & Krainer, 1996).

Inservice teacher education is therefore a complex field dealing with *enormous diversity* characterised for example by elements such as *regional circumstances, participants, designs and philosophies, topics and organizing institutions.* Typical examples of *regional circumstances* are different general conditions for education and different needs of society, schools and teachers, which lead to big differences in students' completion of secondary education (Nebres, 1988) or in class size (Howson, 1994). There is also diversity with regard to *participants:* courses can be confined to special groups of teachers (e.g. 8th grade mathematics teachers or all mathematics and science teachers of a school), but there are also programs such as Family Math (see De la Cruz & Thompson, 1992) in which parents and children work together in cooperative settings to solve problems and engage in mathematical explorations. Further projects exist, like MINERVA in Portugal, which generated a nationwide community of teachers, trainers and researchers that took as their task the "formation of teacher teams and the assertion of a project culture in schools" (Ponte 1994, 161). Inservice courses also have different *designs and philosophies:* A more traditional approach is for experts to come in from outside and tell teachers about new research results; by contrast, there are courses where teachers are seen as co-designers of inservice education in which they are increasingly motivated to take their further education into their own hands, e.g. organizing working groups at the end of the course, where the teacher educators are the participants (Krainer, 1994a). Such courses strive for joint learning of people coming from different institutions, an approach which seems to have become more prominent under the notion of co-reform (Frasier, 1993). Inservice education for mathematics teachers also demonstrates a broad diversity of *topics*, from dealing with mathematics content knowledge or with cross-curricular connections to considering assessment, new teaching methods or reflecting critically on new technology. Diversity of *organizing institutions* is shown when inservice education is organized by the school authority, or by institutions which had also been responsible for the pre-service education of the participants, or by institutions where the connection to the participants is less strong but where other interests have to be negotiated, such as research interests or funding, or by self-organizing groups of teachers such as the MUED in Germany (see e.g. Keitel, 1992).

An additional issue which makes *inservice education* such a complex field is the fact that it *relates our research practice to our teaching practice* and therefore challenges us to apply the theoretical conceptions and philosophies we preach. Thus, it is also our beliefs - and not only those of the teachers - that have to be considered critically. Teacher education can be seen as *our big experiment* and as our continual struggle at the heart of our discipline.

2 Fundamental shifts in mathematics teacher education

Although the recent situation in mathematics teacher education and its related research is far from being a field with well-developed standards, both for theory and practice, the last thirty years seem to have brought considerable *progress.*

First, some brief general remarks on *literature* and *conference programs*: Research on teacher education developed from being "virtually nonexistent in the 1960s and early 1970s" (Cooney, 1994a, 618) to a field with increasing literature, e.g. with the first Handbook of Research on Teacher Education published in 1990 or with the section "Social Conditions and Perspectives on Professional Development" in the International Handbook on Mathematics Education (1996). Conference programs reveal a similar picture. For example, at the International Congresses on Mathematical Education in Quebec (1992) and Sevilla (1996) there were a number of lectures, working groups, and topic groups that focused explicitly on teachers, their work and teacher education. Similar trends can be observed at PME-Conferences (Hoyles 1992, 283) or at recent conferences in mathematics education held in German speaking countries (see e.g. Krainer, 1994b).

Second, two concrete examples of developments from different parts of the world:

a) In the *United States* a lot of efforts towards mathematics teacher education have been made in the last decades. For example, Cooney (1994a) describes the change in teacher education in the last thirty years as a change of paradigm from *analytic perspectives* towards *humanist perspectives* (Mitroff & Kilmann, 1978), from discovering reality to trying to understand the contexts that shape a person's perception of his or her reality (Brown, Cooney & Jones, 1990), having constructivism as an epistemological foundation for mathematics education. Early teacher education dealt primarily with updating teachers' knowledge of mathematics. Research mostly focused on studying connections between student achievement and teachers' characteristics, behaviours and decisions, mostly on a quantitative basis, placing an emphasis on objectivity. Then the focus moved extensively towards interpretative studies describing teachers' cognitions (beliefs, meaning-making processes, etc.) and the contexts that influence cognition. Cooney sees that progress has been made in *discarding false dichotomies* that pervaded teacher education, stating that we are now more aware of the necessity of blurring the distinction between theory and practice, content and pedagogy, researchers and teachers, conceptionalizing the latter as cognizing and reflective agents. He points out that teachers and teacher education have become focal points for research in mathematics education but that we need constructs that can meaningfully guide our research efforts.

b) Another area to examine in looking for progress in mathematics teacher education is the *activities and future plans of institutes in developing countries*. As an example, the Institute for Educational Development (IED) of the Aga Khan University in Karachi (Pakistan) describes its approach to teacher education as follows: "The IED was envisaged neither as a traditional 'school of education' nor 'teacher training college' - models of higher education that seem increasingly out of step with the real needs of teachers and schools, in both the industrial countries as well as in developing nations. The training that would be provided at IED will be guided by some crucial concerns. First, it will be field based, i.e. the training will take place within classrooms. The assumption behind this practice is that effective teaching skills are best acquired 'on the job'. A second distinguishing feature of the training will be its reflective nature, i.e. the aim would be to make the IED students 'reflective practitioners', engaged in continual self-enquiry as practicing teachers. A third major feature will be training in classroom based research." (AKU/IED 1996). The IED establishes Professional Development Centres which focus on the improvement of teaching and learning in schools and classrooms in the region. The research policy of the IED promotes research projects which are realized in collaboration with partner academic institutions from all over the world.

Third, the progress in the field of mathematics teacher education might also be seen as a process of *growing awareness of the complexity of mathematics teaching* (Krainer, 1993b). In a first shift, recognizing that teaching contains more than presenting a pre-fabricated body of knowledge grounded in formalistic theories, research and development activities aimed at yielding a *broader sense of mathematical knowledge*. This included efforts to link mathematics with real life, to place an emphasis on the historical development of concepts and theories, to foster problem solving and to reflect on heuristic strategies, and to question contents with regard to specific and general educational objectives. The increased integration of pedagogical, psychological, social, historical and epistemological aspects into the didactic discussion put the dominance of the subject matter into perspective. This shift might also be seen as the start of mathematics education's struggle towards becoming a scientific discipline in its own right, i.e. a kind of emancipation from its most closely related science, namely mathematics. The teacher's task was seen more and more as creatively engaging students in important mathematical activities like proving, problem solving and modelling. However, very often a strong belief in the "manageability" of teaching through narrowly structured and covert guidance by the teacher remained. A second shift was caused by further research in mathematics education, e.g. on students' thinking and on interaction in classrooms more and more integrating methods and results of related fields; the research showed that teaching cannot be seen as a simple transmission process resulting in pre-determinable learning by the students. This fundamentally *questioned the transferability of knowledge* and partially brought a shift of focus from teaching to learning, placing an em-phasis on students' understanding.

The students are seen less as consumers but more and more as producers and even as researchers. However, this increased awareness of the complexity of learning and teaching was also to have consequences in teacher education. The next shift, therefore, concerns again questioning the transferability of knowledge, this time from us as teacher educators to our prospective and practicing teachers. It marks a step towards meeting demands which teachers formulate in the following sorts of questions: Why do mathematics educators propagate the active and investigative learner, although we the teachers have not been educated in that way, neither in pre-service nor in inservice education (with a few exceptions)? How and from whom do we get support in that direction? It is our task to find ways to take further steps in this direction, both theoretically and practically, and partially in collaboration with teachers.

3 Dimensions of teachers' professional practice: action, reflection, autonomy and networking

The recent discussion in mathematics education shows an increasing interest in teachers' roles, beliefs, knowledge, etc., in many cases emphasising the complexity of teachers' work: Doyle (1986) e.g. characterises the demands of teaching with descriptors such as "multidimensionality", "simultaneity", "immediacy", "unpredictability", "publicness" and "history" (the accumulation of joint experiences). In parallel to this quantitative shift we can also observe a *qualitative shift*: recently more and more publications and conferences deal with topics like "teachers as experts" (Bromme, 1992), as "reflective practitioners" (Schön, 1983, 1987), as "researchers" (e.g. Elliott, 1991) and as "professionals" (Stenhouse, 1975). Several approaches have characterized *basic elements of teachers' knowledge*. Shulman (1986) e.g. proposed seven domains: knowledge of subject matter, pedagogical content knowledge, knowledge of other content, knowledge of the curriculum, knowledge of learners, knowledge of educational aims, and general pedagogical knowledge. Bromme (1992) created a topology of teachers' professional knowledge that attends to the nature of mathematics, pointing out that teaching is primarily a matter of taking "situation-appropriate" decisions based on available knowledge rather than generating additional perspectives for solving newly presented problems. Therefore the focus of teachers' work in the classroom primarily calls for a holistic and integrated view of knowledge rather than the existence of separate solutions to discrete problems. This perspective is supported by Berliner et al. (1988) who found that expert teachers are able to process a greater array of information about students and classroom situations than novice teachers and can therefore demonstrate a greater range of techniques for dealing with individual students. The conception of teachers' professional knowledge cannot be adequately described using the singular category of "knowledge", for their knowledge is a product of many types of knowledge created in quite diverse settings and often rooted in "local theories" (Brown & Cooney, 1991) specific to their classroom situation.

All the approaches sketched above for describing teachers' professional practice mainly focus on teachers' work in the classroom. Given the considerations with which this paper began, it seems a natural consequence not to reduce the quality of education simply to the quality of teaching, but to see the teachers' contribution to the quality of education in a broader context. It seems to be crucial to find dimensions which are general enough to be used in different situations and where both the competence and the attitudes of teachers are given equal consideration. On that basis, the following four dimensions aim at describing teachers' professional practice:

Action: The attitude towards, and competence in, experimental, constructive and goal-directed work;

Reflection: The attitude towards, and competence in, (self-)critical and one's own actions systematically reflecting work;

Autonomy: The attitude towards, and competence in, self-initiating, self-organized and self-determined work;

Networking: The attitude towards, and competence in, communicative and cooperative work with increasing public relevance.

The creation of these four dimensions originally arose from the question of how mathematical tasks relating to the teachers' and learners' roles should be designed in order to promote effective teaching and learning ("powerful tasks", Krainer, 1993a). The main idea is that tasks should initiate active learning processes, closely linked with reflection on action and that tasks both should be well interconnected with other tasks in order to aim at specific goals, and should promote learners to generate further interesting questions for themselves (autonomy). This approach was then broadened for describing mathematics teachers' activities within an inservice course (Krainer, 1994a) and finally for describing teachers' professional practice in general (Altrichter & Krainer, 1996).

Each of the pairs, "action and reflection" and "autonomy and networking", expresses both *contrast and unity,* and can be seen as complimentary dimensions which have to be kept in a certain balance, depending on the context. The importance of the interplay between these dimensions is supported by various theoretical and practical considerations. Here I will confine myself to indicating Schön's (1983) account of "reflective practice" formulating "tacit knowing-in-action", "reflection-in-action" and "reflection-on-action" as different relationships between professional knowledge and professional action, and by citing Stenhouse (1975, 144) who described teachers' professionality as follows: "A capacity for autonomous professional self-development through systematic self-study, through the study of the work of other teachers and through the testing of ideas by classroom research procedures."

There are at least four levels in which these dimensions can be used for reflecting on mathematics teachers' work:

a) With regard to their own further development taking into consideration the standards in their profession, at their school, in their education system, etc. The present paper will mainly fous on this level.

b) With regard to their students' further development, e.g. raising the following questions: In what way does teaching promote students' action and reflection? Which kind of opportunities do they have to work autonomously and also to share their conceptions with other students? How can a teacher's knowledge be effectively linked with the different meanings students have constructed?

c) With regard to their school's further development, e.g. dealing with questions such as: Is there efficient communication among the mathematics teachers in the school? Is there a fruitful collaboration between mathematics teachers and teachers of other subjects? Is mathematics seen as an important learning field at their school? Does the working climate promote innovations in classrooms?

d) With regard to the further development of their profession, their education system and its interaction with the society as a whole, for example by asking: Which role can mathematics, sciences and technology play in our society and which consequences does this role have for further developing mathematics teaching? What kind of influence do teachers have on regulations (curriculum, assessment, etc.), on standards, or on the status of their profession? Is teachers' reflection on their profession seen as a relevant contribution to the education system? Is professional communication and collaboration among teachers promoted? Is it promoted by us? Where do the rewarding effects of closer collaboration between theoreticians and practitioners (universities and schools) lie?

Of course, there are links between these levels. Here is an example which intentionally exaggerates the situation to a certain extent: teachers, who work in an educational system with narrow regulations on curriculum and assessment, who have had no influence on those regulations in the past and who will not be having any in the future, who were educated at universities where lecturing was the dominant teaching method (which leaves the audience to reflect the learned content), currently teaching at a school with a low level of communication among the teachers, and who are now confronted with inservice courses oriented towards their weaknesses, need a very strong motivation not to regard students as "received knowers", in the way themselves have been socialized. On the other hand, too often teachers complain about restrictive regulations that tend to hinder their innovations in classrooms, underestimating thereby the freedom of action they have or could establish. However, in just the same way as research on students' mathematical understanding shows that we systematically underestimate students' creative ways of thinking (when our focus is not restricted to hearing only things we want to hear), we seem to systematically underestimate teachers' creative attempts to improve their teaching. Many experiences in our work with teachers prove that fact.

Given the four dimensions: action, reflection, autonomy and networking, how would we assess mathematics teachers' position in respect of their professional development? Let us consider the following qualitative diagram in which the point in the middle means a balance with regard to each of the two pairs, whereas deviations from the middle can be interpreted as preferences for one or two dimensions (i.e. marking the point more right/higher means more emphasis on action/autonomy).

Based on various experiences, the place of most mathematics teachers (and schools) in this diagram is in the first quadrant. One could say: *there is a lot of action and autonomy but less reflection and networking,* in the sense of critical dialogue about one's teaching with colleagues, mathematics educators, the school authority, the public, etc.

To avoid misunderstandings: this assessment is in no way made with the intention of apportioning blame on teachers or on other people and institutions involved; it should simply identify particular and general problems and possible perspectives which might improve the situation; nor should make the diagram us believe that there would be an ideal position, but rather it should lead us to reflect on how teachers could react flexibly in order to meet the challenges of different contexts. To give an example: Like a medicine working on a patient, a teacher usually cannot take a time-out to reflect on the ongoing process in order to share an opinion with colleagues or to read research literature, he has to act or react immediately. However, this does not mean at all that reflecting and networking are unimportant; by contrast, given situations where time for reflecting and sharing experiences with others are limited, it is decisive to have a rich body of knowledge in which autonomous actions are soundly based on reflections and on the standards of the profession, whereby this knowledge itself is based on having the attitude of a life-long learner.

The necessity for teachers' reflection and networking is underlined by various practical and theoretical considerations. For example, Clark & Yinger (1987) and Peter (1996) stress that combining action and reflection is an essential activity of teachers. Noddings (1992, 206) states that "teachers still labor in isolation, lacking the collegiality necessary for rich professional life". In order to highlight important changes and progress in mathematics teacher education, Grouws & Schultz (1996) describe a wide range of successful projects, studies, systemic initiatives and collaboratives, e.g. stressing the importance of "reflective teaching partnerships" (447), the creation of "collaborative communities of learners - teachers learning new ways to teach and students learning new ways to do mathematics" (449), teachers' reflections "on themselves as learners", the existence of "teacher and school collaboratives, professional development schools" where "the focus of university-school linkages include practice-sensitive researchers at the university and researcher-sensitive teachers in schools ..." (452) and the facilitation of "collaboration among pre-service and in-service teachers" (453) in order to assist teachers in examining their beliefs and actions.

But what are the reasons for teachers' lack of reflection and networking? In the following three functional reasons are sketched which might give some explanation:

a) A first reason is the *culture* in which teachers have to work. In science communities we speak about "publish or perish"; with regard to teaching we might use the slogan "act or perish" (see Krainer, 1994b, 221). Researchers' and teachers' work conditions and agendas differ as researchers' culture emphasizes reflecting, analyzing, writing, making one's ideas public and discussing them with colleagues, whereas the teachers' culture usually emphasizes quickly perceiving and acting with only few contacts with colleagues. Researchers organize their own conferences in which reflection and networking are important dimensions; by contrast, meetings of teachers are mostly not designed as professional exchanges of experiences but as teacher inservice courses led by "external experts" and often organized by the school authority. This makes a difference but also shows a particular way of thinking about progress in teachers' professional development. With respect to cooperation between teachers and researchers the danger of this difference lies in possible one-sided distributions of interests, in forcing one culture on the other. However, the difference of cultures is less a counter-argument against cooperation and more a pro-argument for it because of the opportunities to learn from each other and to build a bridge between the two cultures of theory and practice. More research on the relationship between teachers and researchers is needed (see e.g. Brown, Cooney & Jones 1990; Bishop, 1992; Krainer 1994c).

b) Most teachers' *pre-service* (and often also inservice) *education* did not (and still does not) place any emphasis on reflecting or networking. In many cases teachers feel socialized as "lonely fighters" for their subject matters. Within the process of some of our inservice courses teachers expressed the experience that they firstly had to find a certain distance to mathematics in order to be able to build up a new and constructive relationship to it, allowing them to find a way to appreciate students' thinking. There are more and more international reports (see e.g. Krainer, 1994b; Grouws & Schultz, 1996; Giménez, Llinares & Sánchez, 1996) about involving (practicing or prospective) mathematics teachers into research projects and integrating research components in teacher education courses where reflection and networking are important dimensions.

c) Systematic *reflection* on one's own teaching and *sharing* it with colleagues is *unusual* and costs a lot of time and effort. However, teachers who meet this challenge in general report about positive effects on their teaching and further professional development. The following section highlights some considerations on this issue.

4 Inservice mathematics teacher education as a means of promoting action, reflection, autonomy and networking

One mathematics teacher's *self-critical investigation into his own teaching* while participating in a teacher inservice course will be examined in order to show how the activities are related to the four dimensions mentioned above.

First, some remarks on the *context*. The two-year university course "Pedagogy and Subject-Specific Methodology for Teachers - Mathematics" (PFL being an abbreviation for the German "Pädagogik und Fachdidaktik für Lehrerinnen") offers special inservice education for mathematics teachers in Austria. The PFL-*mathematics* course aims at helping teachers to improve their teaching and at making their innovative work accessible to others, thus promoting professional communication and cooperation among teachers. To meet the interests of the participants the starting point of work within the course in most cases is their practical experience. Because of the complexity of the teacher's task the interconnectedness of pedagogical and subject-specific aspects is a crucial facet. *Action research* (see e.g. Altrichter, Posch & Somekh, 1993), understood as *the systematic reflection of practitioners on action* (i.e. on their professional activities in order to improve them), is used as a framework for achieving a broader situative understanding and for improving the quality of teaching and other professional activities at their school. Within PFL courses the participants are required to do research and to write two case studies in which they have professional developmental interests. The *case study* of the participating teacher will now be discussed. For a detailed description of the philosophy and of activities within PFL-mathematics see Fischer et al. (1985), Krainer (1994a) or Krainer & Posch (1996).

In his first case study in the course, the teacher dealt with the topic *"On the emergence of noise"* in order to investigate the noise level in his classes and to find out means for improving the situation. In order to obtain relevant data, he administrated a questionnaire to his students and wrote a research diary in which he regularly took note of his observations on the topic "noise" in one of his classes for a period of seven months. He found out, to his surprise, that it was primarily he himself who judges his instruction as too loud, and that a considerable part of this "noise" is caused by content-related communication between students. This discovery motivated him, in a second case study, to reflect on possible changes in his approach to teaching and to test them in practice.

How can we interpret the teacher's work with regard to our four dimensions? Let us place an emphasis on the dimensions *action* and *reflection* first: As mentioned above, the course starts out from teachers' practical experiences and needs. For this teacher, "noise" was a problem which influenced his classroom activities enormously. Collecting data and reflecting on this data brought him new information and new insights he would not have got by simply referring to his original "practical theory" of the situation, which mainly said that noise has to be seen as a factor that hinders teaching. The process of reflecting led to a more complex and deeper understanding of the situation, e.g. realizing that noise may be an expression of students' need for content-related communication and that *"noise may emerge through monotonous modes of instruction"* (Kliment, 1994, 1); but this also had consequences on his actions, from an alternative way of dealing with "noise" to starting *"occasionally to design lessons in another way"*. This process shows the impact the close interplay of the teacher's actions and reflections had on his beliefs with regard to teaching and his concrete actions in the classroom. In the following considerations about the teacher's further progress we place our emphasis on the interplay between *autonomy* and *networking.*

For this second study, entitled *"Mathematics instruction for one's different"* (Kliment, 1994), the teacher read literature on teaching and learning objectives, formulated his own objectives and found consequences for his teaching, e.g. stating: *"It is clear that - with regard to the objectives formulated in the preceding section - frontal instruction now plays only a small role. But what are the alternatives? One of the most effective incentives in changing my teaching was a study by colleagues."* Here he refers to a case study written by participants and one staff member of a former course. This shows one advantage of writing down teachers' investigations and of making it accessible to others: teachers' local knowledge can be linked with the experiences of others through being published in studies available for larger community. This means that teachers' autonomous work can be networked networked and therefore used as one contribution to increasing professional communication among teachers.

The teacher increasingly turned to a child-centered, application-oriented and computer-supported form of instruction. He realized his ideas in a teaching experiment which lasted for a period of about 10 weeks (including a written examination). His new way of teaching also had some consequences with regard to assessment: *"Significantly more than before, my teaching gave me opportunities to observe students and to appreciate their involvement ... It is an enormous relief to the students if not everything depends on their performance on two days. It is also advantageous that during examinations a resort to individual or group work is possible. ... "* The evaluation of the teaching experiment was predominantly very positive. In the concluding section "Criticism and outlook" of his study the teacher writes: *"During this school-year I have had numerous experiences. It is no longer my intention to teach year in, year out in the same manner. Now it is time to sift out those methods which have been successful and can be retained. Apart from some details I am content and can with assurance build on the experiences of this school year. It would be arrogant to claim that I succeeded in realizing all my chosen objectives; Moreover, this catalogue of objectives is not definitive. Some changes were not easy for me, old habits had first to be thrown overboard. I did not succeed in encouraging students to participate more actively in the classroom experience. (...) I must further reflect on this question!"*

All in all this shows how motivating and helping teachers to write case studies can improve professional development. More reflection on action improves practitioners' activities which in turn lead to new questions and reflections, etc. But this *interplay between action and reflection* is not only confined to the learning of individual teachers, it can also be used as a starting point for professional exchange among teachers: the learning process is directed towards autonomy as well as towards networking - it is the interplay of both which leads to progress.

Of course, not all teachers of such courses change their teaching in this fundamental way. It was the intention to show here what is possible. Indeed, this is one of the main ideas of the PFL-program: to show teachers (and other interested people) that things can be done, within the existing general conditions or after successfully fighting for their change; it is worth making the good work of teachers visible and available for discussion. More than 100 studies have been written by German, English, mathematics and science teachers within the framework of PFL-courses, which have since been bought by teachers, researchers, schools, etc. and their feedback demonstrate its value.

The teachers' systematic reflections on their own practice can not only improve their own teaching but can also have consequences for the further development of teacher education (see e.g. Krainer & Posch, 1996), for mathematics education (see e.g. Fischer & Malle, 1985) or for the personal and professional development of team members (see e.g. a mathematics educator's reflective paper on his activities within the course; Peschek, 1996).

The fact that writing case studies causes some problems for both the teachers and the teacher educators supporting them, should not be withheld. In writing case studies, teachers have to do at least three things which are rather unusual in their normal practice: They have to gather data and to reflect on them systematically (and not only take action), they have to write down their findings (and not just communicate them orally), and they have to formulate these results for other people (and not just practice something within their own classrooms).

That this is more difficult for teachers than for us - living in a "culture of publishing" - should be taken into consideration. Nevertheless, it seems to be worth promoting teachers' investigations for at least four reasons: Systematic reflection on their own work creates new knowledge which in turn positively influences their teaching; writing down is an additional opportunity to learn; writing a study (to be read by others) increases the opportunities for communicating and cooperating with interested people (teachers, theoreticians, administrators); and finally, it gives us an additional opportunity to learn from them.

However, such an approach is also problematic on quite another level. Inservice teacher education based on voluntary participation is usually confronted with problems of realization and dissemination: Given a good seminar or course, the motivation to change one's mathematics teaching might be high and many participants might try out new things and might apply learned methods and ideas; but it might also happen that they rarely find colleagues who really want to join in their efforts, that their motivation and the perseverance to realize changes are (in the long run) not high enough, that innovative things at schools are often regarded rather critically and cause (open or hidden) resistance or opposition, that the participants on seminars are "always the same" and those who really would need some improvement do not come, and that links between different subjects are used too rarely.

Experience shows that participants engaged in long-term teacher inservice courses which place an emphasis on professional communication among teachers through promoting the discussion of their case studies, more efficiently support teachers' efforts to bring about change, at least during the course. That such a course gives birth to self-organized groups which remain together for a longer period (see e.g. Krainer, 1994a) is more an exception to the rule. However, a lot of participants act as "agents of change" in their region, are engaged in inservice courses or teacher pre-service education, and actively participate in conferences in which innovative work of teachers is presented.

An alternative approach to inservice education which recently has become more popular is school-based inservice. Examples with regard to mathematics education are rare. To sketch the perspective of this approach, a pilot project in this direction will be considered briefly.

5 Continuous work with groups of mathematics teachers at schools

In contrast to working with mathematics teachers from different schools, working continuously with a group of colleagues from one school might yield some advantages which should not be underestimated: the "culture" of this school (as a decisive general condition of what is possible or not) can be taken into consideration, and maybe steps towards changes could be considered; the collaboration among individuals might develop towards the establishment of a group; the teachers now could have the encouragement of others or even colleagues who were ready to join their efforts to improve their mathematics teaching; innovations would be more likely to become a relevant component of mathematics teaching (of the whole school); mathematics teaching could be more visible and could play a greater role at this school.

The necessity of considering the whole entity, in this case the school, seems to be growing in importance, the more so as general conditions change. For example, the growing tendency to more autonomy for schools (including e.g. the question of whether the number of mathematics lessons should be decreased or increased, or mathematics should be combined with other subjects) or due to budget problems a lot of inservice education will be organized at schools to save on travel expenses.

Another argument for placing *greater emphasis on the level of individual schools* is the fact that it allows the context in which the teachers live and work to be taken really seriously, and it provides opportunities where individual and social demands on mathematics teaching meet and can thus be analyzed, discussed and negotiated. This argument is supported by considerations in section one of this paper stating that the quality of education cannot be reduced to the quality of teaching and also by the belief expressed in the preceeding sections that more reflection and networking among teachers are needed.

In the following, we briefly look at the design and the outcome of a recent *pilot inservice seminar* at an urban school in Austria. As agreed at a preliminary meeting, the two-and-a-half-day seminar with the eight participants was based on a "teacher as researcher" philosophy and covered three major issues: 1) Interviews with pupils in order to understand better how they see mathematics, mathematics teaching, etc.; 2) A little experiment towards more "open" mathematics teaching in order to experience new approaches, methods, etc.; 3) Investigating connections between mathematics and other subjects in order to experience the potential of bringing the real world into mathematics teaching. Some of the results were: all teachers intended changes in their teaching, eight weeks after the seminar most teachers reported on concrete realizations of ideas, some indicated preparations for small teaching experiments in the next school-year; a mathematics education journal from which different volumes were analyzed by different teachers during the third part of the seminar was subscribed to after the principal was persuaded that this would contribute to the further development of mathematics at this school; with one participant there was an exchange of articles with regard to connections between geometry and chemistry; most colleagues were interested in commenting on the teacher educators' analyses of the seminar; the group expressed interest in further collaboration with the universitary institute.

6 Summary and outlook

The *promotion of teachers' reflection and networking* seem to be an important challenge for inservice mathematics teacher education in the future. In particular, designers of inservice courses should ask themselves questions like: To what extent do we succeed in motivating the participants to reflect (self-)critically on their own activities and the collaborative work on the seminar and on using it as an opportunity for corresponding learning processes? To what extent do we succeed in promoting deeper communication and collaboration among the participants and in linking individual and social learning experiences meaningfully?

Questions like these express an understanding of inservice education which sees teachers not as receivers of pre-fabricated knowledge and complete solutions but as reflective practitioners who develop their own knowledge and solutions, and fit them into the context in which they work. To avoid misunderstandings: building on teachers' self-critical investigations into their own work does not decrease the importance of research in mathematics education. By contrast, more research is needed, in particular on inservice teacher education. But we should find *new ways* of mediating between theory and practice, of collaborating with teachers on different levels, of taking into consideration the culture in which they live and work, of (re)constructing our beliefs on teacher education while at the same time questioning them thoroughly, and of (re)defining teacher change and inservice education as an inevitable part of professional practice.

References

AKU/IED (1996). *Mission Statement for the Institute for Educational Development (IED), Aga Khan University,* and related material. Aga Khan University, Karachi (Pakistan)

Altrichter, H. & Krainer, K. (1996). Wandel von Lehrerarbeit und Lehrerfortbildung. In K. Krainer & P. Posch (eds.), *Lehrerfortbildung zwischen Prozessen und Produkten.* Klinkhardt, Bad Heilbrunn, 33-52

Altrichter, H., Posch, P., & Somekh, B. (1993). *Teachers Investigate Their Work: An Introduction to the Methods of Action Research.* Routledge, London

Berliner, D., Stein, P., Sabers, D., Clarridge, P., Cushing, K., & Pinnegar, S. (1988). Implications of Research on Pedagogical Expertise and Experience for Mathematics Teaching. In D. Grouws & T. Cooney (eds.) *Effective Mathematics Teaching.* Erlbaum Associates & National Council of Teachers of Mathematics, 67-95

Bishop, A. (1992). International Perspectives on Research in Mathematics Education. In D. Grouws (ed.) *Handbook of Research on Mathematics Teaching and Learning.* Macmillan, New York, 710-723

Bromme, R. (1992). Der Lehrer als Experte. *Zur Psychologie des professionellen Wissens.* Bern-Göttingen-Toronto, Huber

Brown, S. & Cooney, T. (1991). Stalking the Dualism Between Theory and Practice. *Zentralblatt für Didaktik der Mathematik,* 23 (4), 112-117

Brown, S., Cooney, T., & Jones, D. (1990). Mathematics Teacher Education. In W. Houston (ed.), *Handbook of Research on Teacher Education,* Macmillan, New York, 639-656

Clark, C. & Yinger, R. (1987). Teacher Planning. In J. Calderneed (ed.) *Exploring Teachers' Thinking.* London, 84-103

Cooney, T. (1994a). Research and Teacher Education: In Search of Common Ground. *Journal for Research in Mathematics Education,* 25, 608-636

Cooney, T. (1994b). Teacher Education as an Exercise in Adaptation. In D. Aichele (ed.), *Professional Development of Teachers of Mathematics.* National Council of Teachers of Mathematics, Reston, VA, 9-22

Cooney, T. & Krainer, K. (1996). Inservice Mathematics Teacher Education: The Importance of Listening. In A. Bishop et al. (eds.) *International Handbook of Mathematics Education.* Kluwer, Dordrecht

De la Cruz, Y. & Thompson, V. (1992). Influencing Views of Mathematics Through Family Math Programs. Paper presented at ICME 7, Quebec, Canada. (Also cited in C. Gaulin, B. Hodgson, D. Wheeler, & J. Egsgard (eds.) (1994) *Proceedings of the Seventh International Congress of Mathematical Education.* Sainte-Foy (Québec), Les Presses de l'Université Laval, 223.)

Doyle, W. (1986). Classroom Organization and Management. In M. Wittrock (ed.) *Third Handbook of Research on Teaching.* Macmillan, New York, 392-431

Elliott, J. (1991). *Action Research for Educational Change.* Open University Press, Milton Keynes and Philadelphia

Fischer, R. et al. (eds.) (1985). *Pädagogik und Fachdidaktik für Mathematiklehrer.* Hölder-Pichler-Tempsky and Teubner, Vienna and Stuttgart

Fischer, R. & Malle, G. (1985). *Mensch und Mathematik. Eine Einführung in didaktisches Denken und Handeln.* Bibliographisches Institut, Mannheim-Wien-Zürich

Frasier, C. (July 1993) *A Shared Vision: Policy Recommendations for Linking Teacher Education to School Reform.* Education Commission of the States

Giménez, J., Llinares, S. & Sánchez, V. (eds.) *(1996). Becoming a Primary Teacher. Issues from Mathematics Education.* Universities of Tarragona and Seville (Spain), Indugraphic, S.L. (Badajoz)

Grouws, D. & Schultz, K. (1996). Mathematics Teacher Education. In J. Sikula (ed.) *Handbook of Research on Teacher Education.* Macmillan, New York, 442-458

Howson, G. (1994). Teachers of Mathematics. In C. Gaulin, B. Hodgson, D. Wheeler, & J. Egsgard (eds.) *Proceedings of the Seventh International Congress of Mathematical Education.* Les Presses de l'Université Laval, Sainte-Foy (Québec), 9-26

Hoyles, C. (1992). Illuminations and Reflections: Teachers, Methodologies and Mathematics. In W. Geeslin & K. Graham (eds.) *Proceedings of the 16th Psychology in Mathematics Education Annual Meeting.* University of New Hampshire, Durham, NH, V. III, 263-283

Keitel, C. (1992). The Education of Teachers of Mathematics: An Overview. *Zentralblatt für Didaktik der Mathematik,* 24, 265-273

Kliment, F. (1994). Mathematikunterricht einmal anders, Reihe "PFL"- *Mathematik,* No. 10. Universität Klagenfurt/IFF, Klagenfurt

Krainer, K. (1993a). Powerful Tasks: A Contribution to a High Level of Acting and Reflecting in Mathematics Instruction. In *Educational Studies in Mathematics,* 24 (1), 65-93

Krainer, K. (1993b). Understanding Students' Understanding: On the Importance of Cooperation between Teachers and Researchers. In Bero, P. (ed.): *Proceedings of the 3rd Bratislava International Symposium on Mathematical Education,* 1-22, Comenius University, Bratislava

Krainer, K. (1994a). PFL-Mathematics: A Teacher Inservice Education Course as a Contribution to the Improvement of Professional Practice in Mathematics Instruction. In J. Ponte & J. Matos (eds.) *Proceedings of the 18th Psychology in Mathematics Education Annual Meeting.* University of Lisboa, Lisboa, vol. III, 104-111

Krainer, K. (1994b). Zum Wandel von Lehrerfortbildung im Bereich Mathematik. In J. Schönbeck, H. Struve, & K. Volkert (eds.) *Der Wandel im Lehren und Lernen von Mathematik und Naturwissenschaften.* Band I: Mathematik, Deutscher Studienverlag, Weinheim, 203-225

Krainer, K. (1994c). Integrating Research and Teacher Inservice Education as a Means of Mediating. In L. Bazzini (ed.) *Theory and Practice in Mathematics Education.* ISDAF, Pavia, 121-132

Krainer, K. & Posch, P. (1996). *Lehrerfortbildung zwischen Prozessen und Produkten,* Klinkhardt, Bad Heilbrunn

Mitroff, I. & Kilmann, R. (1978). *Methodological Approaches to Social Sciences.* Jossey-Bass, San Francisco

Nebres, B. (1988). School Mathematics in the 1990's: The Challenge of Change Especially for Developing Countries. In A. Hirst & K. Hirst (eds.) *Proceedings of the Sixth International Congress on Mathematical Education.* Bolyai Mathematical Society, Budapest, 11-28

Noddings, N. (1992). Professionalism and Mathematics Teaching. In D. Grouws (ed.) *Handbook of Research on Mathematics Teaching and Learning.* Macmillan, New York, 197-208

Peschek, W. (1996). PFL - Eine wissenschaftliche wie auch persönliche Herausforderung. In K. Krainer & P. Posch (eds.) *Lehrerfortbildung zwischen Prozessen und Produkten.* Klinkhardt, Bad Heilbrunn, 167-180

Peter, A. (1996). *Aktion und Reflexion. Lehrerfortbildung aus international vergleichender Perspektive.* Deutscher Studien Verlag, Weinheim

Ponte, J. (1994). *MINERVA Project. Introducing NIT in Education Portugal.* Ministry of Education, Lisboa

Schön, D. (1983). *The Reflective Practitioner: How Professionals Think in Action.* Basic Books, New York

Schön, D. (1987). *Educating the Reflective Practitioner.* Jossey-Bass, San Francisco

Shulman, L. (1986). Those Who Understand: Knowledge Growth in Teaching. *Educational Researcher,* 15, 4-14

Stenhouse, L. (1975). *An Introduction to Curriculum Research and Development.* Heinemann, London

My greatful thanks go to Tom Cooney, Doug Grouws and Peter Posch for their helpful comments and suggestions.

MATHEMATICS AND GENDER: A QUESTION OF SOCIAL SHAPING?[1]

Gilah C. Leder
Graduate School of Education
La Trobe University
Australia

It's true that Hypatia, the ancient Greek mathematician, was the first eminent woman mathematician ... that anyone seems to know about.... She had a huge following, and distinguished students came from Europe, Asia and Africa to hear her.... Cyril was fearful of her popularity and her religion, and incited a mob of fanatics, who dragged her to a church, murdered her with shells, and then burned her. This happened at the height of her fame, when she was 45. All her writings have been lost. (Woolfe, 1996, p. 7)

Introduction

There is no need, at a meeting of the International Congress on Mathematical Education, to dwell on the intrinsic worth of mathematics as an area for study, nor the important role played by mathematics as a critical barrier to further educational, career, and life opportunities. Nor is it necessary to repeat that mathematics and related occupational fields have been identified, internationally, as areas in which males predomin and females are believed to be disadvantaged. Regrettably, in many countries females' disadvantages go well beyond these areas, however.

Most of the roughly 100 million homeless people in the world are women and children.... (O)f the estimated 1.3 billion people living in poverty, 70 percent are women and girls.... Some 50,000 people - mostly women and children - die daily because of poor shelter, polluted water and bad sanitation... ("End girls poverty", 1996, p. A18)

Educational opportunities are affected by class and ethnicity, as well as by gender. Females from economically and socially advantaged backgrounds are more likely to complete secondary education than males from

---

[1] At the time of writing this paper, I was engaged in a collaborative project with Helen Forgasz (La Trobe University) and Claudie Solar (Université de Montréal). I'd like to acknowledge, with thanks, their influence on this work!

families in poverty. Decisions about continuing with the study of mathematics beyond the compulsory years are also influenced by many, often interacting, factors - including and beyond gender. In other words, research directed at gender issues in mathematics education is contextually situated, whether or not this is acknowledged or recognised by those engaged in these investigations. In the remainder of this paper I want to trace some of the important directions and developments of work conveniently grouped under the label "gender and mathematics education". The focus is necessarily on the broader issues and research dimensions. More detailed and comprehensive reviews of relevant research can be found, for example, in Fennema, 1995; Fennema and Hart, 1994; Fennema and Leder, 1993; Forgasz, 1994; Joffe and Foxman, 1988; Leder, 1992; Leder, Forgasz and Solar, 1996; Linn and Hyde, 1989; Solar et al., 1992; Willis, 1989.

Where should this review begin? It is tempting to start with the life and work of Hypatia "the first eminent woman mathematician ... that anyone seems to know about" (Woolfe, 1996, p. 7). Following the path taken by (Kimball, 1995) also has its appeal. Her more general exploration of the traditions of gender similarities and differences took as its starting point the very different lives, trials and triumphs of Leta Hollingworth and Karen Horney, both born, on different continents, well before the beginning of this century (in 1886 and 1885 respectively). Since current research and debate rely heavily on the psychological and psychoanalytic perspectives within which they worked, such an approach has much to offer. Pragmatically, given the constraints of time and space, it is, however, more appropriate to focus on activities of the past two decades or so.

IDENTIFYING A "PROBLEM"

During the 1970s, much research effort was directed at documenting gender differences in participation in mathematics courses and in performance on mathematical tasks and tests. A then timely "state of the art" summary read as follows:

> Are there sex differences in mathematics achievement? ... No significant differences between boys' and girls' mathematics achievement were found before boys and girls entered elementary school or during early elementary years. In upper elementary and early high school years significant differences were not always apparent. However, when significant differences did appear they were more apt to be in the boys' favor when higher-level cognitive tasks were being measured and in the girls' favor when lower-level

cognitive tasks were being measured.... Is there "sexism" in mathematics education? If mathematics educators believe that there is a sex difference in learning mathematics (as was evidenced in the reviews cited) and have not attempted to help girls achieve at a similar level to boys, then this question must be answered in the affirmative. (Fennema, 1974, p. 137)

SOME EXPLANATIONS

Explanations consistently proposed by researchers for the subtle but persistent performance and participation differences identified in mathematics have included:

* the almost exclusive depiction in mathematics textbooks and related materials of males and activities that appeal to them in contrast to the virtual invisibility of females and their interests
* the setting in which learning takes place
* other organisational structures within the school
* differential (mathematics) course taking and unequal engagement in mathematical activities during leisure times
* liking of mathematics, perceptions of mathematics as useful, worthwhile, and relevant
* expectations of attaining success in mathematics and related fields
* being encouraged by significant others to continue with mathematics
* and less frequently, inherent, genetic differences rather than the environmentally related factors enumerated above.

My own master's thesis, completed in 1972, was typical of the "empirical-scientific-positivist" investigations conducted at that time. It was "concerned with sex differences in mathematics achievement. In particular, the effect of changes in the contextual setting of certain problems on the mathematics performance of a group of ... boys and girls attending Victorian metropolitan high schools (was) examined" (Leder, 1972, p. iii). The study confirmed that boys preferred and performed slightly better on problems set in a "male" context, while girls preferred and performed slightly better on "female" context problems. Furthermore, boys, but not girls, performed better if they were given problems contextualized in their preferred setting. Was this, I speculated at the time, because

the girls have become conditioned to doing mathematics problems with content that is not sex-appropriate for them? ... For them to be given a non-preferred content version is a state of affairs to which they have become accustomed over the years. The boys, on the other hand, have become used to doing problems with sex-appropriate content. Apparently, being given non-preferred content has affected the performance of some boys sufficiently to produce a significant difference in performance. By analogy, this finding could be said to indicate the likely effect on girls' mathematics performance of prolonged exposure to non-preferred content. (Leder, 1972, p. 178)

This line of reasoning suggests:
(i) that males and females have similar learning characteristics and motivations to achieve the same educational goals (the *assimilationist* model)
and
(ii) that the gender differences in learning mathematics, documented in a multitude of investigations, are the result of inadequate educational opportunities, social barriers, or "biased" content and that they can be minimized, if not removed, by compensatory actions and initiatives built into an educational program and typically targeted at females. Thus the removal of barriers, and if necessary the resocialization of females, were seen as paths to equity. Explanations which encompass these thrusts have been labelled a *deficit* model.

The emphasis on the rights of females to equal the achievements of males is consistent with the tenets of *liberal feminism* and of the first wave or generation of feminism. While alternative perspectives have gained in popularity in recent years, our current understandings of gender issues in mathematics owe much to the pioneering studies conceived with this assumption as its central focus.

PRACTICAL INTERVENTIONS

Curriculum initiatives and other intervention strategies aimed at achieving gender equity have attracted considerable research attention as well as significant amounts of funding. Relevant programs can be categorised in various ways. The five-stage model described by McIntosh (1983) and adapted for mathematics education by Rogers and Kaiser (1995) is particularly evocative. Key elements of the three earlier phases of this model are summarised in Table 1.

Table 1: Towards gender equity in mathematics education (1)

PHASES	BRIEF DESCRIPTION	MESSAGES CON VEYED
Womenless mathematics	Mathematics textbooks and other materials focus on males, their interests and activities.	Mathematics is unambiguously portrayed (and typically perceived) as a male domain. This view persists in many contemporary socieites.
Women in mathematics	Portrayals of males and male contexts and themes are supplemented with references to a very small number of exceptional women, who, throughout history have been successful in mathematics. Examples commonly cited include Hypatia, Sonya Kovalevskya, and Emmy Noether.	Female mathematicians are perceived as rare, exotic and exceptional. Valuable contributions by females are scarce. Success in the field is a threat to femininity ; failure an indication of lack of personal worth and ability.
Women as a problem in mathematics	Appropriate intervention programs will raise females to the performance and participation levels of males: e.g., exposing female-friendly settings in text books, single-sex rather than coeducational groupings, highlighting the importance of mathematics as an entry to educational and career opportunities, ...	Females can become successful learners of mathematics. Their deficiencies can be overcome. It is assumed that success and continued participation in mathematics, beyond the compulsory years, is a universal goal. The nature and delivery of mathematics are not questioned.

The presentation of these phases as sequential is simplistic and convenient rather than an accurate chronological representation. Elements of each stage are still present and continue to attract instructional and other interventions. For example, some of the recent studies which have examined gender-stereotyping in mathematics textbooks continue to report a bias towards males. Others have noted that attempts to be gender-neutral seem to have resulted in an overemphasis on numerical questions and a mathematics portrayed as lacking in human dimensions (see Leder et al., 1996 for more details). Attempts to focus on women with exceptional and rare mathematical talents are also not without their problems. Some of these portrayals, it is argued, simply confirm how difficult it is for an "ordinary" (female) student to become an "extraordinary" mathematician, what hardships need to be endured, what challenges to be overcome, what prices to be paid. Preoccupation with the mathematical "deficiencies" of females has been criticized for reinforcing and perpetuating existing stereotypes and for all too readily "blaming the victim" rather than questioning whether the implicit assumptions of using "male" standards as the accepted and most appropriate norms might not more fruitfully be challenged. These alternate perspectives are the focus of later sections.

SUBSEQUENT DEVELOPMENTS

A change in terminology has clearly occurred since the 1970s. *Sex* differences featured in the titles of the early reports and investigations began to be replaced by *gender* differences. This change was of more than linguistic significance. To a sensitive reader, it could be argued, *sex* differences seemed to emphasize innate, genetic characteristics not readily amenable to change. *Gender* differences, on the other hand, instead appeared to highlight the role played by the environment - personal and situational - in which learning occurs. For those engaged in education, it seemed more constructive to concentrate on factors that are at least potentially able to be changed. Thus the current emphasis on *gender* differences signifies the primary interest of those in education with cultural conventions and pressures as well as socialization processes.

With time, the earlier crude comparisons between groups of males and females became more refined: gender differences between- as well as within-groups began to be acknowledged. Simplistic interpretations of "equal" exposure to, and involvement in, mathematics began to be questioned. So, too, were the assumptions that females' norms and preferences were necessarily inferior to those of males and that the largely monocultural definition (white, middle-class, male) of what constitutes worthwhile mathematics are inviolate. No longer was it thought appropriate to ignore the value and diversity of different ways of knowing, nor the harm done in the past, to individuals as well as to larger groups, of denying this diversity. Perhaps, it began to be asserted, it is not females who need to change but mathematics: the way it is conceptualized, defined, taught and assessed. Thus the focus moved to calls for a reconsideration of the nature of the discipline of mathematics and a re-examination of the pedagogical methods used in mathematics. Such lines of reasoning seem to suggest:

(iii) that the goals of education are not necessarily the same for all groups. Learning characteristics may vary within and between groups. These differences should not be regarded as deficits. Rather, the educational environment should be structured to take account of these differences. In this *pluralistic* model, diversity among learners is an expected outcome of the educational process, and

(iv) even more specifically, if justice and equity are to be achieved (the *social justice* model), then differences need to be respected and catered for appropriately. Identical treatment of different groups may be necessary at certain times; different treatment and actions at others.

These models, which value and respect "difference" are congruent with convictions of radical feminist research. Or, to use a somewhat different terminology, the focus on the special attributes of females and the rejection of an uncritical assimilation of females into a male world capture the critical concerns of the second wave or generation of feminism.

THE "PROBLEM" REVISITED

Work conceived and developed in the broader research community has been influential in shifting the directions of those concerned with mathematics education. The themes fuelled by Gilligan (1982) *In a different voice* and the feminist critiques of the sciences and the Western notions of knowledge have been particularly powerful. It is convenient to trace the more recent thrusts to achieve gender equity in mathematics education through the final two stages of the modified McIntosh, 1983 model, referred to earlier. Key elements are summarised in Table 2.

Table 2: Towards gender equity in mathematics education (2)

PHASES	BRIEF DESCRIPTION	MESSAGES IMPLIED
Women as central to mathematics	They system, as well as the contents of mathematics, are changed to be less alienating	Women´s experiences and interests are perceived as central to the

	to females. Rather than expect females to aim for male norms, females' experiences and interests are used to shape the mathematics taught and methods of presentation.	development of mathematics. In this phase the "blame" is shifted away from females through attempts to change not them, but the system.
Mathematics reconstructed	"Cooperation and competitiveness are in balance and mathematics will be what people do" (Kaiser and Rogers, 1995,p.9).	Debate continues about the changes required in the conceptualisation of mathematics, its delivery and applications if the subject is to be (gender) inclusive rather than exclusive

The assumptions of the "women as central to mathematics" phase are not without danger. In particular, programs which value and nourish qualities and characteristics presumed to be exclusively female may imply, directly or indirectly, that these are innate to females and alienate those who do not possess them. This essentialism also risks perpetuating traditional gender stereotypes rather than redressing gender inequities. Nevertheless, recognition that previously unchallenged assumptions, traditions, and cultural exclusivity need to be examined and possibly redefined is overdue.

FURTHER INVESTIGATIONS AND EXPLANATIONS

Recent reviews of research on gender and mathematics education reveal that
* research in the empirical tradition continues to dominate
* quantitative, as against qualitative, studies are more prevalent, irrespective of the country in which the research is located
* affective variables continue to attract considerable research attention
* increasingly authors draw on multiple research methods to plan their studies and analyse their data. This is an important development.
* drawing on publications other than those found in the traditional,

mainstream journals yields a much broader perspective. In particular, work exploring feminist theories is more likely to be found in edited books, collections of articles, and conference proceedings than in mainstream mathematics journals. However, there is some overlap in the authorship, ideas, and studies found in collected volumes of research on gender and mathematics education.

* scholarly evaluations of intervention programs and strategies are all too rarely reported in mainstream mathematics journals

* authors tend to draw on publications written in their own language. Work recorded in English appears to have the most extensive international penetration.

* gender inequities most relevant for those engaged in post compulsory mathematics education are now also attracting research interest.

CONCLUDING COMMENTS

In brief, gender equity concerns represent a significant item on the research agenda of (mathematics) educators in many countries - in highly technological societies as well as developing nations. International comparisons, formal and informal, highlight the role of culture. For a given society, the status of mathematics in the lives of females is linked to their status in that society. Male norms, and acceptance of difference without value judgments, are more likely to be challenged in countries with active and long standing concerns about equity issues. Collectively, the body of work on gender and mathematics education reflects an increasing diversity in the inquiry methods used to examine and unpack contributing factors. More radical feminist perspectives are being adopted, females are less frequently considered as a homogeneous group, and scholarly evaluations of interventions are becoming more prevalent.

There is a continuing need for traditional empirical research which monitors females' participation and performance in mathematics and related educational and career activities. It is important to remember that the various approaches that can be used to extend our knowledge and understandings of females' mathematics learning - whether informed by more classical approaches or by feminist critiques - are complementary, valuable in different ways, and share a common goal: attaining gender equity in mathematics education.

References

End girls' poverty: United Nations. (1996, June 5) *The Age*, p. A 18.

Fennema, E. (1974). Mathematics learning and the sexes: A review. *Journal for Research in Mathematics Education, 5*(3), 126-139.

Fennema, E. (1995). Mathematics, gender and research. In B. Grevholm & G. Hanna (Eds.), *Gender and mathematics education*: An ICMI study (pp. 21-38). Lund, Sweden: Lund University Press.

Fennema, E., & Hart, L. (1994). Gender and the JRME. *Journal for Research in Mathematics Education, 25*(6), 648-659.

Fennema, E., & Leder, G. C. (1993). *Mathematics and gender.* St. Lucia, Queensland: University of Queensland Press.

Forgasz, H. J. (1994). *Society and gender equity in mathematics education.* Geelong, Victoria: Deakin University Press.

Gilligan, C. (1982). *In a different voice.* Cambridge, Massachusetts: Harvard University Press.

Joffe, L., & Foxman, D. (1988). *Attitudes and gender differences: Mathematics at age 11 and 15.* Windsor, Berkshire: NFER-Nelson.

Kaiser, G., & Rogers, P. (1995). Introduction: Equity in mathematics education. In P. Rogers & G. Kaiser (Eds.), *Equity in mathematics education* (pp. 1-10). London: Falmer Press.

Kimball, M. M. (1995). *Feminist visions of gender similarities and differences.* New York: Harrington Park Press.

Leder, G. C. (1972). Sex differences in mathematics achievement: An investigation into the effect of changes in the contextual setting of certain matheatics problems on the mathematics performance of a group of boys and girls . Monash University, Australia.

Leder, G. C. (1992). Mathematics and gender: Changing perspectives. In D. A. Grouws (Ed.), *Handbook of research in mathematics education* (pp. 597-662). New York: MacMillan.

Leder, G. C., Forgasz, H. J., & Solar, C. (1996). Research and intervention programs in mathematics education: a gendered issue. In A. Bishop (Ed.), *International Handbook of Mathematics Education* . Dordrecht, the Netherlands: Kluwer.

Linn, M. C., & Hyde, J. S. (1989). Gender, mathematics, and science. *Educational Researcher, 18*(8), 17-27.

McIntosh, P. (1983). Phase theory of curriculum reform. Wellesley, MA: Center for research on women.

Rogers, P., & Kaiser, G. (1995). *Equity in mathematics education: Influences of feminism and culture.* London: Falmer Press.

Solar, C., LaFortune, L., Kayler, L., Barette, M., Caron, R., & Pasquis, L. (1992). Où en sommes-nous? In L. Lafortune & H. Kayler (Eds.), *Les femmes font des maths* . Montréal: Remue-ménage.

Willis, S. (1989). *Real girls don't do maths.* Geelong, Victoria: Deakin University.

Woolfe, S. (1996). *Leaning towards infinity.* Milson's Point, New South Wales: Random House Australia

SCHOOL STEREOTYPE WORD PROBLEMS AND THE OPEN NATURE OF APPLICATIONS

Pearla Nesher
The University of Haifa, Israel

Introduction

Teaching word problems is an enormous effort in which most of us fail. Why do we continue teaching them? The typical attitude is that by teaching students how to solve word-problems we teach them the applicativity of mathematics; that the heart of learning mathematics is to know when and how to apply mathematics. Unfortunately, many students after struggling with many types of problems, do not consider them to be part of real life, as demonstrated by my favorite example (Nesher, 1980):

In a visit to a second grade in Israel, the teacher has asked the kids to compose their own problems for the mathematical sentence 2+7=9 (which later we will call mathematical model). Here are two examples of their creations:

Joseph: Mother had 2 irons and she bought 7 more, how many irons does mother have now? or,

Rivka: Johnny ate 2 spoons and 7 forks, how many spoons and forks did Johnny eat altogether?

Today, when the math education community is talking so much about 'Realistic Mathematics' (de Lange, 1996, Reusser, 1988, Verschaffel, De Corte et al. 1994) I find it quite absurd to believe this sort of "realistic" problems coming from the children. In fact, the kids have interiorized a habit which seems to be saying something like this: "There is no connection between real life and what the teacher is asking us to do. If we get a 'problem'. i.e., a text with numbers in it, we have to do something with the numbers and to get a numerical reply. The text is irrelevant..."

They also realize that it is not that simple to know what calculation should be done. Many of the little kids will turn to their teacher saying: " I understand the problem well, just tell me whether to add or to subtract".

I am not surprised that this is the case. There is no clear understanding even among math educators what is the purpose of this entire activity. For many decades people felt that it was important to teach word problems, yet, we still don't know how to do it. In a little piece of research that I conducted in an old library at Harvard, I found that nothing has changed concerning the teaching of word problems since the eighteenth century, except for the context. Many problems in the eighteenth century are taken from farm life, or navigation, but they all have a very similar structure, and the children then engaged in the same activities as today's children.

Efforts have been made in the past twenty years to better understand the processes involved in problem solving. Most of these were within the paradigm of cognitive science research. My main thesis in this presentation is that in order to teach problem solving we should learn what cognitive processes are involved and give the children the opportunities to cope with them. Modeling real life situations with mathematical tools means being acquainted with mathematical schemes of actions. School usually starts with the most simple ones (those which unfortunately become stereotyped) and extends to more complex ones. There is a danger that starting with simple stereotyped situations will contradict the open nature of real application. Thus, teaching word problems has two aspects: learning the mathematical tools used for modeling, but at the same time freeing the activities from being artificially restricted.

Findings from Cognitive Research

Most of the findings from cognitive research are well known and have even penetrated to the teaching and learning at the primary level, yet I would like to mention them here in order to get the full picture. It was found that cognitive processes involved in problem solving are driven by schemes. Applications that call for a certain mathematical model have certain characteristics. Research has made these characteristics explicit. Let us examine the additive structure; for example,

Here is a typical word problem text.
.......7......2.....
...........?

This is a typical structure of a simple word problem text (Nesher and Katriel, 1977), This is also how the kids understand this kind of text: namely, ignore the words (the "bla-bla") and do something with the numbers. Unfortunately, without reading the words, one cannot know what to do: to add, subtract, multiply, divide, or else? But once we fill the words, as in the following case:

Johnny had in the morning a certain amount of dollars and he spent some of them. How many dollars does he have now?

We now know for sure that we have to subtract in order to find the answer although no number is mentioned in the text. Thus, the mathematical model is defined by the situation and not by the quantities mentioned in the text. Moreover, a text that has full textual and numerical information such as the following:

In the group there are 4 girls and 8 boys.

will not suffice, and does not have enough information for deciding about the correct mathematical model. Finding the mathematical model will depend on the missing string, which is the question. For example, we can end the above text with one of the following questions:

> *a) How many boys and girls are there altogether?*
> *b) How many more boys are there than girls?*
> *c) How many different couples can one arrange*
>   *in this group?*
> *d) What is the proportion of girls to boys?*

and so on.

Each of the above questions will lead to a different mathematical model. Thus the full information that determines which mathematical model to employ, resides in the full text that on one hand, describes the situation to be modeled and on the other hand, fulfills some requirements that I would like to describe now.

The Additive and Multiplicative Schemes

A semantic analysis of additive texts demonstrates that any text in its minimal form has three strings holding some dependencies among them. Without going into a formal description, the main characteristics of such texts are that if the addition operation is to be selected for modeling the situation, the description is of three sets of objects. Two of these are disjoint sets, the third is a superset of the previously mentioned sets, and no other objects are involved. If more objects are mentioned they will be considered as superfluous information emphasizing the three argument relation necessary for a binary mathematical operation. This actually forms a scheme that is called into action whenever the real situation is like the conditions described above. It is interesting to note that the same conditions also hold for the subtraction operation, since addition and subtraction are two aspects of the same mathematical structure.

Actually, the entire variety of additive word problems should fulfill the above conditions, and these conditions can be described by a variety of linguistic means. Similarly, conditions can be specified for situations in which the multiplicative scheme is called into action and the multiplication or division mathematical operations are to be executed (Nesher, 1988; Vergnaud, 1985).

We, in Israel have, therefore, introduced into primary schools the teaching of schemes, rather than separate mathematical operations. We teach the additive structure which serves as an underlying structure for many arithmetic sentences and the same for the multiplicative structure. After clarifying constrains under which the additive model can fit, it is our responsibility to open it to variety of open situation (CET, 1980-1997).

I would like to present some illustrations of the instruction we use which is based on findings from the above research. In a primary school math program in Israel, we teach (i.e., we give the child an opportunity to be active and construct such schemes). The child is engaged with schemes before he attempts to formal mathematical sentences. Here are some examples of activities for learning the characteristics of the additive scheme.

Children engage in activities in which they have to deal with subsets and supersets that are relevant to the additive scheme; i.e, they should notice, via their activities, whether the subsets are disjoint; the superset includes the same object and nothing else enters the additive scheme. They realize that for deciding about the underlying structure of a text, the numbers are neither sufficient, nor even crucial, while the sets involved are. They realize that the same structure fits both, addition and subtraction, and that one real situation can call for several mathematical schemes (See appendix A for demonstrations).

It is now clearer to math educators which are the real world situations that call for the additive schemes. Three main contextual structures were identified (Greeno 1978a; Nesher, 1982; Carpenter, Moser et al. 1982):

a) Situations where two sets of objects are combined.
(COMBINE).

b) Situations in which one amount is increased or decreased.
(CHANGE).

c) Situations in which two sets are compared.
(COMPARE).

The same holds for multiplication and division. Contexts in which two dimensions are to be arranged or compared, enlarged etc., were identified and became the target of more directed teaching, as preparation for modeling.

More Complex Problems

It was found in the last decade that the basic schemes mentioned above are the building stones of more complex problems. Below, I elaborate on complex schemes, using the illustrations of our instructional program. After becoming acquainted with the two basic schemes, the multiplicative and the additive, it was established (by our group in Israel, and Shalin from LRDC) that when two schemes are combined, some additional constraints appear, and that complex situations have their own structures (Shalin and Bee 1985a; Hershkovitz, Nesher et al. 1990).

Though a problem that combines two full schemes (additive and multiplicative) has in its underlying structure 6 components (strings in the verbal form), in a combined 2-step problem only 3 components are explicitly mentioned and one string states the question. The latent components, which are not explicitly stated, are the main source of difficulty for children.

In analyzing the structure of the 2-step problems we also found that there are only three possible schemes which account for all 28 possible different combination of these two basic mathematical operations (taking into account the order of the operations). For a full exposition of these findings see (Nesher and Hershkovitz 1994).

The question that always bothers researchers in cognitive studies is, are our understandings about the schemes underlying our actions teachable?, Does presenting these structures to students enhance their learning , understanding and performance? I can only hint here about some of our findings, which were the thesis of my Ph.D. student who built two computerized environments to study this issue (Hershkovitz and Nesher 1996). One of the environments represented the schemes approach and the other, though also computerized, represented the more conventional approach. Her tutoring experiment demonstrated that emphasizing the schemes enhances the children's understanding and performance.

The open nature of applications

So far I have succeeded in showing how to reveal the underlying structure of variety of word problems. I also claimed that every well formed problem, where one knows which operation to apply to it, is well defined and can be reduced to a basic underlying structure. Such an analysis seems to lead to stereotyped. behavior. However, this is only one aspect that emphasizes the construction of mathematical tools for modeling. Let us now switch to the other end which is our target in teaching the above tools, i.e., the open nature of applications and how we model them mathematically.

What will be considered an open-ended problem?.

There are several interpretations for the notion of open-ended problems. such as:

1. Problem with no single solution.
2. Problems that lack numerical information
3. Superfluous or missing information.
4. Descriptions of situations with undefined question.
5. An unusual problem
6. Only certain numbers can considered as solutions.
(Verschaffel, De Corte et al. 1994; Greer 1996; Wyndhamn and Saljo 1996)

All the above are important as part of mathematical education. They all call for non-mechanical style of work, but rather for meaningful elaboration which fit a variety of student abilities, as in the following example:

There are 30 children in the second grade. There are more girls than boys. How many boys are there in the class?

Sara: There are 14 boys.
Ruth: It can also be 13 boys.
Eve: There are many possibilities.
Ofra: I know all the possibilities.

These children above kids demonstrated different levels of solutions and generalization However, all of them, when offering a reply have used the additive structure, explicitly or implicitly. Ofra has used it explicitly when she explained her statement.

Let me elaborate now on another problem:

The children in the camp are divided between those who prefer pizza anf those who prefer pita. Pizza costs 4 I.S. each, and pita costs 2 I.S. each. They spent 100 I.S. altogether. What did they buy?

Please note, that there is not sufficient numerical information in the problem. However, if one tries to answer the question, he or she will find that this problem has a well defined underlying structure We gave this problem to 2nd graders and suggested:

Ask your own questions.
Make up your numbers
What else do you want to know

The 2nd graders, usually, gave one solution, but many of them were aware that there are other solutions. Among 5th and 6th graders many could cope with the general structure of the problem, as was demonstrated from their solutions. Some wrote a table of options, the others drew diagrams that demonstrated their level of generalization.

FINAL COMMENTS

In order to help children cope with applications, we should teach the basic **mathematical** schemes and also where and when they apply. Pedagogy is the art of teaching things gradually, of assisting the construction of cognitive tools. The main dilemma is, how to avoid falling into the trap of stereotyping the learning when teaching the basic cognitive tools in a gradual manner. How to first present simple cases and yet keep problems open.

While we are teaching the basic tools of mathematics, we should teach also their constraints, when they apply and when they do not apply. We should present children with problems with missing information, as well as with superfluous information. These are necessary right from the beginning of the learning, as they strengthen the understanding of the mathematical structures. The gist of our teaching should be to have children understand that the game is of finding the mathematical model and not just the numerical solution.

We should not throw the baby with the water. The main role of schools is to enrich the child's cognitive tools, in our case with mathematical concepts, structures and procedures. Being able to cope with open situations successfully means having an enriched set of schemes.

References

Carpenter, T. P., M. J. Moser, et al., Eds. (1982). *Addition and Subtraction: A Cognitive Approach.* Hillsdale, NJ, Lawrence Erlbaum Associates.

CET (1980-1997). *One, two and...three.,* CET.

De Lange, J. (1996). Using and Applying Mathematics in Education. *International Handbook of Mathematics Education.* A. J. Bishop, K. Clements, C. Keitel, J. Kilpatrick and C. Laborde, eds. Dordrecht, Bostob, London, Kluwer Academic Publishers. 49-97.

Greeno, J. G. (1978a). A Study of Problem Solving. *Advances in Instructional Psychology.* R. Glaser, N. J. Hillsdale: Lawrence Erlbaum Associates. **1**.

Greer, B. (1996). "Failing to Model Reality in Mathematics (research report)." *draft.*

Hershkovitz, S. and P. Nesher (1996). "The Role of Schemes in designing Computerized Environments." *Educational Studies in Mathematics* **30**: 339-366.

Hershkovitz, S., P. Nesher, et al. (1990). *Schemes for Problem Analysis (SPA).* Tel Aviv, Centre for Educational Technology.

Nesher, p. (1980). "The Stereotyped Nature of School word problems." *For the Learning of Mathematics* **1**(1): 41-48.

Nesher, P. (1988). Multiplicative School Word Problems: Theoretical Approaches and Empirical Findings. *Number Concepts and Operations in the Middle Grades.* J. Hiebert and M. Behr. NJ, Lawrence Erlbaum Association: 19-41.

Nesher, P. and S. Hershkovitz (1994). "The Role of Schemes in Two-step Problems: Analysis and Research Findings." *Educational Studies in mathematics* **26**: 1-23.

Nesher, P. and T. Katriel (1977). "A Semantic Analysis of Addition and Subtraction Word Problems in Arithmetic." *Educational Studies in Mathematics* **8**: 251-269.

Shalin, V. L. and N. V. Bee (1985a). Structural Differences Between Two-Step Word Problems.

Vergnaud, G. (1988). Multiplicative Structures. *Acquisition of Mathematical Concepts and Processes.* R. Lesh and M. Landau. New York, Academic Press.

Verschaffel, L., E. De Corte, et al. (1994). "Realistic Considerations in Mathematical Modeling of School Arithmetic Word Problems." *Learning and Instruction* **4**: 273-294.

Wyndhamn, J. and R. Saljo (1996). "Word problems and mathematical Reasoning - A study of Children Mastery of Reference and Meaning in Textual Realities." *draft.*

LOS SISTEMAS DE CÁLCULO SIMBÓLICO EN LA ENSEÑANZA DE LAS MATEMÁTICAS

Javier Pérez Fernández
Departamento de Matemáticas. Universidad de Cádiz

Abstract

Symbolic Computation Systems can and must play an important role in mathematics teaching. With adequate planning they can assist in bettering understanding, studying in depth numerous concepts, be a valuable educational instrument in problem solving and influence curriculum planning in terms of content, selection and order. Their use must be placed within what is known as "experimental mathematics teaching" and must not be hidden in activities aimed at learning as a set of fixed Algebra Computer Systems to resolve determined routine exercises. The software in question has been selected on a basis of characteristics accumulated from studies, from students and from other available sources. Alongside an overview of its advantages and inconveniences in relation to its educative tasks, the presentation will incorporate activities directed towards university students.

Introducción

Desde que, hace casi tres años, se fraguara esta conferencia, la evolución del "software" matemático ha sido imparable. Han aparecido sucesivas versiones, mejorando cada una a la anterior, de los distintos Sistemas de Cálculo Simbólico: DERIVE, MATHEMATICA, MAPLE, MACSYMA, etc. La experimentación del uso de estos sistemas para la enseñanza de las matemáticas se ha extendido de forma muy sensible, así como la investigación de su influencia en el proceso de aprendizaje, a las que posteriormente haré referencia.

El debate sobre los efectos del uso de los Sistemas de Cálculo Simbólico como recurso didáctico, en la enseñanza de las matemáticas, a muy diversos niveles y desde muy diversas ópticas, no ha hecho más que empezar. Los profesores de universidad discutimos sobre sus efectos positivos y negativos, sobre la viabilidad de su incorporación sistemática en la labor docente, y muchos profesores de bachillerato (16--18 años) se han incorporado también a la controversia; e incluso aquellos que apuestan por su uso, no llegan a conclusiones unánimes sobre la forma de hacerlo.

Deseo alejarme de esta polémica, circunscrita básicamente a la órbita del uso didáctico de esta herramienta, y abordar la cuestión desde una perspectiva más amplia.

Podemos afirmar que el ordenador es el elemento central del proceso de revolución tecnológica en que vivimos. Desde la primera generación de aquellos, allá por 1945, hasta nuestros días la evolución de la informática ha sido enorme; entre otros avances están: el acceso remoto a máquinas de elevadas prestaciones en multiproceso de tiempo compartido, las redes de comunicaciones informáticas (comúnmente conocidas como autopistas de la información), la extensión del mercado de ordenadores personales de elevadas prestaciones y precios asequibles y un largo etcétera. El avance en la investigación de "software" ha variado sustancialmente los métodos de trabajo a todos los niveles y, por supuesto, los de la investigación de muy diversas ciencias, a la vez que se han abierto nuevos campos de desarrollo científico. Es incuestionable que un objetivo de los sistemas educativos ha de ser capacitar a los alumnos para enfrentarse con adecuada formación a sus futuras actividades profesionales, así como favorecer la necesaria adaptación a los continuos avances de la tecnología.

Desde este punto de vista es claro que la enseñanza de las matemáticas debe asumir y utilizar los recursos tecnológicos de cada momento. Si para abordar muy diversos problemas de la técnica y de la ciencia se están utilizando Sistemas de Cálculo Simbólico, parece adecuado que los alumnos, tanto los de estudios preuniversitarios (16 - 18 años) con una orientación hacia ramas científico-técnicas, como los de estudios universitarios de este mismo campo, tengan una cierta familiarización con este tipo de "software" matemático de propósito general. Por tanto, la incorporación de estos *asistentes matemáticos* a la enseñanza ha de superar su concepción como mero medio didáctico, entre otros recursos, y ha de significar una innovación sustancial que conducirá sin lugar a dudas a profundas transformaciones de los objetivos, contenidos y métodos de enseñanza en los niveles educativos señalados.

2. Matemáticas y Sistemas de Cálculo Simbólico

Si aceptamos la argumentación anterior y, por tanto, la necesidad de la familiarización de los alumnos, en los niveles señalados anteriormente, con los programas de Álgebra Computacional, es claro que éstos deberían tener presencia específica en los curriculos correspondientes, pero ¿cómo hacerlo? Tal vez podría orientar nuestra respuesta el uso que de este tipo de "software" hace el matemático en su investigación.

Creo que es comúnmente aceptado que el fin esencial de la educación matemática es formativo y que radica en el desarrollo de la capacidad de lo que podríamos denominar pensamiento matemático, es decir conseguir que los alumnos hagan matemáticas, cuestión ésta que puede realizarse a muy diversos niveles. Llegar a resolver problemas matemáticos (hacer matemáticas) es el objetivo fundamental de la enseñanza de las mismas, por cuanto en ello se condensa la capacidad de saber usarlas. Consecuentemente merecen especial atención la consecución de capacidades para:
1. Reconocer, seleccionar y saber aplicar estrategias y técnicas como la analogía, la particularización, etc.
2. Reconocer, plantear y resolver problemas a partir de situaciones dentro y fuera de las matemáticas.
3. Aplicar el proceso de formulación de modelos matemáticos a situaciones prácticas, relacionadas con los contenidos curriculares.

En esencia, la forma de hacer matemáticas del matemático y de un estudiante es la misma; varía, eso sí, los conocimientos y el grado de capacitación personal, pero sustancialmente la cualidad del proceso es la misma. Pues bien, ¿cómo los sistemas de Cálculo Simbólico están influyendo en la forma en que hoy se está investigando en matemáticas? y ¿en qué medida ha de traducirse esta situación en la enseñanza de esta disciplina?

Voy a exponer un caso concreto, parte de un problema que un colega mío[1] ha trabajado.

Él estaba interesado en el estudio de las soluciones de la conocida *ecuación de Laplace:*

$$u_{xx} + u_{yy} + u_{zz} = 0,$$

donde u es una función $u=u(x,y,z)$. El objetivo básico era determinar y "clasificar" todas las soluciones que presentan un cierto tipo de invarianza frente a grupos de transformaciones (soluciones de similaridad"), lo que entre otras virtudes le permitiría determinar y construir nuevas soluciones, conocidas otras.

Podemos interpretar una solución $u(x,y,z)$ como una superficie en $\mathbf{R}^3$ x $\mathbf{R}$ y la ecuación de Laplace como una hipersuperficie en el espacio ampliado $\mathbf{R}^3$ x $\mathbf{R}$ x $\mathbf{R}^9$, donde en $\mathbf{R}^9$ se representan las coordenadas dadas por las derivadas de primer y segundo orden: $u_x, \ldots, u_z, u_{xx}, u_{xy}, \ldots, u_{zz}$.

El procedimiento consiste en buscar grupos de transformaciones:

$$x^* = X(x,y,z,u,\varepsilon)$$
$$y^* = Y(x,y,z,u,\varepsilon)$$
$$z^* = Z(x,y,z,u,\varepsilon)$$
$$u^* = U(x,y,z,u,\varepsilon)$$

que dejan invariantes a la *hipersuperficie* y que también preservan las condiciones de contacto, es decir de forma que los *hiperplanos* tangentes sigan siendo, mediante el grupo de transformaciones, *hiperplanos* tangentes, y donde ε es un parámetro. Obviamente a partir de soluciones tan sencillas como $u = k$, con k constante, se pueden determinar múltiples soluciones nuevas. Estas soluciones invariantes por la transformación del grupo se conocen como *soluciones de similaridad*.

Ahora bien, buscar la expresión analítica (exacta) del grupo de transformaciones requiere una cantidad de cálculos extraordinarios, que llevaría días de trabajo (si se aborda sin asistencia del ordenador) y al final no se estaría seguro de no haber cometido errores en el proceso. Los cálculos son de tipo algebraico, es una tarea semiautomática cuya complejidad radica exclusivamente en el volumen de los mismos.

Los sistemas de Cálculo Simbólico en este punto dan adecuada respuesta en pocos segundos. De hecho, a partir de 1988 hay una gran explosión de investigación en el campo de la resolución de ecuaciones en derivadas parciales, gracias al desarrollo de estos asistentes matemáticos.

---

1 José Manuel Díaz Moreno, de la Universidad de Cádiz

En la primera fase de la resolución, el Sistema de Cálculo Simbólico nos devuelve un sistema sobredeterminado de ecuaciones en derivadas parciales de segundo orden:

$$\rho_{xx} + \rho_{yy} + \rho_{zz} = 0,$$
$$\zeta_{xx} + \zeta_{yy} + \zeta_{zz} = 0,$$

$$2\zeta_x - \xi_{xx}^{(1)} - \xi_{yy}^{(1)} - \xi_{zz}^{(1)} = 0,$$
$$2\zeta_x - \xi_{xx}^{(2)} - \xi_{yy}^{(2)} - \xi_{zz}^{(2)} = 0,$$
$$2\zeta_x - \xi_{xx}^{(3)} - \xi_{yy}^{(3)} - \xi_{zz}^{(3)} = 0,$$

$$\xi_x^{(1)} - \xi_z^{(3)} = 0,$$
$$\xi_x^{(2)} - \xi_z^{(1)} = 0,$$
$$\xi_x^{(3)} - \xi_z^{(1)} = 0,$$
$$\xi_x^{(2)} - \xi_z^{(3)} = 0,$$
$$\xi_x^{(3)} - \xi_z^{(2)} = 0.$$

en el que las funciones que aparecen lo son en las variables x, y, z. Su resolución requiere destreza, intuición y cierta maestría, esta es una segunda fase del problema.

Hasta ahora el programa ha actuado como una supercalculadora. Pero ha nacido un campo nuevo de estudio, ¿cómo resolver de forma automática este tipo de sistemas?; este es un problema en el que actualmente se está investigando.

En una tercera fase, se intenta clasificar las soluciones de forma que queden identificadas. Todas las familias de soluciones se distribuyen en clases de equivalencia y se busca un representante de cada clase, entre los infinitos que se pueden elegir. Para esta tarea no hay un procedimiento automático, no existe un algoritmo; el procedimiento estará guiado por la *intuición* matemática, pero los cálculos para verificar la corrección de las sucesivas hipótesis planteadas son muy grandes. El *manipulador simbólico* permite buscar en caminos que sin su asistencia no se podría. El programa ha actuado ahora para permitir la experimentación, para conjeturar y verificar o refutar.

Este no es sino un ejemplo, de los muchos posibles, en los que los Sistemas de Cálculo Simbólico están permitiendo investigación en terrenos hasta ahora inabordables y de cómo la propia existencia de este sofisticado "software" está planteando nuevos campos de investigación matemática.

Se tiende hacia una automatización de procesos de resolución de amplias partes de la matemática. El resultado será que se dispondrá de métodos más fiables y a menor costo, más y mejores herramientas para atacar y resolver problemas y más tiempo para dedicarlo al enfoque de nuevos problemas y ahondar en los misterios de su resolución.

3. Sistemas de Cálculo Simbólico y enseñanza experimental de las Matemáticas.

Algunos profesores estiman que el uso de *Manipuladores Simbólicos* puede representar una pérdida de destrezas básicas e incluso que ésta llegue a ser un obstáculo para un adecuado desarrollo de la capacidad de abstracción y razonamiento. Quienes así piensan (aunque no siempre, ni en todos los casos, sean conscientes de ello) dedican grandes dosis de esfuerzo a la enseñanza de algoritmos y a la realización de ejercicios que tienen una respuesta más o menos inmediata en el uso de uno o varios algoritmos, digamos estándares. La situación actual podría resumirse en el siguiente esquema:

• Se dedica una enorme cantidad de esfuerzo para que los alumnos adquieran destreza en el uso de los algoritmos más usuales.

• Los que fueron alumnos olvidan los algoritmos que aprendieron.

• Muchos algoritmos, de diversos campos de la matemática, pueden construirse sobre "software" científico y particularmente con el lenguaje de programación de diversos sistemas de Cálculo Simbólico y funcionar sobre máquinas baratas.

• Muchos profesores que exponen las virtudes de aprender algoritmos rutinariamente, usan conceptos, procesos y modelos para los que no conocen ningún algoritmo relevante.

Esta situación es lógicamente inestable y presagia profundas revisiones de los sistemas educativos.

Si en el quehacer de un matemático profesional hay elementos importantes de experimentación y ésta alcanza posibilidades inimaginables hace tan sólo dos décadas con los Sistemas de Cálculo Simbólico, parece razonable utilizar este potencial también para la enseñanza. La realización de procesos inductivos, el contraste de hipótesis, la verificación o refutación, el cambio de postulados, el sometimiento de los mismos a nuevas pruebas, la formulación de conjeturas apoyadas en la construcción de modelos que responden a las exigencias del problema, son elementos distintivos de la experimentación matemática. Estos asistentes matemáticos pueden emplearse como recursos didácticos que favorezcan niveles crecientes de pensamiento formal y de adecuada conceptualización matemática. Una tal línea de actuación se inscribiría en la conocida corriente de la "enseñanza experimental" de las matemáticas, que se apoya en las tesis constructivistas y que conecta con la línea metodológica de "resolución de problemas".

3.1 Un ejemplo: La órbita de un satélite

El siguiente problema es uno de los que proponemos a nuestros alumnos de primero de universidad de estudios técnicos [2]. Las prácticas de laboratorio que venimos realizando con nuestros alumnos están centradas en la resolución de problemas, con las necesarias matizaciones y, en principio, son adaptables a distintos sistemas de Cálculo Simbólico, aunque ésta concretamente se ha desarrollado con el programa **MATHEMATICA**. La resolución está orientada y asesora puntualmente, en los momentos que se estiman pertinentes, sobre las órdenes que pueden resultar útiles en el proceso de resolución.

TRANSIT NUMBER 59 SATELLITE
fecha de observación: 15 de Octubre de 1.984

Hora	x	y	z
11h. 13m.	7347.2083	640.4444	-1083.2656
11h. 14m.	7400.8405	614.8864	-647.2850
11h. 15m.	7428.7207	586.8517	-209.0549
11h. 16m.	7430.7346	556.6627	229.9017
11h. 17m.	7406.8609	524.6504	668.0597
11h. 18m.	7357.1717	491.1516	1103.8969
11h. 19m.	7281.8320	456.5073	1535.9001
11h. 20m.	7181.0993	421.0605	1962.5701
11h. 21m.	7055.3220	385.1546	2382.4273
11h. 22m.	6904.9388	349.1307	2794.0170
11h. 23m.	6730.4703	313.3265	3195.9142
11h. 24m.	6532.5472	278.0735	3586.7290
11h. 25m.	6311.8480	243.6957	3965.1112
11h. 26m.	6069.1561	210.5077	4329.7553
11h. 27m.	5805.3269	178.8124	4679.4044
11h. 28m.	5521.2907	148.9000	5012.8552
11h. 29m.	5218.0487	121.0459	5328.9617
11h. 30m.	4896.6697	95.5092	5626.6389
11h. 31m.	4558.2862	72.5316	5904.8669
11h. 32m.	4204.0892	52.3354	6162.6936

Haremos una somera descripción del mismo, señalando los puntos más relevantes, toda vez que un relato pormenorizado requeriría más tiempo del que disponemos.

Deseamos determinar la órbita de un satélite artificial, así como el barrido del mismo sobre la superficie terrestre, determinando su posición minuto a minuto, a partir de 20 observaciones del mismo.

Nuestro punto de partida es un conjunto de 20 observaciones del satélite artificial TRANSIT 59 en coordenadas geocéntricas (en kilómetros), tomadas de [4]. En la tabla anterior aparecen las posiciones del satélite así cómo el día y hora de cada una de ellas. Las coordenadas geográficas (x,y,z), están referidas al siguiente sistema ortogonal

- Su centro (0,0,0) es el centro de la tierra.
- El eje X está situado sobre el plano del ecuador y en dirección Aries (sentido positivo hacia este punto)
- El eje Y está situado sobre el plano del ecuador ortogonal al eje X (el semieje positivo es el que se halla en el sentido contrario a las agujas del reloj desde el semieje positivo de las X).
- El eje Z es la recta norte-sur con sentido positivo hacia el norte.

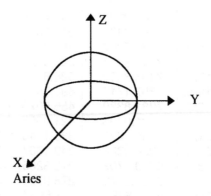

Comenzamos introduciendo la matriz **efemerides** formada por las coordenadas geocéntricas:

In[1]:
efemerides={
{7347.2083,640.4444,-1083.2656} , {7400.8405,614.8864,-647.2850} ,
{7428.7207,586.8517,-209.0549} , {7430.7346,556.6627,229.9017} ,
{7406.8609,524.6504,668.0597} , {7357.1717,491.1516,1103.8969} ,
{7281.8320,456.5073,1535.9001} , {7181.0993,421.0605,1962.5701} ,
{7055.3220,385.1546,2382.4273} , {6904.9388,349.1307,2794.0170} ,
{6730.4703,313.3265,3195.9142} , {6532.5472,278.0735,3586.7290} ,
{6311.8480,243.6957,3965.1112} , {6069.1561,210.5077,4329.7553} ,
{5805.3269,178.8124,4679.4044}, {5521.2907,148.9000,5012.8552} ,
{5218.0487,121.0459,5328.9617} , {4896.6697,95.5092,5626.6389},
{4558.2862, 72.5316,5904.8669} , {4204.0892,52.3354,6162.6936}
};

3.1.1 Arco orbital observado

Durante estos 20 minutos el satélite ha recorrido parte de su órbita que podemos representar usando la orden:

PuntosObservados=Show[Graphics3D[Join[{Line[efemerides]},
Table[Point[efemerides[[i]]],{i,20}]   ]]]

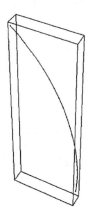

3.1.2. Cálculo de las coordenadas geográficas

Vamos a determinar el ángulo en el momento de la primera observación, para ello se hace preciso la determinación de:

1. El número de días julianos transcurridos y, por tanto, el número de vueltas dadas por la Tierra:

DiaJuliano=Floor[365.25*1984]+Floor[30.6001*11]+
15+(11+13/60)/24+1720994.5+
2-Floor[1984/100]+Floor[Floor[1984/100]/4]

2.A partir del número de días, según el calendario Juliano, se calcula el Tiempo Universal referido al año 2000 (no nos extrañemos, por tanto, del signo) con la fórmula:

TiempoUniversal=(DiaJuliano - 2451545.)/36525.

3. Ahora calculamos la Hora Sidérea, en segundos, con la fórmula:

HoraSiderea=24110.54841+8640184.812866*TiempoUniversal+

0.093104*TiempoUniversal^2-6.2*10^(-6)*TiempoUniversal^3

4. A partir de la hora sidérea, quitando las vueltas completas, determinamos el ángulo en el momento de la primera observación:

AnguloInicial=Mod[HoraSiderea*360/(24*60*60),360]

Se obtiene que el número de grados girado por la Tierra en la primera observación es de 24.1717.

Dado un punto *(x,y,z)* de la trayectoria del satélite podemos conocer la proyección sobre la Tierra hallando la latitud y longitud correspondiente de la siguiente forma:

latitud = ángulo del vector *(x,y,z)* con el plano *XY*
longitud = ángulo, sobre el plano *XY*, del vector
(x,y) con la parte positiva del eje *X* menos el ángulo girado por la Tierra.

3.1.3 Proyección

Para determinar la sombra de los 20 puntos sobre la tierra se procede como sigue:

Latitud[{x_,y_,z_}]:= ArcSin[z/Sqrt[x^2+y^2+z^2]]*(180/pi)

Longitud[{x_,y_,z_}]:=
2*ArcSin[Sign[y]*Sqrt[(1-x/Sqrt[x^2+y^2])/2]]/Degree

El siguiente paso será definir una matriz con las coordenadas geográficas y en donde vamos a tener en cuenta ya el ángulo girado por la Tierra, tanto el inicial como el correspondiente a cada minuto.

Geograficas=Table[
{Latitud[efemerides[[i]]],Longitud[efemerides[[i]]]-AnguloInicial-360/1440(i-1)},
{i,Length[efemerides]}]//N;

Ello nos permite observar la proyección del satélite sobre el mapamundi.

3.1.4 Cálculo de la órbita del satélite

A continuación vamos a determinar la órbita del satélite. La elipse que describe el satélite puede obtenerse como intersección de un elipsoide y un plano, de forma que el punto de coordenadas (0,0,0) debe ser un foco de la órbita, de acuerdo con las leyes de Kepler.

1. Ecuación del elipsoide:

elipsoide[x_,y_,z_]:=
a x^2 + b y^2 + c z^2 + d x y + e x z + f y z + 1000;

2. Ecuación del plano:

plano[x_,y_,z_]:= p x + q y + r z + 1000

Se determinan los coeficientes por mínimos cuadrados. Respecto al plano del ecuador XY podemos considerar dos ramas de la órbita del satélite una superior y otra inferior. Estas ramas se calcularán haciendo la intersección del elipsoide y el plano antes calculados.

Z[x_,y_]:= Solve[plano[x,y,z]==0,z]

Y[x_]:= Solve[elipsoide /. z -> Z[x,y], Y]

Los dos valores obtenidos corresponden con las dos ramas de la órbita. Finalmente se definen dos funciones, correspondientes a cada una de ambas ramas, de forma que para cada valor de x nos da las coordenadas geocéntricas de la posición del satélite.

Rama1[x_] := {x, Y[x] [[2]], Z[x, Y[x] [[2]]]}

Rama2[x_] := {x, Y[x] [[1]], Z[x, Y[x] [[1]]]}

Los valores mínimos y máximos de la variable x serán necesarios para la representación grafica de la órbita. Estos valores se calculan usando el hecho de que son los puntos comunes entre las dos ramas:

{xmax,xmin}=x/. Solve[Y[x][[1]]==Y[x][[2]], x]

Se representa seguidamente la órbita hallada:

**Orbita=ParametricPlot3D[{{Branch1[x][[1]],Rama1[x][[2]],Rama1[x][[3]]},
{Rama2[x][[1]],Rama2[x][[2]],Rama2[x][[3]]}},
{x,xmin,xmax},ViewPoint->{3,1,1},Ticks->None]**

Y obtenemos:

La representación de los puntos observados junto a la órbita nos muestra que tal han ido nuestros cálculos:

Show [{Puntosobsevados,Orbita}]

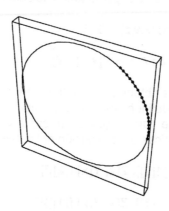

3.1.5 Predicción orbital minuto a minuto

Una vez conocida la órbita del satélite ya estamos en condiciones de encontrar su posición en los minutos siguientes al de las observaciones.Para esto usaremos la segunda ley de Kepler: *el satélite tiene momento angular constante.* Efectuamos una simplificación aproximando el área del triángulo mixtilineo determinado por dos puntos consecutivos de la órbita y el foco por el área del triángulo formado por los tres puntos.

Definamos en primer lugar una función que nos proporcione el área de un triángulo dados dos de sus vértices (el tercero es el foco (0,0,0)):

Area[{u1_,u2_,u3_},{v1_,v2_,v3_}]=1/2 Sqrt[
(u2*v3-u3*v2)^2+
(u1*v3-u3*v1)^2+
(u1*v2-u2*v1)^2
];

Parece razonable considerar, como constante para el área de los triángulos, la media de las áreas de todos los triángulos que se forman con los pares de puntos consecutivos observados. Esto lo hacemos así:

AreaTriangulo=N[Sum[Area[efemerides[[i]],efemerides[[i+1]]],{i,19}]/19]

Posición del satélite en el minuto 21

Procedemos a determinar la posición del satélite en el minuto 21. Esa posición se encuentra en la rama superior **Rama 1** y el triángulo que forma con el punto de la posición 20 debe tener el área calculada anteriormente; así pues, resolvamos la ecuación:

NextPoint=x/. FindRoot[
Area[efemerides[[20]],Rama1[x]]-AreaTriangulo==0,
{x,efem[[20,1]]-5}
]

3835.34

La posición en el minuto 21 será

Rama1[NextPoint]

{3835.34, 17.7762, 6398.92}

Añadimos este valor a la matriz de posiciones

efemerides=Join[efemerides,{Rama1[NextPoint]}];

Determinación completa de la órbita

Realizamos a continuación un procedimiento que nos halle el resto de las posiciones correspondientes a la rama superior:

```
For[i=21,efemerides[[i,1]]-xmin>15,i++,
    efemerides=Join[efem,{Rama1[x]}]/.FindRoot[Area[efemerides
[[i]],Rama1[x] ]-
    AreaTriangulo= =0, {x,efem[[i,1]]-5}          ]
  Print[ efem[[i+1]] ]
    ]
```

{3452.71, -5.59435, 6613.45}
{3058.04, -27.4481, 6805.07}
{2652.69, -47.7089, 6973.09}
{2238.07, -66.3063, 7116.95}
{1815.62, -83.1755, 7236.13}
{1386.83, -98.2578, 7330.23}
{953.181, -111.501, 7398.91}
{516.184, -122.858, 7441.94}
{77.3616, -132.29, 7459.16}
{-361.758, -139.764, 7450.53}
{-799.645, -145.254, 7416.05}
{-1234.78, -148.741, 7355.87}
{-1665.63, -150.212, 7270.18}
{-2090.72, -149.663, 7159.28}
{-2508.55, -147.095, 7023.56}
{-2917.67, -142.518, 6863.49}
{-3316.65, -135.946, 6679.63}
{-3704.11, -127.404, 6472.61}
{-4078.69, -116.919, 6243.16}
{-4439.1, -104.53, 5992.07}
{-4784.06, -90.2788, 5720.23}
{-5112.39, -74.2151, 5428.56}
{-5422.93, -56.3948, 5118.1}
{-5714.6, -36.88, 4789.92}
{-5986.39, -15.7386, 4445.16}
{-6237.34, 6.95602, 4085.02}
{-6466.58, 31.1247, 3710.76}

{-6673.32, 56.6834, 3323.68}
{-6856.81, 83.543, 2925.13}
{-7016.44, 111.61, 2516.5}
{-7151.64, 140.787, 2099.2}
{-7261.92, 170.972, 1674.71}
{-7346.92, 202.059, 1244.49}
{-7406.33, 233.942, 810.038}
{-7439.94, 266.507, 372.88}

Con la orden **Lenght[efemerides]** podemos saber que hemos hallado la posición del satélite durante 56 minutos.

Un procedimiento similar nos permite encontrar las posiciones sucesivas hasta completar la órbita.

La gráfica de la órbita junto a las posiciones observadas y a las calculadas nos muestra que nuestras simplificaciones producen resultados satisfactorios:

AllPoints=Show[Graphics3D[Join[{Line[efem]},
Table[Point[efem[[i]]],{i,106}]]],ViewPoint->{-0.072,-3.381,0.109}]

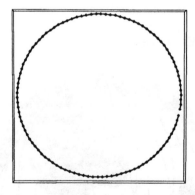

Para completar nuestra aventura vamos a dar vueltas a nuestro satélite suponiendo que su periodo es exactamente de 106 minutos. Damos 14 vueltas.

Turning=Table[efem[[Mod[i-1,106]+1]],{i,106*13}];

Realizamos las transformaciones necesarias tal como hicimos antes:

359

```
Geographics=Table[
{Latitude[Turning[[i]]],Longitude[Turning[[i]]]-InitialAngle-360/1440 (i-1)},
{i,Length[Turning]}]//N;

For[i=1,i<Length[Turning]+1,i++,
Geographics[[i,2]]=Mod[Geographics[[i,2]],360]
];

For[i=1,i<Length[Turning]+1,i++,
If[Geographics[[i,2]]>180,
Geographics[[i,2]]=Geographics[[i,2]]-360
]];

Geographics=60 Geographics;
```

Representamos ahora las 14 vueltas

```
EarthTrace=WorldGraphics[{RGBColor[1,0,0],
Line[
        Geographics
            ]}
                ]
```

Y así obtenemos nuestra última gráfica

```
Show[{mapamundi,EarthTrace}]
```

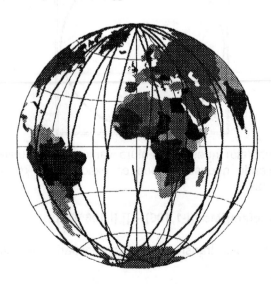

Algunos comentarios

Vemos cómo a partir de datos reales los alumnos, con ayuda de un Sistema de Cálculo Simbólico, se enfrentan a un problema *real,* y cómo mediante la modelización del mismo les lleva a trabajar con variados contenidos matemáticos:

• Geometría en el espacio euclídeo.

• Coordenadas geocéntricas y geográficas.

• Funciones trigonométricas.

• Sistemas de ecuaciones sobredimensionados.

• Mínimos cuadrados.

• Ecuaciones.

En el proceso han podido aprender más acerca del programa en cuestión[2] ; así han tenido que aprender el significado y uso de órdenes como:

Graphics3D, ParametricPlot3D, Table, If, Solve

Sum, Show, For, Mod, QRDescomposition, Length

y el *Paquete WORLDPLOT,* haciendo uso de las órdenes:

WorldPlot, WorldData, WorldGraphics

Por ello, los alumnos se han enfrentado a la tarea de *resolución de problemas* (objetivo primordial de la educación matemática), que al ser de modelización aporta un elemento formativo adicional y una carga de motivación añadida. Además han profundizado en la comprensión de diversos conceptos matemáticos, al tener la necesidad de identificarlos y de aplicar sus correspondientes técnicas de cálculo (éste es el caso de mínimos cuadrados). Finalmente han aprendido mucho acerca del manejo y potencia del programa utilizado.

---

[2] MATHEMATICA

4. Ventajas e inconvenientes del uso de los Sistemas de Cálculo Simbólico en la enseñanza

Aún cuando estos asistentes matemáticos sean poderosas herramientas, muchos profesores están en desacuerdo sobre su utilidad pedagógica. Las razones anteriormente esgrimidas a favor de su uso, pueden parecerles, a algunos, pertenecer más al campo de la mera disquisición que al de la realidad constatable.

Es ya abundante la literatura sobre el uso didáctico de estos programas:

1. Recientes investigaciones (cf. [9], [13], [10], [6], etc.) han puesto de manifiesto en distintos campos de las matemáticas, entre otras, las siguientes ventajas para el aprendizaje:

• Se constata que ayuda a progresar hacia niveles superiores de pensamiento formal.

• La capacidad gráfica facilita la integración de las diversas imágenes conceptuales (en el sentido de Vinner) que son un obstáculo para el aprendizaje.

• La técnica del zoom resulta extremadamente útil para la adecuada conceptualización de los procesos de paso al límite. Estos resultados enlazan con los postulados de la enseñanza dinámica de Gattegno, en la medida que el proceso de visualización se revela como primordial para la abstracción.

• Amplía el abanico de manipulaciones posibles y el de visualización.

• Mejora la actitud de los alumnos frente a las matemáticas.

• Favorece la interiorización de los conceptos y procedimientos, de forma que estos permanecen a más largo plazo.

• Desarrolla nuevas estrategias de razonamiento.

• Es de una gran ductilidad para crear situaciones de trabajo.

• ...

2. Las experimentaciones que en muy diversos lugares y con muy diversas condiciones se vienen realizando (cf. [1] , [4] , [7], etc.) ponen también de manifiesto que:

- Al tratarse de poderosas herramientas de cálculo y representación gráfica, permiten variar el enfoque de los problemas, la cantidad y la cualidad de los mismos, así como abordar problemas de modelización, dando menos tiempo para la adquisición de destreza en el uso de algoritmos y disponiendo de más tiempo para la conceptualización.

- Propician la investigación y el descubrimiento

- Pueden servir para provocar la reflexión y el razonamiento matemático.

- Permiten el trabajo autónomo del estudiante.

- Facilitan el desbloqueo del estudiante en la resolución de un problema, en la medida que le permite experimentar con rapidez y seguridad.

- Su carácter interactivo provoca una retroalimentación inmediata.

- ...

Sin embargo, no hemos de ocultar un cierto peligro tecnocentrista. La conveniencia y necesidad de adaptarse a la realidad tecnológica, el uso de los últimos avances en este campo para la docencia y la aceptación de que ello conlleva cambios curriculares, no significa que ésta tecnología sea el elemento sobre el que se deban vertebrar los cambios en la enseñanza. Un aula con ordenadores *Pentium* con un Sistema de Cálculo Simbólico instalado, en cada uno de ellos, no conlleva por sí sólo una calidad superior en el proceso de enseñanza—aprendizaje. *Los manipuladores simbólicos* no van a solucionar los problemas de aprendizaje que a diario se nos presentan, no es la panacea, pero sí pueden contribuir (integrados dentro de una metodología que contemple propuestas mucho más amplias) a mejorar la calidad de la enseñanza, desde una doble vertiente: como medio para mejorar el aprendizaje y como herramienta con la que los alumnos deben familiarizarse para una adecuada formación para el futuro.

Algunos investigadores y profesores han advertido sobre peligros no desdeñables de un uso inadecuado de estos *sistemas informáticos,* entre ellos:

• Riesgo de que una actitud tecnocentrista convierta al programa en sujeto, en lugar de las matemáticas Las clases podrían llegar a ser clases de un determinado programa.

• Se confíe a la mera interacción entre alumno y ordenador el proceso de aprendizaje.

• Pérdida de destrezas básicas.

• Confianza ciega en la máquina. Se acepta cualquier solución. Creo que todos los que tenemos alguna experiencia en este terreno hemos tenido oportunidad de constatar sobradamente este riesgo.

• Incapacidad para valorar las dificultades de los problemas

• Las dificultades de aprendizaje de un programa determinado lleguen a ser un obstáculo para el aprendizaje de las matemáticas.

• Excesiva dependencia del asistente matemático

5. Dificultades para el uso de los Sistemas de Cálculo simbólico en la enseñanza. Algunas posibles soluciones

No menos desdeñables son las dificultades que algunos señalan para su uso de manera sistemática, entre ellas:

1.Las propuestas de trabajo para los estudiantes no pueden ser exclusivamente, ni principalmente, la realización de algoritmos usuales. Ello representa una dificultad adicional para los profesores: la de diseñar tareas de aprendizaje que no sean triviales ante el medio de que se dispone. Buena parte de los problemas tradicionales, del tipo *hágase tal límite, resuélvase tal integral, calcúlese la inversa de la matriz, resuelva el sistema de ecuaciones, represente tal función, etc.}* son simplemente inadecuados. ¿Qué hacer entonces? Esta situación provoca ansiedad y rechazo por parte de muchos profesores.

2. ¿Cuándo es adecuado el uso de estos asistentes matemáticos?

3. ¿Cómo se evalúa?

4.La formación de los profesores en ejercicio no siempre es la más adecuada para afrontar este nuevo medio.

5. Dificultades logísticas:
   (a) Elevado número de alumnos.

   (b) Escasez de equipos informáticos.

   (c) Las aulas de ordenadores han de atender no sólo los requerimientos de las asignaturas de Matemáticas.

   (d) Organización de la actividad docente. El profesor suele cambiar de clase y resulta complicado trasladar a cada aula el ordenador portátil y la pantalla de cristal líquido (cuando los hay). En los centros de bachillerato la situación suele ser más dura: se carece, en general, de ordenador portátil, de retroproyector de gran intesidad y de pantalla de cristal líquido, con lo que los alumnos sólo podrán acceder al uso de los ordenadores desplazándose al aula correspondiente, con un número de ellos inferior al de alumnos, presentándose además problemas de desdoblamiento de grupos. Por otra parte esta situación provoca que la posible utilización de estos asistentes matemáticos sea puntual, con lo que desaparece la posibilidad real de incorporarlos como recurso didáctico al proceso de aprendizaje.

La realidad es que en la mayoría de los centros de bachillerato el aula de informática no se usa en matemáticas (tampoco en otras disciplinas), limitándose su uso para la docencia de informática.

Incluso en la universidad, la realización de clases prácticas con estos sistemas, separadas de las clases ordinarias, resultan con frecuencia inadecuadas desde una perspectiva estrictamente didáctica. Estos programas, en la mayoría de los casos, no se utilizan sistemáticamente para introducir conceptos, quedando reducidos a su uso como potentes calculadoras.

A mi juicio muchas de las dificultades y peligros señalados son subsanables:

- Algunos, con sólo tener presente el sentido común: este tipo de "software", siendo muy importante, es un elemento más, pero las explicaciones del profesor, con y sin ordenador, los ejercicios con lápiz y papel, el uso de libros adecuados y otros muchos aspectos de una metodolgía ya tradicional son también necesarios.

- Los aspectos logísticos tienen diversas soluciones:

1. Una de ellas, la especialización de aulas por materias, de forma que en éstas dispongamos de los medios necesarios, al menos de un ordenador, un potente retroproyector y una pantalla de cristal líquido.

2. La adecuada integración, dentro del desarrollo de la asignatura, en el uso de los *manipuladores simbólicos* por parte de los alumnos es un tema que la propia evolución tecnológica está resolviendo: ya existen calculadoras que incorporan Sistemas de Cálculo Simbólico, por lo que no tardará mucho en que esta sea tan usual entre los estudiantes como lo es ahora la calculadora científica.

Sin embargo otros obstáculos serán más difíciles de superar. Mientras que los profesores se sientan abrumados por la tecnología que les desborda, ésta estará proscrita. La única solución está en el aumento de bibliografía específicamente diseñada para utilizar en el aula, haciendo uso de estos asistentes matemáticos y unos adecuados programas de formación en ejercicio para profesores.

6. A modo de epílogo

En el número del pasado mes de Junio de la revista *Suma* el profesor Claudi Alsina, presidente del Comité Internacional de Programas de este congreso, publicaba un artículo titulado *Unas reflexiones sobre el ICME--8,* en el que formula algunos interrogantes educativos, entre ellos:

* *¿Cómo podría mejorarse la comunicación en clase, favorecer la motivación y aumentar las actitudes positivas?*
* *¿Qué debe cambiarse de los curricula de matemáticas, cómo hacerlo y por qué hacerlo?*
* *¿Qué tratamiento debe darse a la diversidad?, ... , ¿qué deberíamos ofrecer a los jóvenes con talento?, ¿qué ayuda podemos dar a las personas con dificultades de aprendizaje?*

* *¿Cómo deberían influir las posibilidades tecnológicas en nuestra labor?*

* ***¿Qué nuevas posibilidades ofrece la enseñanza del Cálculo a la luz de las nuevas tecnologías?***

* *¿Deberíamos preocuparnos más por la modelización y matematización de la realidad?*

* *¿El laboratorio de matemáticas es imprescindible?*

• *¿Qué ventajas introducen calculadoras, ordenadores y todas las nuevas tecnologías?*

No cometeré la petulancia de pretender que he contestado a estas ni a otras preguntas sustanciales para la enseñanza de las matemáticas en los años que vivimos, pero unas veces abiertamente y otras de forma implícita hemos tocado, aunque sólo sea tangencialmente, algunos caminos que podrían contribuir, con otros muchos, a dar respuesta a aquellas.

Creo que la penetración de los Sistemas de Cálculo Simbólico es imparable, tenerlos presente en el proceso educativo simplemente una obligación y sacarle el mayor provecho didáctico posible un acto de inteligencia.

Finalmente espero que si al menos no les he contagiado de mi fe en el futuro, al menos no les haya aburrido.

Bibliografía

[1] F. BENÍTEZ, J. M. DÍAZ Y J. PÉREZ (1996). "Experiencia de Laboratorio de Matemáticas en la Universidad de Cádiz". *Matemáticas en Escuelas Técnicas,* 47-58. Servicio de publicaciones de la Univ. de Huelva.
[2] F. BENÍTEZ, J. M. DÍAZ Y J. PÉREZ (1996). *Laboratorio de matemáticas. Prácticas con* **Mathematica.** Departamento de Matemáticas. Universidad de Cádiz.
[3] M. BERROCOSO; M. CATALÁN (1990). "Estimación de la influencia de los armónicos del potencial gravitatorio terrestre en las perturbaciones de las órbitas de los satélites del sistema TRANSIT para el modelo de Tierra GIM 9-10". *Boletín del Real Instituto y Observatorio de la Armada en San Fernando.* **2/90**
[4] A. GARCÍA (1993). "Enseñanza experimental de las Matemáticas". *Epsilon,* 26, 81--92.
[5] A. GARCÍA; A. MARTÍNEZ Y R. MIÑANO (1995). *Nuevas tecnologías y enseñanza de las matemáticas,* Ed. Síntesis, Madrid.
[6] M.K. HEID (1988). "Resequencing Skills and Concepts in Applied Calculus". *Journal of Research in Mathematics Education,* 19(1), 3-25.
[7] J. L. LLORENS (1993). "Un curso de matemáticas con Derive". Epsilon. **26,** 61-80.
[8] J.L. LLORENS (1995) "Una lección de matemáticas con ordenador".*Epsilon.* **31-31,** 81--88.

[9]   J. L. LLORENS (1996). "Aplicación del modelo de Van Hiele al concepto de aproximación local". *Suma,* 13-24.

[10] J. R. PALMITER (1991) "Effects of Computer Algebra Systems on Concepts and Skill Acquisition in Calculus". *Journal for Research in Mathematics Education, 22(2),* 151-156.

[11] J. PÉREZ (1991). "Recursos en el aula de matemáticas". *Actas de las V Jornadas Andaluzas de Educación Matemática* 9-40. Granada.

[12] A. PÉREZ (1994). "Interrogantes en la enseñanza de las matemáticas". *Anais II CIBEM* Blumenau.

[13] S. REPO (1994). "Understanding and Reflective Abstraction: Learning the Concept of Derivative in the Computer enviroment". *DERIVE in Education. Oportunities and Strategies.* (Heugl—Kutzler eds.). Chartwell—Bratt. Kent.

[14] VARIOS (1995). *Actas de las Jornadas sobre enseñanza de matemáticas con Derive.* Santander.

PROGRAMAS DE DOCTORADO E INVESTIGACIÓN ACADÉMICA: EDUCACIÓN MATEMÁTICA EN LA UNIVERSIDAD ESPAÑOLA

Prof. Dr. L. Rico
Departamento de Didáctica de la Matemática
Universidad de Granada

Introducción

Dentro de las Ciencias de la Educación, la Didáctica de la Matemática ha experimentado en los últimos 50 años un desarrollo sostenido tanto en extensión como en profundidad. Este desarrollo es efecto y causa, simultáneamente, de las importantes funciones que desempeña el conocimiento matemático en la sociedad y cultura contemporáneas. La importancia de las matemáticas en los currícula de la enseñanza obligatoria ha provocado, recientemente, una amplia reflexión teórica y un gran esfuerzo de implementación práctica, sostenidos por un cuerpo de investigación en Educación Matemática amplio y sistemático (Romberg, 1992; Popkewitz, 1994).

Los especialistas coinciden en que las características distintivas más apreciables del conocimiento matemático son su carácter formativo y su utilidad práctica, tanto al considerar la dimensión individual como la social (Romberg, 1991; Niss, 1996). La enseñanza de las matemáticas afecta a millones de jóvenes y adolescentes; como campo de actuación profesional son cientos de miles los profesores y educadores que trabajan sobre la enseñanza y el aprendizaje de las matemáticas (OCDE, 1995).

El carácter eminentemente social y cultural de la enseñanza de las matemáticas, junto con la complejidad y dificultades detectadas en el aprendizaje de estas disciplinas, han contribuido a que la preocupación por el estudio de los procesos de comunicación, transmisión y comprensión de las matemáticas hayan interesado a una amplia comunidad científica, que viene realizando desde hace más de un siglo investigación cualificada en este campo (Kilpatrick, 1992).

La investigación, junto con la innovación curricular y la formación del profesorado, concentran la mayor parte de los esfuerzos de la comunidad de educadores matemáticos (Rico y Sierra, 1991).

El despegue de la investigación en Educación Matemática en los últimos años se ha sostenido sobre unas determinadas claves; entre ellas destacan su incorporación a la universidad (Long, Meltzer y Hilton, 1970), el control y la validación académica de sus resultados, el sostenimiento de revistas especializadas con alto nivel de rigor y exigencia científica, la celebración de encuentros y debates periódicos entre especialistas, la delimitación y puesta en práctica de agendas de investigación y el estímulo a los grupos y líneas de investigación en Educación Matemática llevado a cabo por organismos y agencias de promoción de la investigación (Kilpatrick, Rico y Sierra, 1994).

Dentro de este marco general la investigación española en Educación Matemática ha tenido su propio desarrollo en los últimos 25 años.

Antecedentes: Investigación española en los 70

Durante la década de los 70 en España se implanta la Ley General de Educación. Hay dos datos principales, de interés para la Investigación en Educación Matemática:
* una nueva organización del sistema educativo, que desarrolla un currículo basado en las Matemáticas Modernas para todos los niveles de la educación obligatoria (6-14 años) y post-obligatoria (15-18);
* la creación en cada una de las universidades de los Institutos de Ciencias de la Educación (I.C.E.), mediante los que se incorporan la investigación educativa y la formación del profesorado a las competencias universitarias.

Como consecuencia derivada de estas reformas se plantea la necesidad de dar respuesta fundada a los problemas de enseñanza detectados en el Sistema Educativo y justificar la adecuación de los nuevos programas a las necesidades formativas de los escolares. Son varias las iniciativas que surgen en estos años para abordar estos problemas entre las que, por su orientación investigadora, destacamos dos:
* el Equipo de Investigación Granada-Mats, que se constituye en 1971, y
* los grupos de innovación Grupo Cero y Grup Zero, cuyos trabajos se inician en 1975.

Una descripción detallada de la actividad investigadora de estos grupos puede verse en Rico y Sierra (1997).

En el marco de las reformas a que da lugar la Ley General de Educación aparece la disciplina *Didáctica de la Matemática* por primera vez en la Universidad española. Esto ocurre en los nuevos planes de estudio para la formación inicial de los Profesores de Educación General Básica (1971), en primer lugar, y, posteriormente, en la Licenciatura de Matemáticas de algunas universidades (1975). En este contexto hay grupos específicos de investigadores en algunas universidades que comienzan a desarrollar trabajos de investigación en Didáctica de la Matemática; también se logra la valoración académica de algunos de los estudios realizados en este campo. Esto sucede en la Universidad de Granada donde en el año 75, con carácter pionero, se presentan dos tesinas de licenciatura en Didáctica de la Matemática.

Sin embargo, las oportunidades y condiciones institucionales en esta época son restringidas y limitadas, dificultando un desarrollo adecuado de la investigación en Educación Matemática.

La Ley de Reforma Universitaria

En 1984 se promulga la Ley de Reforma Universitaria (L.R.U.). A partir de la nueva estructura universitaria derivada de esta Ley se diversificaron las disciplinas tradicionales en un nuevo catálogo de Areas de Conocimiento, adaptado a un desarrollo actualizado de las ciencias.

La Ley estableció las Areas de conocimiento "como aquellos campos del saber caracterizados por la homogeneidad de su objeto de conocimiento, una común tradición histórica y la existencia de comunidades investigadoras nacionales o internacionales". En este marco surge el *Area de Conocimiento Didáctica de la Matemática* como uno de los campos del conocimiento mediante los que se estructura la Universidad, reconociendo el esfuerzo realizado por la comunidad de educadores matemáticos de nuestro país en años anteriores.

La constitución de Departamentos universitarios en los que está integrada el Area de Didáctica de la Matemática y, en especial, los Departamentos de Didáctica de la Matemática han supuesto un paso importante para la Educación Matemática en España, disponiéndose de nuevos medios personales y materiales y potenciándose la docencia e investigación en el Area.

Pero el punto de partida no resultó fácil; las necesidades y carencias desbordaban ampliamente los medios disponibles y el reto que se asumía parecía estar fuera de cualquier posibilidad de realización. Al comenzar su andadura institucional el área de Didáctica de la Matemática tiene ante sí grandes retos; uno de los más destacados es la investigación académica y la validación de sus resultados mediante tesis doctorales.

Las prioridades de la investigación en Educación Matemática se centran durante estos años, a nivel internacional, en la delimitación, explicitación y enunciado de los principales problemas sobre los que debe trabajar esta investigación (Shumway, 1980; Freudenthal,1981; Wheeler, 1984) y en la conexión necesaria de los resultados de las investigaciones con la práctica escolar (Bell, Low & Kilpatrick 1985). Además, cada comunidad científica nacional tiene que adaptar este programa a las propias condiciones locales, definir sus prioridades, adaptar los medios a los fines e iniciar una propuesta rigurosa de investigación académica. En este contexto se dan los primeros pasos para poner en marcha los programa de Doctorado en Didáctica de la Matemática.

Programas de Doctorado

La nueva ley universitaria establecía que "corresponde a los Departamentos la articulación y coordinación de las enseñanzas y de las actividades investigadoras de las Universidades." Uno de los logros mas importantes derivados de la nueva regulación universitaria ha sido la organización y desarrollo de Programas de Doctorado específicos en Didáctica de la Matemática, como ha ocurrido en la Universidad Autónoma de Barcelona, Universidad de Valencia y Universidad de Granada; posteriormente se han incorporado las universidades de Sevilla y Extremadura.

La importancia de los Programas de Doctorado se resalta en el Real Decreto que regula el Tercer Ciclo de Estudios Universitarios, donde leemos:
"El Tercer Ciclo, como demuestra la experiencia comparada, constituye condición esencial para el progreso científico y, por ello, para el progreso social y económico de una comunidad por cuanto de la profundidad de sus contenidos y la seriedad en su planteamiento depende la formación de los investigadores."

A estos efectos la Ley de Reforma Universitaria se plantea cuatro grandes objetivos en el campo de los estudios de postgrado:
 * Disponer de un marco adecuado para la consecución y transmisión de los avances científicos.

* Formar a los nuevos investigadores y preparar equipos de investigación que puedan afrontar con éxito el reto que suponen las nuevas ciencias, técnicas y metodologías.

* Impulsar la formación de nuevo profesorado.

* Perfeccionar el desarrollo profesional, científico y artístico de los titulados superiores.

Queda claro que el desarrollo de un Area de Conocimiento pasa por el mantenimiento continuado de un Programa de Tercer Ciclo mediante el que se realicen y logren los anteriores objetivos. En este contexto, las Universidades de Granada, Valencia y Autónoma de Barcelona iniciaron durante el curso 88-89, el Programa de Doctorado en Didáctica de la Matemática, que se ha continuado a lo largo de estos años.

Programa de Doctorado en la Universidad de Granada

El Departamento de Didáctica de la Matemática de la Universidad de Granada viene ofreciendo un Programa de Doctorado bianual para la formación de investigadores. Hasta el momento se han desarrollado 4 bienios y va a comenzar un nuevo programa en el próximo bienio 96-98. Según la normativa establecida los Programas de Doctorado deben comprender, con carácter general:

a) Cursos o Seminarios relacionados con la metodología y formación en técnicas de investigación.

b) Cursos o Seminarios sobre los contenidos fundamentales de los campos científico, técnico o artístico a los que esté dedicado el Programa de Doctorado correspondiente.

c) Cursos o Seminarios relacionados con campos afines al del Programa y que sean de interés para el proyecto de tésis doctoral del doctorando.

Siguiendo estas directrices generales, el Programa de Doctorado de Didáctica de la Matemática presenta la siguiente organización de materias para el bienio 96-98:

Curso 96-97
Investigación en Educación Matemática: Avances Metodológicos.
Teoría de la Educación Matemática.
Diseño, Desarrollo y Evaluación del Currículo de Matemáticas.
Seminario de Didáctica de la Matemática I.
Epistemología de la Probabilidad y la Combinatoria.
Análisis de Datos I.
Pensamiento Numérico.

Modelos para Investigación en Etnomatemática, Formación de Profesores y Curricular I.

Curso 97-98:
Seminario de Didáctica de la Matemática II.
Modelos para Investigación Etnomatemática, Formación de Profesores y Curricular II.
Introducción al Análisis de Datos Multivariantes.
Diseño de Investigaciones Educativas.
Investigación en Resolución de Problemas.
Pensamiento Numérico Avanzado.
Semiometría y Ecología de los Objetos Matemáticos.
Creencias y Concepciones de los Profesores, Investigación en Formación de Profesores.
Evaluación en el Aula de Matemáticas.
Epistemología y Didáctica de la Inferencia Estadística.
Estos 18 cursos totalizan una oferta de 52 créditos de formación, y están impartidos por 11 profesores.

Regulación del Programa de Doctorado

El alumno inscrito en los estudios de doctorado deberá cursar y aprobar en el plazo de dos años, prorrogables a tres, un total de 32 créditos (320 horas) mediante los cursos y seminarios incluidos en el programa, así como con créditos obtenidos por la realización de un trabajo de investigación obligatorio, hasta un máximo de 9 créditos. Se exige un mínimo de 16 créditos en materias del área de conocimiento o fundamentales; el resto puede cursarse con asignaturas afines.

El trabajo de investigación consiste en una primera aproximación a la Tesis. El Departamento entiende que la mejor forma de aprender a investigar consiste en realizar un trabajo de investigación, para cuyo fin se estimula a los alumnos a que presenten una Memoria de Tercer Ciclo con los resultados obtenidos en este trabajo. Los alumnos de doctorado han de presentar en el Departamento, antes de terminar el Programa, un proyecto de tesis doctoral avalado por el que vaya a ser su director o directores. La tesis deberá terminarse en el plazo de cinco años desde la fecha de inicio de los estudios, ampliables en otros dos años a juicio de la Comisión de Doctorado(Rico, Batanero y Diaz, 1994). Hasta el momento son 16 las tesis doctorales, 2 tesinas y 12 trabajos de investigación los leidos en el programa de Doctorado de Didáctica de la Matemática de la Universidad de Granada.

Desarrollo de la Investigación

A los cuatro objetivos generales señalados por la ley relativos a la investigación, antes mencionados, el Area de Didáctica de la Matemática ha añadido los siguientes:

* Establecer y mantener un espacio de crítica, debate y comunicación sobre el estado actual y desarrollo reciente de la investigación en el Area de Didáctica de la Matemática, así como de sus avances teóricos y metodológicos.

* Impulsar la delimitación de problemas relevantes en la enseñanza y aprendizaje de las matemáticas para su estudio sistemático, que permita obtener información significativa para su diagnóstico y tratamiento y dé lugar a materiales y recursos adecuados para el aula de matemáticas.

* Constituir grupos de investigación estables, que trabajen metódica y continuadamente sobre líneas específicas de investigación en Didáctica de la Matemática, que sirvan de referencia para los especialistas y estén conectados con la comunidad investigadora internacional.

* Producir investigación propia cualificada, que suponga una aportación específica y original a las cuestiones de indagación prioritarias en el Area de Conocimiento, y presentar regularmente los resultados obtenidos en los foros y medios de comunicación de la comunidad de investigadores de Didáctica de la Matemática.

El logro principal de los Programas de Doctorado en Didáctica de la Matemática no se limita a las tesis doctorales sino que avanza hacia la constitución de grupos estables de investigación y la consolidación de una comunidad de investigadores en Educación Matemática en la Universidad Española. Varios son los datos que avalan esta consideración.

Los profesores del Area de Didáctica de la Matemática se han presentado a las evaluaciones de la actividad investigadora realizadas por el Ministerio de Educación; hay un grupo significativo de estos profesores con tramos evaluados positivamente. En el Plan Nacional de Formación de Personal Investigador se han concedido becas para trabajar en Didáctica de la Matemática.

En las convocatorias anuales para la Promoción General del Conocimiento, convocados por la Dirección General de Investigación Científica y Técnica (DGICYT) se han presentado y aprobado proyectos de grupos de investigadores de Didáctica de la Matemática; igualmente en el Plan Nacional de Investigación Educativa de la Dirección General de Renovación Pedagógica, así como en las convocatorias del Plan Andaluz de Investigación de la Consejería de Educación y Ciencia de la Junta de Andalucia y de otras Comunidades Autónomas.

En los departamentos de Didáctica de la Matemática hay una organización mediante líneas de investigación. Así ocurre en la Universidad de Granada donde el Departamento está estructurado según cinco líneas, con el fin de organizar su actividad investigadora. Estas líneas son:

Didáctica de la Matemática: Pensamiento Numérico

Didáctica de la Probabilidad y de la Estadística

Diseño, Desarrollo y Evaluación del Currículo de Matemáticas

Formación del Profesorado de Matemáticas

Teoría y Métodos de Investigación en Educación Matemática

Cada uno de estos grupos está teniendo un desarrollo considerable, que permite ubicar las investigaciones de los proyectos y tesis doctorales en un marco más general y coordinado, que da continuidad y profundidad a estos estudios especializados.

Las relaciones internacionales son también un rango distintivo de la situación actual. A las invitaciones individuales para impartir cursos y conferencias, hay que añadir que los Departamentos de Didáctica de la Matemática de las Universidades Autónoma de Barcelona, Valencia y Granada tienen firmados convenios entre sí y con Centros de Investigación en Educación Matemática y Departamentos Universitarios de otros países, principalmente de la Comunidad Europea y de Latinoamerica. Estos departamentos han participado en proyectos de la Unión Europea, tales como el Erasmus, Tempus, Sócrates y Alfa, coordinando y formando parte de redes de investigadores en Educación Matemática. La contribución a la formación inicial de investigadores latinoamericanos en Educación Matemática de estos tres centros es sistemática y productiva.

También merece mención la incorporación de investigadores españoles a grupos internacionales (PME, CIEAEM, ICOTS, ICMI-Studies, etc.) y la participación internacional destacada en comités de evaluación, comités científicos y editoriales, paneles de expertos, conferencias, ponencias invitadas, grupos de investigación, redacción de libros, informes de investigación y artículos.

Sociedad Española de Investigación en Educación Matemática

En el marco descrito, las relaciones entre los investigadores españoles en Educación Matemática han ido creciendo y centrándose en los trabajos y tareas de investigación. Todos los debates y actividades realizados han impulsado el sentimiento y han desarrollado la percepción de formar parte de una misma comunidad de investigadores.

Se delimita así un grupo profesionalizado en investigación sobre Educación Matemática, reconocible por sus trabajos académicos, por la pertenencia a grupos internacionales, y por su producción sistemática de trabajos de investigación en este campo, sometidos a la crítica y control de la comunidad.

Este grupo, no muy extenso, necesita su propio espacio de encuentro, debate y reflexión. Surge de este modo la necesidad de una sociedad formalmente establecida, en la que se incardinen y organicen los investigadores profesionales en educación matemática.

La Sociedad Española de Investigación en Educación Matemática se constituye en marzo de 1996. Entre sus principales objetivos están:

* Promover el impulso a la Educación Matemática en los organismos e instituciones relacionados con la investigación. Promover la participación en las convocatorias de ayudas a la investigación, institucionales y privadas.

* Contribuir y participar en el desarrollo, evaluación y aplicación de investigaciones en Didáctica de la Matemática.

* Contribuir a la presentación de resultados de investigación en los foros, encuentros y revistas de Educación Matemática.

* Mantener contactos y promover la colaboración con grupos de investigación en Educación Matemática.

* Favorecer activamente la cooperación e intercambio entre investigación y docencia en todos los niveles educativos.

* Transmitir y divulgar institucionalmente la actividad de la Sociedad.

La Sociedad ha iniciado el debate sobre los campos de investigación prioritarios en Educación Matemática para facilitar la constitución de grupos de trabajo estables en la comunidad.

Tras una revisión y análisis de los tópicos y campos de investigación en los que los investigadores españoles han venido desarrollando sus trabajos, se optó por constituir los siguientes grupos:

1 Didáctica del Análisis. Pensamiento Matemático Avanzado.
2 Aprendizaje de la Geometría y Nuevas Tecnologías
3 Didáctica de la Estadística, Probabilidad y Combinatoria.
4 Pensamiento Numérico y Algebraico.
5 Formación de Profesores de Matemáticas.
6 Metodología de Investigación en Didáctica de la Matemática.

Perspectivas de futuro

Hemos hecho una descripción de los cambios e innovaciones ocurridos en España en el campo de la Investigación en Educación Matemática durante los últimos 25 años, destacando el desarrollo acelerado de los 10 últimos años. Ninguno de estos cambios hubiera tenido lugar con el vigor y profundidad con que se han presentado si no se hubiese producido una evolución en la sociedad española y, en particular, en su sistema educativo que han dado lugar a unas condiciones idóneas para el desarrollo de la investigación.

Entre tales cambios hay que destacar, principalmente, el gran desarrollo cultural y social ocurrido en España y destacar la renovación económica, cultural, política y educativa realizada en estos últimos 25 años.

Para la estabilidad de la comunidad de investigadores en Educación Matemática ha sido determinante que, previamente, se haya consolidado una fuerte comunidad de investigadores en las diferentes disciplinas matemáticas. El hecho de que se investigue en Matemáticas en la Universidad española da sentido a los problemas de su enseñanza y aprendizaje, debido a las dificultades de comunicación y transmisión que se plantean. También es determinante la consolidación de diferentes comunidades de investigadores en las diversas disciplinas que denominamos Ciencias de la Educación, ya que proporcionan marcos de referencia teóricos y metodológicos adecuados y sirven de crítica y contraste a las investigaciones realizadas en Educación Matemática.

Igualmente tiene un efecto determinante para esta investigación la constitución de las Sociedades de Educadores o Profesores de Matemáticas. Estas sociedades han realizado una actividad vigorosa con aportaciones al diseño y desarrollo del curriculo de las matemáticas escolares asi como a la formación inicial y permanente del profesorado. La contribución de las Sociedades de Profesores al desarrollo de la Educación Matemática y, en especial, a la reflexión sobre las conexiones entre teoría y práctica ha sido destacable en España; gran parte del trabajo realizado en investigación se ha planteado y discutido en los encuentros y jornadas organizados por las Sociedades y se ha difundido mediante las actas, revistas y otras publicaciones editadas por estas Sociedades.

La especificidad de los problemas de la Investigación en Educación Matemática desde una perspectiva profesional y académica no deben hacernos olvidar el compromiso y la ineludible conexión con la práctica profesional del educador matemático. Los profesores de matemáticas tampoco pueden contemplar al investigador como ajeno a su trabajo; antes bien, deben exigirle rigor en sus planteamientos, claridad en sus realizaciones y practicidad en sus resultados.

Los investigadores en educación matemática forman parte, por derecho propio, de la comunidad de educadores matemáticos, pero tienen su campo profesional específico al que deben atender con prioridad. Esta situación obliga a reflexionar sobre los problemas comunes, que deben abordarse conjuntamente. La coordinación sistemática entre estos dos colectivos permitirá alcanzar unas señas de identidad bien fundadas y consolidar ambas comunidades.

Todos los educadores matemáticos españoles comparten la misma finalidad: mejorar la calidad de la enseñanza y aprendizaje de las Matemáticas en España y, cada uno, debe asumir este objetivo en el ámbito de sus competencias profesionales. Los investigadores tienen un campo profesional bien delimitado que no pueden eludir. Por razones éticas, cívicas y profesionales han de llevar a cabo el inaplazable desarrollo de la investigación española en Educación Matemática. Se trata de un deber prioritario cuya realización les compete y del que no pueden sustraerse; el éxito o fracaso en esta tarea dará en el futuro la dimensión auténtica de su contribución a la Educación Matemática en España.

Referencias

Bell, A.; Low, B.& Kilpatrick, J. (1985) Theory, Research and *Practice in Mathematical Education.* Nottingham: University of Nottigham.

Freudenthal H. (1981) Major problems of Mathematics Education *Educational Studies in Mathematics.* Vol. 12, nº 2.

Kilpatrick, J. (1992) History of Research in Mathematics Education, En D. Grouws (edt.) *Handbook of Research on Mathematics Teaching and Learning.* New York: Macmillan.

Kilpatrick, J., Rico, L. y Sierra, M. (1994) *Educación Matemática e Investigación.* Madrid: Síntesis.

Lacasta, E.y Rico, L. (1996) *Sociedad Española de Investigación en Educación Matemática Boletin Informativo,* nº 0. Granada.

Long, R; Meltzer, N. & Hilton, P. (1970) Research in Mathematics Education. *Educational Studies in Mathematics* Vol. 2

Niss, M. (1996) ¿Por qué enseñamos matemáticas en la escuela? En L. Puig y J. Calderón (edts.) *Investigación y Didáctica de las Matemáticas.* Madrid: Ministerio de Educación y Ciencia.

OCDE (1995) *Análisis del panorama Educativo. Los indicadores de la OCDE.* Madrid: Ediciones Mundi- Prensa.

Popkewitz, T. (1994) *Sociología Política de las Reformas Educativas,* Madrid: Morata.

Rico, L.; Batanero, C y Diaz, J. (1994) El Programa de Doctorado de Didáctica de la Matemática de la Universidad de Granada.*UNO Revista de Didáctica de las Matemáticas* nº 2, 133-144 .

Rico, L. y Sierra, M. (1991) La Comunidad de Educadores Matemáticos En A. Gutiérrez (edt.) *Area de Conocimiento: Didáctica de la Matemática.* Madrid: Síntesis

Rico, L. y Sierra, M. (1997) Antecedentes del Currículo de Matemáticas. En L. Rico (edt.) *Bases Teóricas del Currículo de Matemáticas en España.* Madrid: Síntesis.

Romberg, T. (1991) Características problemáticas del Currículo Escolar de Matemáticas. *Revista de Educación* nº 294.

Romberg, T. (1992) Perspectives on Schoolarship and Research Methods, En D. Grouws *Handbook of Research on Mathematics Teaching and Learning.* New York: Macmillan.

Shumway R. (1980) *Research in Mathematics Education.* Reston VA: National Council of Teachers of Mathematics.

Wheeler D. (Ed.) (1984) Research Problems in Mathematics Education *For the Learning of Mathematics.* Vol 4.

SEMANTIC STRUCTURES OF WORD PROBLEMS - MEDIATORS BETWEEN MATHEMATICAL STRUCTURES AND COGNITIVE STRUCTURES?

S. Schmidt, Universität zu Köln (Germany)
- Shortened Version -

(1) Introduction

Referring to a considerable body of research on solving word problems in addition and subtraction as well as in multiplication and division by elementary school students (cf.,e.g., Carpenter, Moser & Romberg (1982); Hiebert & Behr (1988)), taking into account epistemological reflections (Ernest (1994), v. Glasersfeld (1995)) and results of neural science (Roth (1995), Kandel et al. (1995)) and - finally - considering the language game perspective of the late Wittgenstein (Wittgenstein (1953)) we discuss this question: What ought to be the role of semantic structures of word problems in mathematics education?

Discussing this question mathematics education is considered in a threefold meaning: as a scientific discipline, as an environment for teacher training, as the background for the activities of the teachers in the mathematics classroom of the elementary school.

(2) Semantic Structures of Multiplicative Word Problems in the elementary School: A Survey of Different Theoretical Frameworks

Concerning semantic structures of simple word problems involving multiplication - and division - in the elementary school different proposals have been made for classifications. Already a global survey of the several classifications of semantic structures of multiplicative word problems reveals: The underlying categorical accentuations are different and there do not exist one-to-one correspondences.

• Vergnaud (1983, (1988)): isomorphism of measures - product of measures - multiple proportion.

• Bell et al. (1989): Multiple groups (repeated addition - sets) - repeated measure (repeated addition - measures) - rate - change of size (same units [enlargement], different units) - mixture (same units, different units).

- Schwartz (1988) (I: intensive quantities; E: extensive quantities): multiplication of I x E = E' - multiplication of E x E' = E" - multiplication of I x I' = I".

- Nesher (1988): mapping rule - multiplicative comparison - Cartesian product.

- Mulligan (1992): repeated addition (types (a),(b),(c)) - rate - factor - array - Cartesian product.

- Schmidt & Weiser (1995): forming the n-th multiple: part-whole structure, iteration structure, multiplicative change, multiplicative comparison, proportion - combinatorial multiplication - composition of operators - multiplication by formula: product structure, quotient structure.

Nesher (1988) presents this example as a paradigmatic one for a "problem describing a 'mapping rule' ":

There are 5 shelves of books in Dan's room. Dan puts 8 books on each shelf.
How many books are there in his room?

According to Schwartz (1988) this example has to classified to I x E = E x I = E': 5 shelves and 40 books interpreted as the extensive quantities E and E', respectively, and 8 books/shelf as an intensive quantity.

Referring to the system of Vergnaud (1983) two interpretations of the category "isomorphism of measures" are possible: using the multiplier 5 as a scalar operator or using it as a function operator.

According to Bell et al (1989) "multiple group" is the appropriate category; Mulligan would classify it to "repeated addition, type (a).

According to Schmidt & Weiser (1995) two interpretations of the category "forming the n-th multiple" are possible depending whether the situation is interpreted as a static one (part-whole structure) or as a dynamic one (iteration structure).

Comparing this example just considered and the following one from Schmidt & Weiser (1995):

Mr. Brown fills the tank of his car with 17 liters of gas. Mr. Miller fills his with 3 times as much. How much gas does Mr. Miller take?

both have to be classified to the same category according to the systems of Vergnaud (1983), namely "isomorphism of measures", and of Schwartz (1988), namely "I x E = E' " [I = 3 I/I, E = 17 I, E' = 3 I/I x 17 I = 3 x 17 I], but to different categories according to the systems of Nesher (1988), namely "mapping rule" or "compare problems", respectively, Bell et al. (1989), namely "multiple groups" or "mixture (same units)", respectively, Mulligan (1992), namely "repeated addition", perhaps "array" or "factor", respectively, Schmidt & Weiser (1995), namely "part-whole structure" or "multplicative comparison", respectively.

Already this short consideration of examples illustrates this: Sometimes one system appears to differentiate more refined, sometimes another one does so.

Evidently the systems of semantic structures under discussion differ from one another: They "tell", in fact, "different stories". And considering empirical results we get to know that not any system of semantic structures reveals the "whole story". How shall we deal with this situation?

Referring to the threefold meaning of "mathematics education" mentioned above we get three questions:

- Shall this situation of theorizing be considered as a deficit situation which has to be overcome towards a unified theory? [*mathematics education question*]
- What appears to be reasonable or recommendable for us when teaching student teachers or when discussing with them? [*teacher question*]
- Which help can a teacher get from research and different theoretical frameworks on semantic structures (of simple word problems)? [*classroom question*]

(3) Semantic Structures - Results of Constructions or Mappings? Or: The Convergence of Epistemological Reflections and Research in Neural Science (on Perceptions and Knowledge)

Nesher (1988) states, that

"it is generally agreed that the main source of difficulty for the learner lies in the transition from the problem given in natural language into its presentation in mathematical language" (Nesher, 1988, p. 19).

For our purpose it is appropriate to transform this statement into this diagram.

natural language: *mathematical language:*

word problem - e.g.:   arithmetical problem - e.g.:

There are 5 shelves of books   [according to Bell et al.,1989]
in Dan's room.
Dan puts 8 books on each shelf.   8   × 5   =
How many books are there in his room? [books]   [books]

↓		student /learner	↑
↓		or her/his	
	→	cognitive structure	↑
	→	*transition*	→

Mr. Brown fills the tank of his car   [according to Schwartz, 1988]
with 17 liters of gas.
Mr. Miller fills his with 3 times as much. 3   × 17   =
How much gas does Mr. Miller take?   [l/l] [l]   [l]

↓		student /learner	↑
↓		or her/his	
		cognitive structure	↑
	→	*transition*	→

One may be inclined to interpret this situation under discussion like this:

- There is something outside the cognitive structure of the student, namely the word problem considered as a set of syntactically correct sentences and - mostly - a concluding question in written form or orally uttered.

And this word problem in natural language is bearing a certain structure - a semantic structure.
- The student has to *extract* the meaning of the word problem, i.e., she/he has to *extraxt* the semantic structure .
- This semantic structure shall help her/him to find and to utter a presentation of this structure in mathematical terms - thus finding a transition from natural language into mathematical language.

Where are the structures?
- Are the semantic structures - 'really'- outside the cognitive

structures of the students and, thus, have to be transferred into the cognitive structures of them?
- And what about the arithmetical structures - where have they to be located?
- Which component can be considered as a mediator between the others - or:
- Must we - finally - take an epistemologically different position?

In the history of epistemology the following questions have been discussed since the time of pre-Socratic philosophy of ancient Greece:

- Is it possible to get objective empirical knowledge?
- Considering this to be the case: How can we get such objective empirical knowledge?

For reasons of brevity we confine to a simple 'epistemological coordinate system' making explicitly only the difference *between* realism and *idealism* that dominated epistemology since the 17th century. Distinguishing between ontological and epistemological realism or idealism, respectively, we already get a certain differentiation.

Thesis of *ontological realism:*
There is a reality existing - and structured - distinctly from human beings experiencing, interpreting or recognizing it.

Thesis of *epistemological realism:*
It is possible to get objective knowledge - i.e., to get knowledge on the independently existing reality. There may be difficulties or constraints to get such knowledge but - at least - in parts we can get knowledge from reality how it actually is.

Thesis of *ontological idealism:*
Reality only consists of human subjects and their ideas:
esse est percipi vel percipere (to be is to be perceived or to perceive).

Thesis of *epistemological idealism:*
Only "phainomena" are objects of our experience.
Phainomena are ideas (Descartes, Locke, Berkeley), sensations, or phenomenons (Kant); phainomena are mental inner objects of human beings - not 'external objects'.

The epistemological realism presupposes an ontological realism. An ontological idealism presupposes an epistemological idealism. Thus an epistemological realism is not compatible with an ontological idealism. But an ontological realism does not imply an epistemological realism: I. Kant (1724-1804) represents a famous combination of ontological realism and epistemological idealism: The "noumena" ("Dinge an sich") cannot be recognized, only their "phainomena" ("Erscheinungen") can be recognized and are processed by the fundamental forms of intuition ("reine Anschauungsformen") of space and time and the categories of reason ("Kategorien", "reine Verstandesbegriffe") - quantity, quality, relationship, modality.

	Epistemological	
	realism	idealism
realism	+	+ (!)
Ontological		
idealism	-	+

Mapping theories of epistemology consider mental objects and their attributes as models of 'real' - external - objects and their 'real' attributes. What would such a 'mapping perspective' mean for our situation under discussion? The interpretation sketched above can be regarded as determined by the mapping perspective: The student has to extract 'the' meaning from the word problem by mapping the semantic structure into her / his own cognitive structure. Then she / he has to map it from her / his cognitive structure into a presentation in mathematical language. Combining an ontological realism with an epistemological idealism must not necessarily lead to a mapping theory - as, e.g., the "Critique of Pure Reason" (1781, 1787) of I. Kant shows. Without discussing the solutions of this combination of ontological realism with an epistemological idealism in the area of philosophy we argue that a convergence is emerging between this philosophical orientation, on the one side, and research in neural science, on the other one.

Regarding the capacity of stimulating and the capacity of interpreting within the human visual system and the neutrality of the neural codes I want to make this plausible.

Considering the different stages of processing of our human visual perception - starting with the photoreceptors and the retina and going on to the primary, the secondary, and the tertiary visual areas of the cerebral cortex there are growing numbers of cells and neurons processing the signals received from rather a small number of ganglion cells in the retina: For one ganglion cell in the retina our human visual system has got 100

000 central neurons. This rate is even more impressive for the auditory system: One hair cell - in the inner ear - corresponds to 16 000 000 central neurons. Not all 200 billion neurons of the brain are active simultaneously: About 100 000 to some millions are active simultaneously, but the patterns of active neurons are perpetually changing. Results of brain research show that objects are not represented by a sole detector cell - the famous "grandma neuron" does not exist nor exists - let us say - a single neuron for detecting the digit "1": There is no single neuron or a set of neurons that can represent a concrete object in all its details and all its different meanings. (For details of this part of scientific discussion cf. Roth (1995, chap. 7,8) or Kandel et al. (1995, Chap. 18,21-25).)

What is important, too, is the neutrality of the neural codes. The different physical and chemical stimulations of our sensory apparatus have to get changed into the 'language' of the brain, i.e., into neuroelectric and neurochemical signals. And those signals are transmitted to the ganglion cells and the neurons in the cerebral cortex and processed there. Considering such neuroelectric or neurochemical signals without any further informations it is not possible to determine whether they have been caused visually or acoustically, chemically or mecanically: Only when knowing in which area of the brain the active neurons are located we can conclude, e.g., that the visual system is activated.

The brain as a neural system gets only its own stimulations in the mode of neuroelectric and neurochemical signals, and it is its task to detect from which sensory system the stimulations come and - being more important - which meaning can be assigned to them. The brain is forced to interpret the received content free signals, i.e., it is forced to give them meaning. All in all the different areas in the brain have to do a lot of work in order to assign meanings to the relatively few informations of the eyes or the ears or the other sensory systems; and there does not exist a unique correspondence between the stimuli of the environment and the processes within the brain. Insofar we get this result:

- Even perceiving is already an active constructing.
And without discussing in detail we state another result:
- The most important part for the assignments of meaning is played by the memory.

These shortly sketched results of brain research can be condensed to this thesis:
The world cannot be mapped by the brain, the world - the knowledge of the world - must be constructed by our neural system on the occasions of sensory stimuli.

Epistemologically speaking this thesis can be interpreted as a support of the combination of ontological realism and epistomological idealism based on results of neural science; and it is quite compatible with reflections of v.Glasersfeld (1995). Using this background we can modify our analysis from the beginning of this section:

> A word problem as a set of written or orally uttered syntactically correct sentences is peripherically coded by our visual or auditory system and then centrally coded into neurochemical or neuroelectrical signals, and after this being processed in the cerebral cortex.

> Referring to our memory a specific interpretation of this "exterior" word problem is established - and it is only this interpretation the human subject can deal with, all further processing is based on this interpretation: There is no direct access to the "exterior" word problem.

> And where are the semantic structures or where can they be? In the process of interpreting the incoming signals and while using the own memory semantic structures may shape the interpretation which is the basis for all further processing in the cortex.

Insofar we get:

> It is always the reader, the listener who constructs meaning: There is "no direct reading either of a text or a diagram, chart or picture" (H. Bauersfeld, 1995, p. 275) nor a direct hearing of a saying. Objects are only objects for a certain - human - subject.

Hence neither a mathematics educator nor a mathematics teacher in the classroom can directly transfer meanings or intentions to the students: Meaning does not travel.

Coming back to the *'mathematics education question'* we can state:
On the epistemological basis of a combination of ontological realism and epistemological idealism it is quite normal and not at all astonishing that there exist different systems of semantic structures of, e.g., simple multiplicative word problems depending on those aspects considered to be relevant for the ordering of a piece of our experiental world. It is quite normal that the systems of semantic structures proposed tell "different stories" and not any tells the "whole story" - the latter because we do not know - and we cannot know - what the whole story is.

What we can do and, of course, what we ought to do is this:
- to make explicitly the foundations and arguments when establishing a certain system of semantic structures, and
- to show what we can achieve when using it.

But, nevertheless, the idea of a *"unified theory"* in the end is - very likely -
only a belief that attracts more epistemological doubts than supports!

What can be the consequences for the *teacher question and the
classroom question?*

The teachers - as reflective practitioners - must learn as well as the
mathematics educators that the diversity of systems of semantic structures
is an epistemologically quite normal situation: A word problem ought better
to be considered as a set of constraints for the problem solver that allows
some - "viable" - interpretations - for instance, some fitting a certain system
of semantic structures.

Sticking too rigorously to certain semantic structures by the teacher can
cause obstacles for the development of the intuitive meanings of, e.g.,
multiplication of the students.

A system of semantic structures is a set of perspectives and using
it we - the mathematics educators or the teachers or the students - can
reduce the vast diversity of one-step multiplicative word problems to a
finite system of types:

> The teacher can analyse students' proposals and ascriptions of
> meanings - but in an open minded manner; she / he can control
> whether the set of problems used in the mathematics classroom is
> of sufficient diversity.
> For the students a prototype like usage of semantic structures may
> serve as an aid in order to become conscious of their own
> interpretations of different situations and to get to know other
> interpretations, for example, of their classmates.

Semantic structures - grounded in whatsoever categories - ought to
be used open mindedly as descriptive notions; the interpretation of them
as normative notions appears to be too narrow and not enough productive.

(4) Knowing and Social Practices - the "Language Game"Perspective of the Late Wittgenstein and Semantic Structures as Suggestions for Practices

In the preceeding section (3) our discussion was focused on the human being as an individual: The cognitive acts of constructing meanings were considered to be personal and to be located within the individual. Now I will turn to the social aspect using as a background the "language game" perspective of the late Wittgenstein. (The "late Wittgenstein" is the author of the "Philosophical Investigations" (PI), 1953 and the "Remarks on the Foundations of Mathematics" (RFM), 1956.)

Let us not enter here into the primacy debate about the individual versus the social; in particular, let aside the discussion of the question: Who is right - Piaget or Vygotsky? As a foundation a position shall be adopted here proposed by the sociologist Elias (1969/1990):

> The single human being ought to be considered as a being that is continuously in an "open process within indissoluble interdependencies with other single human beings" (Elias, 1990, p. LI). As an "open personality" a human being has got only a "relative autonomy" in comparison with the other fellow-beings. Neither are human beings the 'really existing things' beyond society nor is a society the 'really existing thing' beyond the individual human beings: A human being is not 'outside' a society, a society is not 'outside' the individual human being.

In the philosophy of the late Wittgenstein knowledge is not an object any longer for which language is only a box of neutral tools. Language is not considered as an objectively existing mediating factor between the given human subject and the - given - object as it is done in the Aristotelian view. Language is a universal medium - thus it is impossible to describe one's own language from outside: We are always and inevitably within our own language (cf. Hintikka & Hintikka, 1986/96). Knowledge appears as knowing, and knowing is always performed in language games. Language as languaging or playing a language game is equal to constituting meanings and, thus, constituting objects. There are no objects without meaning, and meaning is constituted by a specific use of language within a respective language game:

> "For a *large* class of cases - though not for *all* - in which we employ the word 'meaning' it can be explained thus: the meaning of a word is its use in the language" (Wittgenstein, PI, 43).

"Every sign *by itself* seems dead. *What* gives it life? - In use it is *alive*" (Wittgenstein, PI, 432).

"I shall call the whole, consisting of language and the actions into which it is woven, the 'language game' " (Wittgenstein, PI, 7).

"There are countless kinds: countless different kinds of use of what we call 'symbols', 'words', 'sentences'. And this multiplicity is not something fixed, given once for all; but new types of language, new language games, as we may say, come into existence, and others become obsolete and get forgotten. (...)
Here the term 'language game' is meant to bring into prominence the fact that speaking of language is part of an activity, or of a form of life" (Wittgenstein, PI, 23).

Language games are "systems of communication" between human beings in which the connections between
- language (as languaging),
- (non-verbal) actions, and the
- environment of the utterances count.
Language games are always parts of a social practice, and non-linguistic components become a necessary condition for the understanding of a language - even gestures and pictures or patterns can be important components of a language game.

Accepting the 'language game perspective' as a productive and challenging perspective for analyzing teaching-learning processes in mathematics as well as for the teacher's activities in the classroom

- also mathematical knowledge ought to be considered as a part of a - specific - social practice;
- and it is by communicating - by playing a language game - that we give witness for the existence of a particular use - be it use of a formula, of a definition, of a theorem, or something else. Thus it is by communicating - in a language game - that we give witness to a certain meaning.

How do students - in the elementary school - use simple word problems? When pupils are asking - for example - "Is it to add, Miss?" or "Is it to multiply, Miss?" or when children consider the verbal cue "times" as indicating multiplication or the cue "more" as indicating addition we can interpret such - and similar - questions and such 'cue hunting' as indicators for a certain language game in the classroom, for a certain social practice

- namely: Word problems are only hidden arithmetical problems, and how to use them is equal to reveal the hidden arithmetical problem whereby the teacher is the institution to evaluate the proposed solutions and where you have preferably to look for certain cues. This social practice is a result of the practice in the classroom and is - rather often - supported by the textbook used.

If we want to alter a social practice, if we want to initiate another language game - thus assigning a new meaning to word problems, e.g. - this can be done by initiating another set of social practices:

"Social practices can be readily criticized: by appeal to another set of social practices. The possibility of criticism resides in diversity" (Bloor, 1974-75, p. 185).

We have to bear in mind: New language games are not initiated by learning new rules but - vice versa - it is by mastering a language game that we learn new rules. Insofar it does not make sense when teaching student teachers or elementary school students, respectively, to make them learn descriptions of semantic structures first in order to start a new language game. Moreover, we - the teachers - first ought to use the semantic structures as an implicit background in order to practice an 'anti cue hunting' language game when dealing with simple word problems.

The wit of a 'cue hunting' language game with word problems is to produce an arithmetic sentence in symbolic form the teacher is satisfied with. The wit of a 'modelling oriented' language game with word problems is to answer questions like these:

- How can I / we interpret a word problem situation in a contextual and in an arithmetical (mathematical) meaningful manner?
- Which interpretation
    - fits certain non-mathematical contextual aspects (criteria),
    - fits certain arithmetical (mathematical) aspects (standards, criteria),
    - is intended (by the author(s) of the word problem presented)? (These references may be in conflict with another!)
- Which procedure(s) or strategy(ies) to solve a word problem - or certain interpretations of it - appear to be appropriate?
- Does a comparison of several procedures or strategies help me / us to construct more powerful procedures or strategies?

Working within such framing can result in making explicitly certain semantic structures thus making them explicit 'rules' for this language game, and having them available - on the other hand - can enable the learner to work more effectively by using these 'rules' consciously.

Concluding this section we hold: Playing such 'modelling oriented' language games - taking this as a 'didactical demand' for teachers in the classroom as well as for the mathematics educators - is our proposal for the threefold guiding question as a whole.

(5) Concluding Remarks

Concluding this paper I want to focus on two points aiming at the *mathematics education question* and at the *teacher and the classroom question* all at once.

The following statements of Bernstein (1983) and of Kuhn (1970) are adopted as appropriate descriptions concerning the situation of the choice of models or theories:

"Theory-choice is a jugdemental activity requiring imagination, interpretation, the weighing of alternatives, and the application of criteria that are essentially open" (Bernstein, 1983, p. 56).

"There is no neutral algorithm for theory-choice, no systematic decision procedure which, properly applied, must lead each individual or group to the same decision" (Kuhn, 1970, p. 200).

In educational environments in Germany this Latin saying is well known: Docendo discimus - it is by teaching that we are learning. As an important complement we can add: Communicando discimus - it is by communicating that we are learning.

References

Bauersfeld, H. (1995): "Language Games" in the Mathematical Classroom: Their Function and their Effects. In: Cobb, P., Bauersfeld, H. (Eds.): *The Emergence of Mathematical Meaning: Interactions in Classroom Cultures.* Hillsdale, NJ: Erlbaum, 271-291

Bell, A., Greer, B., Grimison, L. Mangan, C. (1989): Children's Performance on Multiplicative Word Problems: Elements of a Descriptive Theory. In: *Journal for Research in Mathematics Education*, 20, 434-449

Bernstein, R.J. (1983): *Beyond Objectivism and Relativism: Science, Hermeneutics, and Praxis.* Philadelphia: University of Pennsylvania Press

Bloor, D. (1973): Wittgenstein and Mannheim on the Sociology of Mathematics. In: *Studies in History and Philosophy of Science*, 4, 173-191

Carpenter, T.P., Moser, J.M., & Romberg, T.A. (Eds.) (1982): *Addition and Subtraction: A Cognitive Perspective.* Hillsdale, NJ: Erlbaum

Elias, N. (1969): *Über den Prozeß der Zivilisation. Soziogenetische und psychogenetische Untersuchungen. 1. Bd.: Wandlungen des Verhaltens in den weltlichen Oberschichten des Abendlandes* (15. Aufl., 1990). Frankfurt/Main: Suhrkamp

Ernest, P. (1994): *Constructing Mathematical Knowledge: Epistemology and Mathematical Education.* London: The Falmer Press

Glasersfeld, E. von (1995): *Radical Constructivism. A Way of Knowing and Learning.* London: The Falmer Press

Hiebert, J. & Behr, M. (Eds.) (1988): *Number Concepts and Operations in the Middle Grades,* vol. 2. Reston, VA: NCTM.

Kandel, E.R., Schwartz, J.H., & Jessell, Th.M. (Eds.) (1995): *Essentials of Neural Science and Behavior.* East Norwalc, USA: Appleton & Lange

Kant, I. (1781/1787): *Kritik der reinen Vernunft* [Critique of Pure Reason, first edition: 1781; second edition: 1787]. Hamburg: Meiner Verlag (1956)

Kuhn, T. (1970): *The Structure of Scientific Revolutions* (2nd edition). Chicago: University of Chicago Press

Mulligan, J. (1992): Children's Solutions to Multiplication and Division Word Problems: A Longitudinal Study. In: *Mathematics Education Research Journal*, 4, 24-41

Nesher, P. (1988): Multplicative School Word Problems: Theoretical Approaches and Empirical Findings. In: Hiebert, J., Behr, M. (Eds.): *Number Concepts and Operations in the Middle Grades, vol. 2.* Reston, VA: NCTM. 19-40

Roth, G. (1995): *Das Gehirn und seine Wirklichkeit. Kognitive Neurobiologie und ihre philosophischen Konsequenzen.* Frankfurt/Main: Suhrkamp (second edition)

Schmidt, S. & Weiser, W. (1995): Semantic Structures of One-Step Word Problems Involving Multiplication or Division. In: *Educational Studies in Mathematics*, 28, 55-72

Schwartz, J.L. (1988): Intensive Quantity and Referent Transforming Arithmetic Operations. In: Hiebert, J., Behr, M. (Eds.): *Number Concepts and Operations in the Middle Grades,* vol. 2. Reston, VA: NCTM. 41-52

Vergnaud, G. (1983): Multiplicative Structures. In: Lesh, R., Landau, M. (Eds.): *Acquisition of Mathematics Concepts and Processes.* New York: Academic Press, 127-174

Vergnaud, G. (1988): Multiplicative Structures. In: Hiebert, J., Behr, M. (Eds.): *Number Concpets and Operations in the Middle Grades, vol.* 2. Reston, VA: NCTM. 141-161

Wittgenstein, L. (1953): *Philosophische Untersuchungen* [Philosophical Investigations]. Ludwig Wittgenstein. Werkausgabe, Bd. 1 (9. Aufl., 1993). Frankfurt/Main: Suhrkamp, 225-580

ON ACQUISITION METAPHOR AND PARTICIPATION METAPHOR FOR MATHEMATICS LEARNING

Anna Sfard

1. Introduction: Theories as metaphors

Theories as metaphors. In the moving novel *Ardiente Paciencia* (turned into an unforgettable movie *Il Postino -- The Postman*), the author, Antonio Skarmata, tells the story of the Chilean poet Pablo Neruda who explains the concept of metaphor to his young admirer Mario, the postman. To Mario's question : "[Metaphor], what kind of thing is this?", the poet replies: "In order for you to have some sense of it, let's say that this is presenting something by help of something else". Quite a classic treatment, so far. It is the uneducated postman rather than the sophisticated poet who, after a little sampling and additional explanations, draws a conclusion similar to the one which in this talk is going to be grounded: "The entire world is like a metaphor of something else". The immediacy of Mario's insight indicates that one does not need more than scrutinizing look around to realize the ubiquity of metaphors and their power to create for us the world in which we live.

Although the indispensability of the metaphors may render them practically transparent, philosophers of science agreed quite a long time ago that no kind of research would be possible without them (see e.g. Ortony, 1993). As Scheffler (1991) put it, "The line, even in science, between serious theory and metaphor is a thin one -- if it can be drawn at all.... there is no obvious point at which we may say, 'Here the metaphors stop and the theories begin'" (p. 45). Indeed, there are no clear boundaries which would separate the metaphorical from the literal; there is no background of genuinely non-figurative expressions against which the metaphorical nature of such terms as "cognitive strain", "closed set" or "constructing meaning" would stand in full relief. The fact that concealing the metaphorical origins of ideas is a mandatory part of the scientific game makes the figurative roots of scientific theories fairly difficult to reconstruct. As an aside let me notice how the basic distinction between "literal" and "metaphorical" loses its ground when it comes to concepts that grew out of metaphors.

Conceptual metaphors. Quite often, when we choose a concept, say *teaching*, and then look carefully at the language in which we use to talk about it, we are able to notice a striking phenomenon: while there may be a great variety of common expressions concerned with this concept, a sizable subset of these expressions takes us in a systematic way to a certain well-defined domain which does not seem to be a "natural setting" of the concept at hand. Thus, for example, whether we talk about 'conveying ideas', 'delivering [getting] a message' or 'putting thoughts into words', we make it clear that our image of *communicating* is borrowed from the domain of *transferring) material goods.* This observation was first made in late seventies by Michael Reddy (1978) in his seminal paper entitled *Conduit metaphor.* Since then, systematic conceptual mappings came to be known as *conceptual metaphors* and became an object of a vigorous inquiry (Sacks, 1978; Lakoff & Johnson, 1980; Lakoff, 1987, 1993; Johnson, 1987). What traditionally has been regarded as a mere tool for better understanding and more effective memorizing, was now recognized as the primary source of our conceptual systems.

The strikingly systematic character of conceptual mappings such as the ones presented above, and the fact that such mappings can only arise and be dissipated through language, point out to the social, supra-individual character of conceptual metaphors. Being by-products of interpersonal communication rather than of a solitary effort of a lone thinker, they enjoy the status of public possessions. No wonder, then, that deeply rooted metaphors such as the one that ties human communication to transferring goods are often thought of as externally determined, natural, and mind-independent. As such, they also tend to be "dead" metaphors, their metaphorical nature being hardly recognizable behind their apparent self-evidence. Another noteworthy aspect is the cultural embeddedness of metaphors -- their being a product of associations that are specific to the culture within which they arise. One may say, therefore, that metaphorical projection is a mechanism through which the given culture perpetuates and reproduces itself in a steadily growing system of concepts.

Elicitation of the metaphors which guide us in our work as mathematics teachers and as mathematics education researchers is the aim of the present paper. Before I proceed, however, let me remark that the things I am going to say (as well as those I have said already) are, in themselves, metaphorical. For those who accept the claim about the constitutive role of metaphor, this fact should be easily understandable: if we create our conceptual systems with the help of metaphors, then the mechanism of metaphor is essentially recursive -- self-referential. Or, as Ricoeur (1977, p. 66) has observed, "The paradox is that we can't talk about metaphor except by using a conceptual framework which itself is engendered out of metaphor".

2. Learning mathematics: The *Acquisition Metaphor* vs. *Participation Metaphor*

In the quest after metaphors that guide our work as mathematics teachers and as researchers I decided to make a search of professional literature, looking for characteristic expressions and keywords. It did not take much effort to notice that there seem to be two leading motifs in what we do and what we say. In fact, mathematics education research seems to be caught in between two metaphors, which I decided to call *Acquisition Metaphor* and *Participation Metaphor*. Both these metaphors are simultaneously present in most recent texts, but in any given paper one of them is usually more dominant than the other. In my search I quickly noticed that the Acquisition Metaphor is likely to be more prominent in older texts while the Participation Metaphor took the lead mainly in the more recent studies. It is also quite obvious that at present, some researchers are making a strenuous effort to free themselves from the former metaphor for the sake of the latter.

Acquisition Metaphor. Ever since the dawn of civilization, human learning is conceived as an *acquisition* of something. Indeed, *The Collins English Dictionary* defines learning as "the act of gaining knowledge". Since the works of Piaget and Vygotsky, the growth of knowledge in the process of learning has been analyzed in terms of *concept development*. Concepts are to be understood as basic units of knowledge which can be accumulated, gradually refined, and combined together to form ever richer and ever more complex cognitive structures. The picture is not much different when we talk about the learner as a person who *constructs meaning.* This approach, which today seems self-evident and natural, brings to mind the activity of enriching oneself with material goods. The language of 'knowledge acquisition' and 'concept development' makes us think about human mind as a container to be filled with certain materials, and about the learner as becoming an owner of these materials.

Once we realize the fact that it is the metaphor of acquisition that underlies our thinking about learning mathematics, we become immediately aware of its being present in almost every common utterance on learning. Let us have a look at a number of titles taken from publications that appeared over the last two decades: *Acquisition of mathematical concepts and processes, Building up mathematics, Rachel's schemes for constructing fraction knowledge, The development of ... ratio concept, Children's construction of number, Extending the meaning of multiplication and division, On having and using geometric knowledge, The development of the concept of space in the child, Conceptual difficulties ... in the acquisition of the concept of function.* The idea that learning means acquisition and accumulation of some goods is evident in all these titles. They may point to a gradual *reception* or to an acquirement by *development* or by *construction*, but all of them seem to imply gaining ownership over some kind of self-sustained entity.

There are many different types of entities that may be acquired in the process of learning. One finds a great variety of relevant terms among the keywords of the frameworks generated by the Acquisition Metaphor: *knowledge, concept, conception, idea, notion, misconception, meaning, sense, referent, schema, fact, representation, material, contents, mathematical process, mathematical object.* There are equally many terms which denote the action of making such entity one's own: *reception, acquisition, construction, internalization, transmission, attainment, development, accumulation, grasp.* The teacher may help the student to attain her goal by *delivering, conveying, facilitating, mediating,* etc.

This impressively rich terminological assortment was necessary to mark differences, sometimes substantial and sometimes quite subtle, between different schools of thought. Over the last decades, many different suggestions have been made as to the nature of the mechanism through which mathematical concepts may be turned into the learner's private property; however, in spite of the many differences on the issue of "how", there was no controversy about the essence: the idea of learning as gaining possession over some commodity persisted in the wide spectrum of frameworks, from moderate to radical constructivist, and then to interactionist and socio-cultural theories. The researchers have offered a range of greatly differing mechanisms of concept development. First, they were simply talking about passive 'reception' of knowledge (thus of concepts), then about its being actively constructed by the learner; later, they analyzed the ways in which concepts are transferred from a social to individual plane and interiorized by the learner; eventually, they envisioned learning as a never-ending, self-regulating process of emergence in a continuing interaction with peers, teachers and texts. As long, however, as they investigated learning by focusing on the 'development of concepts' and on 'acquisition of knowledge', they implicitly agreed that this process can be conceptualized in terms of the Acquisition Metaphor.

Participation Metaphor. The learning-as-Acquisition Metaphor is so deeply entrenched in our minds that we would probably never became aware of its existence if another, alternative metaphor did not start to develop.

Indeed, when we search through recent issues of professional journals (e.g. *For the learning of mathematics, Learning and Instruction*) and newly published books, the emergence of a new metaphor becomes immediately apparent. Among the harbingers of the change are such titles as *Reflection, communication, and learning mathematics; Democratic competence and reflective knowing in mathematics; Developing written communication in mathematics; Reflective discourse and collective reflection; Discourse, mathematical thinking and classroom practice; Mathematics as being in the world. New researcher talks about learning as a legitimate peripheral participation* (Lave and Wenger, 1989) *or as apprenticeship in thinking* (Rogoff, 1990).

A far-reaching change is signaled by the fact that although all these titles and expressions refer to learning, none of them mentions either "concept" or "knowledge". The terms which imply the existence of some permanent entities have been replaced with the noun "knowing" that indicates action. This seemingly minor linguistic modification marks a remarkable ontological and epistemological shift in the research on learning (compare Smith, 1995; Cobb, 1995). The talks about the *states* have been replaced with attention to *activities*. In the image of learning that emerges from this linguistic turn, the permanence of *having gives way to a constant flux of doing.* While the concept of acquisition implies that there is a clear end-point to the process of learning, the new terminology leaves no room for immutable states and halting signals. Moreover, the ongoing mathematical activities are never considered separately from the context within which they are taking place. The context, in its turn, is rich and multifarious, and its importance is pronounced by talks about *situatedness, contextuality, cultural embeddedness, and social mediation.* The set of new keywords which, along with the noun *practice*, prominently features the terms *discourse* and *communication*, signals that the learner should be viewed as a person interested in *participation* in a certain kind of activities rather than in accumulating private possessions. To put it differently, learning mathematics is now conceived as a process of *becoming a member of a mathematical community.* This entails, above all, the ability to *communicate* in the language of this community and acting according to its particular *norms.* The norms themselves are to be *negotiated* in the process of consolidating the community. While learners are the newcomers and potential reformers of the practice, the teachers are the preservers of its continuity. From a lone entrepreneur the learner turns into an integral part of a team.

For obvious reasons, this new view of learning can be called *Participation Metaphor.* The decision to view learning an integration with a community in action rather than as an attempt to enhance an individual possession gave raise to quite a number of different approaches, the *theory of situated learning* (Brown et al, 1989; Lave and Wenger, 1991), the *discursive paradigm* (Foucault, 1972), and the *theory of distributes cognition* (Salomon, 1993) being the best known among them. As I will soon explain in a more detailed way, all these are theories of a new kind, differing from the old doctrines not only in their vision of learning but also, and perhaps most importantly, in their basic epistemological beliefs and the underlying assumption on the mission of the research on learning. The profoundness of the change and its revolutionary quality is sensed by many, but its exact nature has yet to be understood and made explicit. It is by no means restricted to research in mathematics education. For example, one relevant attempt at capturing the revolutionary character of the "discursive turn", which is the direct derivative of the change of the metaphor, has recently been made by Harre and Gillett (1995) in the book entitled *The Discursive Mind.* While presenting the latest developments in the study of human thinking as an emergence of *discursive psychology,* the authors name this event "a second cognitive revolution, the final apotheosis of the New Paradigm". According to their account, this second cognitive revolution" aims to accomplish what the first one failed to achieve, namely to "push the transformation of psychology right through" freeing it from the shortcomings of the behaviorist approach as well as of those inherent in the computer metaphor mind.

Twilit zone -- mathematics education in between metaphors. It is now worthwhile to pause for a moment in order to reflect on what is happening to us, mathematics teachers and educational researchers, in the twilight zone in between the two metaphors.

Perhaps the most salient indication of the switching allegiances is the change of the professional language. Since such change can only be gradual, initially one can hardly avoid linguistic hybrids. This period is also marked by the appearance of an interim language, where inverted commas around an old word are used to signal its demoted status. It is obvious that this word will only be left in the discourse for as long as proves necessary to find an eligible replacement. This is how we use today the words "fact", "knowledge", "real" world, etc.

Another way to preserve the existing terminology is to provide the old words with new definitions. Thus, Lave and Wenger (1991) propose to re-define the old terms *learning and knowing* as "relations between people in activity in, with, and arising from the socially and culturally structured world" (p. 51). With Foucault (1972) we can re-describe the term *concept* in discursive terms and say that it is a virtual entity "constituted by all that was said in all the statements that named it, divided it up, described it, explained it, traced its developments, indicated its various correlations, judged it..."

Such a "face-lifting" job on the old terminology may be not acceptable, however, in the eyes of the most devoted adherents of the new metaphor. They would claim that the switch to a new metaphor cannot be regarded as complete until the professional discourse is thoroughly purged from words that bring to mind the old metaphor. Thus, for example, they would object to preserving the words "knowledge" and "concept" as the central elements of the language of Acquisition Metaphor (see Bauersfeld, 1995; Smith, 1995). Harbingers of revolutions tend to believe that the old and the new are mutually exclusive. Are they really? Let me leave this question open, at the moment. For now, I will only remark that it is only natural that the profound change like the one we are witnessing nowadays is marked by a doze of single-mindedness and zealousness. One must declare his or her full allegiance to the new metaphor if the other metaphor -- the one by which we lived for centuries -- is to be ever elicited and questioned.

A schematic comparison between the Acquisition and Participation Metaphors is presented in Figure 1.

Fig.1: The metaphorical mappings

individual enrichment	**goal of learning**	community buding
acquisition of something	**learning**	becoming a participant
recipient (consumer), (re-)constructor	**student**	peripheral participant apprentice
provider, facilitator, mediator	**teacher**	expert participant preserver of practice/discourse
property, possession, commodity (individual, public)	**knowledge concept**	aspect of practice/discourse/ activity
having, possessing	**knowing**	belonging, participating, communicating

3. What does the Participation Metaphor change?

The Acquisition Metaphor is the one which underlies probably all the theories of cognitive development. Up to now, this metaphor has been promoting research molded in the image of natural sciences (after all, natural science is the place the metaphors of acquisition and development come from). Such research considers human cognition in its "pure" form and does not leave a room for any "noises". This means, among others, that in the acquisition-based theories almost no space is left for the role of the genuine interests of those who learn, those who teach, and those who decide what should be taught. It is therefore quite obvious that if one expects these other issues to be considered as well, quite a different kind of theoretical endeavor must be undertaken. Since the Acquisition Metaphor can hardly be expected to remain sufficient when this other kind of purpose is being pursued, the need of re-consideration, and then of another metaphor for learning becomes evident.

The shift from the Acquisition Metaphor to the Participation Metaphors makes an essential difference in almost every possible aspect of both theory and practice: it means a new epistemology, a different type of theory, a reformed visions of mathematics, of its learning and teaching, and a novel research paradigm. Let me say a few words on some of these shifts.

For one thing, our thinking about learning has always been plagued by epistemological and ontological quandaries which would not yield to the finest of philosophical minds. Further, the teaching of mathematics that followed the lead of the Acquisition Metaphor has invariably been producing to disappointing results while continuously deepening our sense of helplessness. Moreover, for some time now it has been becoming increasingly clear that in the pragmatically-minded post-modern world, the idea of a solitary activity aimed at accumulation of some esoteric goods that can hardly be shared with others is rapidly losing its allure. Let me now give a closer look to each one of these problems.

Foundational change. Nowadays it is quite obvious that the critical reconsideration of the Acquisition Metaphor can no longer be put off. First, there is a foundational dilemma that was first signaled by Plato in his dialogue *Meno* and came later to be known as *the learning paradox* (Berieter, 1985; Cobb et al., 1992). Although appearing in many different disguises throughout history, the quandary is always the same and its gist is embarrassingly simple: How can we want to acquire a knowledge of something which is not yet known to us? Indeed, if this something does not yet belong to the repertoire of the things we know, then being completely unaware of its existence we cannot possibly want it or inquire about it. Or, to put it differently, if we can only become aware of something by recognizing it on the basis of the knowledge we already posses, then nothing that does not yet belong to the assortment of the things we know can ever become one of them. Conclusion: learning new things is inherently impossible.

Thinking about the epistemological and ontological foundations of our conception of learning intensified a few decades ago, when the doctrine of radical constructivism entangled psychologists into a new dilemma. Without questioning the thrust of the Acquisition Metaphor, the constructivists offered a new conception of the mechanism which turns knowledge into a private possession of a person. In their hands, passive recipients of knowledge turned into builders of their own conceptual schemes. This image of the learner was forcefully promoted by many contemporary thinkers, notably by Piaget and by Vygotsky who, although divided on the questions of the role of social interaction and of the primary sources of learners' inspiration, were nevertheless in full agreement as to the constructive nature of learning. It is this central idea of the individuals as constructing or re-constructing their private conceptions from external materials which, at a closer look, turns problematic. Whatever version of constructivism is concerned -- the moderate, the radical or the social, the same dilemma must eventually pop up: how do we account for the fact that the learners are able to build for themselves concepts which are fully congruent with those of other people? Or, to put it differently, how do people bridge between individual and public possession?

The Participation Metaphor liberates us from these paradoxes by *disobjectivation of knowledge,* namely by providing an alternative to the talks about learning as making an acquisition. In doing so, this new metaphor does not *solve* the old quandaries by rather pulls the ground from under the vexing questions and renders them meaningless. Within its boundaries, there is simply no room for the dichotomy between internal and external (concepts, knowledge), which is the basis of the objectification. The new metaphor replaces the old selective outlook with the attention to the whole, and with the view of the learner as being a part of a community in a most essential way. Consequently, science or mathematics cannot be considered as self-contained entities anymore; rather they have to be regarded as aspects of ongoing social activities. The researchers must no longer insist on isolating knowledge from the totality of social interactions.

The change in the vision of learning mathematics. For the sake of later comparison, I will begin with drafting *the picture of learning as conveyed by the Acquisition Metaphor.*

There is hardly a more forcible expression of the vision of mathematics as an accumulable commodity and there is no better source for insights about the metaphor's entailments than the classical pamphlet "A Mathematician's Apology" by the Cambridge mathematician G.H. Hardy. For Hardy, mathematical knowledge is a means for a personal advancement and success. Many times in his brief essay he speaks about the *superiority and seriousness* of mathematics, thus stressing the superiority and seriousness of people who have an access to this special commodity. Like material goods, mathematics has the permanent quality, which makes the special merits and the privileged position of their owner equally permanent: Thus, learning mathematics means insuring one's future with the help of one's past. In fact, according to Hardy it means not less than immortality: "Immortality may be a silly word, but probably a mathematician has the best chance of whatever it may mean" (p. 81).

Within the acquisition paradigm, not only the mathematical knowledge, but also the *means* for gaining it count as a private possession of the learner. "Man's choice of a career will almost always be dictated by the limitations of his natural abilities" (p. 69) says Hardy, implying that one has to have a special mathematical *talent* to become a successful learner or creator of mathematics. This characteristic is believed to be given, not acquired. It is a person's permanent 'quality mark'. Student's achievements may depend on environmental factors, but the teachers feel they can tell students' *real* (permanent) potential from their actual performance.

Let me now try to show how the Participation Metaphor changes the overall picture. According to Rorty (1991, p. 21), there are two principal ways in which people can give sense to their lives: they can do it by describing themselves "as standing in immediate relation to a nonhuman reality" or by "telling the story of their contribution to community". Clearly, Hardy has chosen the first of these ways. Adherents of the Participation Metaphor opt for the other. They seem to be saying, together with Rorty, that "whatever good the ideas of 'objectivity' and 'transcendence' have done for our culture can be attained equally well by the idea of a community which strives after both intersubjective agreement and novelty" (*ibid*, p.13).

While the Acquisition Metaphor puts forward human personal ambitions as a principal drive for learning, within the participation framework the most important prerequisite for learning is student's wish to be a part of a certain community. Further, while Acquisition Metaphor presents *cognitive skills* as a most valued characteristic of a learner, the Participation Metaphor stresses qualities which till now, have been regarded as social rather than intellectual, and as such have not been an integral part of research on learning: being able to negotiate norms of behavior and then observe them, being able to develop a good communication with other members of the group, having a good influence on others and, preferably, leadership qualities.

Another important change induced by the Participation Metaphor is the fact that there are no more talks about permanence -- permanence of human possessions or of human traits. The new metaphor promotes an interest in people in action rather than in people "as such", and views the reality as being in a constant flux. The awareness of the constant change means refraining from any permanent labeling. It is action that can be clever or unsuccessful, not the actor. For the learner, all the options remain open in spite of failures of the past. To sum up, the Participation Metaphor brings a much more optimistic message for the learner. Since nothing is viewed as permanent anymore, and there are no more talks about factors that determine the learner's fate once and for all, the new metaphor's main message seems to be that of an everlasting hope: today you act one way, tomorrow you may act in quite differently.

It the light of all this, it is quite obvious that the Participation Metaphor has a potential to lead to a new, more democratic practice of learning and teaching mathematics. It is significant, however, that I said "has a potential to lead" rather than just "leads to". It is extremely important to understand that the outcomes of the use of a metaphor are not inscribed in the metaphor itself but rather are a function of the intentions and skills of those who harness the metaphors to work. All this is obviously true also about the NCTM's *New Standards* for teaching and learning mathematics, which seem to favor the Participation Metaphor, but which cannot bring the desired change by their mere existence. In the final account, it is up to those who translate ideas into practice rather than to the legislators, whether the introduction of the new metaphor will, indeed, lead to a democratization of learning and to the improvement of learner's condition.

4. Concluding question: Is this either-or choice?

In this talk I have elaborated on the drawbacks of the Acquisition Metaphor and on the advantages of the Participation Metaphor. It would be a mistake, however, to let you leave this room with the impression that I have preached a clear-cut preference for the latter while suggesting the abandonment of the former. Nothing could be farther from what I really intended to say. If I did not put any effort in showing the advantages of the Acquisition Metaphor, it is only because this metaphor, being still the default option for the majority of researchers, did not seem to me in a need of defense; and if I tried to show the bright sides of the Participation Metaphor, it is because of its being a relatively new idea, and as such --- in a need of explanation and justification. But now, it is time to remind ourselves that the Acquisition Metaphor does have much to offer, while the Participation Metaphor has shortcomings which, if not controlled, may lead to undesirable consequences (see e.g. Sierpinska, 1995; Thomas, 1996). Besides, even if we don't like the objectifying quality of the Acquisition Metaphor, we can hardly escape it. The perceptual, bodily roots of all our thinking compel us to talk in terms of objects and processes that can be applied to these objects even when we reach the regions of pure abstraction. I committed the "objectification crime" in this very papers when presenting its central notion -- the metaphor -- as a "conceptual transplant".

It is my deep belief that most powerful theories are those that stand on more than one metaphorical leg (compare Sfard, 1996). Metaphorical pluralism seems to me an absolute necessity. An adequate combination of metaphors would allow for bringing to the fore the advantages of each one of them while keeping their respective drawbacks under control. I fully agree with Freudenthal (1978) who said that "education is a vast field and even that part which displays a scientific attitude is too vast to be watched with one pair of eyes" (p. 78). The Acquisition and Participation Metaphor, when combined together, run a good chance of gratifying all our needs without perpetuating the drawbacks of each one of them.

Considering the fact that the two metaphors, while offering competing outlooks and conflicting ontological claims about the same phenomena, seem to be mutually exclusive, one may wonder how the suggested metaphorical crossbreeding could be possible at all. The problem, however, is definitely not new, and it is not restricted to the research on learning. We can turn to contemporary science for many more examples of similar dilemmas, as well as for ways in which the difficulty can be overcome (think, for example, about the Niels Bohr's complementarity principle which settled the ontological debate in physics without resolving the wave-particle controversy; or of chemistry and physics which deal with the same natural phenomena , but they do it in completely different ways).

Whichever of the possible solutions is adopted, one thing transpires from the dilemma itself and from the assortment of ways in which it may be tackled: one can only arrive at a peace of mind if one accepts the thought of reality constructed from a variety of metaphors. The metaphors we use while theorizing are good enough to fit small areas, but none of them can suffice to cover the entire field. We have to satisfy ourselves with only local sense making. Realistic thinker knows she has no choice but to give up the hope that the little patches of coherence will eventually combine into a consistent global theory. It seems that the sooner we accept the thought that our work is bound to produce a patchwork of metaphors rather than a unified, homogeneous theory of learning, the better for us and for those whose lives are likely to be affected by our work.

References

Bauersfeld, H. (1995). "Language games" in the Mathematics Classroom: Their Function and their Effects. In P. Cobb & H. Bauersfled (eds.), *Emergence of Mathematical Meaning: Interaction in Classroom Cultures,* Lawrence Erlbaum Associates, Hilsdale, NJ, 271 - 291.

Berieter, C. (1985). Towards the solution of the learning paradox. *Review of Educational Research,* 55, 201-226.

Brown, J.S., Collins, A., and Duguid, P. (1989). Situated Cognition and the Culture of learning, *Educational Researcher,* 18(1), 32-42.

Bruner, J. (1986). *Actual minds, possible worlds.* Cambridge, Mass.: Harvard University Press.

Cobb, P. (1996). Continuing the Conversation: A Response to Smith, *Educational Researcher* 24(7), 25-27.

Foucault, M. (1972). *The Archaelogy of Knowledge,* Harper Colophon, New York.

Freudenthal,H. (1978). *Weeding and sowing.* Dordrecht, Holland: D. Reidel.

Hardy, G.H. (1940/1967). *A Mathematician's apology.* Cambridge University Press.

Harre, R. and Gillet, G. (1995). *The discursive mind.* Thousand Oaks: SAGE Publications.

Johnson, M. (1987). *The Body in the Mind: The Bodily Basis of Meaning, Imagination, and Reason,* The University of Chicago Press, Chicago.

Lakoff, G. (1987). *Women, Fire and Dangerous Things: What Categories Reveal about the Mind,* The University of Chicago Press, Chicago.

Lakoff, G. (1993). The contemporary theory of metaphor. In Ortony, A. (ed.) (1993), *Metaphor and Thought, Second edition* . Cambridge: Cambridge University Press. pp. 202-250.

Lakoff, G. and Johnson, M. (1980). *The metaphors we live by.* Chicago: The University of Chicago Press.

Lave, J. and Wenger, E. (1990). *Situated Learning: Legitimate Peripheral Participation,* Cambridge University Press, Cambridge.

Lerman, S. (1996). Intersubjectivity in mathematics learning: A challenge to the radical constructivist paradigm? *Journal for Research in Mathematics Education,* 27(2), 133-150.

National Council of Teachers of Mathematics. (1989). *Curriculum and evaluation standards for school mathematics.* Reston, VA: National Council of Teachers of Mathematics.

National Council of Teachers of Mathematics. (1991). *Professional standards for teaching mathematics.* Reston, VA: National Council of Teachers of Mathematics.

Ortony, A. (ed.) (1993), *Metaphor and Thought, Second edition.* Cambridge: Cambridge University Press.

Reddy, M. (1978). The conduit metaphor: A case of frame conflict in our language about language. *Metaphor and Thought, Second edition.* Cambridge: Cambridge University Press. pp. 164-201.

Ricoeur, P. (1977). *The rule of metaphor.* Toronto: Toronto University Press.

Rogoff, B. (1990). *Apprenticeship in thinking: Cognitive development in social context.* Oxford: Oxford University Press.

Rorty, R. (1991). *Objectivity,Relativism, andTruth,* Cambridge University Press, Cambridge.

Sacks, S., Ed. (1978). *On metaphor.* Chicago: The University of Chicago Press.

Salomon, G., Ed. (1993). *Distributed cognitions: Psychological and educational considerations.* Cambridge: Cambridge University Press.

Scheffler, I. (1991). Educational Metaphors. In *In praise of cognitive emotions,* pp.45-55. New York: Routledge.

Sfard, A. (1996). Commentary: On metaphorical roots of conceptual growth'. To appear in English, L. (ed.), *Mathematical reasoning: Analogies, metaphors, and images.* Erlbaum.

Sfard, A. (1997). On two metaphors for learning and the danger of choosing just one. (in preparation).

Smith, E. (1996).Where is the mind? "Knowing" and "knowledge" in Cobb's constructivist and sociocultural perspectives. *Educational Researcher* 24,23-24

Sierpinska, A (1995). Mathematics "in Context", "Pure" or "with Applications"?, *For the Learning of Mathematics* 15(1),2-15.

Thomas, R (1996). Proto-mathematics and/or real mathematics. *For the learning of mathematics,* 16(2), 11-18.

CRITICAL MATHEMATICS EDUCATION
- SOME PHILOSOPHICAL REMARKS

Ole Skovsmose

Introduction

If mathematics education can be organised in a way so that it will challenge undemocratic features of society, it can be called critical mathematics education. This education does not provide any recipe for teaching. Nor does it provide a recipe for researching mathematics education.

Critical mathematics education refers to educational concerns. The notions of students' interest and of reflective knowing are important in clarifying those concerns. Students' interest cannot be described in terms of students' background only, but must be discussed with reference to students' foreground as well. Reflective knowing is introduced as a constituent of the notion of mathemacy. Reflecting knowing refers to a broad range of considerations having to do with already developed understandings and misconceptions.

A *thought experiment*: Imagine that I am a dictator. I run this country. I decide everything. Imagine that you are the, rather naive, people of the country. You are naive because you want to do what I ask you to do. You are very kind and try to please me in every respect. Nevertheless, it is not an attractive job for me to be a dictator, at least not in this country with these naive people. I write down what I want my people to do, but unfortunately my people are not able to read my orders. Everybody ask me to explain what they have to do. So I decide to teach my people how to read and write. It turns out to be a successful educational programme, and now I do not find difficulties in getting my orders carried out.

However, the dictator has run a risk. When the people was taught how to read and write, they also acquired a competency which can be used for a different purpose. The competency of literacy can be used to interpret the situation in which the learner is engaged. Seen with the eyes of the dictator, it is 'risky' to develop literacy as a general competency. The people may use this competency and reinterpret the power relationships of society. Literacy can be used for critical purposes, and the nature of a dictatorship may be put on the agenda. Literacy is a double-edged-sword competency.

Nevertheless, the story is favourable to the dictator. He is not overthrown. Even though literacy may have a double-edged-sword quality, it need not be applied. The dictator can live peacefully together with his people, who continue to follow his written orders.

Industrialisation and the need for modernisation also reach this peaceful dictatorship. Representatives of the new industry show nice things which can be produced if the country is industrialised. The dictator decides to develop his country in accordance with these new suggestions. All sorts of glittering machinery are installed, but the people look at the machinery and at the dictator. What are they supposed to do?

The dictator starts to teach the people how to handle this technology, and this of course presupposes that he teaches them mathematics. The dictator introduces mathematics at all levels of the curriculum, and the entire work-force acquires the competency needed in order to meet the demands of industrialisation. Mathematical knowledge and literacy become the two pillars of the educational system of the dictatorship.

Does the dictator run any risks introducing mathematics into the curriculum? Will mathematical knowledge turn into a double-edged-sword competency? The dictator includes 'everything' in the mathematical curriculum: set theory, functions, graphs, algebra, group theory, calculus, etc. The people really learn mathematics. But is this learning a threat to the dictatorship?

This question concerns the possibility of establishing a critical mathematics education. If mathematics education can be organised in such a way that it challenges undemocratic features in society, we can call it *critical mathematics education.*

1 The notion of critical mathematics education

Critical mathematics education does not provide methods for teaching and researching. Critical mathematics education refers to educational *concerns.*

In the chapter, 'Critical Mathematics Education', from the *International Handbook of Mathematics Education,* Lene Nielsen and I outline such concerns. They have to do with: (1) preparing students for citizenship; (2) establishing mathematics as a tool for analysing critical features of social relevance; (3) considering the students' interest; (4) considering cultural conflicts in which the schooling takes place; (5) reflecting upon mathematics which as such might be a problematic tool; (6) communication in the classroom, as personal interrelationships provides a basis for democratic life.[1]

The emphasis on these concerns can be explained with reference to the technological paradox: Technology can be interpreted as a response to human needs, but the very attempt to solve problems is itself an instrument for creating problems. In the middle of this paradox of technology we find mathematics.[2]

In 'Cultural Framing of Mathematics Teaching and Learning', Ubiratan D'Ambrosio states the paradox in the following way: "In the last 100 years, we have seen enormous advances on our knowledge of nature and in the development of new technologies. ... And yet, this same century has shown us a despicable human behaviour. Unprecedented means of mass destruction, of insecurity, new terrible diseases, unjustified famine ... are matched only by an irreversible destruction of the environment. Much of this paradox has to do with an absence of reflections and considerations of values in academics, particularly in the scientific disciplines, both in research and in education. Most of the means to achieve these wonders and also these horrors of science and technology have to do with advances in mathematics."[3]

Could mathematics as such be considered problematic? On the other hand: Could anybody imagine a more critical thinking than the mathematical? However, the notion of critique cannot be restricted to certain forms of logical reasoning, nor to a problem-solving competency. Critical thinking cannot be reduced to a form of strict reasoning. The interpretation of critical thinking as logical reasoning has its roots in rationalism. René Descartes has emphasised that all truths can be grasped by reasoning and by reasoning alone. But the paradox of technology indicates that a more fundamental interpretation of critical thinking is necessary.

Human reason has not grasped the nature of its own creation.[4] To the rational eye, the social implications of technology are hidden below the

---

[1] See Skovsmose and Nielsen (1996).
[2] For a discussion of the relationship between mathematics and technology see also Keitel (1989, 1993), Keitel, Kotzmann and Skovsmose (1993) and Skovsmose (1994, Chapter 3).
[3] See D'Ambrosio, 1993, p. 443.
[4] The Vico-paradox refers to this phenomenon, see Skovsmose (1994, Chapter 3).

horizon. Therefore, critical reasoning must be developed in a much broader way. This will be an educational task, if mathematical understanding is to be developed as a double-edged-sword competency.

Mathematics education as a global concern assigns educators a particular responsibility. Mathematics education provides, on the one hand, an introduction to participation in the technological development but, on the other hand, this education might provide a basis for criticising this particular development. This challenge calls for a critical mathematics education.

I do not think of critical mathematics education as a special branch of mathematics education. It is a global concern which reminds us that we cannot develop mathematics education on a blind assumption that mathematical knowledge, as such, ensures critical thinking.

2 The extended family of critical mathematics education

Critical mathematics education has different roots. One is found in Europe. As a reaction to the Second World War, the idea developed that education must invite students into a democratic life.[5] Education must prevent the upbringing of followers: Why did so many accept the Nazi way of thinking? How was it possible to turn technology into a production of mass-destruction? It was suggested that education should be part of a democratic life. Education should mean education for citizenship as well. This leads to the notion of critical education.

According to Paulo Freire, education is also a way of grasping the political and social constrains in which the learners are situated. In particular, these constrains are leftovers from colonialism. In this way education can be seen as a reaction to imposed social structures[6]. Ethnomathematics can be interpreted along similar lines of thought.[7] A particular development of critical mathematics education, with reference to the work of Paulo Freire, has been carried out by Marilyn Frankenstein.[8]

---

[5] See Adorno (1971) and in particular the chapter 'Erziehung nach Auschwitz' ('Education after Auschwitz') which was published in 1966.

[6] See Freire (1972, 1974).

[7] See for instance D'Ambrosio 1985), Borba (1990) and Knijnik (1993).

[8] See Frankenstein (1983, 1989).

I am involved in a project in South Africa, which has to do with establishing frameworks for research in mathematics education.[9] From a South African perspective, it becomes obvious that it does not make sense to import a European variant of critical mathematics education. Nor does it make sense to import an ethnomathematical perspective. The prefix 'ethno' has an awkward connotation in South Africa.[10] Critical mathematics must be rethought anew.

This is the present challenge of critical mathematics education: To rethink its conceptions and concerns in terms of new challenges to education. Are we able to, in this new situation, to identify a competency, mathemacy, which can support critical thinking?

Can mathemacy, similarly to literacy, be developed as a double-edged-sword competency? Is it possible to relate both literacy and mathemacy to sociological imagination which means to imagine that a given situation could be formed differently. [11]

3 Two warnings

Let me give two warnings concerning critical mathematics education:
(1) Critical mathematics education cannot be imposed on students nor on teachers. The only possibility seems to be to make an invitation to being critical. Critique cannot be itemised and incorporated bit by bit into a curriculum.
(2) It is not possible to provide a specific description of a certain amount of knowledge which contains the essence of being critical. Mathemacy, as part of critical mathematics education, must be searched for as a complex network of understanding.
In what follows I shall concentrate on two issues: the notion of students' interest, keeping in mind that critical competency cannot be imposed on students; and the notion of *reflective knowing* in order to emphasise the complexity as well as the fragility of knowing.

---

9 The persons involved in the project are Jill Adler, Mathume Bopape, Jonathan Jansen, Herbert Khuzwayo, Mzwandile Kibi, Cassius Lubisi, Manikam Moodley, Anandhavelli Naidoo, Nomsa Sibisi, Renuka Vithal and John Volmink.

10 For a further discussion of the notion of ethnomathematics, see Vithal and Skovsmose (in press).

11 See Mills (1959).

4 'Energy'

Before going into this discussion, let me shortly mention an example of classroom practice. The example (together with other examples) is described in my book *Towards a Philosophy of Critical Mathematics Education*. The examples in my book are not to be thought of as examples of critical mathematics education. However, I certainly conceive them as interesting, and it is possible for me to explain some of the idea of critical mathematics education by referring to them.

Here I have chosen the example 'Energy', which was planned and carried out by the teacher, Henning Bødtkjer. As it is described in details elsewhere, I shall make only a brief summary.[12]

In the project 'Energy', students discussed the input-output figures for the 'use of energy'.[13] The first part of the project work concerned the students' own breakfast. What energy supply is contained in an ordinary breakfast? This energy-supply was calculated using statistics about the 'energy-content' of bread, butter, cheese, etc. 'Use of energy' consisted in a ride on a bike. By means of certain formulas, including the parameters, velocity, time and 'front area of the cyclist', it was possible to calculate the use of energy during the ride.[14]

The project then turned to input-output figures for farming. First: What energy input is needed to grow barley in a specific field? The input includes, for instance, the use of petrol for ploughing. The students then calculated the energy supply contained in the harvested barley. The result of these calculations showed that the energy-output in the barley produced is six times the energy-input. The farmer used the harvested barley as pig food, and the input-output figures for pig-breeding were finally calculated. The result was that the energy output was five times less than the energy input. Therefore, according to the students' calculations, pork-production is very expensive, seen from the perspective of energy supply. Finally, these results were interpreted in a global perspective.

---

[12] See Skovsmose (1994), Chapter 7. In Skovsmose (1996) the project 'Energy' is discussed with reference to 'meaning in mathematics education'.

[13] Physics states that energy does not disappear but changes from one form to another. Naturally, it is this phenomenon of changing which is referred to by the everyday expression 'use of energy'

[14] Three different formulas could be used to determine the 'bike resistance' r which depends on the type of bike, the velocity v, and the 'frontal area' a:
Normal bike: $r = 1.1av^2 + 7$
Sports bike: $r = 1.0av^2 + 6$
Racer: $r = 0.7av^2 + 5$

5 Students' interest

With reference to research in ethnomathematics it has been suggested that mathematics education must consider the cultural background of the students as a source for developing mathematical activities. The students cannot be 'objects' of an educational process. They must be seen as participants, and *students'* interest therefore plays a crucial role.

The concern for students' interest is important. Let me, however, add a few comments on the notion of background. There is a difference between paying attention to the students' background and respecting the students' interest. Students' interest cannot be described in terms of students' background only. We do not do students a favour by relating the content of the curriculum solely to their background.

My father was a tailor, and I can assure you that much mathematics, especially geometry, is involved in tailoring. Mathematicians have faced a tremendous task in projecting the three-dimensional globe into the two-dimensional map. But tailors are involved in the complicated task: projecting the two-dimensional cloth unto the three-dimensional body. Let us imagine that some ethnomathematicians had come to my place. They studied my background and the mathematical content of my father's work. They could tell him that in fact he was doing very advanced mathematics. He would not understand a single bit of what they were saying. (Maybe he would have asked the ethnomathematicians if they wanted him to make them a new dress.) Assume that the ethnomathematicians had suggested to my teacher that he was to develop some special mathematics for me, based on (the so fascinating and advanced) tailor's mathematics. I would feel insulted. I am sure that I would not want to be treated differently in this respect.

The point of this story is not to say that students' interest is unimportant. It is essential to consider the students' interest. But the interest cannot be examined simply in terms of the background of the students. Equally important is the *foreground* of the students.

By foreground I refer to the students' interpretation of opportunities which society reveals as opportunities for the students. The foreground contains hopes and aspirations. Instead of tailor's mathematics it might have been just as rewarding to introduce me to pilots' mathematics (although I had no idea that I would ever become a pilot). The students' interest is not to be reduced to 'background'.

The frontal area was estimated by each student individually by using a video print of themselves riding towards the camera. To get the right scale each student had attached a little piece of cardboard on which were drawn a few squares, one dm^2 each. The top of the cardboard was fixed to the student's sweat-shirt by two safety pins. This meant that the cardboard took a vertical position independent of whether the student was sitting in an upright position or bent forward when riding the bike towards the camera. The whole video print was divided by drawing a lattice of squares over it, and that made it possible to count the number of squares needed to cover the whole picture of the person. The front area a has to be measured in m^2 and the velocity v in m/s. The formulas then gives the bike resistance r as measured in N (Newton).

The project 'Energy' was developed with aim of relating it to the students' interest. Is it possible for the teacher (and other planners of the educational process) to design a project and then claim, so to say, that they have considered the students' interest? This is a difficult question. I do not think a simple answer exists, which again means that I think it is possible for the teacher to plan a project considering the students' interest.

For me it is essential that the project 'Energy' is presented within a framework making sense to the students. It should be possible for the students to negotiate the purpose of doing different things. For me the question is not simple how student' interest can be used as a source of motivation. I do not think in terms of using students' interest as a device for planning and managing the curriculum. It is essential that students' interest is respected, which again implies establishing projects the relevance of which can be challenged by the students.

The project 'Energy' was planned by the teacher who presented the topic to the students. However, the topic was presented in a way that provided opportunities for the students to question the points of the different tasks.

We can separate two different notions of understanding. The students might come to understand *how* a certain algorithm works. They might also come to understand *why* certain algorithms are used and exercised. Respecting students' interest means ensuring an understanding not only directed towards mathematical concepts and algorithms but also towards the nature of the educational tasks. What was learned in the project 'Energy' was not linked to the students' background nor immediate interests. While the introduction of the topic, breakfast-biking may be seen as part of a motivational device, the kernel of the project, coming to grasp the essential elements of input-output figures of farming, refers to a different interpretation of students' interest.

This interpretation of interest has to do more with students as citizens. Such long-term interests are also real interests, and the students will also be aware of these, if they are involved in projects facilitating discussions of the meaning of educational tasks.

6 Reflective knowing

Mathematics educators are very concerned about students' development of mathematical knowledge and, in specific, about students' understanding (or lack of understanding) of mathematical concepts. However, much more is on stake in mathematics education than mathematical knowledge.

This is the reason why I have introduced the notion of *reflective knowing* as an important constituent of mathemacy.[15] Mathematical knowledge in itself does not provide a double-edged-sword competency.

The students can reflect upon many things. Let us relate to the example of 'Energy'. Some formulas were used for the calculation of bike resistance. They contained different parameters: What do the different parameters mean? Is the result reasonable? How are the results justified? How are the formulas justified?

The students may reflect on how they did the calculations: How do we calculate the energy supply in the field? They may consider their own modelling activity: Have we considered the relevant features? Are some aspects forgotten?

The students may reflect upon the actual results of the modelling process: What can the input-output figures for farming tell us? Are our results similar to other results? Are other 'official' results reliable?

The students may consider their results in a global perspective. Their reflections may take the form of exemplary thought: What does this mean for the food production of the earth?

The students may also consider their own activity: Maybe the project was not that interesting but what did we actually learn? The reflection may consider the whole school situation.

---

[15] The notion of reflective knowing is developed in Skovsmose (1994). See also Skovsmose (1990).

The activity of reflecting is essential in the development of knowing. I do not see reflecting as similar to the notion of reflective abstraction which plays a critical role in Jean Piaget's genetic epistemology. Piaget concentrates on the description of the development of mathematics knowledge, and he studies operations as the basis for mathematical knowledge. However, I am not only interested in the development of mathematical knowledge. My concern is the development of the much broader competency of mathemacy. In this competency, mathematical knowledge is only one of the elements. Reflecting knowing refers to a broad range of considerations having to do with already developed understandings and misconceptions.

The concern of mathematics education cannot be simply to produce mathematical knowledge. To develop a reflective knowing is a much wider concern which calls for the development of a mathemacy.

7 Conclusion

As already emphasised, there is no recipe for critical mathematics education. We must be open to an experimental practice, and such practice might give ways to identifying ideas for the further development of critical competencies.

Why are the competencies important? This has to do with the paradox of technology which indicates that conditions for democracy may be hampered by the actual technological development for which mathematics education serves as a preparation. This is the challenge of a critical mathematics education.

A *thought experiment*: Imagine we are joining a Middle Age conference concerning religious education. Sitting in the dim light in the conference centre, we are listening to many and interesting lectures. One lecturer makes an exegesis of the teaching of the Holy Trinity. He explains that he has investigated also the sources of the holy text and come to new conclusions concerning the basic structures of the Trinity. He suggests that the curriculum in religious education, including the teaching of how to pray, is changed in accordance with his findings. Instead of relating to a patch-work of information about the Trinity, the prayers can simply be structured, and a few basic prayers can serve as 'mother-structures' in the development of all sorts of advanced praying. To change the curriculum in accordance with this insight would make sure that the children were better equipped for further education (which also means further praying).

Another lecturer has found it possible to interpret the basic concepts expressing the structure of the Trinity in a way comprehensible to every child, independent of the child's intellectual development. This lecturer has obviously already been listening to the first one. Other lectures announce that they have produced textbooks in accordance with these new ideas about how to teach the Holy Trinity.

A critique, however, is passed about. Why not listen to the way children already produce simple rhymes? Children are already preoccupied with praying. The only thing needed is to push the children smoothly in the direction of praying for the real Trinity. In this way the teaching of the Holy Trinity can be based on already established rhymes of the children.

This suggestion is supported by scholars, obviously not living in the city of the conference. They explain that in their country they have observed many sorts of old and well-established prayers. Already long before the praying for the Holy Trinity was institutionalised, people have been praying, and in many respects these old prayers anticipate the prayers for the Holy Trinity. In fact, they are to be conceived as genuine prayers. The foreign scholars suggest that the religious curriculum take into consideration these good old prayers, and on the basis on these the teaching can move in direction of paradigmatic prayers for the Holy Trinity. But why, in fact, call some prayers 'right' ones? Why stick to the old paradigm? All sorts of prayers seem equal.

During the happy hour of the conference somebody raised the questions: Why this concern for religious education? Why teach children to memorise players? What are the social and political functions of teaching everybody to pray? What is the purpose? Why not discuss the actual function of religious education? This might be the voice of critical religious education.

Acknowledgment

I want to tank Elin Emborg for comments and suggestions for improving the manuscript.

References

Adorno, T. W. (1971): *Erziehung zur Mündigkeit*, Suhrkamp, Frankfurt am Main.
Borba, M. (1990): 'Ethnomathematics and Education', *For the Learning of Mathematics* 10(1), 39-43.

D'Ambrosio, U. (1985): 'Ethnomathematics and its Place in the History and Pedagogy of Mathematics', *For the Learning of Mathematics* 5(1), 44-48.

D'Ambrosio, U. (1994): 'Cultural Framing of Mathematics Teaching and Learning', in Biehler, R. et al. (eds.): *Didactics of Mathematics as a Scientific Discipline*, Kluwer Academic Publishers, Dordrecht, 443-455.

Frankenstein, M. (1983): 'Critical Mathematics Education: An Application of Paulo Freire's Epistemology', *Journal of Education* 165(4), 315-339. (Reprinted in Shor, I. (ed.): *Freire for the Classroom*, Boyton and Cook Publishers, Porthmouth, New Hampshire, 1987, 180-210.)

Frankenstein, M. (1989): *Relearning Mathematics*: A Different Third R - Radical Maths, Free Association Books, London.

Freire, P. (1972): *Pedagogy of the Oppressed*, Herder and Herder, New York.

Freire, P. (1974): *Cultural Action for Freedom*, Penguin Books, London.

Keitel, C. (1989): 'Mathematics and Technology', *For the Learning of Mathematics* 9(1), 7-13.

Keitel, C. (1993): 'Implicit Mathematical Models in Social Practice and Explicit Mathematics Teaching by Applications', in Lange, J. de et al. (eds): *Innovations in Maths Education by Modelling and Applications*, Ellis Horwood, Chichester, 19-30.

Keitel, C., Kotzmann, E. and Skovsmose, O.(1993): 'Beyond the Tunnel-Vision: Analysing the Relationship between Mathematics, Society and Technology', in Keitel, C. and Ruthven, K. (eds.): *Learning from Computers: Mathematics Education and Technology*, Springer Verlag, Berlin, 243-279.

Knijnik, G. (1993): 'Culture, Mathematics, Education and the Landless of Southern Brazil', in Julie, C., Angelis, D. and Davis, Z. (eds.) (1993): *Political Dimensions of Mathematics Education 2: Curriculum Reconstruction for Society in Transition*, Maskew Miller Longman, Cape Town, 149-153.

Mills, C. W. (1959): *The Sociological Imagination*, Oxford University Press, New York.

Skovsmose, O. (1990): 'Mathematical Education and Democracy', *Educational Studies in Mathematics* 21, 109-128.

Skovsmose, O. (1992): 'Democratic Competence and Reflective Knowing in Mathematics', *For the Learning of Mathematics* 2(2), 2-11.

Skovsmose, O. (1994): *Towards a Philosophy of Critical Mathematics Education*, Kluwer Academic Publishers, Dordrecht.

Skovsmose, O. (1996): 'Meaning in Mathematics Education', Research Report 4, Department of Mathematics, Physics, Chemistry and

Informatics, Royal Danish School of Educational Studies, Copenhagen. (Will be published as part of the BACOMET-4 project.)

Skovsmose, O. and Nielsen, L. (1996): 'Critical Mathematics Education', in Bishop, A. (ed.): *International Handbook of Mathematics Education*, Kluwer Academic Publishers, Dordrecht, 1257-1288.

Vithal, R. and Skovsmose, O. 'The End of Innocence: A Critique of "Ethnomathematics"', *Educational Studies in Mathematics 34 (1997) 131-157.*

MATHEMATICS FOR WORK - A DIDACTICAL PERSPECTIVE

Rudolf Straesser,

> *"... mind is an extension of the hands*
> *and tools that you use and of the jobs to*
> *which you apply them."*
> *Jerome Bruner 1996*

0 Slogans on mathematics for work and its learning

Here are some slogans which are frequently offered to comment on the role of mathematics at work and the way of learning to prepare for the workplace:

> - The world of work is full of Mathematics.
> - Abstract Mathematics is the most powerful mathematics for work.
> - Computer use implies sophisticated mathematics at work.
> - The average employee / worker must learn (no) mathematics for her/ his work.
> - The best way to learn mathematics for work is training on the job.

After briefly describing the most important concepts - namely "work" and "vocational education", the lecture reviews some research findings on mathematics for / at work and identifies consequences, problems and potentials of vocational mathematics education.

1   Work and Learning for Work: some basic "definitions"

The "Advanced Learner's Dictionary of Current English" offers the following two first (of seven) definitions of "**work**":
- "bodily or mental effort directed towards doing or making something; the expenditure of energy (by man, machinery, forces such as steam, electricity, etc. or by forces of nature)" and
- "occupation; employment what a person does in order to earn money"
(p. 1492 in Hornby et al. 1960, 11th impr.).

From this definition, it is obvious that "work" is one of the central human activities - if not *the* central one as in certain philosophies. The lecture comments on the role of mathematics in this human activity and on learning mathematics related to these activities. Following the definition, I will concentrate on work with an identifiable purpose and within a certain social system to secure one's own life. Consequently, I will not go into details on "informal", everyday-activities related to mathematics or topics like "out of school mathematics" or "Ethno-Mathematics" which nevertheless are somehow related to the subject of my lecture.

In this lecture, learning mathematics for work will be referred to as "learning mathematics in technical and vocational education" - following the definition given more than a decade ago. According to the terminology of UNESCO, technical and vocational education is
> "the educational process ... (which) involves, in addition to general education, the study of technologies and related sciences and the acquisition of practical skills and knowledge relating occupations in various sectors of economic and social life"
> (UNESCO 1978, p. 17).

On purpose, the lecture will start from aims, problems and potentialities inherent in mathematics at work and vocational mathematics education. As a consequence, only minor attention is paid to general psychological competencies fostered or destroyed by vocational mathematics education. Nevertheless, by analysing mathematics at work and vocational mathematics education, general mathematics education could be informed on fundamental issues of using and learning mathematics. In my view - and somehow in contrast to the UNESCO-definition, vocational education is not an addition or a field of application of general education. To the contrary: general education tends to present too narrow a perspective on education, a perspective hampered by the concentration on schools, classrooms and mathematics watered down to school mathematics. Vocational mathematics broadens this narrow perspective by opening a window on mathematics at work, deeply intertwined with its applications and social life.

2 Mathematics for Work: findings on workplace practice

In this paragraph I present three cases in mathematics for work and its learning in order to show the variety of relevant situations as well as some features which I think are most pertinent to learning mathematics for work. I start with "street mathematics" at work, then present a study on geometry in technical drawing and finish this paragraph with research on mathematics in the banking sector. "Street mathematics" is a reminder of the omnipresence of mathematics at work, while the other two cases analyse standard professional use of mathematics in economic enterprises. These activities are firmly institutionalised in a workplace hierarchy and executed to earn one' s living. Both cases serve to look more deeply in major features of mathematics at work. Technical drawing in some sense presents the "usual" potentials and problems of mathematics at work while mathematics in the banking sector throws some light on the role of modern technology, especially computers, with mathematics at work.

2.1"Street Mathematics" at work

"Street mathematics" is usually not analysed under the heading "work" but under the heading "out-of-school" or "informal" mathematics. If you recall the definition given above, it nevertheless is quite obvious that it is a case of "mathematics for work".

What I have in mind is the series of studies undertaken by Carraher, Nunes and Schliemann (and a whole lot of co-workers) recently published as a book entitled "Street mathematics and school mathematics" (cf. Nunes et al. 1993). I do not want to rephrase all the findings and careful analyses of the book. From this material it is obvious that mathematics can and - sometimes - must be learned at the workplace, that mathematics learned at the workplace seems to be somehow different from school mathematics and that mathematics learned in school sometimes even seems to hinder workplace activities. As an illustration I want to read out only one quote from the study on "Mathematical Knowledge Developed at Work: The Contribution of Practice Versus the Contribution of Schooling" where Schliemann&Acioly (1989) analyse the use and understanding of mathematical knowledge among Brazilian bookies working in a special lottery game:
"Procedures to solve problems for which bookies do not have a ready answer are usually oral procedures not taught in schools. ... experience in solving problems at work can be a source of mathematical knowledge" (op.cit., p. 217).

As a consequence, we start from the assumption that participation in a workplace community of practice seems to foster learning for work - even learning mathematics for work. Nunes et al. even go further, concluding a study on the concept of proportionality and its transfer by stating:
"... this series of study demonstrates that the concept of proportionality does not have to be taught. It can develop on the basis of everyday experience. The resulting conceptual schema ...

models relationships in everyday situations but clearly surpasses the procedures used in everyday practice. It is not unidirectional, as everyday practices tend to be, and it can be applied to new situations"
(Nunes et al. 1993, p. 126).

Is this true for every type of mathematics at work ? Does this also hold for the qualified technician ? Are we entitled to dissolve all technical and vocational schools and colleges around the world in favour of learning at the workplace ? The next case will shed some favourable light on this wrong assumption.

2.2 Mathematics for the qualified technician: Geometry and technical drawing

To learn more about the actual use of mathematics, especially geometry, at work, we "climb up" the qualification ladder and look into a study with technical drawers in metalwork analysing the role of geometry in technical drawing (for a detailed report cf. Bromme, Rambow & Straesser 1996). As a consequence of difficulties in identifying mathematics at work, the study in technical drawing approached the problem of finding mathematics at work by individually interviewing thirty draughtspersons near their workplace and during their usual working time. All but one interviewee had passed an examination as a qualified draughtsperson. They had 2 to 32 years of professional draughting experience (median: twelve years). At the time of the interviews, thirteen of them did not use CAD-techniques at their workplace.

A prepared set of sixteen technical drawings was offered to the draughtspersons who were asked to classify them in a way they would classify if they had to draw these. In order to relate the drawings to the work of the interviewees, the drawings were selected to represent three dimensions: measurement versus no measurement in the drawing, symmetry or non-symmetry of the pieces drawn, and type of drawing (projections versus orthogonal views).

With two possibilities in each dimension, 16 drawings can have two drawings for every combination of possibilities (cf. Fig. 1 showing two sample drawings). When the interviewees had formed groups with the drawings, they were asked to comment on their classification by giving a short description, at least a catchword to every group they had formed.

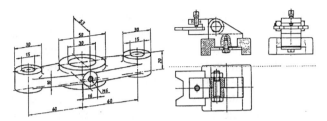

Fig. 1: Two sample drawings

The groupings and catchwords of the draughtspersons can be summed up as follows:

• Symmetry does not play a role in the mental representation of the technical draughtspersons, while type of representation of the drawings shown is respected by the interviewees and measurement seems highly important to them.

• On average, the draughtspersons give a classification which can be represented by the following two-dimensional drawing with the "standard" catchwords given.

This classification rather well duplicates the two ex-ante dimensions of measurement and type of drawing. One could even say: the draughtspersons rather well respected two major mathematical classifications "hidden" in the drawings.

• Nevertheless the "standard"-descriptions illustrate that the interviewees more or less classify according to similar uses of the drawings (such as production, fitting, or presentation of tools) and only once in four "standard" descriptions relay on categories from descriptive geometry - a subdiscipline from applied geometry, if classified in disciplinary mathematical terms. What is most important to the draughtspersons is the professional, the production aspect of the drawings.

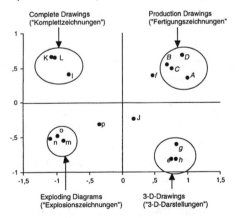

Fig. 2: Classification of drawings in a 2D-space
(Drawings with measurement are represented by italics,
orthogonal views are represented by capital letters)

In order to know more about the actual workplace situation, the draughtspersons were also asked to evaluate the respective importance of vocational training against workplace-experience and aspects of technical drawing which they came to learn at the workplace. We asked the interviewees to linearly rank qualifications according to their importance for an experienced draughtspersons. With nine qualifications offered, the draughtspersons came up with three qualifications rather clearly ranked most important. "Comprehension of the purpose and functioning of the object to be drawn" was clearly ranked in the first place (mean: 1, mode: 1), while "comprehension of geometrical relations of the drawing" (mean: 3, mode: 1) and "comprehension of a sketch or an order" (mean: 3, mode: 2) were ranked behind. The result is some sort of confirmation of the utmost importance of production-related aspects of a technical drawing - while mathematics, esp. geometry seems to be embedded in workplace matters. According to the interviewees, this "vocational mathematics" is better learned at the workplace than in colleges.

Interpreted more globally, the study clearly shows that mathematics and vocational knowledge are intimately interwoven at work. Workplace practices do not distinguish mathematical knowledge from other knowledge helpful to cope with the professional problem. It is by means of a "problem-oriented integration of concepts" from various sources (cf. Bromme et al. 1996, p. 166) that the draughtspersons cognitively organise their work. A separation and piecewise analysis and piecewise learning seem to be inappropriate.

2.3 Information technology and mathematics for banking

To come to the topic of vocational use of mathematics when the professional activity is deeply characterised by use of modern information technology, I turn to a recent study by Noss & Hoyles (1996) analysing the mathematics of banking. They were asked to help with a problem in a London bank. The senior management thought that

"many employees did not have a robust grasp of the mathematics underpinning their work — they had little feel for the mathematics which would enable them to appreciate the models on which financial instruments were based and to recognise their limitations. There was apparently a widespread reluctance to think mathematically about transactions, and a recipe-book mentality which relied on technology without understanding what it could and could not do" (loc.cit., p. 6).

To illustrate the situation, Noss & Hoyles (loc. cit., p. 8) quote from a meeting with an employee:
> In short, ... 'I press the button and see what it says'.
> What then?
> 'I look at the answer. If it seems to indicate what I think we should do, I use the number to justify my decision. If not, I ignore it, or put in figures which will support my hunch'.

Noss & Hoyles accepted to work on the problems and took a twofold approach:
> "First, we set out to understand more clearly what was the essence of the problem. ... What did employees do that was (or was not) mathematical? ... What would be a useful and valid way to simplify and mathematise the banking situation for learnability? ...
> Second, we agreed to implement an educational programme which could begin to tackle the problem." (loc.cit, p. 7)

The most difficult part of the study was to identify mathematical relations in the practice of the bankers, to handle the dialectics of the specific procedures used by the bankers and the mathematical commonalities underpinning their transactions. Noss & Hoyles took the concept of function as a bridge between banking procedures and the mathematical models. They decided to place modelling by programming at the core of their course in order to foster the mathematical culture of the employees. The conceptual focus was on percentages and graphs which where (re)presented by simple program procedures which could be changed and linked in co-operation between the employees and the mathematics educators.

I will not go on with Noss & Hoyles' description of the course they designed to make the bankers better comprehend their banking mathematics. More important here are two aspects of the use of modern technology:

(1) If nothing is prepared to counterbalance the 'natural' development, application of modern (computer) technology seems to imply an additional step to a total invisibility of mathematics at the workplace. Even in the number driven world of banking, numbers and commercial arithmetic disappear from the consciousness of the average employee. Mathematics hide in computer algorithms which are applied without paying attention to the underlying mathematical model of the banking process. Even somewhat complicated procedures (like calculating the present value of a treasury bill by discounting from face value in

dependence of the day of maturity) go unrecognised by the average employee who relies on the programs designed by an unknown specialist in an unknown software house or department.

"... these models were almost entirely hidden from view. Understanding and reshaping them was the preserve of the rocket scientists; the separation between use and understanding was absolute and the models' structures were obscured by the data-driven view encouraged by the computer screens"
(cf. Noss & Hoyles 1996, p. 17).

The use of modern (computer) technology implies the use of so-phisticated mathematical models - but this normally goes without recognition by the average employee.

(2) Nevertheless this practice of using sophisticated mathematics can be brought to the foreground and consciousness of the user by appropriate courses designed to open up the black boxes of the programs and partially degreying these boxes. And it is modern computer technology and appropriate software again who can be successfully used in this process to really explore and understand the underlying banking mathematics.

To put it differently: Modern computer technology itself has a dual role in the process of using mathematics at the workplace: It can be used as a way to hide mathematics in sophisticated software. Mathematics as a tool disappears in workplace routines - and modern technology speeds up this disappearance. On the other hand, the very same technology can be used to foster understanding of the professional use of mathematics by explicitly modelling the hidden mathematical relations and offering software tools to explore and better understand the underlying mathematical models.

3 Vocational Mathematics Education: Learning for work

The last remark on technology's potential to further understanding brings me to my second important topic: What about learning mathematics for work ? What about vocational mathematics education ?

If we look for the organisational patterns of technical and vocational education around the world, we find a whole variety of models from full-time technical colleges organised by the government (as in France) over part-time colleges partly run by governmental agencies (e.g.: some areas of vocational education in Germany) to isolated activities in colleges and/or private enterprises (as for instance in England or the USA). Sometimes, a mix of all these ingredients is offered (see e.g. Australia, showing the typical feature of a country which only recently acknowledges the potential of technical and vocational education). The so-called developing countries often have no technical and vocational education at all.

3.1 Two Pedagogies: Modelling versus Legitimate Peripheral Participation

Taken as an indicator of the underlying pedagogy, the organisational features show two extremes of learning principles and the standard oscillation and insecurity of political decisions on this matter.

Classroom type of vocational mathematics education tends to present mathematics as a separate body of knowledge, sometimes even structured along a disciplinary system from mathematics. In this case, mathematics has to be linked to work and workplace practice by building mathematical models and applying mathematics by the well-known modelling cycle of "situation - (mathematical) model - interpretation of the situation". The situation is to come from the workplace, the mathematical model rests upon mathematical structures and algorithms known before or taught on the spot and the solution of the model hopefully can be interpreted in a way to cope with the given professional situation (for a summary of this approach see Blum 1988, related Theme or Topic Groups at various ICMEs and the series of conferences under the "ICTMA" heading). In this pedagogy, mathematics can come first and can be taught / learned along its own, disciplinary structure while applying it to work via modelling may come second, sometimes never or inappropriately. As can be seen from this description, the modelling approach clearly distinguishes two types of knowledge - namely professional and mathematical knowledge, which have to be brought together by the individual to cope with the professional problem. In most cases, modelling vocational problems by applying mathematics is a major difficulty for the future worker - especially the extraction of the mathematical model from a professional situation at hand.

The other extreme and contrasting pedagogy is training on the job, where learning takes place at the workplace whenever it is needed by the workplace practice and its problems. The focus is on coping with the situation at hand - and mathematics may come in or not when solving a workplace problem. Apprenticeship may offer a chance to gradually develop from a beginner to an expert at the workplace. With this approach, learning may be identified with taking part in a "community of practice" and gradually developing from a beginner to a full practitioner by means of situated learning (for thorough discussion of the underlying concept of "legitimate peripheral participation" see Lave & Wenger 1991). This pedagogy starts from a uniform concept of knowledge present in a community of practice (not in individual workers),

"knowing is inherent in the growth and transformation of identities and it is located in relations among practitioners, their practice, the artefacts of that practice and the social organization and political economy of communities of practice"
(Lave&Wenger 1991, p. 122).

As a consequence, mathematics can continue to go invisibly, embedded in the workplace practice and serving as a tool used to cope with professional problems if needed. A problem-oriented integration of concepts tends to hide mathematical relations under the uniform workplace practices. Following this approach, studies on "street mathematics" (like Nunes et al.) had to detect and bring back to light the mathematical procedures in workplace activities, to describe them and to show the competence of the practitioners in using mathematics.

3.2 Transfer - a Focus of the Didactical Debate

The starting point of the research on "street mathematics" was a twofold observation: (a) With little or no schooling, the children working in the streets were able to solve their "mathematical" problems at work. (b) Even if the children had attended school, children successful at work could not or worse solve "isomorphic" college type word problems. How to understand this obvious lack of transfer from classroom to work ?

After more than a decade of research (cf. the monographs Lave 1988, Lave & Wenger 1991, Nunes et al. 1993, Saxe 1991), the protagonists of situated learning in a community of practice can easily understand the dilemma described above: Mathematics used in the street is learned there, is efficient in solving the street problems and fundamentally different from the one learned in school or researched in a mathematics department at university. To rephrase it in a more general way: Mathematics learned in a specific context is part of a subjective domain of experience (cf. Bauersfeld 1983) and cannot easily be isolated, taken away, transferred and applied in a different situation.

In contrast to that, the "mathematical modeller" starts from the assumption that a piece of mathematics once learned will come to mind whenever it models (adequately) a given situation, that - after appropriately modelling the situation - it can be applied easily and will offer a decent way to cope with the problem at hand. In fact, reality seems to be less convenient: The learner usually has difficulties to mobilise her/his knowledge in so-called isomorphic situations, s/he has problems to transfer a procedure, a solution from one situation to a different, maybe unknown, one. The widespread and well documented lack of easy transfer definitely contradicts the plea for modelling and easy application.

3.3 Training on the Job versus Learning in Vocational Colleges

As a consequence of this preference for the situated learning and community of practice approach, why not dissolve any classroom type of training at least in vocational mathematics and totally rely on training on the job for vocational mathematics? I want to draw your attention to a finding which might be forgotten when closing vocational / technical colleges: In the study on Brazilian bookies, the protagonists of street mathematics state :

"... the influence of schooling is not limited to topics explicitly taught in classrooms but ... school experience provides a different way of analyzing and understanding everyday activities. ... Schooled bookies ... seem to have a different attitude toward procedures for solving problems as a result of their schooling. ... school experience has an effect on how people deal with more academic questions, such as explaining their everyday procedures or making explicit the mathematical structures implicit in their everyday activities. School experience is also related to better performance on solving problems that differ from those usually encountered at work" (Schliemann&Acioly 1989, p. 216 ff).

Obviously, classroom type of activities can offer an opportunity to broaden the perspective of the future worker, to empower her/him with solving problems not common to workplace practice and to foster understanding of the workplace procedure. Classroom type of activities can offer an understanding which goes beyond the narrow confines of the actual situation, which transcends the situation and the problem where and when knowledge is developed. Classroom type activities in schools or colleges can show mathematics as a way to transcend the context with more general problem solving strategies and structures. But how to cope with the transfer dilemma described in part 3.2 ?

As far as I can see there is a "way out". Modelling with the help of mathematics should not be taken as a means to get rid of the dirty specialities of the concrete workplace to solve the abstracted problem by means of pure mathematics. It is by exploiting the interplay of the professional, concrete situation and the structural, mathematical model that one can cope with the given professional problem. In doing so, one can develop a mathematical structure maybe adaptable to a variety of different problems linked to the initial professional situation. Noss & Hoyles in their paper call this to set up a "domain of abstraction" where the "dialectic between concrete and abstract" closely ties together mathematical ideas and practical knowledge of the professional domain (Noss & Hoyles 1996., p. 27). In doing so, mathematics is not reduced to the general type of activity of theorising, analysing language and seeing structures implicitly devaluing situated learning as learning no mathematics (for a recent claim of this reduced point of view cf. Sierpinska 1995, p. 5).

If mathematics is taught as a bridge between the concrete, maybe vocational situation and the abstract, maybe systematic structure, even classroom vocational education can show mathematics as a "general" tool which is of larger an importance than just coping with the narrow tasks of the everyday work practice or the inculcation of algorithms. If college type education aims at presenting (vocational) mathematics in this way, one condition for success seems to be that mathematics is taught in a way it is "meaningful to the individual" who is learning. Technical and vocational colleges then have to strive for problems from the workplace which are as realistic as possible. And the problems should be taught in a way as close as possible to the actual concerns of the students (for an elaboration of this cf. Boaler 1993).

An additional case for learning mathematics not in a too narrow workplace context is expressed in a reminder I would like to place at the end of this section:

"Mathematics in vocational education is serving more as a background knowledge for explaining and avoiding mistakes, recognising safety risks, judicious measurement and various forms of estimation. ... Not practice at the workplace but deepening of the professional knowledge, education to a responsible use of tools and machines and the understanding of and coping with everyday mathematical problems legitimise mathematics in vocational education"

(Appelrath 1985, p. 133/139; translation R.S.).

4 The slogans revisited

To end the lecture, I will comment on the slogans of the beginning of my talk.

"The world of work is full of Mathematics."

Indeed, the world of work is full of mathematics, but vocational mathematics is different from disciplinary mathematics - insofar as it is interested in solving the workplace problems, not disciplinary mathematical problems.

Vocational mathematics is also different from "school mathematics" in general education - insofar as it is always specific to the workplace in question, hardly interested in links to other mathematics and sometimes far more complicated than school mathematics.

"Abstract Mathematics is the most powerful mathematics for work."

Mathematics at work is not primarily interested in structures and logico-mathematical statements per se. It is not used the way mathematics is developed within its discipline. At work, it is used as algorithms, black boxes, prepared forms like worksheets etc.

"Computer use implies sophisticated mathematics at work."

Computer based mathematics is developed by few specialised people in a sophisticated way - to give it to the majority of workers encapsulated in algorithms and black boxes. Computers and appropriate software normally work to hide mathematical structures, but can be used to enhance understanding the practice of the workplace.

"The average worker must learn (no) mathematics for her/his work."

The mathematics of the average worker depends on the vision one has of a worker. To train the qualified and autonomous worker, you have to give the opportunity of learning and understanding ("legitimate peripheral participation" together with understanding algorithms and "degreying" black boxes). This is not only the case in the presence of modern (computer) technology, but also holds in traditional workplaces and societies.

"The best way to learn mathematics for work is training on the job."

Training on the job is a very good way to learn vocational mathematics. Nevertheless, learning deeply related to, but within a certain distance from actual workplace practice offers the opportunity to develop a broader understanding of the task to be mastered. There may be even technological and/or social conditions of work where learning is only feasible and affordable in a certain distance from productive work, e.g. in simulation scenarios. If "peripheral" is realised in an empowering way - not necessarily in classrooms, legitimate peripheral participation may be the best way to learn mathematics for work.

As a reminder of the more general aspiration of my lecture, I would like to offer you a slight change of my title's wording. Why not change from "Mathematics for Work - a Didactical Perspective" to "Vocational Mathematics Education - a New Perspective for Mathematics Instruction" ?

References

Appelrath, K.-H. (1985). Zur Verwendung von Mathematik und zur Situation des Fachrechnens im Berufsfeld Metalltechnik (dargestellt an zwei Unterrichtsbeispielen). In P. Bardy,W. Blum, & H. G. Braun (Eds.), *Mathematik in der Berufsschule - Analysen und Vorschläge zum Fachrechenunterricht.* (pp. 127 - 139). Essen: Girardet.

Bauersfeld, H. (1983). Subjektive Erfahrungsbereiche als Grundlage einer Interaktionstheorie des Mathematiklernens und -lehrens. In Bauersfeld et al. (Eds.), *Lernen und Lehren von Mathematik* (pp. 1 - 56). Köln: Aulis-Verlag Deubner.

Blum, W. (1988). Theme Group 6: Mathematics and Other Subjects. In A. Hirst & K. Hirst (Eds.), *Proceedings of the Sixth International Congress on Mathematical Education* (pp. 277 - 291). Budapest: János Bolyai Mathematical Society.

Boaler, J. (1993). The Role of Contexts in the Mathematics Classroom: Do they Make Mathematics More "Real"? *For the Learning of Mathematics,* 13(2), 12 - 17.

Bromme, R.,Rambow, R., & Sträßer, R. (1996). Jenseits von 'Oberfläche' und 'Tiefe': Zum Zusammenhang von Problemkategorisierungen und Arbeitskontext bei Fachleuten des Technischen Zeichnens. In H. Gruber & A. Ziegler (Eds.), *Expertiseforschung - Theoretische und methodische Grundlagen* (pp. 150 - 168). Wiesbaden: Westdeutscher Verlag.

Bruner, J. (1996). *The Culture of Education.* Cambridge, Mass. - London: Harvard University Press.

Hornby, A. S., Gatenby, E. V., & Wakefield, H. (1960, 11th ed.). *The Advanced Learner's Dictionary of Current English.* London: Oxford University Press.

Lave, J. (1988). *Cognition in Practice.* Cambridge, Mass.: Cambridge University Press.

Lave, J., & Wenger, E. (1991). *Situated learning: Legitimate peripheral participation.* Cambridge - New York - Oakleigh: Cambridge University Press.

Noss, R., & Hoyles, C. (1996). The visibility of meanings: Modelling the mathematics of banking. *International Journal of Computers for Mathematical Learning,* 1(1), 3 - 31.

Nunes, T., Schliemann, A. D., & Carraher, D. W. (1993). *Street mathematics and school mathematics.* Cambridge - New York - Oakleigh: Cambridge University Press.

Saxe, G. B. (1991). *Culture and Cognitive Development: Studies in mathematical understanding.* Hilldale, NJ: Lawrence Erlbaum.

Schliemann, A. D., & Acioly, N. M. (1989). Mathematical Knowledge Developed at Work: The Contribution of Practice Versus the Contribution of Schooling. *Cognition and Instruction,* 6(3), 185 - 221.

Sierpinska, A. (1995). Mathematics: "in Context", "Pure", or "with Applications" ? A contribution to the question of transfer in the learning of mathematics. *For the Learning of Mathematics,* 15(1), 2 - 15.

Sträßer, R., & Zevenbergen, R. (1996). Further Mathematics Education. In A. Bishop et al. (Eds.), *International Handbook on Mathematics Education* (pp. 647-674) Dodrecht: Kluwer.

UNESCO (1978). *Terminology of technical and vocational education - Terminologie de l'enseignement technique et professionnel.* Paris: UNESCO.

Acknowledgements: I would like to thank my colleague Falk Seeger for helpful and constructive comments on an earlier draft of this paper.

UNA TEORÍA DE PROCESOS Y SISTEMAS GENÉRICOS EN LAS MATEMÁTICAS Y EN LA EDUCACIÓN MATEMÁTICA

Carlos E. Vasco (Colombia)

1. Introducción

La enunciación de categorías ontológicas explícitas pareció quedar desacreditada después de Aristóteles por los desarrollos neo-platónicos; pero reapareció con toda su fuerza en la filosofía escolástica. Esas categorías fueron rechazadas nuevamente por los filósofos y científicos de la Ilustración, pero reaparecieron en el ingenioso intento de diseñar nuevas categorías que instauró Immanuel Kant. Los neo-positivistas y los empirstas lógicos desacreditaron todo tipo de ontología como metafísica sin sentido. Pero esa breve historia puede significar también que ya está maduro el tiempo para intentar una nueva organización de las categorías del discurso contemporáneo.

Un primer intento de este estilo fue la Teoría General de Sistemas de Ludwig von Berthalanffy, que derivó del lenguaje de la biología en los años treinta, y tuvo gran florecimiento en los sesenta y setenta. Pero fue criticada duramente por los existencialistas y por los neo-marxistas, hasta el punto de que en los años ochenta y noventa se experimenta ya como pasada de moda.

Un esfuerzo por repensar todas esas objeciones a la Teoría General de Sistemas y por recuperar muchos aspectos válidos de ella me llevó a proponer una teoría general de procesos, en la cual los sistemas juegan un papel secundario, pues sirven sólo como modelos para esos procesos que parecen escaparse de nuestra comprensión. La he llamado indistintamente 'Teoría General de Procesos y Sistemas' o 'Teoría de Procesos y Sistemas Genéricos', según si el énfasis está en la generalidad de la teoría o en la genericidad de los procesos y los sistemas de que ella trata. Para esta conferencia voy a utilizar la segunda manera de nombrarla, haciendo énfasis en los procesos y sistemas genéricos y por ello, para abreviar, me referiré a ella como 'la teoría PSG'.

La inspiración para esta teoría la obtuve de la lógica matemática, que estudia todas las ramas de las matemáticas por medio de la teoría de modelos, utilizando un dispositivo muy sencillo, que los matemáticos suelen llamar 'una estructura', y que consiste de un conjunto básico de elementos o universo de la estructura, un conjunto de operaciones y un conjunto de relaciones. El nombre de 'estructura' es cuestionable, pero la idea es lo suficientemente sencilla y poderosa para intentar ensayarla en disciplinas diferentes de las matemáticas, desde la biología y la ecología hasta la sociología y la ciencia política. También resultó muy adecuada para describir la actividad de los matemáticos y para diseñar proyectos de investigación y materiales curriculares en la educación matemática.

Esta conferencia intenta hacer una breve descripción de esta teoría, omitiendo los aspectos puramente filosóficos y concentrándonos en las descripciones y esquemas que se vuelven posibles desde la teoría PSG cuando tratamos de capturar las maneras como tanto los matemáticos como los investigadores en educación matemática conducen sus investigaciones, y en las implicaciones que esto tiene para el trabajo curricular en matemáticas en todos los niveles, desde el Jardín Infantil hasta la Escuela de Postgrado.

Para decirlo de una vez, no estoy hablando de meras aplicaciones futuras de esta teoría PSG. Ya fue utilizada para desarrollar todo el currículo de matemáticas para los grados primero a noveno de la reforma de la educación colombiana que fue adoptada en 1984 para los dos primeros grados, y extendida luego grado por grado hasta alcanzar el noveno en 1993.

Un informe sobre este tratamiento del currículo de matemáticas se publicó en inglés en un libro sobre experiencias transculturales de educación apoyado por el Proyecto de Potencial Humano de la Universidad de Harvard y la Fundación Bernard van Leer, que salió en 1985 y fue traducido al español en 1990. Dirigí un seminario sobre ese tema en la Universidad de Harvard en 1986, y he publicado una serie de trabajos en español sobre esta teoría PSG, tanto respecto a las matemáticas como a la educación matemática, así como a otras disciplinas.

En esta conferencia voy a exponer la última versión de la teoría PSG que acaba de ser publicada en febrero pasado en el segundo volumen de una serie de siete tomos que contienen las contribuciones de la Misión de Ciencia, Educación y Desarrollo de la Presidencia de la República de Colombia, de la cual Misión tuve el honor de haber sido miembro y comisionado coordinador.

2. La teoría PSG

Para las matemáticas, la idea básica de la teoría PSG es que un matemático selecciona mentalmente un subproceso específico de entre los muchos y muy complejos procesos que vive, siendo él mismo o ella misma un subproceso más que se entrelaza con el subproceso seleccionado. La investigación original en matemáticas involucra ante todo la creación de modelos mentales de esos subprocesos, con el fin de reproducir, a través de la manipulación mental de esos modelos y a través de la manipulación de símbolos externos para ellos, los esquemas y patrones que se observaron en esos subprocesos. La tarea de construcción de modelos de esos subprocesos fue bautizada por Hans Freudenthal como 'matematización', palabra que ya es usual entre los educadores matemáticos. Pero con la ayuda de la teoría PSG podemos decir mucho más que el nombre de esa actividad matematizadora: podemos describir precisamente los productos de ese esfuerzo. El producto de un esfuerzo de matematización es un sistema conceptual con uno o más universos básicos, que llamo el substrato o el aspecto material del sistema; con ninguna, una, dos o más operaciones, posiblemente de ariedades diferentes (o sea no sólo binarias, sino tal vez unarias, ternarias, o hablando en general, n-arias), que llamo la dinámica o el aspecto activo del sistema, y con una, dos o más relaciones, que también pueden ser unarias, binarias, ternarias, o en general n-arias, que llamo la estructura o aspecto formal del sistema.

Utilizo con frecuencia la analogía de los juegos de salón para explicar lo que son los sistemas matemáticos: el substrato o aspecto material de un juego está compuesto por las fichas y el tablero; la dinámica o aspecto activo del sistema está compuesto por las jugadas válidas del juego, y la estructura o aspecto formal está compuesto por la red de relaciones definida en las reglas del juego.

Por lo tanto, insisto en distinguir el sistema de su substrato, distinción que ya es común entre los matemáticos, quienes saben cómo construir sistemas matemáticos diferentes utilizando el mismo conjunto básico de fichas; por ejemplo, con un conjunto de sólo cuatro fichas básicas se pueden construir dos grupos no isomorfos, 48 grupos superficialmente diferentes, y más de cuatro mil millones de grupoides. Pero también insisto en distinguir claramente la estructura del sistema de lo que es el sistema mismo, con el argumento de que es necesario mantener la distinción de los aspectos material y formal, o sea del substrato con respecto a la estructura o red de relaciones. Así pues, la palabra 'estructura' se refiere a esa red de relaciones que hace que un juego dado sea diferente de otros que utilizan las mismas fichas. Un argumento fuerte para apoyar esta distinción está tomado del lenguaje matemático mismo: se puede decir correctamente que un sistema tiene una estructura particular, pero no tiene mucho sentido decir que una estructura tiene un sistema particular. En el ejemplo de los grupos de cuatro elementos, hay sólo dos estructuras de grupo diferentes, cada una de ellas compartida por 24 grupos superficialmente diferentes pero isomorfos. Tiene pues mucho sentido decir que los 24 miembros diferentes de una clase de isomorfismo tienen la misma estructura, pero no tiene sentido decir que tienen el mismo sistema.

También distingo claramente la estructura de la dinámica. Hay sistemas puramente relacionales, con estructura pero sin dinámica, como los conjuntos parcialmente ordenados. Pero no hay sistemas puramente operacionales que no tengan estructura. Es verdad que uno puede presentar un sistema en una forma puramente operacional, como lo voy a mostrar más tarde con el ejemplo de la teoría de categorías; pero cada operación crea estructura a través de la relación (n+1)-aria que corresponde a cada operación n-aria. Por lo menos esta estructura implícita siempre existe. Pero el hecho mismo de que haya sistemas puramente relacionales, es decir, sistemas con estructura y sin dinámica, nos obliga a admitir que la estructura es diferente de la dinámica de un sistema dado. La estructura es algo más pasivo y estático; la dinámica es algo más activo y cinemático. Y esta distinción es muy poderosa cuando se trata de construir materiales curriculares, porque los estudiantes prefieren los aspectos dinámicos a los estructurales, y los textos prefieren lo estructural a lo dinámico. La misma distinción es muy útil para revisar y planificar investigaciones sobre el aprendizaje de las funciones, pues los estudiantes las entienden principalmente como transformadores, que son dinámicos y activos; pero los libros de texto las definen como un tipo especial de relaciones, o hasta como un tipo especial de conjuntos, a saber, conjuntos de parejas ordenadas. Pero tanto las relaciones como los conjuntos son pasivos y estáticos, y no capturan las construcciones activas y dinámicas que los estudiantes producen a partir de los sistemas concretos con los cuales ya están familiarizados.

Se puede decir que la potencia de una teoría se puede comparar con el poder de resolución de un microscopio o telescopio: es tanto más poderosa, cuanto mejores y más generadoras sean las distinciones que permite esa teoría. Otra distinción importante que permite la teoría PSG viene de la observación de que los sistemas matemáticos aparecen en tres capas de profundidad diferente: la capa superficial o visible está compuesta por sistemas simbólicos externos, que tienen sus propios elementos, operaciones y relaciones: la capa central o nuclear está compuesta de sistemas conceptuales, y la capa inferior o generadora está compuesta de sistemas concretos o familiares para los sujetos activos que construyen sistemas conceptuales a partir de ellos.

La diferenciación de esos tres niveles de sistemas matemáticos se puede visualizar como un rayo de luz que pasa a través de un prisma: el espectro está compuesto de sólo tres bandas de colores: la superficial, la central y la inferior (ver figura 1).

Un rayo de luz ya refractado a través de un prisma en general no se vuelve a partir cuando pasa a través de un segundo prisma. Pero en este caso podemos visualizar los tres tipos de sistemas como rayos de luz que atraviesan un segundo prisma y que producen a la derecha otro espectro de tres bandas: el conjunto de universos básicos en donde viven sus elementos o fichas del juego, que constituyen su substrato, el conjunto de operaciones básicas que constituyen su dinámica, y el conjunto de relaciones básicas que constituyen su estructura (ver figura 2).

Este artificio sencillo, tomado de la teoría de modelos, pero con la distinción clara entre los tres niveles de sistemas, y entre los tres aspectos de cada sistema, ayuda a tratar todos los temas de las matemáticas de manera coherente desde el Jardín Infantil hasta la Escuela de Postgrado.

3. Algunos ejemplos de utilización de la teoría PSG

La teoría PSG ayuda a distinguir entre operaciones y relaciones. Esta distinción es muy enriquecedora cuando se trata de formular proyectos de investigación sobre preconcepciones de los alumnos o sobre posibles estrategias curriculares.

La reducción usual de las operaciones binarias a relaciones ternarias brilla con luz propia, lo que permite extenderla a la reducción de operaciones unarias a relaciones binarias, de las operaciones ternarias a relaciones cuaternarias, y en general, de las operaciones n-arias a relaciones (n+1)-arias, pero distinguiendo claramente la reducción de la confusión.

A su vez, se puede ver que las relaciones ternarias también pueden reducirse a operaciones n-arias externas, que producen un resultado en un clasificador, por lo general en el clasificador booleano Verdadero-Falso usual, pero también podrían utilizarse otras semánticas. Esta distinción entre relaciones y operaciones, con las dos posibles reducciones que ella habilita, me ha resultado muy fructuosa para tratar los problemas que tienen los estudiantes con las matemáticas de las calculadoras de bolsillo y los computadores, y para aclarar el carácter operatorio que tienen las conectivas lógicas, incluida la implicación material, como diferente del carácter relacional que tienen otras construcciones lógicas como la implicación semántica y la sintáctica, que no son conectivas, pues son relaciones implicativas y no operaciones, como sí lo es la implicación material.

Otro ejemplo tomado de la lógica: la distinción entre las oposiciones medievales entre proposiciones cuantificadas, que es una tripla de relaciones binarias, y las operaciones respectivas, me ayudó a descubrir un nuevo grupo piagetiano en la lógica elemental, a aclarar las misteriosas oscuridades del grupo INRC de Piaget, y a distinguirlo de otro grupo isomorfo a él, pero diferente, que actúa únicamente sobre las implicaciones.

La utilización de la teoría PSG para revisar cuidadosamente la epistemología y la psicología genéticas de Piaget me ayudó a construir una filosofía de las matemáticas, que llamo 'el constructivismo genético', con su contraparte pedagógica, basada en la actividad de construcción de modelos a partir de esquemas recurrentes que se observan en procesos concretos y familiares.

Para explicar el aspecto genético de la teoría PSG voy a utilizar otro ejemplo de lógica. En lugar de introducir las conectivas lógicas usuales por medio de sus tablas de verdad, comienzo con el sistema concreto y familiar de las discusiones entre estudiantes acerca de las distintas interpretaciones de las reglas del fútbol o de otro de sus deportes favoritos. El intento de construir sistemas consistentes que reproduzcan algunos de los esquemas recurrentes en estas discusiones produce en primer lugar una lógica de conectivas temporales, diferentes de las usuales. Por ejemplo, la 'y' temporal no es conmutativa. Trátese de conmutar la frase: 'Me quito los zapatos y me quito las medias'. Es bastante difícil hacerlo en el orden inverso. Pero se puede construir un modelito simplificado de conectivas atemporales, y si se distingue adecuadamente entre las operaciones internas de tipo sintáctico sobre proposiciones, que producen una proposición nueva, y las operaciones externas de tipo semántico sobre las proposiciones hacia el clasificador usual Verdadero-Falso, que producen un valor de verdad, los estudiantes reconstruyen sin mucha dificultad las tablas de verdad y utilizan apropiadamente las conectivas usuales, sin necesidad de obligarlos a aprenderse de memoria esas tablas de verdad.

Tomemos otros ejemplos de la geometría. Los procesos espaciales, como moverse en un salón, moldear arcilla, construir mesas y casas, dibujar decoraciones en hojas de papel, etc., son muy familiares y concretos para la mayoría de las personas. A partir de esos subprocesos se pueden construir muchos modelos diferentes, con el fin de producir los esquemas recurrentes que aparecen cuando esos subprocesos se van desarrollando en el tiempo. Piaget anotó que regresar al punto de partida de un movimiento, o llegar al mismo sitio por medio de caminos diferentes, son procesos que preparan la construcción de los conceptos de invertibilidad y de asociatividad, lo que permite la construcción del concepto de grupo sin necesidad de introducir definiciones formales o axiomas. Lo mismo se puede decir de cualquier sistema matemático relacionado con la geometría.

En realidad, ¿que es una geometría? Desde el punto de vista de la teoría PSG se puede decir que una geometría es un sistema que tiene un substrato con al menos dos universos diferentes, estructurado por relaciones de incidencia que los conectan. Se pueden pues desarrollar geometrías puramente relacionales finitas e infinitas. Al agregarles transformaciones, que en general son operaciones unarias sobre puntos o sobre conjuntos, se está marcando la transición de las geometrías clásicas a las modernas, incluida la topología. Recuérdese que la sola introducción de una operación binaria activa, llamada 'adición', guiada por una ecuación cúbica dada (que es una relación estática), transformó la teoría de las curvas elípticas.

Esta visión filosófica de la geometría, tomada de la teoría PSG me permitió introducir desde el curriculo de primer grado hasta la escuela secundaria un tipo de geometría dinámica que no es la geometría de transformaciones usual. Una breve reseña de esta geometría apareció en las pre-memorias de la Conferencia del ICMI que tuvo lugar en Catania el año pasado, y una versión más completa aparecerá en el libro sobre enseñanza de la geometría que está preparando Vagn Lundsgaard Hansen.

4. Presentaciones de los sistemas

Así como los modelos no son únicos ni unívocos, dada la creatividad de los sujetos que los construyen, así también las presentaciones de un sistema conceptual no son únicas: cada tema matemático puede presentarse por medio de distintos tipos de sistemas. (La palabra 'presentación' está tomada de la teoría de grupos presentados por medio de generadores y relaciones).

Por ejemplo, en la teoría de categorías es posible presentar cada categoría como un sistema puramente relacional, con dos universos diferentes (objetos y flechas), dos relaciones de incidencia diferentes entre flechas y objetos (ser fuente y ser meta), una relación binaria de componibilidad entre flechas, y una relación ternaria que represente la composición; pero también puede presentarse la misma categoría como un sistema puramente operacional, pensando los objetos como productos de operaciones unarias sobre flechas (la fuente de y la meta de), y postulando sólo una operación binaria, la composición de flechas. (Técnicamente hasta se podría eliminar el universo de los objetos, identificando cada objeto con su flecha de identidad).

La teoría de modelos nos ahorra mucho tiempo, al proveernos de modelos para muchos campos conocidos de las matemáticas, y darnos ideas de cómo podemos modelar los nuevos. Pero siempre es muy instructivo tratar de presentar cada sistema por medio de otros tipos no ortodoxos de sistemas.

Por ejemplo, los espacios vectoriales se pueden presentar como sistemas con un universo único y una sola operación binaria interna, bajo la cual forman un grupo abeliano, que tiene también un rico conjunto de operaciones unarias, cada una de las cuales es un endomorfismo, y que forman ellas mismas un cuerpo bajo las operaciones apropiadas; pero también puede presentarse como un sistema con dos universos, uno para un grupo abeliano y otro para un cuerpo, con sus operaciones internas respectivas, más una operación binaria externa que conecta los dos universos.

Esta diversidad de presentaciones nos ilustra uno de los postulados básicos de la teoría PSG: los procesos son lo primario; los sistemas son siempre secundarios, como estrategias subjetivas que son para representar, intervenir o predecir la evolución de los subprocesos, y por lo tanto son variables, incompletos, siempre perfectibles y desechables.

5. Las fracciones y la teoría PSG

Estudiemos ahora una aplicación de la teoría PSG a los sistemas numéricos. La distinción entre los sistemas simbólicos externos, los sistemas conceptuales y sus sistemas concretos de donde provienen, me ayudó a producir una visión más clara de lo que llamo 'el archipiélago fraccionario', basado en la teoría de Thomas Kieran sobre las fracciones como operadores y como partidores. Esta visión le quita las arrugas a esa teoría y ayuda a planear una revisión completa de la investigación sobre fracciones y sobre números racionales que existe en la literatura, pues las fracciones pertenecen a los sistemas simbólicos externos y los números racionales forman por lo menos un sistema conceptual, y probablemente muchos.

Les propongo un acertijo que muestra algo del poder de la teoría PSG en estos aspectos de la investigación sobre fracciones y números racionales. Piensen en esta paradoja: un número racional no tiene numerador ni denominador. ¿Qué les parece?

Si los tuviera, yo pregunto si el numerador de la fracción mitad es par o impar. Puede ser cualquiera de las dos cosas: 1/2 o 2/4. Por lo tanto, lo que llamamos equivocadamente 'la fracción mitad' no es una fracción, sino algo más profundo: un objeto de un sistema conceptual que no tiene numerador ni denominador, y las fracciones no son objetos de ese sistema conceptual, sino de otro sistema simbólico externo para los mismos números racionales como sistema conceptual.

Los decimales son otro tipo de sistema simbólico externo para el mismo sistema conceptual, y también los son los sistemas de rectángulos cuadriculados y los sistemas de pizzas sectorizadas que son tan frecuentes en los libros de texto de matemáticas elementales.

Por ello podemos hablar de fracciones equivalentes: porque hay varias maneras simbólicas de representar el mismo racional. Así deberíamos hablar de rectangulaciones equivalentes y tal vez de 'pizzaciones' equivalentes (ver figura 3). Pero ninguna de ellas es el número racional del sistema conceptual relevante.

La falta de una adecuada distinción entre los subprocesos familiares a los estudiantes, como partir chocolatinas en partes iguales de volumen, o partir rectángulos en partes iguales de área, o partir segmentos de recta en partes iguales de largas (que son procesos no equivalentes); los sistemas conceptuales que los maestros quieren que sus alumnos construyan (los sistemas de números racionales) y los sistemas simbólicos externos que pueden utilizarse para representarlos (el verbal, el gestual, el decimal, el fraccional, el porcentual, el rectangular y el sectorial, entre otros) es lo que hace tan difícil elaborar proyectos de investigación consistentes acerca del aprendizaje de los fraccionarios, y lo que hace más difícil todavía diseñar los currículos, elaborar los listados de contenidos, escribir los libros de texto o programar el software educativo. Manejar esta distinción fundamental no es que haga fáciles esas tareas, pero sí las hace mucho menos difíciles.

6. ¿Dónde quedó el álgebra?

La eliminación de las fracciones de la lista de sistemas conceptuales importantes en el currículo colombiano de matemáticas elementales fue una jugada radical. Pero la teoría PSG me permitió atreverme a hacer una jugada más radical todavía: la eliminación del álgebra del currículo de matemáticas de la educación secundaria en Colombia. En realidad, en los programas de matemáticas de la renovación curricular en Colombia no aparece nada que se llame 'el Algebra'. Es que para mí, desde el punto de vista de la teoría PSG no hay ningún sistema conceptual matemático que se llame 'el Algebra', así escrita en singular y con mayúscula. Habrá tantas álgebras como sistemas simbólicos operatorios podamos inventar para representar cada tipo de sistema conceptual. Por ejemplo, habrá un álgebra lineal para los espacios vectoriales; habrá una o varias álgebras lógicas para los sistemas conceptuales de la lógica; hay al menos un álgebra conjuntista para la teoría de conjuntos, etc.

Al comienzo de los cursos de álgebra de la secundaria, se puede comprobar que lo que se considera como aprender álgebra es sólo un aprendizaje de un juego particular con un sistema simbólico externo para el sistema conceptual de los números reales. Por ejemplo, la letra x se usa para un número real genérico, y es más una incógnita que una variable real. No tendría sentido preguntar cuál es la derivada de x. No tiene derivada, porque las derivadas sólo están definidas para las funciones.

O los profesores de secundaria no caen en la cuenta de que sólo están enseñando a manipular símbolos sin ningún sistema conceptual subyacente, o sí caen en la cuenta de que lo utilizan para los números reales, pero pronto se olvidan de ello, y se deslizan inconcientemente hacia los símbolos para las funciones. De todas maneras, al nivel de los cursos de cálculo, ya los profesores están utilizando lo que ellos llaman 'álgebra' para representar funciones, pero no le dicen a los estudiantes lo que están haciendo. Por ejemplo, ¿han visto Uds. a algún profesor de cálculo que explique que ahora la letra x se utiliza para representar la función idéntica sobre los reales? En realidad así se utiliza, y por ello tiene como derivada la función constante uno (no el número uno).

La teoría PSG le ayuda a uno a ver que las funciones reales, o sea de valor real, de una variable real son precisamente las operaciones unarias de los sistemas de números reales, y que ellas mismas como objetos de un nuevo universo forman el substrato de un sistema de orden superior. Esto parece un hecho obvio, pero no aparece así en ninguno de los libros de cálculo que conozco. En realidad, en ellos las funciones se reducen a relaciones binarias de cierto tipo, o aun a conjuntos de parejas ordenadas. Pero esto no está de acuerdo con el sistema conceptual subyacente que ha sido construido a partir de las operaciones unarias sobre los números reales. Se puede ver esto muy claramente al estudiar los capítulos sobre relaciones y funciones que aparecen en los libros de cálculo, si se utiliza la teoría PSG para distinguir las relaciones binarias de las operaciones unarias, que son las funciones. Este análisis de los textos usuales de cálculo (y he revisado más de veinte de ellos) muestra que, con una sola excepción, hay un error en la transición del capítulo de relaciones al capítulo de funciones, o aun dentro del mismo capítulo, de la sección sobre relaciones a la sección sobre funciones, error que sólo se notaría si se asignaran ejercicios combinados de relaciones y funciones, ejercicios que prácticamente ninguno de los libros propone.

Tomemos por ejemplo la relación de ser raíz cuadrada. Sea 'xRy' una abreviatura de 'x es raíz cuadrada de y'. La pareja ordenada (x,y) debería estar en el grafo de la relación R. Pero ensayemos con (2,4). Ya habrán adivinado que (2,4) no está en el gráfico usual de la relación raíz cuadrada (ver figura 4). Peor todavía: si analizamos esa relación R por medio de las definiciones usuales, resulta ser funcional. Tomemos un número específico x y tratemos de encontrar otros dos números diferentes, y y y', tales que se cumpla tanto xRy como xRy'. No existe tal pareja de números diferentes, y según las definiciones en el capítulo de relaciones, eso quiere decir que la relación R es funcional.

Lo que sucede es que, más tarde, en el capítulo de funciones, cuando se trata de invertir las funciones, se señala que una función que no es inyectiva, al invertirse, no produce una función sino una relación no funcional; si se trata de invertir la función cuadrado, resulta una relación no funcional. Eso es correcto dentro del capítulo de funciones, pero al compararlo con el capítulo previo sobre relaciones, hay una contradicción clara, pero que pasa desapercibida para los profesores, los estudiantes, los editores de textos, y hasta para sus críticos.

Ensayemos ahora un ejercicio combinado de relaciones y funciones. Sobrepongamos el gráfico de la relación > correspondiente a 'x es estrictamente mayor que y' y el gráfico de la función cuadrado. Tomemos la intersección de esos dos gráficos, y la proyección sobre el eje de las x. Esto debe producir el conjunto de los números reales que tienen su cuadrado estrictamente mayor que ellos mismos. Hagamos la superposición y la proyección (ver figura 5). Podremos ver que ese conjunto consiste precisamente de aquellos números reales cuyo cuadrado es estrictamente menor que el número inicial. ¿Qué sucedió?

Así pues, la famosa álgebra de secundaria no es una verdadera disciplina matemática porque no es un sistema conceptual. Es sólo un sistema simbólico externo. Hay un álgebra para los números reales, que debe estudiarse para poderlos tratar a fondo y familiarizarse con ellos. Luego se introducen las operaciones unarias sobre el cuerpo de los números reales, y se las estudia por medio de calculadoras, computadoras, tablas, gráficos, instrucciones y algoritmos, y por medio de otros dispositivos gráficos que llamo 'molinos de moler números', con el fin de familiarizar a los estudiantes con los sistemas cuyos objetos son las operaciones sobre los antiguos objetos llamados 'números racionales' y 'números reales'. Cuando los estudiantes se pueden ya olvidar de esos objetos antiguos y trabajar directamente con esos monstruos activos que se alimentan de ellos, entonces sí se puede empezar a manejar un nuevo sistema simbólico para las funciones que sea apropiado para ese nuevo sistema conceptual. Ese nuevo sistema simbólico será un álgebra de funciones, que se parece mucho al álgebra de números reales, pero no es el mismo ni tiene la misma referencia.

Toda la literatura sobre investigaciones en educación matemática acerca del álgebra debe revisarse desde el punto de vista de la teoría PSG para tratar de especificar qué es realmente álgebra para números reales y qué es álgebra para funciones y para distinguir más precisamente los sistemas conceptuales de los simbólicos. Todo el currículo de pre-álgebra, álgebra y cálculo debe reestructurarse de acuerdo con esta teoría.

7. Conclusión

Así lo hice no sólo para el álgebra, sino para todo el currículo de la escuela elemental y de la escuela secundaria en Colombia. Se identificaron siete tipos distintos de sistemas conceptuales como dignos de atención en los programas curriculares de los grados primero a noveno, y uno más para los grados sexto a noveno.

Los tres tipos de sistemas más importantes para todos los grados son los sistemas numéricos, los sistemas geométricos y los sistemas métricos (y la distinción entre sistemas geométricos y sistemas métricos es crucial para el currículo, y muy clara desde el punto de vista de la teoría PSG). Además de éstos, están los sistemas de datos, los sistemas conjuntistas, los sistemas lógicos y los sistemas generalizados de orden superior, cuyos elementos son las operaciones o las relaciones de otros sistemas precedentes. Entre estos sistemas generalizados, se selecciona como el más importante para la secundaria el sistema cuyo substrato está formado por las operaciones unarias sobre los números racionales y reales, o sea por las funciones reales de una variable real.

Se recomienda tratar los sistemas de datos desde el primer grado en adelante. Los sistemas conjuntistas, los sistemas lógicos y los sistemas generalizados de relaciones y funciones (a excepción de los sistemas analíticos), se tratan sólo como herramientas, y no como objetos, según la distinción introducida por Régine Douady, hasta los dos o tres últimos años de la escuela secundaria.

Hablando en broma, y otras veces no tan en broma, algunos profesores de matemáticas en las escuelas secundarias de Colombia han dicho que a mí me recordarán en la historia de la educación colombiana por haber tratado de eliminar del currículo las fracciones y el álgebra, que son para ellos los temas más importantes y los que saben enseñar mejor. Pero yo no las eliminé del currículo: sólo las eliminé de la lista de sistemas conceptuales relevantes. Y lo hice porque no lo son: las fracciones son sólo uno de los muchos sistemas simbólicos para el sistema conceptual de los números racionales, y el álgebra usual en secundaria es sólo uno entre otros sistemas simbólicos para los sistemas conceptuales analíticos, cuyo substrato está formado por las funciones.

Espero haberles proporcionado algunos avances enriquecedores sobre las posibilidades que nos puede proporcionar la teoría de procesos y sistemas genéricos para hacer más comprensible la maravillosa empresa que son las matemáticas, para hacer más transparente la relación de ellas con la educación matemática, para hacer más visible y clasificable el currículo de las matemáticas escolares, y para captar que los programas de investigación en educación matemática pueden desplegarse e interconectarse en forma más orgánica y, sobre todo, mucho más hermosa.

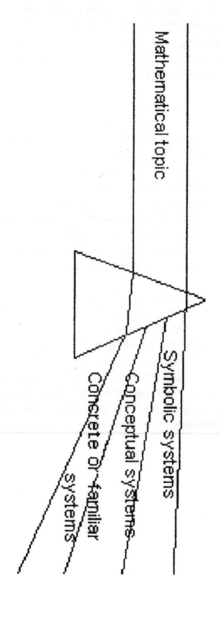

Figure 1

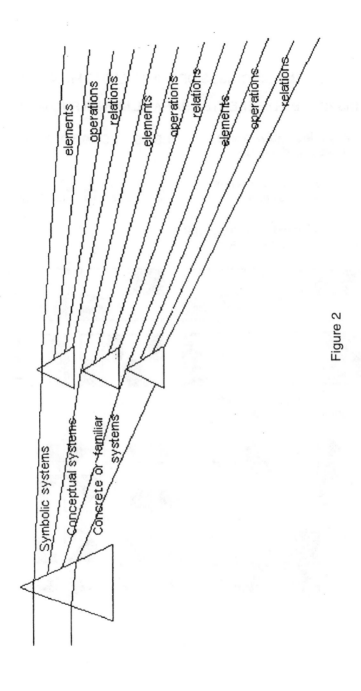

Figure 2

DIFFERENT DISGUISES OF THE HALVING MONSTER

DISFRACES DIFERENTES PARA EL MONSTRUO MITAD

Decimales equivalentes Equivalent decimals	0.5 .5 0,5 0.50 0,500

Fracciones equivalentes
Equivalent fractions

$$\frac{1}{2} \quad \frac{2}{4} \quad \frac{3}{6} \quad \frac{5}{10} \quad \frac{50}{100} \quad \frac{500}{1000}$$

Rectangulaciones equivalentes
Equivalent rectangulations

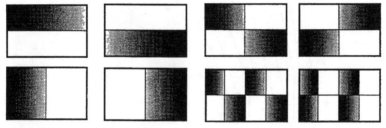

Pizzaciones equivalentes
Equivalent pizzations

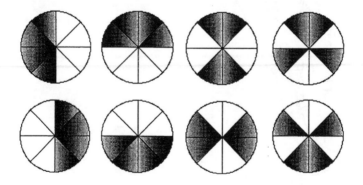

Figure 3

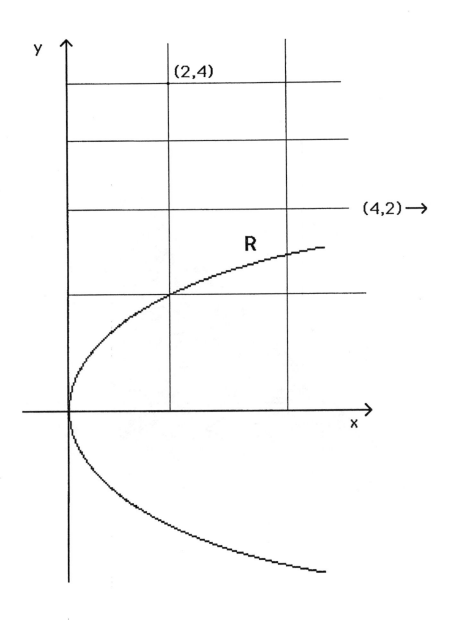

Figure 4

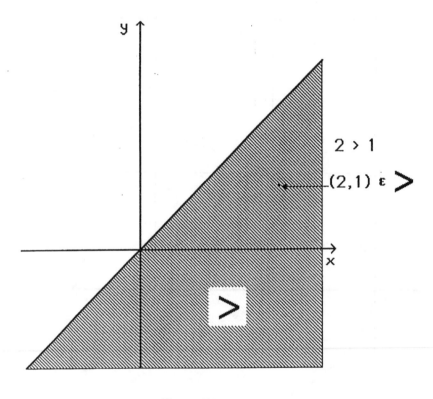

Figure 5a

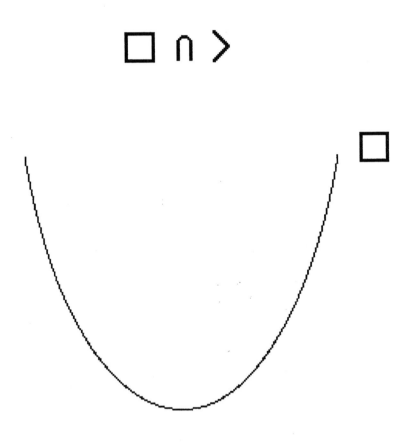

Figure 5b

PHILOSOPHY OF MATHEMATICAL EDUCATION: A PHENOMENOLOGICAL APPROACH

Maria Aparecida Viggiani Bicudo
Geo-Science and Science Institute
Rio Claro - Paulista State University - UNESP

I. EXPLICITING THE MEANING OF PHILOSOPHY MATHEMATICS

1.1. A little bit of history

In 1980 I begun to work with Philosophy of Education with students of a course of teachers of Mathematics. Such a experience made me wonder about the possibility of naming this school subject of *Philosophy of Mathematical Education*. I, then, suggested it to university professors who had already worked with the Teaching of Mathematics. They guaranteed me that papers having this name had never been presented either in congress or in international or national meetings. They also guaranteed me that it was very common to have papers, articles, books which focused upon Psychology of Mathematical Education, Didactic of Mathematics and specific topics of teaching Mathematics. Nevertheless, they had never seen *Philosophy of Mathematical Education* as topic of research before.

From that moment on I attempted to find out the work which had been carried out in such area of teaching and research. I realized that many themes treated by Philosophy such as Epistemology, Ontology and Axiology used to be merged in arguments and discussions in those school subjects without being highlighted and treated in accordance with the strictness and theoretical basis of Philosophy itself.

In January 1982, in the path I had followed inquiring and doing research about relevant topic to Philosophy of Mathematical Education, for the very first time, I came to know of a work which had been named Philosophy of Mathematical Education. It is a doctorate thesis of Eric Blaire[1], presented at the Institute of Education of the University of London in December 1981.

---

[1] Blaire, Eric *Philosophy of Mathematics Education*. London. Institute of Education, University of London. 1981 (Doctorate Thesis)

It is a study which joins Philosophy of Mathematics. In its first section, while it takes on questions about mathematical objects on epistemological and ontological basis, it describes the three traditional schools in Philosophy of Mathematics, logicism, formalism and intuitionalism, aiming at constructing a fourth one which is named hypothetical in the lights of Pierce's and Lakatos ideas.

In its second section, it presents different ways of teaching Mathematics and identifies logical connections and some times contingents which the author realizes between the philosophies of Mathematics addressed in the first part and these teaching practices. It draws four perspectives, the teaching of Mathematics as language, the teaching of Mathematics as a game, the teaching of Mathematics as a member of natural sciences and the teaching of Mathematics oriented to technology. The author argues that it is possible to draw a fifth perspective as teaching of Mathematics recognized as an interdisciplinary perspective.

In its third section, it draws attention to the concept of Education, to the objectives of Education and points out what is essential to be treated in courses addressed to teachers of Mathematics.

This way, Blaire works the Philosophy of Mathematical Education, based on the Philosophy of Mathematics and on the Philosophy of Education which provide him with the support to the analysis of teaching practices of Mathematics and to introduce pedagogical proposes which focus on the formation of teachers of Mathematics.

From 1982 to 1992, I carried out my work on Philosophy of Mathematical Education. In the meantime, I came to know important pieces of research and far reaching books by authors worldwide known and recognized in the area of Education of Mathematics without having mentioned the Philosophy of Mathematical Education, however.

In order to mention some, amongst the most meaningful ones, I point out Hans Freudenthal, mainly his book on *Didatical Phenomenological of Mathematical Structures*,[2] the work *Theory of Mathematical Education* which was one of the ICME-5 topics, joining researchers such as H.G. Steiner, N. Balacheff, J. Mason. H. Steinbring, L.P. Steffe, H.Brousseau, T.J. Cooney, B. Christiansen.

---

[2] Freudenthal, Hans. *Didactical Phenomenological of Mathematical Structures.* Dordrecht: D. Reidel Publishing Co. 1983.

I would also point out Gila Hanna, Michael Otte, Ubiratan D'Ambrósio, whose studies discuss aspects concerning the Mathematical reality, the epistemology which underlies the doing and the teaching of Mathematics. They also analyze and criticize the pedagogical practices, mathematical practices and the tendencies of teaching of Mathematics, providing explicit positions on the topics addressed.

In 1992, owing to ICME-7, I found the book under the particular name of *The Philosophy of the Mathematics Education*[3] by Paul Ernest. In this book, Ernst takes the task of explaining the title, and borrowing Higginson's[4] postulations "(he) identifies a number of subjects of foundations to Mathematical Education, including the Philosophy. A perspective of Mathematical Education, he argues, gathers a different set of problems from those regarded from any other point.[5] "

Based on this elucidation, he distinguishes, as the most relevant, four sets of problems and questions to the Philosophy of Mathematical Education, as follows:

• Philosophy of Mathematics which addresses questions such as: what is Mathematics and how can we explain its nature? Which philosophies of Mathematics were developed?

• The nature of learning, focusing on questions as such: which philosophical statements, possibly the implicit ones, underlie mathematical learning? Which epistemology and theories of learning are assumed?

• The objectives of Education, emphasizing questions as such: which are the objectives of Mathematical Education? Are its objectives valid? Who benefits and who loses?

• The nature of teaching, focusing on: which philosophical assertions, possibly the implicit ones, bear mathematical teaching? Are these assertions valid? Which means are adopted to achieve the objectives of mathematical teaching?[6]

---

[3] Ernest, Paul, *The Philosophy of Mathematics Education*. London. New York. Philadelphia. The Falmer Press. 1991.

[4] Higginson, W. "On The Foundations of Mathematics Education" *For the Learning of Mathematics*. 1 (2) (1980) pp.3-7.

[5] Ernest, P. op.cit. P.XII

[6] cf. Ernest, P. op.cit. p.XII and XIII

Ernest divides his books into two parts. The first one addresses the Philosophy of Mathematics, focusing on the logicism, the formalism and the intuitionalism in accordance with the category of the Philosophy of Absolutistic Mathematics, exposing his criticism, arguing about the implicit fallacy in these philosophies and enlarging the scope of understanding with the arguments of the falibilistic vision of Mathematics. He draws out the grounds for his criticism about Lakatos' work and about Constructivism, working out a conception of one Philosophy of Mathematics which is supported by Social Constructivism.

In the second part, he exploits the Philosophy of Mathematical Education, showing that many aspects of Mathematical Education lie on philosophical assertions.

In 1994, I came to know of the book by Ole Skovsmose intitled *Towards a Philosophy of Critical Mathematics Education.*[7] The title itself indicates that the author takes the Philosophy of Mathematics Education as being critical, according to his conception. Skovsmose attributes to the criticism the meaning of an Education which is kept as social and political power in a society whose nature is critical, punctuated by crises and conflicts.

He is based on the works by contemporaneous authors such as Adorno, Habermas and Paulo Freire, without losing the sight of a historical vision of the term *criticism* shown in Kant and Hegel, interpreted by Marx. He goes farther concerning the meaning of the term, visiting the authors of the School of Frankfurt, mentioning Max Horkheimer, Herbert Marcuse.

In order to elucidate the idea of critical Education, he highlights crises, criticism and emancipation.

To Skovsmose[8] criticism has a double meaning: it means criticism of some opinion and criticism of some real situation, of some aspect of real life. Crisis "is a metaphor to a situation to which people are to react through criticism"[9] . Emancipation has various aspects. It refers to the liberation of stereotypes of thought, when it would be the result of an ideological

---

[7] Skovsmose, Ole. *Towards a Philosophy of Critical Mathematics Education.* Dordrecht, Klumver Academic Publishers. 1994

[8] idem. chap. 1.6.

[9] idem.

criticism. It also refers to the liberation of material obstacles, as it is the case of setting people free from slavery.

The author builds his concept of critical Education based on these aspects, in a way that, being critical, Education should be aware of social inequities, trying to abolish them and without lengthening the existent social relationship. He exposed the different ways through which Education could react to the critical nature of the society. He sums up his thought, stating that critical Education involves two major interests: it has to recognize the different ways through which society is reproduced, it has to attempt to compensate these reproductive forces, it has to offer an equal distribution of what school can offer, it has to provide children with competence which enables them to identify and to react to social repression. Thus, in his book, he shows how he develops topics of Mathematics, in order to provide students with competence to react to social repression, being critical.

1.2. Explaining the meaning of philosophy of mathematical education

The meaning I have given to the Philosophy of Mathematical Education has been built throughout my work with Philosophy of Education itself.

While working with Philosophy of Education I have always highlighted Education as the main focus of my attention, bringing the systematic of philosophical doing to help me to understand this phenomenon, Education, in its complexity.

What does that mean?

It means I regard Education as phenomenon and I try to see its different perspectives of taking place: in school, in family, in books, in media, in multimedia, in life. After all, I try to understand what is shown in the real life in order to understand what characterizes it and then interpret it in the lights of the ways it takes place and in the lights of the world where it occurs.

Hence, Education is not regarded through filters, that is, through theoretical conceptions which define it previously, such as those that seek for these conceptions in Philosophy, in Psychology, in Anthropology, and so forth. Education itself is regarded as the focus of the investigation which is carried out in a multi-disciplinary way.

This procedure is sustained by the systematic of work of Philosophy which has as its focus a reaching, systematic and reflexive thinking. It focuses the everydayness life of Education, providing topics to the aspects of educational doing such as the relationship between teacher and student, teaching, learning, evaluation, curriculum, school, describing the ways through which this doing takes place, analyzing them and reflecting about the meanings which are constructed. The doing of Philosophy of Education allows me to understand and to interpret what is done while education takes place. It allows me to understand pedagogical proposals and the sense that theories which study educational issues make. It is undoubtedly a meditative doing which leads to self knowledge, to self criticism, and, therefore, to the knowledge and criticism of the world.

It is important to emphasize that in the conception of Philosophy of Education which I assume, reflection only takes place if it focuses upon an action properly analyzed in its genesis. It does not take place on the top of abstract thinking, in the sphere of subjectiveness of a subject, apart from the lived reality. Accomplishing it already takes place in the process of an intervening action in the educational reality. Hence, its characteristic doing does not reject what exists, but it assumes it as being the world where action occurs and where the analyses and the reflection can be possible. Therefore, Philosophy of Education is constructing knowledge and, at the same time, it is a continuous evaluation and criticism of this construction.

This work demands the presence of the others, researchers, authors who have already written about the studied topic, subjects present to the educational studied situation. This work always takes into account the presence of the world, horizons of interpretations, field of lived experiences.

In this perspective, Philosophy of Education is characterized as a criticism of education. This criticism is understood in the philosophical sense which has reflection as its focus, and which accomplishes knowledge of the genesis, i.e. of the creation of ideas, pedagogical proposals and educational action present to the investigated everydayness life. This task is important to prevent the agents of Education from getting lost in fashionable theories, in words of command determined by political discourse, in the density of the school world, helping them to keep lucid, understanding their doing, being able to choose and defining the path to be followed.

This conception and procedure in Philosophy of Education has delimited my work in Philosophy of Mathematical Education.

I understand Philosophy of Mathematical Education as a reaching, systematic, and reflexive study of Mathematical Education, as it appears in everyday life. Mathematical Education is the main focus. Understanding it demands having it reflected on what is done. Therefore, in this perspective, Mathematical Education is regarded as a whole which appears in different ways, down the streets, in theories, in culture, in curriculum, in legislative rules, in the educational policy, in media, in multimedia.

To ask "WHAT IS MATHEMATICAL EDUCATION?" leads to the way of the investigation, in the sense of seeing what is common to the different ways through which it appears, keeping it as Mathematical Education. This investigation demands analyses and interpretation of data, a logical work to reunite what is constant in the multiple appearances and in the reflexive work to accomplish criticism, searching for the sense of what is taken in the world of Mathematical Education.

Philosophy of Mathematical Education cannot be taken as Philosophy of Mathematics, nor even as Philosophy of Education. It can be distinguished from the former for it does not have the theme reality of mathematical entities nor the construction of their knowledge as its goal. It can be distinguished from the latter because it does not deal with specific issues, nor even with the ones that are peculiar to it, such as: purposes and aims of Education, nature of teaching, of learning, of school, and of school curriculum. Nevertheless, in spite of being distinguished from both - Philosophy of Mathematics and Philosophy of Education - Philosophy of Mathematical Education is sustained by their studies, deepened in specific themes which can be detected in the interface which it has with both areas. It supports both of them with their own research and reflection, as it is supported by them, at the same time.

Philosophy of Mathematical Education deals with the issues studied by Mathematical Philosophy, regarding them from the point of view of Education. This way it focuses topics like reality of mathematical entities, knowledge of mathematical objects, value of mathematics, characteristics of mathematical sciences by studying them through the mathematical perspective. In order to work in this perspective it is necessary to be based on studies and reflexive analyses of Philosophy of Education. By doing this it gets the necessary strength to understand how having the conceptions of reality and of knowledge of mathematical entities take place in the way the teacher of Mathematics teaches and evaluates his/her students, in the proposed curriculum, in the ways people deal with their everyday work, such as building houses, preparing and organizing the soil for plantation, trade exchanges and manipulation of technology.

From the point of view of the value of mathematical entities or of Mathematics, Philosophy of Mathematical Education approaches the matter of the position of Mathematics in the school curriculum, in the way the society values it and, how this valuation interferes in the school evaluation and in the selection of the most capable ones in a particular community. This is a study which cannot be carried out without comprehension of the ideology which is present in the way of seeing, of evaluating Mathematics, interfering, therefore, in the conceptions of the reality of mathematical entities and of the knowledge of these objects.

Hence, Philosophy of Mathematical Education imposes itself as a thinking about reaching themes to cover the field of Mathematical Education. This does not mean that it can be reduced to Philosophy of Mathematical Education. It only means that the last one reflects and thinks reflexively the Mathematical Education, trying to know and to interpret what has been and what is being accomplished. This a meditative thinking which leads to self knowledge, to self criticism, and also outlines the identity. It is in this way that Mathematical Education is strengthened and, at the same time, it discerns future perspectives and provides support to its choices.

In the field of activities of Mathematical Education, I understand that the following topics represent convergence to be taken as center of reflexive and critical analysis by the Philosophy of Mathematical Education:

- conception of Education and of the Mathematical Education;
- conception of reality and of knowledge;
- conception of reality of mathematical entities;
- attitude and pedagogical didactic aims of the teaching of Mathematics work.

2. Approaching mathematical education in a phenomeno logical perspective

I will resume the topics appointed as important to the Philosophy of Mathematical Education in order to treat them according to the phenomenological concept, demonstrating how the Phenomenology addresses them. I have decided not to establish a parallel between the conceptions and the relevant guiding to Phenomenological Attitude and those of **Natural Attitude**[10] , but to show conceptions of Phenomenology which support pedagogical practice and its analysis and reflection.

2.1. Conception of education and the mathematical education

In the phenomenological conception, Education is taken as phenomenon which is shown to consciousness which, in its intentionality, comprises it, making its sense to take place in its diverse ways of showing up.

Phenomenon means what is shown, what is manifested to consciousness. The meaning of counsciousness will be carried out in the next item 2.2

The essence of the *phenomenon Education* is understood by Phenomenology as being the care taken with the project[11] of human being taking him in his possibilities of being wordly and temporal. Project which throws man in his being, hence, in his acting.

The interpretation of this statement is constructed in the network of meanings attributed by Phenomenology to Ego, to Other, to truth, to reality of the life-world. These issues make the nucleo of the development of phenomenological thinking exposed in the works by Edmund Husserl, Martin Heidegger, Hans G. Gadamer, Paul Ricoeur and Maurice Merleau-Ponty, just to mention the most renowned founders.

The life-world[12] is the universal field of lived experiences, it is the horizon where one is always conscious of objects and of other fellows. In the school life-world there are students, teachers and cultural objects

---

10 The Natural Attitude is characterized by conceiving the things of the natural world as positive contents thought as distinct of the phenomenon and its manifestations. Either the thing which becomes object to the subject, or the mind which operates the relationships of knowledge. In the Phenomenological Attitude, the thing is not taken as having objective existence in itself, thus a) it is not beyond its manifestations and, therefore, it is relative to perception and dependent of consciousness; b) consciousness is not part or region of a field larger, but it itself is a whole which does not have anything out of it. It is by being understood and comprised the world that it makes the world make sense to subject. (cf. Moura, C.A.R. *Crítica da Razão na Fenomenologia* - São Paulo - Nova Stella & EDUSP, 1989)

11 Pro-ject is the act of throwing ahead, permitting the human possibilities to be updated.

12 cf. Husserl, E. *The crises of European Sciences,* Evanston. North Western University Press. 1970.

which are already given to the consciousness of those who live in this horizon. The last ones are given as intentional objects, therefore, comprised by consciousness activity. The *others* are others of each *Self* making themselves present in their own body and in their psyche[13]. Each student, being Ego, is a pole of intentionality, a zero-origin from which the perspective of the world is drawn. This is an existential comprehension which everyone develops from himself, pole of identity, incarnated body which is modility, intentionality, desire, communication and also comprehension of *other* which makes sense by being with in the life-world, horizons of meanings of existence and the of cultural objectives.

The school life-world is in the *School,* secular institution which is history and whose meaning has been constructed over the years. The meaning of School takes place in school everyday life experienced by its agents: teachers, students, member of the family, clerks, pedagogical and technical staff, etc. Therefore, this sense takes place in teaching, in learning, in evaluation, in wish, in want, in repudiation. It takes place where the ideal[14] objects permeate pragmatically contents from which they are transmitted by spoken language, by images and sounds, gestures and writing.

The Phenomenology works the educational project in the everydayness of school. It pursues the sense which actions of the school life-world make to their subjects and it sends the thinking of this sense in a vigorous and systematic way, putting forward to the analysis and criticism and self-criticism. This is the real work of Philosophy of Education: being aware of action or being conscious of what is done, analyzing and reflecting the done in a systematic and rigorous way, pointing out possible paths and their implications in the educational project.

The highlighted aspect in the phenomenological approach is to understand the essence of Education as human project. It means the Phenomenology does not address Education as a natural object, possible to become known by the means of the representations by language signs or signs possible of being decomposed into parts of a process programmed in sequences of aims and operations displayed in time. It means it works Education as opening, as possibilities which are accomplished in the human temporality in which actions and decisions outline paths,

---

[13] cf. Husserl, E. *Cartesian Meditations*, op. cit.
[14] The mathematical objects are idealities, according to the exposed in Husserl, E. "The Origin of Geometry" in Husserl, E. *The crises of European Sciences,* op. cit.

making history. Possibilities, decisions and signs reflected, by searching, the Education, the consciousness of the sense which world and life make to each one and for everyone at the same time.

Therefore, the Phenomenology does not have as its starting point a concept of Education or of a particular educational proposal as the most plausible and valid one. But it searches in the school life-world itself for the sense of what one does, the sense of time and of history, and the sense of ideologies, of theories and of pedagogical practices which permeate and base accomplished action.

The Mathematical Education is also seen as phenomenon by Phenomenology. Thus, as a totality which is shown in the everyday life-world through perceptions of subject aware of it. Hence, Mathematical Education is a human being project which is projected in the possibilities of man being worldly and temporal, and understanding mathematical relationships perceived in the life-world, expanding them creatively by using in the interventive action in everydayness lived.

To assume a Phenomenological attitude when we work with Mathematical Education means to search for the sense of what is done while teaching and learning, the sense of the mathematical contents transmitted in culture, those of common sense and of the everydayness lived by subjects, those transmitted by books, specialized magazines and in the academy. The sense of ideologies permeate the network of the meanings of mathematical conceptions, of pedagogical conceptions, of educational practice. It is on attempt to understand the sense which the world makes to each participant of a particular process of teaching and learning, searching for points of intercession of the horizon of comprehension. It is to be aware of *other, co-subject* of the life-world, observer of the comprehended and nuclear presence in self-knowledge process. It is to proceed constantly and systematically to the analysis, to the reflection and to the criticism of the acceptable truth.

2.2 Conception of reality and of knowledge

In the phenomenologial perspective the real is given as an everyday temporal and historical dynamic whole, perceived in the man-world encounter, not apart from that who perceives it, who speaks of it, who interprets it, constructing a network of meanings in the inter-subjectiveness by sharing and communicating interpretation. In the preface of *Phenomenology of Perception*, Marleau-Ponty states:

"The real is a closed woven fabric. It does not await our judgement before incorporating the most surprising phenomena, or before rejecting the most plausible figments of our imagination."[15]

The solid woven fabric which is given to the lived experience. And this is the world: lived, reflected, communicated and shared experience. "The world is not what I think, but what I live through."[16] The reading of this statement leads to the interpretation that the world is not what is postulated about it or what is stated about it or an object susceptible to be owned or represented. But, "it is natural setting of and field of all my thoughts and of all my explicit perceptions."[17]

The real is understood as reality lived in spatiality and temporality of the life-world. Therefore, in the perceived perception of time and space and its convergences which join modalities of perception of each subject and of several subjects.

From reality, the subject is integrated and constituent part who perceives together with other subjects, mates and co-subjects of this reality. Subject and reality do not separate from each other. There is a constant movement between perception and acts which generates meanings attributed to the perceived one, to the perceived thing. This movement is the noesis - *noema* process - *noesis* refers to perception of acts, of providing sense, of logical organization of those data and *noema* refers to the perceived one.

All this process is worked by Husserl under the name **transcendental reduction**[18] , that exposes how understanding of the world takes place. Being so, to clarify the meaning of reality in the phenomenological approach implies to expose meaning to knowledge.

I am going to focus on some nuclear topics of phenomenological conceptions of knowledge and of reality, considering the impossibility of treating, in this article, the transcendental reduction in its complexity and with the strictness which Husserl treats it in his several works.

---

15 Merleau-Ponty, M. *Phenomenology of Perception.* London and Henley. Ronthege & Kegan Paul New Jersey. The Humanities Press. 1978 P. X
16 Idem. p.XVII
17 Idem. p. XI
18 cf. Husserl, E. *The crises of European Sciences.* op.cit.

The emphasis has to be given to consciousness and reflection, since to understand these allows me to understand the way through which Phenomenology conceives the real and the superation of momentaneous of *noétic* acts.

To Phenomenology consciousness is intentionality.[19] It is the act of being aware of..., of being drawn to... Intentionality is the essence of consciousness. It comes from the Latin verb *intento, tendi, tentum, ere* which means to be inclined to a direction, to enlarge, to be inclined to open, to make one aware of, to support, to provide intensity, to state boldly[20]. These meanings allow me to understand consciousness as expansion to the world, being opened to... In this aspect lies the difference between understood consciousness, in the natural attitude, as thing, as recipient, as modelling as part of the world and consciousness understood by Phenomenology as intentionality, as movement of being understood to...[21] This *something* to which consciousness is expanded to is not only something visually present, but it comprehends wish of acting, of effecting itself in which the existence takes place.

Hence, consciousness does not have anything out of it, for the movement of being expanded to it involves objects of its existence and because of it these objects are always intentional.

It is in this aspect that lies the core of the difference between Natural Attitude and Phenomenological Attitude. To Phenomenology, every object is an intentional object. This is a *noésis-noema* synthesis, or rather, of existential acts and of their products.

The consciousness is also expanded to it itself, to its own acts. This is a reflexive movement, through which it understands its own existence, allowing itself lucidity of its acts. Through this movement, there is the possibility of consciousness include self comprehension, self knowledge, self criticism. It is a retrospective perception focusing on manifestations of primary perceptions. This is the sense of *Erlebnis*, or of experiencing.

To reflect is an act. And as such, it is susceptible of becoming an intentional object whose acts of reflection can be focused on. It is a movement of going one step behind and regarding the lived, the done, and

---

19   Husserl, E. *Ideas* op.cit. p. 198
20   Gaffiot, F. *Dictionnaire Latin / Français*. Paris. Hachette, 1934.
21   Husserl, E. *Ideas*. op. cit. p.199

the accomplished one. This involves the distance and, at the same time, the reflection on lived experience. This is the sense of *transcendence*, in Phenomenology: a retrospective perception of the invariance of the lived one. Hence, the Transcendental Phenomenology is posed as a criticism of knowledge and, also, as a criticism of the totality of human experience which has self-criticism as a founding one.[22]

This reflexive movement which leads the consciousness to self-knowledge enabled the interpretation that Phenomenology operates in an introspective way and that what it does, even if proceeding strictly to the *transcendental reduction*,[23] is to reach to a solipsist *Self* which is self-comprehended and that creates the world.

However, the possibility of a conception of solipsist ideality of the *Self* and of reality is definitely overcome when the husserlian Phenomenology considers the presence of the *other* in the life-world.

Before addressing the theme of *Other* and of intersubjectiveness, we shall focus on *perception*, for it is the key of the encounter man-world and, thus, of knowledge and of construction of worldly reality, in the phenomenological perspective.

It is important to make it clear that Phenomenology perception is not taken as sensation and it is not susceptible of being decomposed into parts and made by the sum of sensations either. In *Phenomenology of Perception*[24] and in *Primacy of Perception*[25] Merleau-Ponty carries out a very deep study of this theme, exposing philosophical consequences deriving from the attitude of admitting perception as primacy of knowledge of the world. To this author, perception does not reveal the ideal and the necessary, not even the transitory occurrence free from chains and independent of the world. He states that it occurs in scope of the whole. The subject who perceives and who takes a seen point is the incarnated-body, field of perception and of action, who makes syntheses in his aimed horizon.

---

[22] Zaner, Richard M. *The way of Phenomenology. Criticism as a Philosophical Discipline.* Indianopolis. The Bobbs Merril Co. Inc. 1970. p.194

[23] Merleau-Ponty, M. *Phenomenology of Perception.* op. cit.

[24] Idem

[25] Merleau-Ponty, M. "The primacy of Perception and its philosophical consequences" in Merleau-Ponty, M. *The primacy of Perception .* Northwestern University Press - USA, 1964. p.12-43

The perception offers truth as *presences*. This means, according to Merleau-Ponty, that our relationships with the world is not that of a thinker with the object of thought or that of the unit of the perceived thing, perceived by many consciousness, that is that one which is given in proposal. It does not mean that the perceived is comparable to the real either.

Presence is to take part of the moment in which things, truths, values are constituted. It is the instant in which the sense takes place. Owing to this, Merleau-Ponty states that perception is constituted as a nascent logos.[26] The statement that *"the matter of perception with its pregnant of its form*[27] comprises the idea that every perception takes place in an horizon, in the world and in the action of the incarnated body itself. Thus, the distinction classically made between *matter* and *form* does not proceed. The matter is already pregnant with its form, for it is in the action, in the moment that the perception unifies, that the form is constituted with the matter. This unification is, according to Husserl, a synthesis of transition or of the identity which processes the unity of the perceived objects.[28] Therefore, it does not refer to an intellectual synthesis which apprehend the object as possible or necessary, but it is a synthesis in which the object is given as a series of perception in profiles, though, in its totality, it is not given in any of them. Thus, in the perception the object can be given in deformed way. It refers to the deformation deriving of the perceptible taken from the zero-origin, which is that point of the incarnated body.

However, in this point of view, although the perceived **thing**[29] is shown in multiples ways, it is not lost in the multiplicity of perceptions. According to Husserl[30] there is always an unit which permeates the multiple ways through which perception of things takes place, formed by *synthesis of transition.*

This game between multiplicity, typical of perception, which is by profile, and identity of intentional object defines transcendence of object

---

26   Idem p.25

27   Idem p.15

28   Husserl.

29   Thing is not something which is imposed as true to all inteligence, not something felt in privacy of individual perception, but it is what is there in its concrete aspect, in the texture of its qualities itself. cf. Merleau-Ponty, M. "An Unpublished Text" in Merleau-Ponty, M. *The Primacy of Perception*. North Western University Press. 1964, p.48.

30   cf. Husserl, E. *Cartesian Meditations*, op.cit.

related to psychological aspects. Thus, intentional object is polo of identity intrinsic to lived experiences. However, it is also transcendent to these existence by being perceived as identical or invariant in temporal flow of lived experiences.

To Husserl, the activity which joins multiplicity, so that the identical is perceived, is the *essential intuition*. It is in this act that *essence*, is intuited, enabling the essential evidence of the phenomenon. The essence defines an intentional object with characteristics, for it is given in the *essential intuition*. These are the acts which generate the ideal objects or idealities. *An empirical intuition or individual can be converted into essential intuition (ideal)*[31] *and the essential intuition is also intuition and not a representation.*[32]

Although idealities are generated in the *essential intuition*, they acquire form, they are kept and perpetuated in an objective way in language, in the relationships between subjects, in culture and in history. That is why idealities of ideal objects exceed psychological existences and perspective multiplicity, in which the phenomenon is shown to the subject. They are taken from the subjective sphere, projected to the intersubjective and to the objective ones through language and through the presence of the *other*, in the horizon of life-world. Hence, in phenomenological perspective, the idealities do not exist in the abstract level, subjective or not, and non-temporal, but they are cultural objective realities, temporal and worldly.

To move on to the sphere of intersubjectivity and of objectivity, we are withdrawing from the possibility of interpreting husserlian Phenomenology as abstract and founded in solipsism of a pure Self. And here I emphasize that the *Other* and the *Intersubjectiveness,* also central themes of conceptions of knowledge and of reality, in this approach.

For Husserl, perception is temporal, worldly and carnal.[33] He states that the act of perceiving takes place in the present. However, it always takes place in a temporal horizon where past and future are also present in a continuous flow of retention and of procrastination. Perception and perceived thing take place in horizon-world, in perspectives, when the sense gains space and the perception is processed. It is like this that inten-

---

31 Husserl, E. *Ideas*, p.20
32 Husserl. E. *Cartesian Meditation*, op. cit. 116/117.
33 Husserl, E. *Cartesian Mediattions*. op. cit. p. 116 / 117.

tional objects gain existence to the consciousness having meanings attributed to them through the way they happened in the horizon-world. It in this way that the reality of the the life-world goes through subjectiveness and that certainty of the world is established.

This subjectiveness is considered by Husserl as carnal, as being the one of the incarnated body which moves, feels, desires and which perceives the movement of the physical bodies, in its concreteness with the others, present in a corporeal way, thus, intentionally.

Other, living bodies which are made present in perceptions which are communicated, making the network of intersubjectiveness, are co-subjects of experience of the world, making the horizon where the encounter of *Self* - and oneself and with the *Other* is possible.

The *other* is not made present to consciousness in a direct and primordial way, but always through his incarnated body. In this intervention the Ego is perceived in a "worldly" way. It is a process which involves analogy from body to body, lived in a existential way which enables the formation of the peer Self-Other, supposition of a strange life to *Self* which is confirmed in gestures, in expressions, in *others'* behaviors, imagination of itself and of the *other,* as a being in the place of the *other,* who is up-to-date with an experience as if the *Self* were there.[34]

The intervening notion which enables the passage of identity from a body to what is common between the *Self* and the *Other* is the perspective notion. The body itself is the zero-origin of a point of view which gives a certain orientation to its system of experience. It understands that the *other* has another perspective which orients his experience in a different way of that through which the *Self* orients his. The body of the *other* belongs concomitantly to the system of experience of the *Self* and of the *Other* and that makes possible to understand that the same object can be seen from different perspectives.

In the husserlian thinking, however, the *Other,* or the *Self* does not appear only as flesh, as incarnated body, but also as *psyche,* others that are separated and different and which are linked in the fabric woven by constructing a common world made by a community of inter-egos or of co-subjects. This is the way to the construction of all the intersubjective communities and, also, its foundation. In the common project of man, the

---

34   cf. Husserl. E. Fifth Meditation. in Husserl, E. *Cartesian Meditations,* op. cit

world and the time provide base to the union of men and transform the union of their bodies in an indissoluble cohesion. In this way, surrounding cultural worlds are made as if they were personalities of a higher level.

Those are *Lebenswelt's* and *Geist's* notions, or the life-world and of the spirit.[35] The *geist* separates the boarding line between nature and culture. The latter is then constituted by the intersubjectiveness which leads to higher personalities.

The core of the life-world and of culture is in the language, in the history and in the tradition.

Language, in the Phenomenology, is not only understood as communication between subjects but also and mostly as organizer and structure of thinking. The affirmative of Mealeau-Ponty that *perception is a nascent logos*[36] makes sense when language is thought as a process which organizes the acts which generate the sense and the meaning, as expositor of these meanings generated in speech, as articulator of the perceived sense, as vehicle of senses, as maintainer of senses, as structure of the world commonalized and of the perception itself in its thinking process.

Hence, all language is founded in a discourse[37] , that is, in the articulation of the sense that the world makes to the perceiver subject. The written text vehiculates this articulation. The reader has to search for the sense which the text makes to him in the horizon-world of his comprehension, which is also that of the *others*, of culture. This is a work of hermeneutical interpretation, that is, the one of the reading which focuses on the sense and the comprehension of cultural meanings, which are historical. They are historical, for they are made in the perspective of time, in the interlacement of intentional acts in the life-world, in the network of objective meanings kept as cultural objects, altogether with all subjects in the world.

That is the network of the real worked out by knowledge. That is weft *Lebenswelt*.

In this weft, HOW CAN THE TRUTH BE UNDERSTOOD?

---

[35] cf. Husserl. E. *The crises of European Sciences*, op.cit.

[36] cf. Mealeu-Ponty. *Primacy of Perception*. op. cit. p.25

[37] Discourse is understood according to Martin Heidegger, cf. Heidegger, Martin,*To be and Time*. Trad. M.S. Cavancanti. Rio de Janeiro. Ed. Vozes. 1988.

In phenomenological view truth is not understood as adequacy between the representation and the represented one, but it is understood as *aletheia,* that is, unveiling.

It is the truth given in perception, which unveils or shows without veiling the presence of the world. It is the truth exposed in the discourse which unveils the sense that the world makes to the one who interprets and communicates the interpreted. Therefore, one cannot work on Phenomenology with truth itself, a non-temporal, absolute truth which reveals sharpness. One works on convergence of unveiling got in accordance with the reality attained through perspectives.

2.3 Conception of reality of the mathematical entities

The mathematical entities, in according with phenomenological view, are ideal objects. They are constituted in the essential or eidetical intuition, thus in the psyche subjectiveness. However, its ideality exceeds this sphere and, by the means of intersubjectiveness, it is presented objectively in the life-world, and so, they are present to consciouness.

Emphasizing what has already been postulated in the previous item concerning the ideal objects, the ideality of mathematical entities is not kept in the level of abstractness apart from the lived experiences in the life-world. But it becomes wordly in the intersubjectiveness and it is embodied in the language and it is kept in *History* and in *Tradition.* It is intentional objects, but, through essential intuition exceed the psychological existences and the perspective multiplicities given by perception. The ideality of mathematical entities is kept as objective and susceptible of being perceived and developed by means of evidence, imagination, logical reasoning, practical and theoretical doings.

They are projected to the intersubjectiveness sphere and given as objectives in culture through language, which can be exposed in differentes ways: speech, exposing propositions, interconnecting judgements, enchaining reasoning. It is the writing which registers what is said in symbols through common language and in particular mathematical symbols, gesticulation which communicates through corporeal gestures of whats is understood by subjects and through pictorical language which communicate through figures; plastic language which exposes the understood through art, etc.

To guarantee the permanence of mathematical entities it is necessary to take into consideration to the life-world, horizon of civilization where the *other* is, fellow to whom we are always virtually thoughtful and to whom we are always present as own body and as psyche. It is also necessary to count with the structural characteristic of spoken language and the possibility of its structure be confirmed through writing.

In accordance with Husserl the evidence got in the essential intuition, generates the mathematical entity and it is susceptible of being communicated to other through mental structures of communicators agents, subjects co-present to the same community. Being repeated in many productions and communications, by the means of spoken language, this structure becomes an ordinary structure to the community, keeping the objectiveness of ideal objects.

Besides being objective, the mathematical entities are lasting. Its lastingness is guaranteed by linguistical documentation, throught writing.

The writing brings in itself a transformation concerning the way of being of the structure and of the sense of the ideal objects. While in oral and gesticulated communication the structure of mathematical entities can be transmitted through empathy and fellowship, reinforcing the linguistical structure which communicates the discourse, that is, the articulation of the sense that the world makes to its interlocutor subject, the written language incorporates and perpetuates that structure. Logic is inlaid in this language, understood as Theory of Sentences or of the propositions in general .[38]

To Husserl, to the reader is opened the possibility of renewing the lived in the evidences which incorporate the ideality of the ideal mathematical entities or of being reduced through language. In the former, the most general experiences should be reactivated by the sense which the idealities make to him. Going beyond Husserl, but still remaining in the phenomenological thinking, I can postulate that the reader, while searching for the sense in the written text, still has to search for the discourse which provides base to this text. In this case, I am concerned with an hermeneutic work which privileges the sense, the perception of perspectives which is made concrete in the horizon of temporality and that of the spatiality of the subject who reads, interpreting the text from the life-world and that also previleges the interpretation of cultural and social meanings of what is written. It provides dimension to it in History and in the region of mathematical and that of the sciences.

---

[38] cf. Husserl. E. "The Origin of Germany", op. cit.

In the case of the reader who remains seduced by the language I have a more passive reading, more restricted to repetition, to mechanical and pragmatical application of the mathematical entities, which is possible through the formula and practical doings.

2.4 Didactic pedagogical attitudes and proposals for mathematics teaching

A phenomenological didactics of Mathematics considers that the school world in its concrete worldhood and experiences lived in it form the reality in which the work of teaching is accomplished. It works with perception, exploiting the ways the mathematical entities are shown to the subjects, to each student, to the teacher and to others, also present to the teaching / learning situation. It considers the ways through which everyone feels, in accordance with his possibilities and how everyone sees the world and Mathematics, from the zero-origin given by his own body and by his culture. This regard is an incarnated one, therefore, it brings with it the action, the thought, the speech ..., after all the ways through which the subject is in his world with the motility with others. Thus, the ideality of mathematical entities is presented either in books, texts and specific articles on mathematical sciences or on teaching of mathematical sciences, as in everydayness ordinary practical doings lived by students and teachers. It is shown in perspectives.

To emphasize the perception, the pedagogical work of the teacher of Mathematics gives preference in the present moment and temporal horizon making possible that teacher and students be alert to past, to future and to their own existences which take place in the present. So, they can realize themselves feeling, reasoning, remembering, speaking about the perceived, moving around, in other words, acting. Hence, the sense of the accomplished one is presented to them, each of them considered as an individual ego and the meaning keeps on being processed.

This procedure contributes so that the life-world makes sense. The certainty of the world reinforces the knowledge of its reality, through subjectiveness, through intersubjectiveness and reaching the cultural objectiveness, without mystery.

Moving ahead towards the understanding of the reality of the ideal objects, the work of the teacher of Mathematics elects activities which enable him / her to reunite to the given multiplicity in the perception and in the individual experiences. This activity should privilege attention to similar aspects between classmates expositions and experiences individually lived by the students. It is mandatory to listen to the *Other* attentively, seeing what he does and speaks, trying to interprete it, searching for convergencies. It also is mandatory to listen to oneself trying to interprete his own feeling, doing, speaking etc.

Hence, the pedagogical doing of the teacher of Mathematics works on the *Self* and on the *Other* by the means of his own body and not in an introspective way. It privileges the perception of the *Self* and of the *Other* which are perceived as incarnated bodies making movements, wanting, acting, answering, speaking, listening, and interpreting. The perspective, the temporality are existencially understood in a primary level, and worked little by little in the sphere of cultural meanings and in the sphere of sciences.

The mathematical text - either the one produced by students or the one produced by authors - is part of these activities. To understand the meaning of writing, managing to register their own mathematical understandings of the world, sharing with learning-situation mates their evidences, the ones already elaborated and communicated through language, listening to what the *other* has to say are activities which take place in the core of mathematical doing and in the core of mathematical science. They subside the development of an active attitude of reading, participative and critical reading of texts written by other authors.

These activities generate the *trans-doing*,[39] for they re-create the data and what is already done in an endless chain of constructing the unfinished one, what is in movement, assuming that we ourselves are the horizon-world, the culture, the History after all.

Another point to be highlighted in the pedagogical practice which has Phenomenology as proposal of regarding the world is *reflection*. It involves everyday school activities which require students and teachers drawing attention to their own experiences, either the individual or the group ones in order to understand them, analysing them and criticizing them properly. In classes of Mathematics, these activities

---

[39] Trans-doing, recreating term which does not have the same meaning of dialectics. The trans-doing refers to how the human being as an individual feels the world and from it attributes meaning. It means to go beyond, to overcome a simple doing. It is an endless re-creating, always unfinished one, for the human being is always a being of possibilities." (cf. Marins Joel (org. Vitória H.C. Espósito). *Educação como Noises*. São Paulo, 2ed.Cortez, 1992.

comprehend the exposition of operated reasoning, the analysis of the starting point, of its sequence and of anticipation of other possibilities through imagination. Or they comprehend the presentation of figures which represent the past, moving them in the depth which the regard in perspective enables one to project light and shadow and to reporting the seen thing. They comprehend the analysis of text, of programs of informatics etc.

Going backwards and returning to the accomplished thing is the turning point to learn how to regard the world phenomenologically, or rather, not taking oneself and the classmates as natural object, given objectively and susceptible of being handled, reproduced and represented according to pattern of truth. But it is by taking them as incarnated bodies to whom the world makes sense and which questions this sense itself, as well as the *self* and the world, always searching for the truth as explanation, as a clear regard or evidence of essence or essential intuition which gathers the multiplicity of ways of focusing according to perspectives.

The reflection lies in the core of strictness of phenomenological procedures which have research as goal. To work this strictness pedagogically helps the formation of a thoughtful reflexive and critical researcher. It also helps the formation of a citizen who interferes in the reality in a conscious and consequent way.

The evaluation, in accordance with the perspective assumed here, is qualitative and based on the process in which the sense and the meaning take place and which they elaborate their temporal and cultural dimension. It is always accomplished by subjects presented to the reality in which evaluated activities take place and in which they claim themselves and the others as authors and as subjects aware of their own action.

In the school world, the product of evaluation is preferably presented in a propositional language which provides values of judgement, and are objectivated in texts susceptible to be interpreted, making sense to the subjects involved.